UNDER WIDE AND STARRY SKIES

UNDER WIDE AND STARRY SKIES

50 Sailing Destinations in Seas Less Travelled

NICHOLAS COGHLAN

ADLARD COLES

LONDON · OXFORD · NEW YORK · NEW DELHI · SYDNEY

ADLARD COLES
Bloomsbury Publishing Plc
50 Bedford Square, London, WC1B 3DP, UK
29 Earlsfort Terrace, Dublin 2, Ireland

BLOOMSBURY, ADLARD COLES and the Adlard Coles logo are trademarks of
Bloomsbury Publishing Plc

First published in Great Britain 2025

A catalogue record for this book is available from the British Library

Library of Congress Cataloguing-in-Publication data has been applied for

ISBN: PB: 978-1-3994-1375-6; ePDF: 978-1-3994-1376-3; ePub: 978-1-3994-1374-9

2 4 6 8 10 9 7 5 3 1

Typeset in Adobe Caslon Pro by Phil Beresford

Printed and bound in India by Replika Press Pvt. Ltd.

To find out more about our authors and books visit www.bloomsbury.com and sign up for our newsletters

CONTENTS

PART II: SOUTH PACIFIC

105° E
120° E
135° E
150° E
165° E
180°
60° N
45° N
30° N
15° N
0°
30° S
45° S
NORTH PACIFIC
7. Mitarai
6. Kabashima
8. Shimoda
5. Guam
4. Pohnpei
35. Christmas Island
31. Lola Island
29. Twin Waterfall Bay
34. Possession Island
30. Port Mary
25. Apia
36. Cocos Keeling Atoll
33. Lizard Island
28. Port Havannah
24. *
32. Middle Percy Island
27. Port Resolution
26. Kavala Bay
*Niuatoputapu
N
W E
S

165° W
150° W
135° W
120° W
105° W
90° W
75° W
60° N
10. Nellie's Rest
9. Geographic Harbor
11. Kliuchevoi Bay
13. Rose Harbour
12. Summers Bay
48. Anse Aux Petites Iles
14. Hollywood Passage
47. Quebec Harbour
45° N
15. San Miguel Island
1. Isla Guadalupe
30° N
2. Isla Clarion
15° N
3. Isla Canal de Afuera
0°
23. Palmerston Atoll
15° S
22. Aitutaki
20. Aukena
21. Motu Haamu
19. Easter Island
30° S
18. Robinson Crusoe Island
SOUTH PACIFIC
45° S
17. Puerto Edén
16. Caleta Brecknock
165° W
150° W
135° W
120° W
105° W
90° W
75° W

75° W   60° W   45° W   30° W   15° W   0°   15° E
60° N
45° N
30° N
0°
15° S
30° S
45° S
75° W   60° W   45° W   30° W   15° W   0°   15° E
NORTH ATLANTIC
SOUTH ATLANTIC
N
W   E
S
48. Anse Aux Petites Iles
50. Cayo Herradura
49. Man O'War Bay
43. Fernando de Noronha
42. Ascension Island
41. St Helena
44. Praia Cantagalo
39. Lüderitz
38. Kraalbaai
45. Puerto Deseado
46. Spaniard Harbour

30 ° E
45 ° E
60 ° E
75 ° E
90 ° E
105 ° E
60 ° N
45 ° N
30 ° N
15 ° N
0 °
15 ° S
30 ° S
45 ° S
40. Alkwasir Island
35. Christmas Island
36. Cocos Keeling Atoll
37. Rodrigues Island
INDIAN OCEAN
30 ° E
45 ° E
60 ° E
75 ° E
90 ° E
105 ° E

INTRODUCTION

If you own a sailing boat, no matter how small or unsuitable, chances are that you've wondered what it would be like to throw in your job, cast off and sail over the horizon. Maybe you've already chartered a yacht in the Mediterranean or the Caribbean but were disappointed to find the anchorages crowded, the locals jaded and over-exposed to foreign cruisers. Or you've spent a season or two out there, and you're now ready to break away from the Coconut Milk Run and try waters less travelled.

Here are 50 out-of-the way destinations to encourage you to sell up and go (or just to divert) with practical tips including formalities, the prevailing weather and GPS positions. Every anchorage featured is accessible in a small to moderate production vessel equipped with the basics and stocked for offshore. None is in a truly extreme location such as the Arctic or Antarctic, or (with two hopefully temporary exceptions) in waters notorious for piracy or hostile governments. But none can be reached in a charter yacht or by a daysail; you will need your own boat.

The selection made – after 70,000 miles of cruising with my partner Jenny in our two successive 27-footers – is highly personal. Some anchorages (St Helena, Cocos Keeling) are classic yet remote destinations that have been favoured by circumnavigators ever since the days of Joshua Slocum. Others (in Japan, Patagonia or the Pacific Northwest) have been chosen more as indicators of the attractions of those regions than as indisputable standouts. Common denominators are protection from the weather, scenic beauty, historic and/or human interest. And the fact that, while solitude is not guaranteed, you won't be troubled by the arrival of a cruising flotilla or by a novice dragging anchor onto you.

The destinations are organised first by ocean: North Pacific; South Pacific; Indian Ocean; South Atlantic; Caribbean/North Atlantic. Then, where there is more than one destination within a single country, they are grouped by country.

Each anchorage is introduced by an essay that describes not just the place, its history and people (if any…) but recounts the author and his crew's adventures in getting there and away. The essays span the 40 years since Jenny and I began sailing offshore and – taken together – tell a story of mistakes made, lessons learned, unforgettable highs and a few frightening lows. They can be dipped into and read in any order. But the opening destination (Guadalupe Island, Mexico) was the first truly remote anchorage we visited under sail and might best be read first. In many ways the cruising scene has changed radically since that voyage to Guadalupe in 1984. Cruisers are older, wealthier and have larger boats; GPS has eclipsed the dark art of celestial navigation and paper charts have all but disappeared; international entry formalities have become more cumbersome. But in other ways, things are much the same. There are no more long-distance sailors out there today than there were in the heyday of ferrocement home-builds. The must-see destinations are still Tahiti, the Windwards, and the Virgin Islands. Which means that places that were out of the way then remain so today. Adventures are still to be had.

Following each introductory essay is a sketch of the highlighted anchorage. Every effort has been made to ensure the accuracy of these drawings and of the characteristics of navigational aids in the neighbourhood, but they should only be used in conjunction with more detailed electronic or paper charts. In many instances, especially in coral waters, it may also be useful to deploy Google Earth/Maps or an equivalent such as Satellites Pro.

Then comes a set of practical tips. When there is more than one destination in a given country, then information relevant to the whole country is presented following the first destination to be described.

Entry Formalities. These were up to date at the time of writing and are largely web-accessible. But they are subject to constant change, especially in light of political and health-related developments. In many cases advance notification of arrival in a new country on a yacht is required, which presupposes internet access while at sea or at the previous port.

Under the heading **Getting There** are hints on the optimal direction of approach for a sail-powered vessel, along with information on how the location may be reached by other means (air, ferry etc). This section should be read in conjunction with **Distances** (the mileage to other major destinations in the region) and **Weather**, which summarises

West into the sunset

prevailing winds, including the risk of cyclones. All references to miles should be considered as nautical miles (1 nautical mile = 1.15 statute miles or 1.85 kilometres).

Under **Anchorages**, the principal anchorage described in the introductory essay is given, along with a GPS position (*Degrees and Decimal Minutes* or DDM format, eg 29°09'.682N 118°16'.652W) and approximate low-water depth in metres. Where there are obvious alternatives within easy reach and/or if other locations have also been described, positions for these anchorages are also provided. If Google Maps/Earth are not in tune with nautical charts (which may occur in the case of older paper charts), the positions noted are correct vis-à-vis Google Maps/Earth. As always, GPS positions should be taken as strictly advisory; in case of doubt, the Eyes Always Have It.

The section entitled **General** comprises other information related to the location: the availability of key services; points of historical or geographical interest; security considerations.

The final sections are entitled **Charts** and **References**.

Paper charts are nearly extinct. But hydrographic agencies are all moving at differing speeds and not necessarily in the same direction as they convert to electronic varieties. For the sake of brevity and consistency – and in recognition of the fact that many cruisers still have paper charts on board – the index number of the relevant paper chart(s) is given. For more detailed commentary on charting, including links to the catalogues of the world's major hydrographic agencies, please see the Note on Charts at the end of this volume.

It is assumed that mariners will already be familiar with the relevant Sailing Directions/Pilot Books for the destinations in question; these are not listed (US Sailing Directions for the whole world are available online for free). Where there are cruising guides or relevant narratives, the latest editions are given. For some areas – notably Venezuela – the old go-to cruising guides have not been updated for many years; for a few destinations there exists no published guide. A wide variety of cruising blogs can also be found online.

The topic of security is an appropriate one with which to close this Introduction.

Non-sailors may think it is foolhardy to leave home and go cruising when the world today seems to be such a dangerous place. It is true that such voyaging incurs perils beyond reefs, high winds and rough seas. But this has always been so. In the 1980s, the waters off southern Indonesia were notorious for pirates; more recently it has been the Horn of Africa. At one point the Suez Canal closed for eight years (1967–75), the Panama Canal for a shorter time, in both cases because of political turmoil. Colombian waters were considered too dangerous for cruisers for 30 years. Now that country is back on the circuit, only for Venezuela to inherit its unfortunate reputation.

Land-based hazards should be investigated and weighed up before you undo that last mooring line. But don't be distracted. All you really need to accomplish your dream is a sound boat, health, a few charts (electronic if you wish to be new-fangled) and a GPS.

Don't dally too long. It is always Later Than You Think.

At anchor, Caleta Yaghan, Chile

PART I

NORTH PACIFIC & NORTH AMERICA

ISLA GUADALUPE

MEXICO

Like everyone who ventures offshore in their own small boat for the first time, we had no shortage of dreams. But we had plenty of doubts, too. How would we deal with leaving the sight of land for the first time? What about seasickness? Cooking while underway? And, while we'd practised celestial navigation with an artificial horizon in our island-bound home waters, would we really be able to take sun sights from the pitching deck of a small sailboat, with the sun dodging behind clouds?

Before quitting our jobs and telling friends and family, we decided to test the waters. We scrutinised the 'Crew Wanted' pages of San Francisco's freebie sailing magazine, *Latitude 38*, and quickly came to an arrangement with John, who wanted to take his 32-foot Cheoy Lee *Jacaranda* south from San Diego to Cabo San Lucas (Mexico), sometime around the Christmas period.

In navigational terms, things did not start well. We'd agreed by phone to meet John the night before departure. None of the first three taxi drivers we tried could tell us where the Valley High restaurant might be. One commented that it sounded more like the name of a school than an eatery. The fourth put us right: 'I guess you mean the Bali Hai, right?'

John was what we needed: he dropped us right in the thick of things.

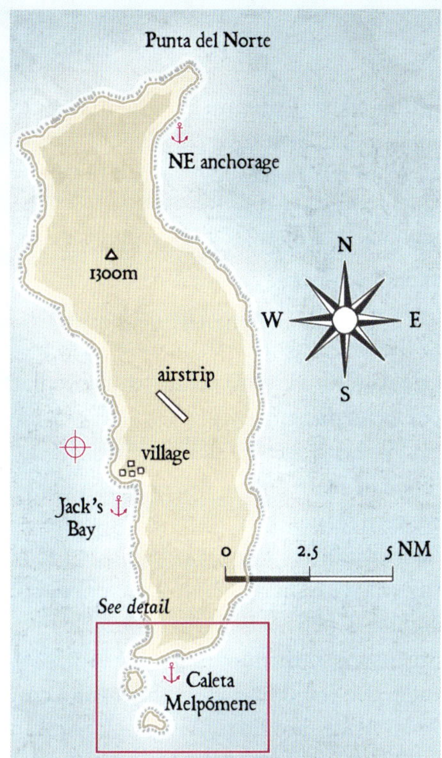

Isla Guadalupe, Mexico
29° N 118° 20' W

Within a few minutes of our leaving the Shelter Island marina the following evening, he'd handed me the wheel, warning me only to stay well clear of the navy submarine pens. He then beckoned Jenny below. Pointing first to a pile of charts on one of the bunks, then rummaging around to find a pencil, dividers and parallel rule, he said, 'Your job is to plot a course for Ensenada. It should come out as 60 or 70 miles.' And he disappeared into the forepeak for a nap.

In hindsight, our first night of offshore sailing was straightforward. At the time it seemed terrifying. We struggled in turn to steer a course by the dimly illuminated compass, while peering over the side to estimate our speed (for *Jacaranda* had no knot meter) and checking off the many navigational lights inshore against the chart. And then there were the ships: an aircraft carrier was a few miles out, practising take-offs and landings. At least, I thought, I would come into my own – as a Spanish speaker – when we reached Mexico in the morning.

Ensenada was not a scenic spot in 1984. We landed on an oil and garbage-covered beach where I impressed John by successfully negotiating with an eight-year-old boy terms for watching over our dinghy. More challenging was the hour shuffling papers at the offices of the port captain and immigration, where questions that I had to relay to John concerned the horsepower of *Jacaranda*'s diescl, her registered tonnage and the unmarried name of John's mother, all these asked in a lisping

Previous pages: Evening at Rose Harbour, British Columbia

Jacaranda at anchor, Melpómene Cove

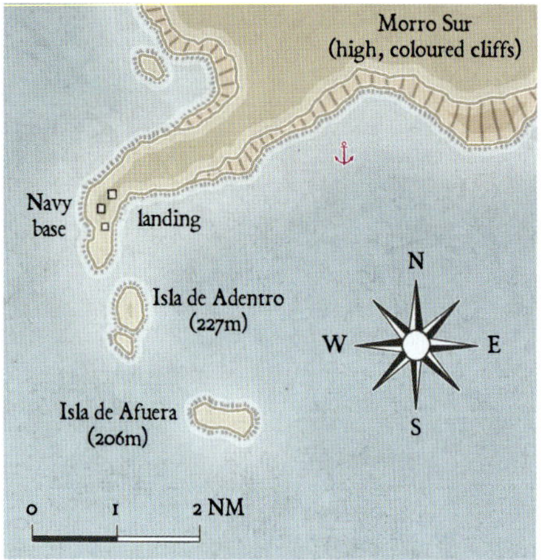

DETAIL: CALETA MELPÓMENE

version of Mexican Spanish with which I was not familiar.

As we sat over the obligatory Corona at Hussong's Cantina, John suggested we ignore the cruising herd hugging the coast southbound:

'You wanted a feel for offshore sailing; and you wanted to test your navigation, right? So let's give Guadalupe a shot.'

We learned how to pole the genoa, how to brace with every roll of the boat, how to compensate with the wheel as we slewed down the front of the waves. And with the dozen or more sun sights we took, we steadily reduced the time it took to plot a line of position from 90 to 30 minutes. The star sights were more challenging: it would be several days before we were skilful enough to shrink the 'cocked hat' triangle within which *Jacaranda* must lie to a size smaller than Switzerland.

Prior to dawn on our second night out Jenny spent time, under John's tutelage, figuring out at what distance we should see Isla Guadalupe, which rises to over 1,200 metres. When it showed up in the morning haze there were further calculations with the sextant to figure out our exact distance off.

With sail area reduced, we spent much of the morning rolling down the western shoreline of this 32-kilometre-long island. The coast was high and rugged, with spectacularly coloured red and black cliffs. About two-thirds of the way along, at the foot of a dry alluvial valley, we could make out about a dozen small white dwellings. As we compared what we were looking at with the chart – which indicated the possibility of anchorage just south of the village – an outboard-powered launch puttered out. A cheerful man in oilskins shouted a greeting, held up a squirming lobster and, as he manoeuvred to keep clear of our rolling topsides, we had a discussion on what we might have to offer in exchange. The skipper of *Pila* wasn't interested in money. 'There's no shop here!' he laughed. A packet of 20 cigarettes sealed the deal and he tossed the lobster up to us.

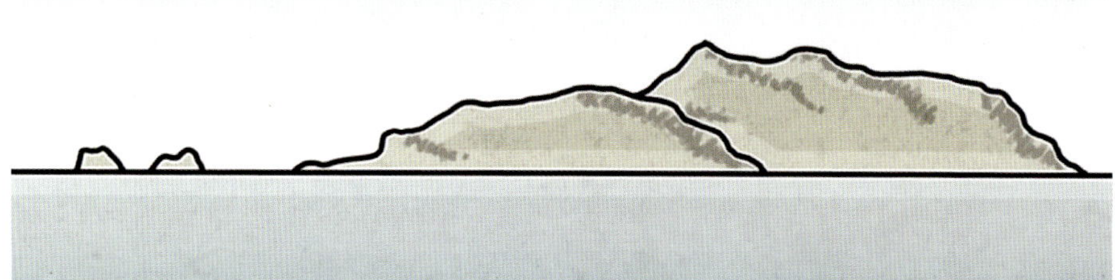

ISLA GUADALUPE
BEARING 343°, 26 NM

Cliffs at Melpómene Cove

'What about the village anchorage?' we asked.

He looked away to windward and shrugged. '*Malo*. We pull our boats up on the beach. And on a day like today, there'll be a big swell running. You'd be better off at Melpómene,' and he pointed in the direction we were headed, to the southern tip of the island.

Melpómene (pron. Mel-POM-enay) Cove is cliff-bound, with excellent protection from the north and north-west – the direction of the prevailing winds – but it's completely open to the south. We anchored a long way out, and in what (to us novices) seemed to be deep water. John explained to us that even if the wind stayed in the north, as was likely, we could easily find ourselves in heavy swell generated by some storm many hundreds of miles to the south, in which case it was advisable to be well clear.

On the west coast of North America, whenever you come across a nautical place name that is from Greek mythology (Melpomene was one of the nine Greek Muses, patron of Tragedy) chances are it was on account of a Royal Navy vessel of the same name. HMS *Melpomene* was in these waters in 1912.

But the island had been frequented by humans long before that. Russian and American sealers found rich pickings on its rocky volcanic beaches starting in the late 1700s, hunting the Guadalupe fur seal and the northern elephant seal almost to extinction. There are the remains of an old sealing station on the eastern shore of the island.

We spent 36 hours at this lonely bay, our first offshore destination. John landed us through breakers – he preferred to stay on board *Jacaranda*, keeping an eye on the weather and the rattling anchor chain – and we explored the black sand beach. Truth be told, there was too much happening here to tempt us far inland. An energetic bull elephant seal, the rolls of blubber around his thick neck scarred by countless fights with rivals, was doing his best to ward off raiders on his harem. Adolescents and other young males lurked offshore or on the margins of the beach, waiting impatiently for the chance to dash in and steal a female.

In the late afternoon, we looked out over the now silver sea and saw John, coming back to pick us up in the dinghy. I thought: 'This is it. This is what I want to do.'

IF YOU GO...

ENTRY FORMALITIES

Guadalupe and Clarion are Mexican territory. There is no official port of entry in either location; they should only be visited following the completion of formalities on the mainland (see below).

Most visitors to Mexico do not require a visa and are granted permission for a 180-day stay. See **https://embamex.sre.gob.mx/ finlandia/index.php/traveling/visas**.

All persons arriving in Mexico by yacht must check in (before landing anywhere else) at the immigration office at an official port of entry and obtain a *Forma Migratoria Múltiple – FMM*; a fee is payable. You must also visit the office of the port captain.

In addition, the captains of vessels over 15 feet in length must obtain a Temporary Import Permit (TIP) for their boat. This is valid for ten years and is transferrable if and when ownership of the vessel changes. It can be obtained in advance at Mexican consulates, online, or in person on arrival. Among documentation required for the issuance of a TIP is proof of insurance.

If you intend to fish in Mexican waters, a licence is obligatory: **https://tramites. ebajacalifornia.gob.mx/ventanillaunica/ tramites/pesca/pesca-deportiva** or **www.sportfishingbcs.gob.mx**. Lobster fishing (by visitors) is illegal.

Both Guadalupe and Clarion are part of the National Parks system. The Revillagigedo archipelago is also a UNESCO Marine World Heritage site. To visit any and all National Parks, a permit is required, entitled *Pasaporte de la Conservación*. Validity one year; fee payable. For UNESCO's description of the archipelago, see: **https://whc.unesco.org/en/ list/1510/**.

A convenient summary of all formalities can be found at:

www.marinadelapaz.com/wp-content/ uploads/2024/06/boatinginmexico2024.pdf.

Note: It is neither legal nor advisable to arrive at Guadalupe or Clarion without documentation in order; you will almost certainly be seen and approached. Penalties for non-compliance are severe and may include seizure of your vessel. If your next destination after either island is in another country – eg USA – the authorities may not be able to give you official clearance papers.

GETTING THERE

Under sail, Guadalupe is most easily reached from the north or north-west. The island has a 1,200-metre dirt airstrip; there is no scheduled air service, but occasional private charters come in. Dive companies run liveaboard boat charters out of Ensenada (18 hours by sea), to dive with Great White Sharks.

DISTANCES

Ensenada to Melpómene Cove, 215 miles. Melpómene to Cabo San Lucas, 580 miles.

WEATHER

So as to avoid the risk of hurricanes further south, few sailboats will wish to approach Guadalupe (from the north) before late November. Through the winter, 75 per cent of winds are from the north and north-west, at an average force 4. Winds from the south and south-east (to which Melpómene is exposed) are rare; heavy swell from storms in the south is possible May to November but less common in winter.

ANCHORAGES

Melpómene Cove, GPS 28°53'.208N 118°16'.260W; depth 20 metres. Subject to williwaws. Landing on the narrow black sand beach may be difficult if there is swell running; it is easiest on the rocks in the extreme west of the cove, below the navy station. Elephant seals (which often crowd the beach) are generally placid but should not be approached closely; fur seals are more aggressive. Other options: Jack's Bay (aka West Anchorage, off Campo Oeste): GPS 28°58'.088N 118°17'.713W; depth 8 metres; marginal. North-east anchorage: GPS 29°09'.682N 118°16'.652W, depth 10 metres; on a shelf, close to the beach, 1.5 miles south and in the lee of Punta del Norte.

GENERAL

The island is 35 kilometres long with a maximum width of 9.5 kilometres. Rocky, arid and largely barren, Guadalupe was denuded of vegetation by a population of feral goats that, at its peak, reached 100,000. By 2007 these had been eradicated and vegetation is now recovering. This was the last refuge of the Guadalupe fur seal and the northern elephant seal, hunted almost to extinction by the 1890s; they have now made a significant recovery. See **https://en.wikipedia.org/wiki/ Guadalupe_Island_Biosphere_Reserve**.

The only permanent civilian settlement is Campo Oeste, on the west coast; about 100 fishermen and their families live here. There are no services or shops. On the south point, west of Melpómene Cove, is a detachment of Mexican navy personnel that functions as a weather station, known as Campamento Sur. Rough tracks join the two population centres and the airstrip (4 kilometres north of Campo Oeste); it is a full day's walk from Melpómene to the village. Water for Campo Oeste is provided by a desalination plant; this should not be relied upon as a water source by visitors.

For an account of a voyage under sail to Guadalupe (2010), see **https:// oceannavigator.com/isla-de-guadalupe/**; for more general information see **https:// en.wikivoyage.org/wiki/Guadalupe_Island**.

CHARTS

USA (NGA) 21661, Islas de Revillagigedo, Guadalupe and Escollos Alijos. Longitude references on this chart, which dates originally from 1874, may not be accurate; charting of the north coast of Clarion is very approximate (compare with Google Maps/Earth).

REFERENCE

Scott, Holly. *Charlie's Charts: Western Coast of Mexico and Baja.* Blue Lake, USA: Paradise Cay Publications, 2015 updated edn.

ELEPHANT SEAL

ISLA CLARION

MEXICO

Four and a half years and 26,000 miles after Guadalupe, we had almost completed a circumnavigation on our own *Tarka the Otter*, an Albin Vega 27. We'd taken the classic route from western Canada, via the South Pacific, Australia, South Africa and the Caribbean. After a slow meander back up to Mexico from Panama, we'd made a pit stop in Acapulco, and now we planned to set off on the long haul to Hawaii and, hopefully, home to British Columbia.

On a Thursday morning (we'd adopted the sailors' superstition of never leaving on a Friday) we spent our last Mexican pesos on a blowout breakfast at the Vaca Negra, behind the swanky Club de Yates de Acapulco, and informed the Dragon Lady at the club's front desk that we were leaving. She was clearly relieved: foreign cruisers were cheap and lowered the tone. For the first time she cracked a smile, as she wished us '*Buen viaje*' and put her hand out for our club pass. In light winds we ghosted out of magnificent Acapulco Bay.

The Great Circle route to Hilo (Hawaii) would take us past the Revillagigedo Islands, some 800 miles on, which sounded like an interesting stop.

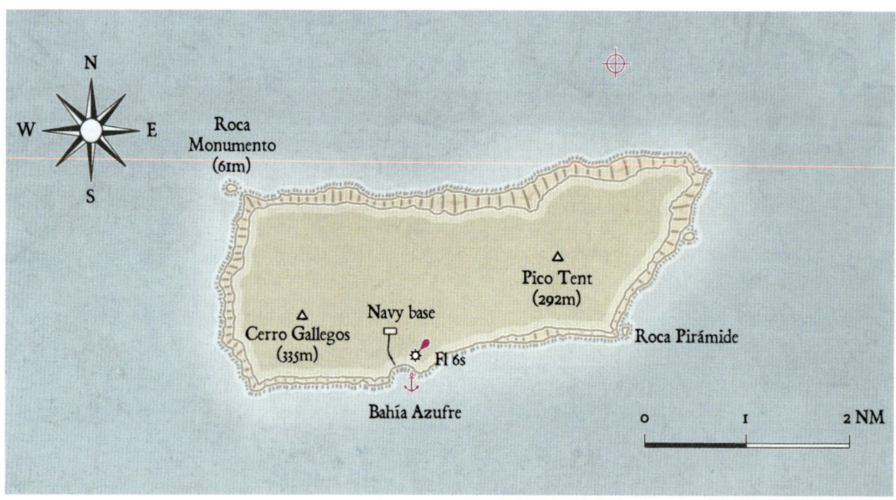

Isla Clarion, Mexico
18° N 114° 42' W

But before we could reach the islands we met with an important moment.

The first few days passed slowly, with the wind rarely over 10 knots. With the sun exactly overhead at this time of the year, we experimented with an esoteric technique learned from our navigation textbook, by which it was theoretically possible to derive a position – not just a line of position – from a single sun sight. Several times, when becalmed, we went swimming to cool off, but only one at a time and after craning our necks to check there was nothing hiding beneath the boat. A close encounter with a large shark off Costa Rica had rendered us cautious.

On the eighth day, we were extra careful in taking the daytime sights which, combined with our estimate of the distance run, would give us our evening position. We double checked them against Rigel, Sirius and Arcturus at dusk. Carefully, on our ink and coffee-stained 'Kodiak to Cabo Corrientes' chart, we marked a tiny 'x'. Steering west-north-west as we were, in about 20 miles' time we would cross our outward track: the path we had taken from Manzanillo to the Marquesas, three years earlier.

At precisely 02:08 – it was her watch – Jenny woke me up to say we had done it. We had sailed around the world.

Thirty-five years on, I often think of that moment. We sat together in the cockpit in silence for a few minutes, as the water rustled slowly past, the windvane creaking as it nudged the tiller first one way then the other. The dimly lit red compass card was swinging hypnotically, but always returning to 285 degrees magnetic. There was no moon, the stars were bright. I was struck by the

Celebrating the circumnavigation, en route to Clarion

obvious: we'd been steering west – on and off – for three years, and now we were back at the very same lonely spot in the ocean. The world seemed suddenly small, our place in it even smaller.

We celebrated properly later in the day, unearthing a bottle of cheap Venezuelan 'champagne' we'd been saving for the occasion. We hoisted the courtesy flags of all the countries we'd visited and toasted ourselves as the sun sank ahead of us. When I look today at the picture of that moment, I'm reminded of how long ago it was: there's Jenny hoisting the old flag of apartheid South Africa up to the spreader.

At daybreak on Day 15, 860 miles out from Mexico, Clarion Island showed itself over the bows. Everything looked brown and barren. Against the blustery early morning sky, this was a forbidding place. As we edged in, following the

The crew of Kialoa II *welcome us aboard*

chart to a semi-circular indentation marked as Bahía Azufre (Sulphur Bay), a single, low white building, set back 200 metres from the bay, came into view. This was the home of a small naval garrison, who made up the place's only human inhabitants.

There was a fishing boat rolling gently at anchor and the wreck of another – the *Conte Bianco* – on the beach. It had been lost in Hurricane Paul, which had devastated Cabo San Lucas in 1982. We didn't hurry to land: we could see the white foam of breakers all along the shoreline. Instead, Jenny dived in and set to work, scraping from our waterline the surprising number of gooseneck barnacles that had accumulated during the two-week voyage from the mainland.

When we later made it through the surf by dinghy, a young sailor met us and escorted us politely up the track to meet his Comandante. Things were informal. Victor (as he introduced himself) wore a Brazil soccer T-shirt and jeans, and everybody called each other by their first names. We signed the log book. There

had been half a dozen boats through Clarion over the past six months, the last two of them registered in Victoria. As we chatted, Victor had the junior sailor make up what he called a Cóctel Clarión: thick, grimace-inducingly spicy and strangely glutinous. Victor smiled and listed the ingredients: 'Garlic; salt; lots of chilli. And a raw turtle egg.' Having only just arrived, it didn't seem diplomatic for us immediately to express concern for the island's turtle population.

Victor redeemed himself with his evident love of the local wildlife. We went first to see the nesting sites of Clarion's large colony of boobies ('bobos' in Spanish, which also means 'fools'): hundreds dotted the scrub-covered hillsides. '*Bobos enmascarados*' (masked), I commented to Victor in a superior fashion, but he corrected me. These were actually much rarer Nazca boobies.

When, after a two-hour walk, we reached the northern edge of Clarion we realised it was even more rugged than it had appeared on the lee side. Cliffs plunged almost 300 metres into the ocean and sharp, isolated pinnacles offered a second line of defence. This would be no place to be caught in a strong norther. Victor agreed and, passing his binoculars, showed us the remains of another fishing boat, hard up against the cliff.

Back at Bahía Azufre we were surprised to find another sailboat had arrived: Victor told us he had never seen two here at the same time. It turned out to be an exhibit from yachting history: *Kialoa II*, one of the original great 'maxis' and winner of countless ocean racing honours. We have never raced offshore, never will, and – like many ocean cruisers – regard racers as a different breed. But Frank, *Kialoa II*'s millionaire owner, was in cruising mode these days. He and his crew reciprocated our invitation for Earl Grey in *Tarka*'s tiny cockpit, with iced margaritas and a lobster dinner aboard *Kialoa II*.

We said a reluctant goodbye to Victor and his team a few days later. Among the friends we had made at the barracks were Blackie and Petunia, two very large pigs kept in a fenced-in enclosure. They especially liked to be scratched behind the ears.

'It's a pity you can't stay for the fiesta next week,' said Victor, and he nodded his head towards Petunia. I must have looked puzzled. 'Yes, it's been a long time coming. We're really looking forward to it; she's the guest of honour.'

On the beach, Bahía Azufre

IF YOU GO…

For information on entry formalities, charts and references see Chapter 1, pages 22–23.

GETTING THERE

There are four islands in the widely spread Revillagigedo group: Socorro, San Benedicto, Roca Partida (the 'Inner Group') and – 200 miles further west – Clarion. Only Socorro and Clarion are inhabited and have acceptable anchorages. Under sail, approach is easiest from north through east. There is an airstrip on Clarion that is used very rarely, and a helicopter pad. The most frequent external visitors are liveaboard dive boats. Naval vessels call in at Socorro, less frequently at Clarion. Note: While the Spanish word for the kind of trumpet known as a clarion is spelled *clarión* the island is named after an American sailing ship, hence no accent should be used.

DISTANCES

Acapulco to Clarion, 856 miles; Manzanillo to Clarion, 596 miles; Cabo San Lucas to Clarion, 410 miles; Socorro to Clarion, 195 miles.

WEATHER

Clarion is subject to hurricanes from May to October. Frequency is highest in August (average 4.3 tropical storms annually). Although Clarion is within the north-east trade wind belt, if approaching from Manzanillo or Acapulco, vessels can expect a significant proportion of westerlies for the first 100 to 200 miles.

ANCHORAGE

Bahía Azufre (Sulphur Bay): GPS 18°20'.642N 114°43'.843W, depth 15 metres, off the white sand beach, north-west corner of the bay.

Land at the foot of the visible track. A marked passage for small boats has also been blasted through rocks to an inner lagoon. With a swell running, landing may be difficult.

GENERAL

Clarion – rectangular in shape; 8.5 kilometres east to west, and 3.7 kilometres north to south – is named after an American brig active here in 1820 but had been sighted by Spanish sailors as early as 1542. There are nesting colonies of Nazca boobies, red-footed boobies and great frigatebirds. Introduced rabbits, feral sheep and – lately – pigs have greatly damaged the environment. Diving is excellent. The only population is six to eight Mexican navy personnel. No services are available, but the navy may help in an emergency; there is a larger navy presence on Socorro.

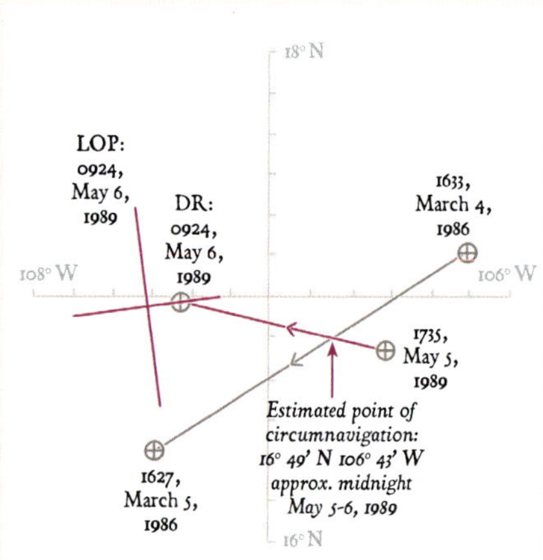

CELESTIAL PLOTTING SHEET FOR THE NIGHT OF CIRCUMNAVIGATION

ISLA CANAL DE AFUERA

PANAMA

For most of our ten-day crossing of the Caribbean, from Montserrat to Panama, it had blown force 7, even 8. We'd only had a few sun sights and the last one showed us that we'd overshot Colón, at the entrance to the Canal. Grimly, we'd put the third reef in the mainsail and spent most of the day beating back.

It was dusk by the time we made out the red and green lights of the entrance to the harbour; they were difficult to see against the bright lights of the city waterfront. But the wind fell sharply once we were inside. We breathed a sigh of relief and, down in the cabin, Jenny smoothed out the chart we'd need to find the approved yacht anchorage, in an area known as The Flats.

With the engine now on, I described aloud what I could see, from one buoy to the next. After a while, the lights on shore gave way to near-total darkness ahead. Something was wrong, I thought; we should have been at The Flats some time ago. Then, looking up, just below *Tarka*'s starboard spreader, I made out a single green light, and below the port spreader a red light. There was a large freighter coming right for us. Its sheer bulk had blocked out the lights of Gatún Locks, just beyond.

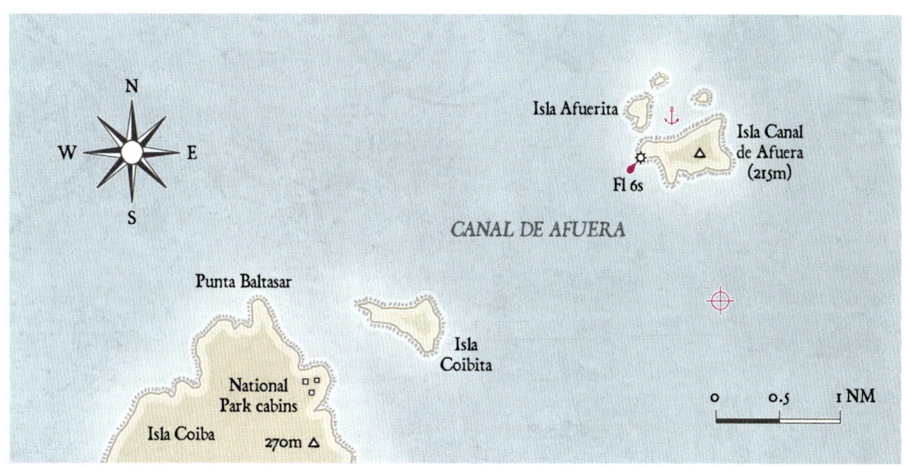

ISLA CANAL DE AFUERA, PANAMA
7° N 81° 37' W

Somehow, we had misread the chart and we were right into the Canal.

I rammed the tiller over and pushed the throttle so hard that I smelled smoke. We shot out of the buoyed channel to one side. A quick glance at the chart indicated there was only a metre of water here, but better to go aground than be run down. After a short, edgy exchange between helmsman and navigator as the freighter glided silently past, we turned tail and made for The Flats. In stunned silence we found a suitable space among the yachts already at anchor and dropped the hook.

Next morning, as we ate breakfast in the cockpit with mutual civility restored, I closely examined the chart from the previous night. In the area which we had motored through after our close call was the interesting notation 'Tree Stumps'. I was about to point this out to Jenny when a neighbouring skipper hailed us:

'Hey, you guys, I was so impressed… What a team! The way you came in last night and anchored without even speaking – fantastic!'

After this adventure, our transit of the Canal was straightforward. We rounded up three other yachties to serve as line-handlers, paid our transit fees – it cost us US$9, based on our estimated cargo capacity of 2 cubic metres – and, at the appointed hour, welcomed our pilot, David, on board. He sagely advised us to have a couple of six-packs of Budweiser beer on hand to send up to the shore-based line-handlers and asked: 'You know you have to be capable of running at 6 knots?'

'Mmm…', I murmured noncommittally. 'Yes, I heard that.'

In the last of the three 'up' locks at Gatún, rafted to a larger Australian yacht, we coincided with a cruise ship called the *Crown Odyssey* in the parallel 'down' set. It seemed that every one of the 2,000 or so passengers aboard was out on deck. Over the PA system, we could hear the captain making an announcement: '…and coming the other way, you can see two sailboats. I can't make out the flag on the larger one, it's blue I think, but the little white boat, she's flying the Canadian maple leaf.'

A huge cheer went up on the ship. We were starting to feel a bit better about the Canal now. But once we were up onto Gatún Lake it became evident that our engine, mutinous after the previous night's experience, could barely manage 4 knots, let alone 6. David sighed; it obviously wasn't the first time this had happened to him.

'Give me the chart, please.' He indicated the Banana Cut, parallel to the main channel, shallower but quite open: 'We can sail in here if it means we go faster.'

At anchor, Isla Canal de Afuera

We did go faster but we still had to spend the night at anchor, mid-Canal. David went ashore, but it was cosy with five of us on board for the night. The rest of the transit was painless and it was with a sense of exhilaration that we motored under the Bridge of the Americas, back into our home ocean: the Pacific.

We had at least six months before the weather dictated we should be back in Canada. A clutch of little-visited islands to the north-west of Panama City, in the Gulf of Chiriquí, looked tempting. The 200-mile sail took us nearly four days with the wind rarely rising above 10 knots.

It remained calm in the islands. Most of our time we spent at Isla Canal De Afuera (Outer Channel Island). In our well-protected bay there was a choice of three sandy beaches on shore, snorkelling and shallows to explore, kingfishers and scarlet macaws in the lush forests behind the anchorage. Occasionally a fishing boat would join us for a few hours, sometimes overnight. There was a family living in a straw shack at one end of the main beach; they directed us to some freshwater pools where we loaded up our tanks, and that afternoon brought us some crabs.

One night I awoke suddenly at around 1am. I'd heard something and the

Sharing one of the down-locks, Panama Canal

boat was rocking very gently. I got up, looked around in the darkness. There was no moon. All I could see was the dim anchor light of a small fishing boat that had pulled in that evening. Everything was now still. But the next morning we were dismayed to find that our dinghy, bobbing astern, was half-deflated. We pulled it aboard and found a neat 3-centimetre gash in one side. It was very difficult to see how this could have occurred: there was nothing protruding

from our boat, and our beach landings had all been on soft sand.

We spent the early morning repairing the damage. Then a military launch pulled in. There were four soldiers on board, in olive-green uniforms, all armed. They went first to the fishing boat. After a few minutes' conversation, the fisherman moved forward and began pulling up his anchor. He gave us a wave and headed out. The launch buzzed over to us next.

'Buenos días Señor capitán…'

The officer politely explained that 36 hours earlier, six prisoners had escaped from the maximum-security jail on Isla Coiba, the big island 4 miles to the south-west. They'd constructed a raft and were considered highly dangerous; certainly they were carrying knives. He politely suggested we move on.

Later we found that Coiba was notorious as a Panamanian Devil's Island, with a reputation for austere conditions, brutality and torture. It was shut down in 2004 and is now a nature reserve. We never found out who or what had caused that gash in the dinghy, but a knife was entirely plausible.

Meanwhile, whenever one of us tempted to make a night entry into an unknown harbour, in the hope of a quiet night at anchor, all the other has to say is: 'Remember the approach to Panama.'

As we proceed in the up-lock, the Crown Odyssey is heading down

IF YOU GO…

ENTRY FORMALITIES AND PANAMA CANAL TRANSITS

Formalities for entry into Panama and for transiting the Canal are separate.

ENTRY INTO PANAMA

Citizens of most countries do not require a visa and are permitted to stay up to 180 days.

Yachts arriving from the Caribbean should call Cristóbal Signal Station on VHF Ch 12 or 16 immediately prior to arrival; they will be directed to an anchorage location or to the Shelter Bay Marina, in Limón Bay at the foot of the Fort Sherman breakwater (**www.shelterbaymarina.com**); GPS 09°22'.1767N 79°56'.9683W. Shelter Bay has immigration officials on site. The previously favoured Panama Canal Yacht Club was demolished in 2022. On the Pacific side, yachts should call in to the Flamenco Signal station; the Balboa Yacht Club has moorings for visitors.

You need to check in both with immigration and the port captain (*Autoridad Marítima de Panamá*). The port captains in Colón or Balboa can issue Cruising Permits.

For further details see **www.noonsite.com/place/panama/formalities/**.

TRANSITING THE CANAL

You will need four line-handlers, in addition to the skipper; an 'advisor' (pilot) is also obligatory. Many yachties volunteer to help another boat first, so as to gain experience, then take the train or bus back. Costs have risen greatly: starting January 2024, fees for yachts under 65 feet were slated to be US$1,935, rising to US$2,130 in 2025. There are additional (lesser) fees for admeasurement, lines and line-handlers (if you cannot find your own) and a security deposit. It will take

Sailing in the Banana Cut, Gatún Lake

three to four days before admeasurement can be completed and a time slot assigned. For detailed regulations see **www.noonsite.com/report/panama-canal-transit-information/**.

GETTING THERE (ISLA CANAL DE AFUERA AND OTHER ISLANDS IN THE GULF OF CHIRIQUÍ)

Vessels hugging the coast eastwards from Costa Rica will experience light westerlies; yachts coming from Balboa/Panama City will have strong to moderate northerlies for much of the way. Dive operators based in David or Santa Catalina (on the mainland) occasionally visit Coiba. Other islands have small temporary populations of fishermen. The nearest large settlement on the mainland is David, accessible by air from Panama City.

DISTANCE

Isla Taboga (off Balboa) to Isla Canal de Afuera, 220 miles.

WEATHER

At 08 degrees north, this area is hurricane-free. The dry season (January to May) is windier than the wet, but it is hot all year (25–30°C+). In the Gulf of Panama (Pacific side) the prevailing winds are the same as on the Caribbean side – ie in the dry, strong northerlies. Starting in June, northerlies in the Gulf weaken, the possibility of southerlies and westerlies increases. West of Cabo Mala, in the Gulf of Chiriquí, westerlies are more common all year and northerlies are much lighter; high mountains act as a shield from Caribbean weather.

ANCHORAGES

Off the middle of three sand beaches on Isla Canal de Afuera, east of Isla Afuerita. GPS 07°41′.99N 81°37′.93W, depth 8–10 metres. Good shelter except from due north.

OTHER ANCHORAGES

Isla Cebaco, Caleta Cayman, GPS 07°29′.56N 81°13′.53W; open to the SW; Islotes Cativo, off the easternmost red sand beach: GPS 07° 42′.47N 81°29′.19W; depth 8 metres; Bahia

Honda, east of Isla Talón, GPS 07°44′.8268N 81°30′.6157W; depth 12 metres; Isla Brincanco: GPS 07°52′.01N 81°47′.62W; depth 13 metres; and Isla Cavada, part of the Islas Secas group, half a mile north of the small village: GPS 07°59′.2484N 82°01′.7768W; depth 16 metres.

GENERAL

Isla Coiba and adjacent islands (including Isla Canal de Afuera) now comprise a national park; Coiba has a ranger station and basic cabins. A permit is required to land; see **www.coibanationalpark.com**. There are no officials on any of the smaller islands.

CHARTS

BA 2145 – Cabo Mala to Bahia Elena; BA 1928 – Cabo Mala to Punta Burica.

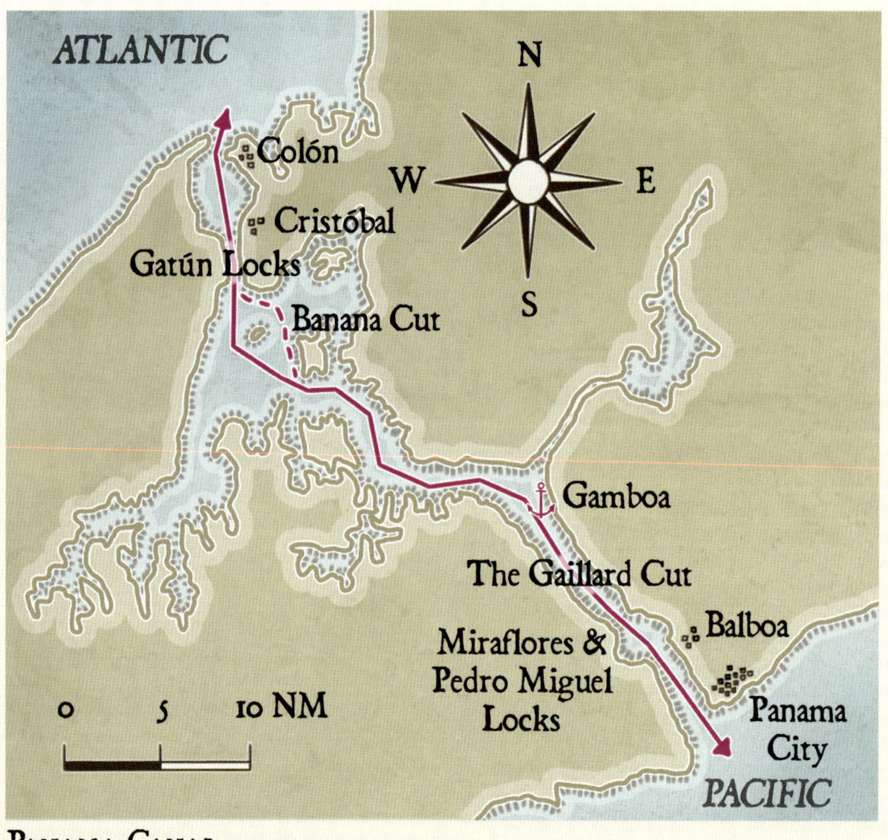

PANAMA CANAL

POHNPEI

FEDERATED STATES OF MICRONESIA

From our anchorage in the Solomon Islands north to the island of Pohnpei, in Micronesia, it was 844 miles. The passage across the equator was slow, but by flying every inch of canvas that we had, we made 119 miles on our last day. We reached the entrance pass through the reef off the north coast, below a huge square-topped mountain, just as dusk was coming on.

The port captain sent out a launch to guide us to a safe outer anchorage before darkness engulfed us. Next morning, we motored the final couple of miles into the port and, among dozens of Chinese and Taiwanese fishing boats, checked into the Federated States of Micronesia (FSM).

As we lay alongside the high harbour wall, pondering on the chart the tortuous route to the inner anchorage, along came a bearded, white and half-naked Good Samaritan in his rubber dinghy:

'Hi! I'm Ted. From *Aloha*. First time here? When you're ready, just follow me. And welcome!'

Pohnpei is one of four large islands –

Kayaking at Nan Madol

the others being Kosrae, Chuuk (formerly known as Truk) and Yap – that, along with their associated atolls, now make up the FSM. The nation's modern history is complicated. Spain was the first outside power to claim these islands, calling them the Carolines, but they soon sold the group on to Germany. After the First World War, control in turn passed to Japan, as a prize for having fought on the Allied side during the conflict. Many Japanese people quickly settled. With war imminent again in the 1930s, Japan established a seaplane base and heavily fortified the area around Pohnpei's only town, Kolonia. The town was bombed, but there was no attempt at an American landing here.

From 1945 to 1979 the USA administered the Carolines as part of a larger Trust Territory. American rule consisted of benign neglect. Everything went into gentle decline and this became known informally as the Rust Territory. In 1979 a vote was held that resulted in Chuuk, Yap, Pohnpei and Kosrae holding together to form the FSM as an independent country in 1986.

Visible reminders of the short era of Japanese control are ubiquitous. One afternoon we walked up to the top of Sokehs Ridge, which dominates the yacht anchorage, and explored the rusting old anti-aircraft installations. And the locals maintain a taste for Japanese cuisine, especially sashimi.

But the USA continues to make investments in all four islands under a succession of agreements known as Compacts, and the people look very much to America today. FSM'ers have full and free access to the USA (and vice versa), and many take advantage of this to enlist in the military and send home their wages. All about town we saw bumper stickers reading 'My Son's a Marine' or 'Go Army'.

An important source of income is offshore fishing licenses. Every two or three nights we would be awakened at around midnight by the roar of a large jet landing at the nearby airport, and again departing an hour or so later. I knew it wasn't the scheduled Continental Airlines milk-run service along the island chain; that departed in the middle of the day.

'Oh yes,' said *Aloha* Ted. 'It's a cargo plane. They load up here with frozen tuna

The airport and commercial port, Pohnpei

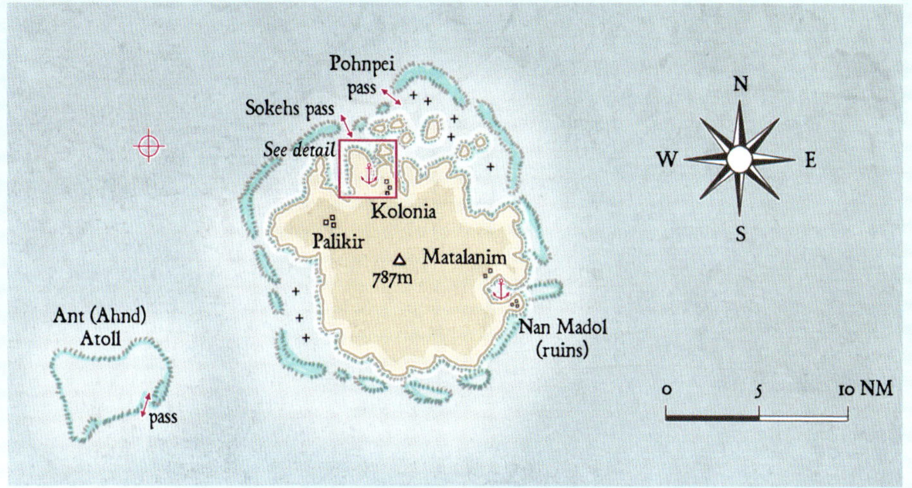

Pohnpei / Ponape, Federated States of Micronesia
7° N 158° E

and fly direct to Tokyo, in time to make it for the morning auction.'

Ted was a long-term liveaboard. His story was sad but not untypical of tales you hear in remote and apparently idyllic harbours around the world.

'My wife Lynn and I, we'd always had the dream, to sail away for ever… We saved and saved, bought our boat. We didn't really know how to sail, but a friend came with us from San Francisco to Hawaii. It seemed straightforward enough, so we carried on alone. Well, you know how things go. Stuff started to go wrong. I'm practical and I could fix most things. But Lynn got spooked. We were a day or so out of here, had a big blow. One thing after another broke, one of those sequences. When it was over, I couldn't get the engine going.'

Lynn had got a job on land as a teacher. It had been a year now that they had been here. Ted tinkered on *Aloha* but, it seemed to us, in a dispirited way.

'She doesn't want to go on. And I can't blame her. But we can't go back either. We've nothing to go back to, you see.'

Cruiser hangouts in foreign ports shift year by year, often according to the price of beer. A favourite in Pohnpei was Rusty's, located in a post-apocalyptic ruined apartment building overlooking the harbour, with an appropriately rusty anchor over the doorway. Here the island's expat band – Wetter Than Seattle, a meteorologically correct reference to the local climate – performed every couple of weeks. The real locals, meanwhile, drank a form of kava called Sakau and the preferred cultural activity was cockfighting, at which vast bets were laid every Sunday afternoon, after church.

Aside from the Japanese dishes, the cuisine was unimpressive, but there was one surely unique specialty: Ramen seasoned with purple grape-flavoured Kool-Aid powder: 'Jim Jones' favourite noodle dish,' joked one of the regulars at Rusty's.

One day we chartered a speedboat and its owner and zigzagged through several miles of reefs and shallows to Nan Madol. This is a long-abandoned city, built on artificial islands within Pohnpei's lagoon; it was constructed around 1200 CE, deserted 400 years later. What makes it unique is that the streets are all shallow canals, best navigated today by kayak. The walls of the buildings are constructed of basalt columns laid on their sides in such a way that they resemble logs; the columns were extracted from a volcanic plug on the far side of the island. It is an odd place

World War Two era Japanese tank

On the northeastern coast of Pohnpei

– no crops ever grew here and there is no nearby source of fresh water – and very little is known about the Saudeleurs, the then-ruling dynasty of Pohnpei.

Our boat driver was Billy. Muscular, with a buzz cut, he had one thick forearm tattooed with the word 'Desert,' the other with the word 'Storm.'

'You guys heard of Moo?'

We both must have looked puzzled.

He spelled it out: 'Em-you. You know, the lost continent of Mu. It's kinda like Atlantis …'cept this one's real, and it was here.'

Later we looked it all up. Over the years, various characters with interesting names – Augustus le Plongeon, Ignatius Donnelly, Etienne Brasseur de Bourbourg – have placed the mythical Atlantis in many locations. Some have suggested that Atlantis, Mu and Lemuria (the supposed origin of lemurs) were all the same place and gave rise to the great civilisations of Greece, Egypt and Easter Island. One of the most prolific and imaginative writers is James Churchward. He states that Pohnpei's Nan Madol is 12,000 years old and was one of Mu's seven great cities; he adds that Mu had a total population of precisely 64 million.

Jenny glowered at me in warning as Billy gave us a version of this, but years as a diplomat had accustomed me to take in wild ideas while maintaining a straight face. We nodded judiciously and said nothing.

We hoisted the kayaks Billy had lent us into the water and wended our way around the vegetation-choked canals, climbing ashore occasionally to inspect Nan Madol's massive structures. Few tourists ever come here, we'd been told. It was oddly quiet, sinister even. Only occasionally we could hear in the distance the tinny tones of Radio Pohnpei. Billy was listening to an evangelical preacher who seemed especially fond of the Books of Leviticus and Revelation.

IF YOU GO...

ENTRY FORMALITIES

No visa is required for US citizens wishing to visit the FSM; non-US citizens are granted entry for 30 days, extendable to 90 if requested in advance. It is necessary to check in/out of each of the four Federated States separately.

Apply well in advance (ie months) for a Cruising Permit to the Chief of Immigration, PO Box PS105, Palikir, Pohnpei, Federated States of Micronesia, FSM 96941. Phone: 320 2606, Fax: 320 2234; Emails: **fmk.mallen@gmail.com, imhq@mail.fm**. Some insistence may be needed; keep a record of your correspondence as proof of application. On arrival, tie up at the main wharf for customs/immigration.

GETTING THERE

Pohnpei is best approached under sail from north through east to south. United (formerly Continental) Airlines flies three times weekly, each direction, to Guam and Honolulu. There are also flights to PNG.

Awaiting entry clearance at the commercial port, Pohnpei

DISTANCES

Gizo (Solomon Islands) to Pohnpei, 1,015 miles; Kosrae (FSM) to Pohnpei, 300 miles; Pohnpei to Chuuk (FSM), 380 miles; Pohnpei to Guam, 900 miles.

WEATHER

Pohnpei is on the southern edge of the typhoon belt; storms spawn here but are usually less severe than in Yap and Chuuk. The main season is May to November, with a peak in August/September, but there was a catastrophic typhoon in April 1904. For the remainder of the year the north-east trades predominate.

ANCHORAGE

Yachts should enter the island's encircling barrier reef by the Main (Sokehs) Pass, to the north-north-west of the town; there is a lit range. Temporary anchorage inside the reef is possible by buoy #6, at GPS 06°59'.669N 158°11'.728E, depth 25 metres. For customs/immigration tie up at the main wharf, GPS 06°58'.7668N 158°12'.0628E. Then proceed with care (missing marker stakes, many shoals) to the well-sheltered inner anchorage at GPS 06°57'.714N 158°12'.060E. Land at the Mangrove Bay Hotel at the head of the bay.

OTHER ANCHORAGES

Ant (or Ahnd) Atoll, fve miles off the south-west tip of Pohnpei, has a narrow entrance pass and has excellent diving. It is uninhabited; advance permission to land is required (obtainable in Kolonia). Anchorage is possible at Matalanim (for Nan Madol) if you have already cleared in at Pohnpei, GPS 06°51'.680N 158°19'.195E.

GENERAL

Pohnpei (formerly known as Ponape) hosts the capital of the FSM, Palikir. Population 37,000. The major town is Kolonia; Palikir (close by) is much smaller. Most services, including a US post office and an Ace hardware store, are in Kolonia. Nan Madol is on a complex of islands south-east of the principal island. It can be reached from the main anchorage by shallow-draught vessels remaining within the reef, or by exiting and re-entering. Most of the waters inside the reef are obstructed by coral heads.

CHARTS

USA (NGA) 81435 (Senyavin Islands); USA (NGA) 81453 (Pohnpei Harbour).

REFERENCES

(1) Hinz, Earl. *Landfalls of Paradise: Cruising Guide to the Pacific Islands (5th edn)*. Hawaii, USA: University of Hawaii Press, 2006.

(2) Clay, Warwick. *South Pacific Anchorages (2nd edn)*. St Ives, UK: Imray, Laurie, Norie and Wilson, 2001.

(3) Cregeen, Phil. *Migrant Cruising Notes, Micronesia*. Auckland, NZ: South Pacific Cruising Services, 1995.

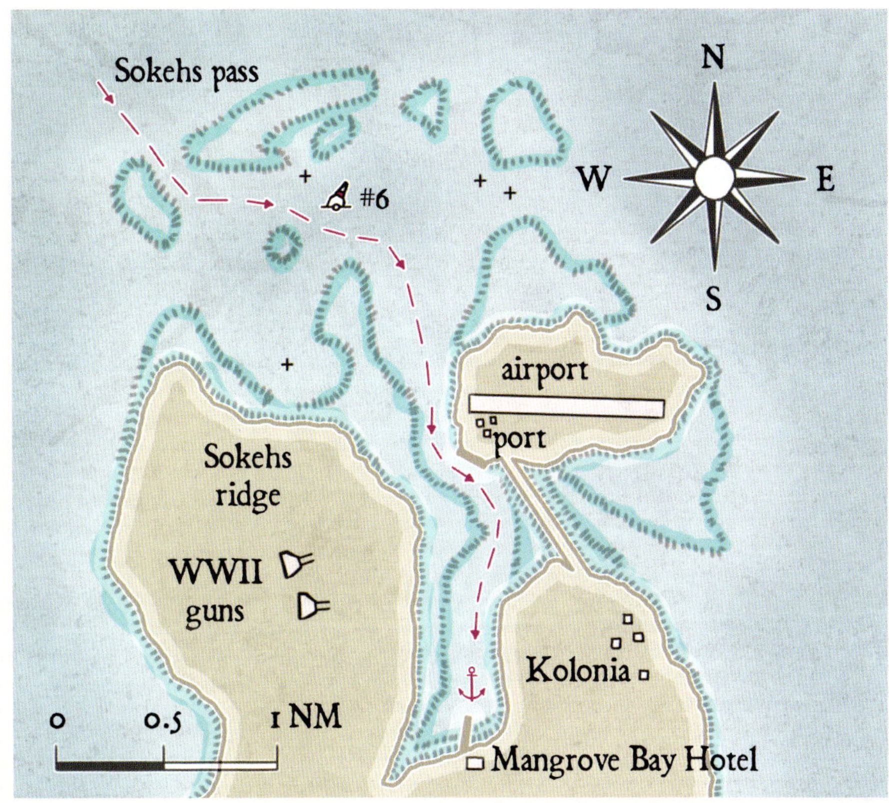

DETAIL: POHNPEI / PONAPE

GUAM

USA

It had been six days since we had left Pohnpei. After a slow start we were now rolling along downwind at 5 knots, with 800 miles on the log. It had been an ideal passage, enlivened by dolphin sightings and successive nocturnal visits from the same large brown booby. In another day or so, we should be off the US Territory of Guam. But there was something I wanted to check now.

Reading from the GPS, Jenny called out our position to me: '12 degrees 46.9 north, 145 degrees 38 east … I'd say we're about there.'

'What depth is the chart plotter showing?'

'It's just dark blue … but the paper chart has us in about 9,600 metres.'

We were over the Mariana Trench, the deepest water in the world. I'd always wanted to go for a swim right here. But the seas were breaking; getting back on board could be tricky and it seemed a pity to waste the wind by stopping. Instead, we rustled up some loose change and I recorded Jenny ceremonially dropping two Canadian quarters overboard. Later I skimmed through pages of arcane discussion on the web:

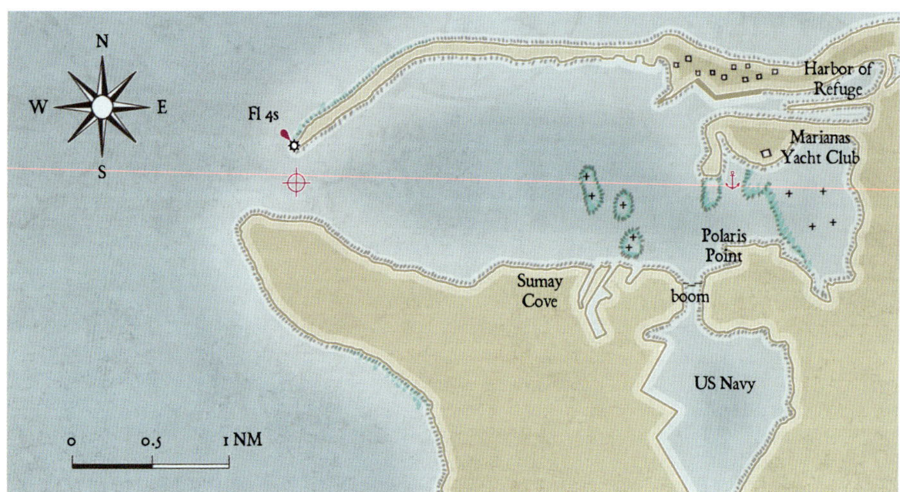

APRA HARBOR, GUAM, US TERRITORY
13° 27' N 144° 37'.5 E

Monument to Magellan's landing, Umatac Bay

the conclusion was that it would take three to four hours for a coin to reach the bottom.

Magellan, of course, knew nothing of the unusual depth of the ocean when he passed this way with the *Concepción*, *Trinidad* and *Victoria* on 5 March 1521, on the first voyage around the world. They were three months out from Patagonia and had crossed the entire width of the Pacific. In this time the men had seen only one small atoll (from a distance) and so low were their rations that by now they were soaking their boot leather in water and eating it.

When they landed in Guam, the first contact between Europeans and Pacific islanders did not go well. The Chamorros had no concept of private property and, after initially friendly encounters, made off with whatever they could find aboard the ships. In retaliation Magellan's men shot several of them dead with their crossbows. The Spaniards sailed on almost immediately, having been unable to re-provision. In disgust the Admiral named Guam and its neighbouring islands the Islas de los Ladrones (Islands of Thieves), a name that stuck until Spain formally claimed the archipelago in 1667, renaming the group the Marianas.

As we motor-sailed into a stiff north-north-east breeze up the supposedly lee side of the main island, we were nervous about two things (but not the modern Chamorros, known to be friendly and peaceable). First, although there was cooling water entering our venerable Bukh diesel engine, there mysteriously seemed to be none exiting overboard. Second, we knew that Guam hosted a massive American military presence; our reception might be brusque.

The matter of the disappearing cooling water was clarified when Jenny reported steam rising from the bilge, inside the cabin: there must be a leak of some sort in our exhaust's water trap, allowing the near-boiling exhaust water to run below. This was not reassuring. But the problem could be resolved temporarily by frequent (manual) pumping of the bilge. The crew, accordingly, did not see much of the coastline over the next several hours.

As for the navy, as we drew near Apra Harbour we were approached by a grey high-speed military launch. The captain, after shouting instructions via a bullhorn, shepherded us past great booms that block the entrance to the navy dockyard and pointed towards a set of mooring buoys off the Marianas Yacht Club. The dummy Polaris missile mounted in one corner of the bay was a clue as to what lay behind those booms. On shore,

One of the sites of American landings, 1944

officials kindly came to meet us at the club bar, wished us welcome to the USA and mentioned in passing 'the terrible news from Japan'.

We now learned that a week earlier, when we were 300 miles out from Pohnpei, a devastating tsunami had struck the east coast of Japan's largest island, Honshu. It had flooded the Fukushima nuclear plant and caused incalculable loss of life. In Guam those nuclear subs had strained at their moorings for a few minutes, but that was all. At sea a 1-metre wave must have passed under *Bosun Bird*'s keel, but we would not have noticed it in the trade wind conditions. By phone we reassured distant shore-bound friends that we were fine. This development gave us pause for thought, certainly. But 95 per cent of the coast of Japan – our next destination – was unaffected. Callous though it might sound (and it did, to some friends) we could see no reason to change our sailing plans.

Exactly where Magellan landed is open to doubt. But the conventionally accepted site, marked by a small white memorial, is at Umatac Bay in the south-west of this hilly, 70-kilometre-long island. After an entire day squeezed inside our cockpit lockers, fixing that water trap, we rented a rusty Toyota to visit. There was an unimpressive whitewashed obelisk in the quiet village and a bar named Magellan's Landing; its Budweiser-sponsored sign stated enigmatically that 'Responsibility Matters'. On the hillside above the bar were some more imposing ruins from a Spanish fort of a later date. But as we looked down on the small bay we thought it unlikely that Magellan would have been able to fit his three caravels into this cramped space.

Much-better documented, as you would expect, is Guam's pivotal role in the Second World War. The fighting over this island, along with neighbouring Saipan and Tinian, was desperate, but not every Japanese soldier was killed or captured. Just around the corner from Umatac was a tacky hamburger joint called Jeff's Pirate's Cove. Near here, Jeff himself told us, Sergeant Yokoi of the Imperial Japanese Army stepped onto the road one day in 1972, after 28 years hiding in the hills of the interior. After he was apprehended, he was shown newspapers from 1945. But only when he received authority from Tokyo would he formally surrender. Yokoi received US$300 in back pay and was flown home to a media frenzy, to which he responded by saying only: 'It is with much embarrassment that I return.'

On the sandy landing beaches at Asan and Agat, the Japanese flag now flew alongside the Stars and Stripes.

Unlike in Normandy, there were no American graves here, but artillery pieces had been preserved and black-and-white photographs on the front gave an impression of the organised chaos of the landings of 21 July 1944.

At the Marianas Yacht Club, I picked up an old copy of *Latitude 38*. The Letters section was always interesting. One in particular caught our attention. It was from a singlehander whom we knew as Freeloader Bob. He mentioned meeting up with another solo sailor from Japan – Chinami – a friend we'd made, first in Tonga, then in New Zealand. Responding, the magazine editor noted that Chinami and his 35-foot sloop had gone missing near Cape Horn and were presumed lost. I passed the magazine over to Jenny. She read the comment and we sat in silence for a few moments. We rarely discussed the dangers of what we were doing; we'd both internalised them long ago.

'Time to be off?' I suggested eventually.

She nodded. We rowed out in silence to *Bosun Bird*. An hour later, as we motored out of the harbour, I answered her anxious look of inquiry by bending over the stern.

'Yes, there is water coming out of the exhaust.'

IF YOU GO...

ENTRY FORMALITIES

Visitors to the USA from most European countries do not require a visa (for the list see https://travel.state.gov/content/travel/en/us-visas/tourism-visit/visa-waiver-program.html) but still need permission under the Electronic System for Travel Authorization (ESTA); Canadians and citizens of Bermuda require neither.

Foreign yachts entering the USA for the first time must check in with Customs and Border Protection (CBP) at the first possible port of entry; see www.cbp.gov/travel/pleasure-boats-private-flyers/pleasure-boat-locations. In many locations, the first requirement is to phone in; you may then be required to wait on board for a face-to-face interview.

Following an initial entry, boaters may apply to go through one of three Alternative Inspection Systems (AIS) for subsequent visits; see www.cbp.gov/travel/pleasure-boats-private-flyers/pleasure-boat-overview. Vessels over 30 foot are required to make application for a private vessel decal (ie Cruising License); fee $27.50.

When approaching Apra – the only port of entry – call the harbourmaster on VHF Ch 16; the harbour is under the control of the US Navy and a launch may be sent to guide you in. On arrival at the designated moorings off the Marianas Yacht Club, call customs and immigration and they will come to the club (overtime fees apply after 17:00 and on weekends). Customs: (Marine) 472-8426, (Airport) 642-071; Immigration: (Marine) 472-7265, (Airport) 642-7611.

GETTING THERE

Guam is best approached by sail from the east. United Airlines offers frequent service to/from the US mainland and to/from Japan.

DISTANCES

Pohnpei (FSM) to Guam, 885 miles; Honolulu to Guam, 3,320 miles; Guam to Okinawa (Japan), 1,240 miles; Guam to Kagoshima (Japan), 1,340 miles.

WEATHER

Guam is firmly within the easterly trades. Typhoons are frequent; they may occur at any time of year but especially July to November. On average, one typhoon per year passes within 100 kilometres of Guam, two to three more within 290 kilometres.

CROSSING THE MARIANA TRENCH
13° 30' N 150° E

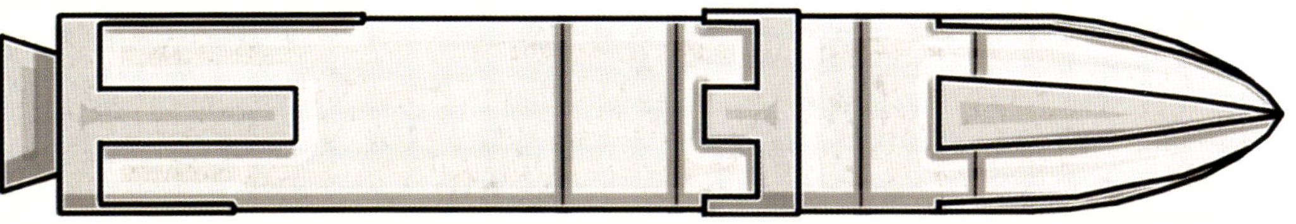

Dummy Polaris missile, Polaris Point

ANCHORAGE

Apra Harbor, on the west side of the island and protected by a long breakwater, is the only all-weather anchorage. A range leads vessels through the entrance, then a second range leads to starboard towards Polaris Point (the entrance to the navy facility). There are large reef patches on the final approach to the Marianas Yacht Club; take care. Mooring buoys are available for visitors, free for the first three days, then US$7 daily; GPS 13°27'.1186N 144°40'.2697E. For details regarding services at the Yacht Club see **www.marianasyachtclub.org**.

To the north of the Yacht Club, in a cut between Cabras Island and Drydock Point, is the Harbor of Refuge, intended as a typhoon shelter; moorings (depth 2.5 metres) should not be relied upon without prior underwater inspection. The marina at Sumay Cove, on the south side of the harbour, is open only to military personnel.

GENERAL

This is a standalone Unincorporated Territory of the USA; Guamanians are American citizens but have limited representation in Washington. Population 170,000. All services are available, at US mainland prices. There is a heavy presence of the US military:

Andersen Air Force Base in the north of the island services B-52 bombers and there is a large (off-limits) submarine base in Apra Harbor. Public transport is poor and it is some distance from the Yacht Club to the nearest shops. If staying more than a day or two, it may be practical to rent a car. The United Seamen's Service Club (M111 Cabras Hwy, Piti; tel (671) 472-2370) is within walking distance; it has a restaurant; they may help in an emergency.

CHARTS

USA (NOAA) 81048 (Guam); USA (NOAA) 81054 (Apra Harbor).

REFERENCES

(1) Hinz, Earl. *Landfalls of Paradise: Cruising Guide to the Pacific Islands (5th edn).* Hawaii, USA: University of Hawaii Press, 2006.

(2) Clay, Warwick. *South Pacific Anchorages (2nd edn).* St Ives, UK: Imray, Laurie, Norie and Wilson, 2001.

(3) Cregeen, Phil. *Migrant Cruising Notes, Micronesia.* Auckland, NZ: South Pacific Cruising Services, 1995.

(4) Hawkings, Francis, and RCC Pilotage Foundation. *The Pacific Crossing Guide (4th edn).* London: Adlard Coles, 2024.

KABASHIMA, GOTO RETTO ARCHIPELAGO

JAPAN

One of the reasons cruisers often give for taking to the high seas is that you become master of your own destiny: you break free of the ever-encroaching rules and conventions that bind us in daily life on shore. This overlooks the fact that if you ever want to land anywhere there will be paperwork again. *Bosun Bird* and its crew take a more sanguine view: dealing with foreign officials and bureaucracy, often in a language of which we have little or no command, is all part of the experience of travel and of learning about different cultures.

But Japan did put us to the test.

First there was the requirement that we fax to the officials at our intended port of entry all our details along with an exact time of arrival. No, we were told politely, email would not do.

'Who has a fax machine these days?' we asked ourselves.

Fortunately, the United Seamen's Club, a charitable outfit in industrial wasteland adjoining Guam's Apra Harbor did, albeit long since disconnected and gathering dust.

And who can predict an exact arrival time for a 27-foot boat facing a 1,350-mile

bash upwind? We entered a random time and date into the fax and thought no more of it as – en route to Kyushu – we weaved our way around a developing typhoon and puzzled over powerful ocean currents that were not behaving as predicted.

When we finally approached the designated yacht moorings at Kagoshima after a bumpy, wet and fast passage, Jenny pointed out a line of men in bright blue blazers, peaked caps and white gloves, all standing to attention on the edge of a high concrete breakwater. I made an off-colour remark, recalling those old Toyota ads involving joyous Japanese men in such blazers. But more seriously I wondered if we were inadvertently crashing some formal event.

The process of tying up was novel and confusing: we were required to position ourselves within a rectangle formed by four mooring buoys, bows in to a wall, with landing at the high quayside to be achieved from an unstable foam and plank raft. It took some time but once we were secure, we looked up again. The men were still there, now looking down at us. We realised belatedly that this was our reception committee. And that they were here because we had, by a one in a

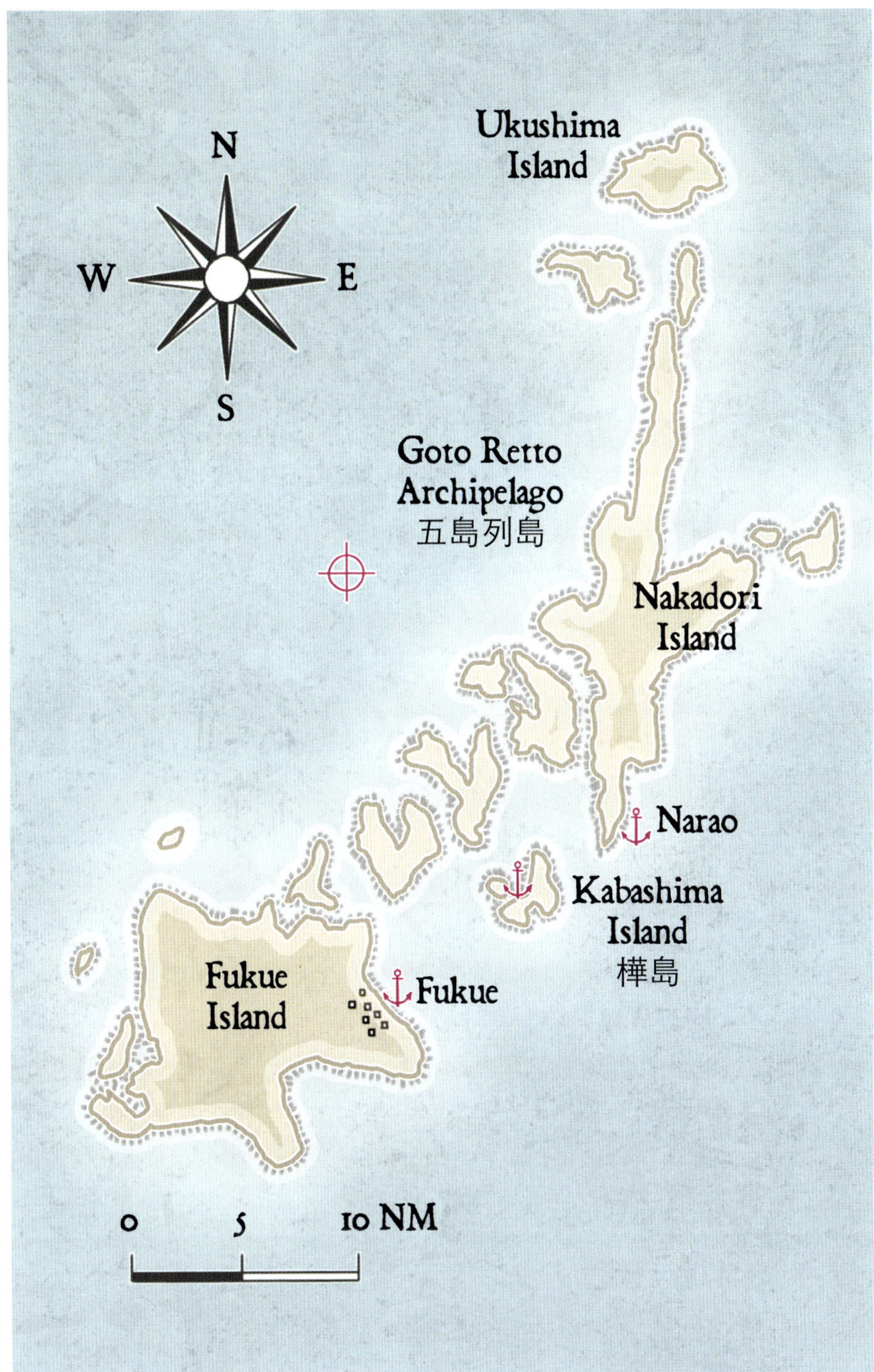

KABASHIMA & GOTO RETTO ARCHIPELAGO, JAPAN
33° 128' N 50° E

thousand chance, arrived when we said we would.

The officials boarded two by two, gamely braving a vertical steel ladder and the wobbly raft in their shiny black shoes and impeccably creased trousers. We soon lost track of which government department they represented – immigration, agriculture, the port authority and so on – but they were all unfailingly polite. And they all required that we fill in the same form: the aptly named General Declaration. Several offices in Japan now have the names of all eight of our long-deceased grandparents on record.

The bureaucracy done with, we were overwhelmed with kindness. Cases of beer, watermelons, sushi: almost every day we would come home to *Bosun Bird* and find that complete strangers had deposited gifts for us on the quayside.

We were taken everywhere. Our new best friend was Mi-Chan, who filled miscellaneous functions at the Kagoshima boatyard. She was our guide to Onsen and Sento (spa/bath) etiquette: where you undress, how you put your clothes in a locker, how you must shower sitting down before you enter the main pool, the need for a small washcloth: 'Not hide parts,' she emphasised with a giggle and after checking her electronic dictionary. 'Put cloth on head.'

Several times Mi-Chan accompanied Jenny while I went in the men's side. We found the experience of public nudity oddly liberating. Until, that is, a few days later.

The Onsen (spa) in question was one we had already visited with our friend just the previous day, so we felt confident enough to go alone, carefully repeating the rituals we'd been taught. After half an hour, I was floating contentedly and by myself in my hot pool, half asleep; Jenny was presumably doing the same, on the ladies' side. Then I heard the door slide open. There was that classic Japanese sound: a sharply indrawn breath. A completely naked middle-aged woman – those washcloths leave little to the imagination, even if you do try for concealment – was looking at me open-mouthed, in horror. She closed the door and fled. A few minutes later, in through the steam came a uniformed man – another blue blazer – looking bashful, his hands together in the classic gesture of apology: 'So sorry. Here is woman's side…'

And the manager explained that on account of the better view from one window of the Onsen, the men were assigned the view one day, the women the next. Thus, we learned to recognise our first two Japanese ideograms: 女 – woman; and 男 – man.

Back at the marina as we prepared to move on, more gifts were showered on us. Oota San – his visiting card read '*Wind Word* – I am Boss – Captain Oota' – gave us a small solar-powered lantern and a plastic folder with a set of Google Maps/Earth photos of harbours and anchorages. Captain Maika of *Summertime* supplemented this with a typewritten suggested itinerary, complete with estimated distances and times.

The itinerary seemed typically Japanese, unnecessarily precise, we thought. But we thanked Maika anyway. Then, the day before departure, Mi-Chan came to us looking flustered. The marina boss was worried that there was still a set of officials we had failed to see. The Ministry of Transport, which is responsible for the Coastguard, now required that we submit a list of all 'Closed' ports we intended to visit, with a view to developing a customised cruising permit.

'What is a Closed Port?' we asked.

Pretty much all small harbours in Japan are Closed Ports, it turned out. The term harks back 500 years to when, after centuries of isolation, Nagasaki was authorised by the authorities in Edo (today's Tokyo) as the only location where foreign traders might enter and do business. Everywhere else was deemed Closed. Over the years, and only after American gunboats threatened to force access in 1854, a few more places made the Open list.

This is where Maika's itinerary now came in. We submitted it unchanged and, after a few days, back came an impressive permit in kanji characters that would take us up at least half the coast of western Kyushu. We were confused by the dates on our vellum scroll, which seemed to be wrong to the tune of several decades.

'Ah yes, traditional, imperial calendar,' explained Maika as he examined it.

To begin with, we were only asked once or twice to show the permit. Then, after an overnight sail west from Nagasaki we came to the little visited archipelago of Goto Retto (Five Islands) in the East China Sea. We tied up to a float at Fukue, on the main island. A typhoon was forecast to pass within 200 kilometres, so we thought it would be a good idea to have a chat with the Coastguard and seek their advice on

places to shelter. For half an hour, we pored over charts with the uniformed officers, finally plumping on a narrow nearby inlet as the best option. Then a slim folder was passed by a flunkey to our helper. He opened it, and by reading upside-down I could see it contained a copy of our cruising permit, as well as the General Declaration. There was a drumming of fingers, then.

'Very sorry…' He turned the folder towards us and pointed halfway down the list of our approved stops. 'Please see. Typhoon hole … not on list.'

The only remedy – this was said with a fixed smile – was to sail back to Nagasaki and seek a new permit.

'But by that time, the typhoon might be here…'

'*Sou desu ka…*' That is so.

In the end the storm veered away. But we had learned our second big lesson in Japan: when preparing your sailing itinerary, cover yourself bureaucratically by including every possible stop, however unlikely.

New friends Yoshinori and Matsumoto owned the only two sailboats in Fukue. When the time came to leave again, they pointed us to their favourite weekend cruising destination: the island of Kabashima. Like everywhere else

The breakwater at Kagoshima, Sakurajima volcano in the background

in Japan (for every promising-looking inlet or bay has a harbour of some sort and swinging free at anchor is almost unknown), we would need to tie up. Conveniently there was a floating pontoon at Kabashima that, in their experience, was never fully occupied.

Their recommendation was a good one. The small, hilly and wooded island a few miles north of Fukue had two tiny villages and the bay was eerily quiet, save for the chirping of cicadas in the woods and the distinctive call of kingfishers in the trees. At its head was a set of sixties-era concrete buildings. It must be a school, we decided. But on the first morning only a few cars

Tied up at the pontoon, Kabashima

drew up and there were no children to be seen. Then a young man, leading by the hand a six-year-old boy, came down to our pontoon and shyly introduced himself.

'I am Hideki, elementary school teacher; this is Kenji; Kenji please say hello.'

Kenji and Hideki stayed for tea and cookies. We had been correct. The buildings were Kabashima's elementary and junior high schools, with a shared gymnasium. But there was only one pupil in each school. The once populous islands of the archipelago were now almost empty, Hideki told us. Nobody was having children anymore, everyone had gone to the cities.

As we talked, Kenji was looking at us intently; it was evident he had Down's syndrome or some similar disability.

'Yes,' said Hideki. 'He is a nice little boy, but he has some problems. His mother lives at Fukue, with a new man; … she cannot look after Kenji. So, he lives here on Kabashima with his grandmother.'

Hideki pointed to the very top of the mountain where you could make out the curling and gold-painted eaves of a small wooden temple among the trees. Seventy-seven-year-old Grandma was a soothsayer – we had to look up the word in the dictionary, when Hideki had trouble explaining it – who made a small living by telling the fortunes of the occasional pilgrim who climbed to her eyrie.

The old fortune teller and the lonely boy, living in a temple on a hill on a small island: I thought there might be an enigmatic Japanese novel or arthouse movie there.

IF YOU GO…

ENTRY FORMALITIES

Most nationalities are eligible for tourist visas, valid for 90 days; many cruising sailors are able to extend their stay by briefly leaving by ferry or air, then returning (eg to/from South Korea). The vessel is not subject to the 90-day limit, see **www.mofa.go.jp/j_info/visit/visa/index.html**.

Entry by sailboat can only be made at designated Ports of Entry (Open Ports). In south-western Japan these include Okinawa, Chichijima, Kagoshima, Nagasaki and Fukuoka (the last three all on the island of Kyushu). For the full list of Open Ports, see **www.mlit.go.jp/common/001257673.pdf**.

Application forms for entry should be sent in advance from your last port of departure to the appropriate office of the Japan Coast Guard, which is affiliated with the Ministry of Land, Infrastructure and Transport (MLIT). You should update your arrival information no later than one working day before your actual arrival. Email is now accepted. More information and the necessary form can be found at **www.kaiho.mlit.go.jp/ope/apply/hoanoo-e.html**.

Some Japan Coast Guard contacts: Kagoshima (Kyushu) **jcgakagoshimakotsu1-2c2a@mlit.go.jp**; Naha (Okinawa) **jcgbnahakq3-8f5m@mlit.go.jp**; Chichijima (Ogasawara) **jcg3ogasawara-9q3p@mlit.go.jp**; Wakayama (Osaka Bay) **jcg5wakayamakotsu2-7g2d@mlit.go.jp**; Shimoda, (Shizuoka) **jcg3shimodakq1-9t8x@mlit.go.jp**.

Sailing up the east coast of the Goto Retto archipelago

ONWARD FORMALITIES

All ports in Japan are deemed to be either 'Open' or 'Closed'. Until recently, cruisers had to apply at an Open Port, with the Maritime Bureau of MLIT for permission to visit each and every Closed Port on their subsequent itinerary. This process has now been simplified, and a single Cruising Permit can be issued at the port of entry. A minimum of one week's notice is required. See: **www.mlit.go.jp/ en/maritime/specialpermission.html**, but also see **www.mlit.go.jp/common/001420113. pdf**, which explains that you do not need to list every Closed Port.

GETTING THERE

It is usually a reach or a run from Nagasaki to the Goto Retto archipelago. The islands can also be reached by ferry from Nagasaki and Sasebo, by air from Nagasaki and Fukuoka. Smaller inter-island ferries run.

DISTANCES

Nagasaki to Fukue, 60 miles; Fukue to Kabashima, 9 miles.

WEATHER

The eastern shores of the archipelago are well sheltered from the open waters of the East China Sea. In general, the winter brings dry, northerly winds; in summer, more moist, warmer southeasterlies prevail. Typhoons can occur at any time, but most frequently between May and October; Kyushu is often hit hard. For a regional overview, see **www. data.jma.go.jp/gmd/cpd/longfcst/en/ tourist/file/Northern_Kyushu.html**.

ANCHORAGE/MOORING

Kabashima. Tie to the large pontoon at GPS 32°45'.491N 128°59'.317E; well protected. Other nearby anchorages: Fukue: inshore end of a pontoon, near the Coastguard building, GPS 32°41'.786N 128°51'.020E'; Narao: pontoon on the south-west wall in the almost deserted northern harbour, at GPS 32°50'.810N 129°03'.482E.

GENERAL

There are two small villages on Kabashima with very few services, one 1.5 kilometres to the west, the other 1.5 kilometres north; both have harbours. Most services are available at Fukue, on the main island. There are a number of interesting churches to visit from Fukue – these islands hosted a clandestine Christian population at a time when the religion was banned in Japan.

CHARTS

BA 359, Western Approaches to Kyushu; JHA W1212, Goto Retto.

REFERENCE

Coghlan, Nicholas. *Sailing to the Heart of Japan.* Florida, USA: Seaworthy, 2024

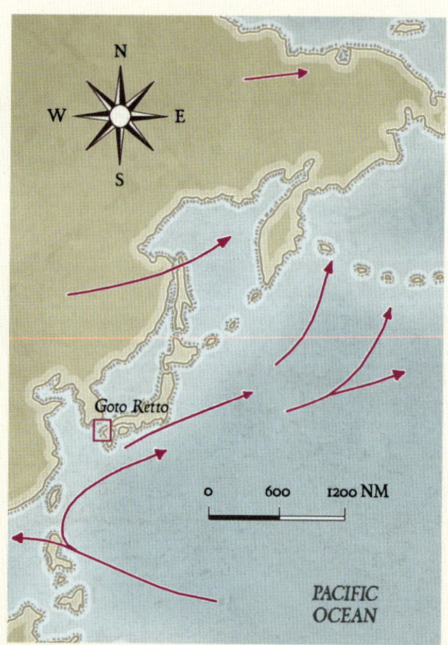

Typical typhoon tracks in June in the northwestern Pacific

7

MITARAI, INLAND SEA

The Inland Sea – Seto Naikai in Japanese – is a vast, island-studded seawater lake, protected from typhoons and ocean swells by the three great islands of Kyushu, Honshu and Shikoku that encircle it.

For hundreds of years, pilgrims, traders and envoys have used Seto Naikai as a thoroughfare. At Hirado, a stop we made soon after Kabashima, a 5-metre-long ancient parchment on display in the local museum shows the route the feudal lord – the Daimyo – would take every few years to pay obeisance to the Shogun in Edo. The retinue would first thread Kanmon Kaikyo (the narrow, tidal strait that gives access to the Inland Sea from the Sea of Japan), then sail from one island to the next, dodging dragons, devils, sea monsters and whirlpools all the way to Osaka, where the Daimyo would climb into his palanquin to continue overland.

This was the path we would now follow.

At Kanmon Kaikyo there are no dragons anymore and great LED sign boards allow the navigator to read the strength and direction of the current, so as to avoid the worst of the whirlpools. But there are monsters still: 200,000-ton tankers take advantage of slack water to manoeuvre awkwardly in and out of berths in the dockyards that line the Strait. Tugs buzz rapidly from one side to the other. Small fishing boats studiously ignore (until the very last moment) the bigger vessels making their way up and down.

The industrial landscape is grim – Kitakyushu City, to our starboard side, was the primary target for the second atomic bomb, spared by cloud cover that August day – but there was an arresting sight as we reached halfway:

'I can't believe it,' said Jenny, looking

Karatsu castle, north shore of Kyushu

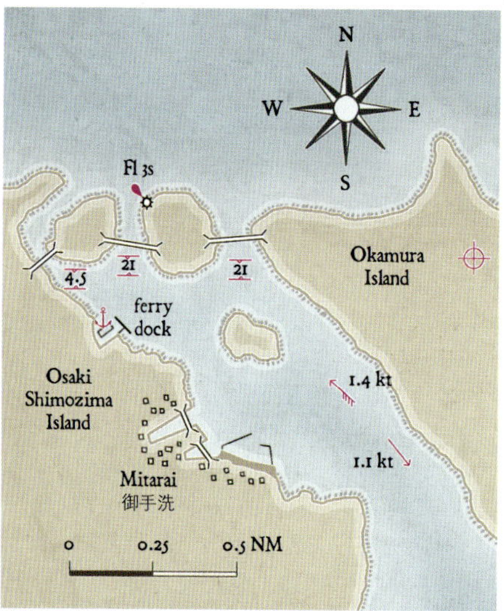

MITARAI – 御手洗, JAPAN
⊕ 34° 11'.5 N 132° 52'.5 E

through the binoculars. 'It's St Mark's, Venice, but half-size…'

A wedding palace, we deduced. As well as having a traditional Shinto ceremony, many young Japanese couples like to have a western-style wedding in a European-looking venue, complete with the white dress and veil, Mendelssohn (possibly a little Celine Dion), and an English-speaking clergyman officiating. The 'clergyman' is usually a foreign English Language teacher looking to make some extra cash; these weddings are for show only.

Once we were through the narrows, we left all that blight behind. As spring became summer, we meandered from one bucolic and verdant island to the next, making the odd detour to larger towns on the Honshu mainland, usually because there was some colourful local festival that friends pressed us to see. The winds were light; often we'd only make 5 or 6 miles in a day. We rarely anchored. Every nook had a little fishing harbour at its head, but most were quiet and semi-abandoned; it was easy to find space on the wall or on a pontoon.

On Kurahashi Jima (Jima/Shima means island), the self-appointed yacht greeter doubled as a Buddhist priest. He treated us to lunch and took us up in the hot afternoon to his temple. In the woods behind was a small granite plaque, with a poem dating from about 1200 CE; it described this very spot, with the rustle of the same stream and the clicking of the cicadas. Time had truly stood still.

Halfway along the Sea, we came to the town of Mitarai, and a square concrete basin into which a floating pontoon with two short fingers had been crammed. There was room (just) for four yachts. For a change, we had company.

'Hello, I am Olive,' said the suntanned, liver-spotted and rather frail-looking man from the neighbouring yacht.

We realised after a few minutes that *Olive* was in fact the name of his boat. Mr Olive was well into his eighties. He'd bought his boat 25 years ago, he said, and had done a lot of sailing around the Japanese islands.

'Yes, I wanted to sail to America,' he said wistfully. 'But now is too late. And my wife … yes, she is still alive, but she has never liked to sail. So, I have no crew.'

Mr Olive was in many ways typical. He had bought his boat in boom years (the 1980s), but Japan's work culture had allowed him little time to enjoy it. He was married but sailed alone; a mystery to all our Japanese friends was how I had ever persuaded Jenny to step onto a boat.

Mitarai's boom time was the 18th century. The port served then not just as a waystation, but as a deluxe resort for the Daimyo of Hiroshima. Part of the

The Waka Ebisu-Ya, last surviving Tea House of Mitarai

entertainment was a plentiful supply of prostitutes. The girls of Mitarai were known as Oiran (花魁), which literally means 'queen of flowers'. Back then there were four Oiran houses, each home to a dozen girls and their servants.

One of the most famous was Yae Murasaki. Every day before meeting her guests she would have her young maid, Shige, help her blacken her teeth. This was the fashion of the day. A special kind of pitch was needed, and it had to be of the right consistency if it was to cling to damp, shiny teeth. One day, Shige just could not get the mixture right. Clients were calling Murasaki from the next room. In her anger and impatience, the Oiran grabbed the cup of pitch and forced the boiling liquid down Shige's throat. In her death agony Shige brushed the wall with her blood and pitch-soaked palm. Murasaki was thereafter haunted. Whenever she took up her mirror, there was the face of the dead child looking at her.

You can still see Shige's tiny palm print high up on the adobe wall of the Waka Ebisu-Ya, the largest and only one remaining of Mitarai's four teahouses.

It was Lucy, an expatriate American who served as a volunteer guide for the few English-speaking visitors who pass through Mitarai that told us the story. She pointed out a dusty pile of wooden-backed books on a shelf and took one down. Here was the life story of one of the Oiran, from the day she entered the teahouse as a maid; here in these columns were her earnings, the lists of her clients, her debts; here was recorded the day she died.

We ambled through the narrow, deserted back streets to the old fishing harbour where there were some unusual-looking wooden boats with hard angles and covered-in decks. From the weed on their mooring lines and the flaking white paint, they looked as though they had been unused for many years.

'Orange boats,' Lucy explained. 'These islands have always been famous for growing mandarin oranges. You've probably seen those odd little funicular railways that run up and down the hills; those are so that the farmers can reach the steepest slopes. And the boats were designed to be able to pack in the maximum number of orange wooden crates. They didn't have to be seaworthy, they sculled them from island to island with those long hinged oars.'

In the fading light Lucy took us home for tea at her rickety bungalow behind Mitarai. We took turns luxuriating in her cedar hot tub. Her Japanese husband worked during the week and many weekends on the mainland. To our unspoken question, she answered quietly: 'I read a lot. I look after the oranges… I suppose you could call it a Japanese marriage. It's not like a western marriage. I'm not unhappy.'

INLAND SEA — SETO NAIKAI — 瀬戸内海
34° 45' N 132° 20' E

IF YOU GO…

For information on entry and onward formalities see Chapter 6, page 53.

GETTING THERE

In summer, winds are sufficiently light that Mitarai can be reached under sail from any direction. A series of bridges allows for overland access from Honshu, where the nearest large towns are Hiroshima and Fukuyama. Many small ferries also link the islands.

DISTANCES

Mitarai, on Osaki Shimozima Island, is about halfway (east-west) along the Inland Sea. Hiroshima to Mitarai, 35 miles; Mitarai to Kobe, 200 miles.

WEATHER

Japanese weather forecasts cover the entire Inland Sea as a single zone. This is of limited use: many local effects apply. The only lighthouse reports are from Kobe (at the east end) and on the outer (Pacific) coast of Shikoku Island, where things are usually a lot windier than inside. The prevailing summer winds are easterly, generally less than 10 knots, but higher near Kanmon Kaikyo; calms are common. Fog is common starting late July. Typhoons can occur any time but especially between May and October; the island of Shikoku shelters the Inland Sea from the worst effects; most well-protected marinas would be adequate in case of a moderate typhoon.

ANCHORAGE/MOORING

Were it not for the fact that nobody (ferries, fishing boats) expects it, it would be possible to anchor in the well-protected channel between Osaki Shimozima and Okamura Shima. However, at GPS 34°11'.313N 132°

The waterfront, Mitarai

51'.160E is a tiny four-slip marina, just to the north-west of a large and underused ferry pontoon. Beware of an area of shallow water inside the breakwater, to starboard as you enter. Check in (no fee) at the nearby shop.

GENERAL

There are significant currents in the vicinity. See **https://www1.kaiho.mlit.go.jp/TIDE/ pred2/CurrPred/iCurrPred.htm**. When visiting the Inland Sea, it is rewarding to have on hand Donald Richie's travel masterpiece, *The Inland Sea* (Kyoto: Weatherhill, 1971).

CHARTS

JP1108 (ie English language), Aki Nada and Hiroshima Wan; Chartlet book H-804W, page 48.

TORII — GATEWAY TO A SHINTO SHRINE

SHIMODA

JAPAN

A haiku requires three lines of five, seven and five syllables respectively; a juxtaposition of two images; and a seasonal reference. I spent the night hours as we sailed up the Pacific coast of Honshu towards Tokyo Bay composing a bad haiku:

Shimoda by sail:
All those ships, how black the night,
My hair turned quite white.

Jenny was not impressed. But she had not taken in my clever use of the adjective 'black': Shimoda, our destination, was famous for what is known as the episode of the Black Ships.

In 1854, US Commodore Perry, much to the consternation of the Shogun in nearby Edo, appeared here out of nowhere, with several powerful black-painted warships. He demanded that Japan end its 200-year-old policy of isolation and permit commerce with the USA. Subsequently a Treaty of Amity was signed at Shimoda, and the first western consul was installed in a convenient Buddhist Temple. Japan never looked back.

Fortuitously, we tied up at the very location where Perry had first landed, and even more luckily, we found that we had arrived at the start of the annual three-day Black Ship Festival. There were Japanese and American warships at anchor and the place was flooded with shore-leave sailors in their best whites. American and Japanese flags festooned the streets; there were marching bands and majorettes; parading Boy Scout troops from US forces high schools; and a civic delegation from Newport (Rhode Island), Perry's hometown. Local students staged a costumed re-enactment of Perry's arrival, which we watched from our cockpit. In the streets, traditional

"Commodore Perry"

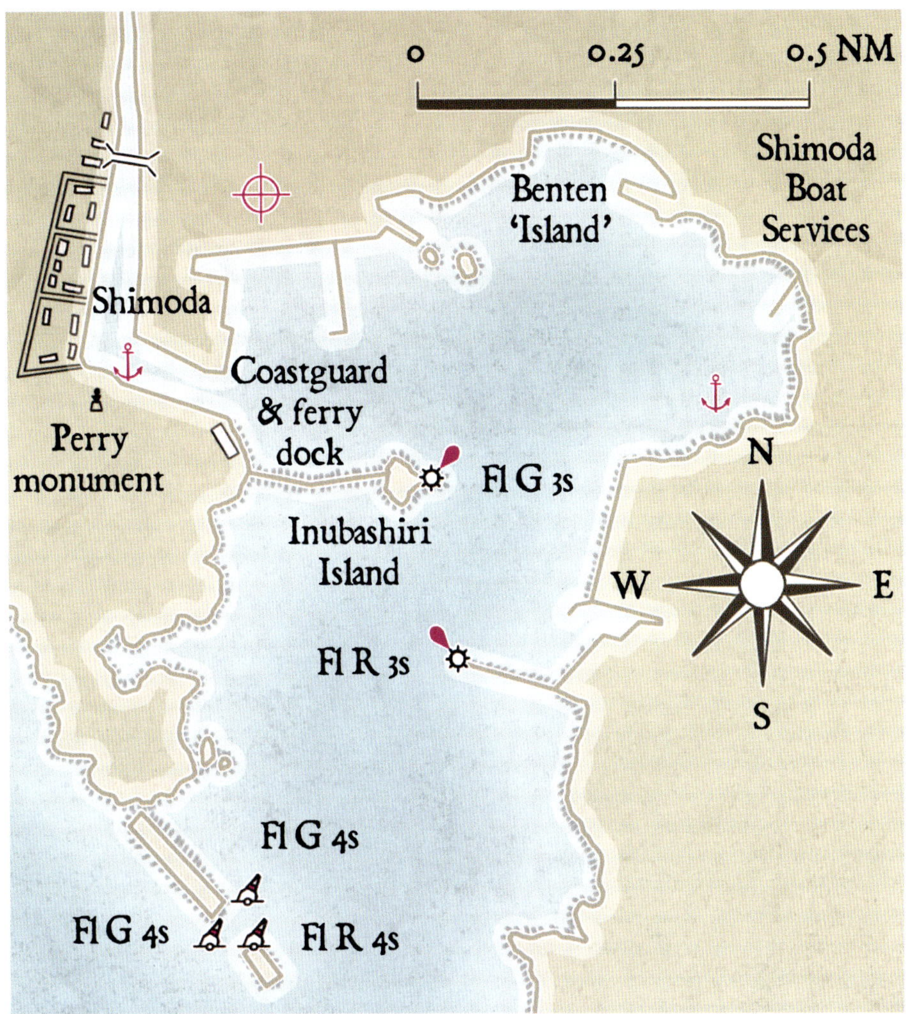

Shimoda — 下田市, Japan
⊕ 34° 40'.5 N 138° 57' E

dancers from all over the country paraded and performed daily.

We planned to leave Shimoda for Alaska. But after the festivities, a long stretch of contrary easterly winds set in. There were two early typhoons that passed to the south and made us glad that we had not rushed to sea. What we were now waiting for was the *Baiu* or *Tsuyu* ('Plum Rain'), a wet front that traditionally arrives when plums are ripening. As it reaches the Japanese archipelago, then drifts north, it brings in its wake the southerly and westerly winds we needed.

Itoh San, who ran Shimoda Boat Services and was one of the City Fathers, plied us with many cups of green tea as we mused over the weather. Every day he would print off the day's meteorological chart. Every day it seemed to be the same:

'Low,' he would say, tapping with his pen at an area to the south. 'Need low up here. Maybe tomorrow,' he'd conclude with a big toothy smile.

Itoh introduced us to one of his good friends. Mrs Nakamura ran a coffee shop called Okawaya Fruits, which had been in Shimoda since 1811. She was also an accomplished translator/interpreter and an elementary school teacher.

Nakamura San introduced us to her Grade 5 and 6 English students, and we gave talks about our sailing experiences. Mostly, the questions were what you would have expected of North American Grade 5s:

'Did you see any monsters?'

'How many pirates did you meet?'

The most thrilling picture was one we showed of a coral snake that had come on board up our cockpit drains in Vanuatu: one of the little girls screamed.

As Grade 5s are, they were also interested in earthy matters, such as how the marine toilet worked and how we showered (standing out in the rain). We were impressed with the careful preparations made by the teachers in case of natural disasters. Tsunami and earthquake drills were held regularly, and the children must always have their white helmets at hand. In one school, the Grade 5s were responsible for looking after the school's rice paddy, seeing the whole cultivation process right through from planting to the annual production of some 60 kilograms of prime rice.

Shimoda still would not let us go. Twice, three times a day, we would get out our chart for the North Pacific, measure out the curving route to Alaska, plot the weather systems that lay in

Shimoda

our path and any embryonic storms lurking near Taiwan. Our nervousness grew. In the evenings, to pass the time, we watched movies on our laptop; we'd copied these from friends over the past two to three years and often their titles meant little to us.

One day we cranked up *The Guardian.* The dramatic opening sequence has a sailboat sinking at night in heavy seas as a red-and-white rescue helicopter clatters overhead. The husband and wife jump overboard. Then the desperate husband fights the wife to be the first into the rescue basket that has been lowered. The chopper finally gets underway, with both of the shivering yacht crew aboard, while navy diver Kevin Costner glowers at the unchivalrous and snivelling husband. The first words of the movie are spoken by the pilot, into his radio: 'Kodiak base, Kodiak base; we're on our way…'

We were not reassured. Kodiak was our precise destination.

There came word that a super typhoon called Guchol was on its way.[1] Fishing boats from all over south-central Honshu streamed into Shimoda, for the tight, safe river moorings it provided. For two or three days the place was a hive of activity as lines were led across the river in spiders' webs, in such a way that when arrangements were finally complete, you could not have left if you had wanted to. An air of tension filled the town. Everything went silent as the skies darkened, the rain began and the winds built up. The fishermen all went home to watch TV and see where Guchol would make landfall. Every vessel except ours

Temple on the Kii peninsula

was left deserted. There was nobody on the streets; the steel shutters were down.

The storm struck early on the evening of 19 June at Kushimoto, a port we had stopped at a few weeks earlier. It was the first typhoon to hit Honshu in June in a decade. But in Shimoda we dodged the eye by 100 kilometres or so. The winds rose to 60 knots, causing the pontoon to which we were lashed to snake uneasily from side to side. As swells in the outer bay increased, it began undulating as well. We hardly slept. Our lines strained and creaked, the wind howled in our rigging and we heeled from one side to the other. Even the town streetlamps went out, adding to the sense of doom.

---

1 The World Meteorological Organization maintains a roster of potential names for storms, from submissions by regional member countries; Guchol means Turmeric in the language of Yap.

By morning all was quiet, the river turbid and full of debris. A second storm (Talim) followed two or three days later. We reconsidered our options. The Pacific High was still distant. We would face moderate easterlies for several days after we left Japan, but it looked as though we now had a week to spare before another typhoon might start cartwheeling towards us. It was time to take the plunge.

Soon before casting off, we went in search of wi-fi, to send a final batch of emails. McDonald's obliged. Hours after we had gone to bed – it was past two o'clock in the morning – there was a shy knock on the hull and an even more tentative call.

'Police, please!'

In alarm, I grabbed some clothes and climbed out into the cockpit. A young uniformed woman officer apologised profusely for waking us. She held out her hand, with Jenny's wallet. It had been found at McDonald's and handed in, she said.

'But how did you know to find us?' I asked.

'Oh, is very easy.' She opened the wallet to show us. 'I find card inside. It has address and telephone of Mr Ishii San, from Kobe. I think he your friend. So I call him just now. He tell me two Gaijin on Yotto, so I come to find only Yotto in Shimoda… Everyone know you are here.'

Needless to say, all our money and valuables were intact. It seemed a fitting story to remember Japan by.

Traditional dancers at the Black Ships Festival

IF YOU GO…

For information on entry and onward formalities see Chapter 6, page 53.

GETTING THERE

Under sail, Shimoda is most easily reached from the west through south. It is accessible by land (train, bus) from Tokyo (130 kilometres) and Shizuoka (70 kilometres).

DISTANCES

Shimoda to Yokohama, 110 miles; Shimoda to Shizuoka, 40 miles.

WEATHER

In this area, north winds are dominant in winter but by mid to late summer, following the arrival of the Baiu/Tsuyu front, winds from the south and south-west begin to predominate; see 'Summer' at **www.data. jma.go.jp/gmd/cpd/longfcst/en/tourist/file/ Kanto_Koshin.html**. This coastline is exposed to typhoons, which may occur at any time but are most common from April to November.

ANCHORAGE/MOORING

Shimoda Boat Services maintains a mooring field in the north-east corner of the bay, with a nearby landing at GPS 34°40'.3532N 138°57'.7568E, as well as the downtown pontoons at GPS 34°40'.290N 138°56'.777E. See **https://en.riviera.co.jp/marina/shimoda/ index.html**. The owner of Shimoda Boat Services is an experienced ocean racer and was involved in the Japanese America's Cup challenge of 1992.

GENERAL

The annual Black Ships Festival starts on the third Friday in May.

CHARTS

BA 953, Omae Saki to Tokyo Wan; JHA W096 (Shimoda Ko and approaches); Japan Chartlet book H-801, page 74.

Fishing boats jam the harbour as a typhoon approaches

GEOGRAPHIC HARBOR, ALASKA

USA

Our passage from Japan to Kodiak was slow: 42 days for 3,600 miles, nearly all of them fogbound, much of it on the wind. The damp got everywhere; our carefully saved paperbacks swelled up and we had to place them on top of the stove to dry out (giving a new meaning to the phrase 'cooking the books'). But by the time we were coasting by the mountains of the great island's east coast, the seas were glassily calm and the skies clear. The Laysan albatross that had been following us for weeks disconsolately settled on the water, an orca nosed over.

Entry into the USA was surprisingly low-key. At the office for the St Paul fishing harbour at the town of Kodiak, where we tied up, the manager was welcoming but looked blank when we asked what formalities we needed to follow.

'Not quite sure what you mean. There's a washroom around the corner … laundry at Walmart. Customs? Immigration? Nah, there's none of that here, but I can give you a phone number in Anchorage if you really want to speak to them…'

Back down on the dock we were also surprised when, once or twice a day, tourists would knock on our hull and politely ask where they might find Wild

At anchor, Long Island, Kodiak

Bill or Captain Corky. We eventually worked out that these were the stars of a TV reality series – *The Deadliest Catch* – that featured local crab-fishing boats at work in the Bering Sea in winter. It was a massive hit in the Lower 48 and episodes ran in a constant loop in the town's two bars.

We never did meet Wild Bill, but daily life in and around the harbour was colourful all the same. The crab fishers were hard-working and just as free-spending and hard-living. One morning there was yellow 'crime scene' tape around the marina washroom; there had been a drug takedown by state troopers in the early hours. One fisherman told us darkly that dealers caught up in turf wars had been known to end up on the bottom in one of those large crab traps we'd seen on TV. And that odd-looking boat at anchor, with an enormous square stern cabin overhanging the water?

'Oh yeah…' said the harbour manager. 'Pole-dancing. Russian, Ukrainian gals. See, the town council won't allow it, but they get around that by doing it in the harbour. On bad nights there's always people falling in, coming and going after a drink or two.'

We would spent three summers cruising the spectacular waters of Kodiak – which is the USA's second largest island, after Hawaii – and we scarcely saw another sailboat.

A favourite destination was Long Island. More than 5,000 troops were stationed here in the Second World War. You can hike out to see the massive guns that were installed to guard the approaches to Kodiak, and in the dripping woods are crumbling Nissen huts and rusting old jeeps. The Japanese did take two of the Aleutian Islands and bombed Dutch Harbour, but it's said that there was always too much cloud over Kodiak to allow for an attack here.

Exploring the inlets on Kodiak's western shores – reached through tidal rips in Ouzinkie Passage and Whale Passage – we'd ride out the gales that roll through every three days, at anchor off abandoned canneries or in lonely, steep-sided granite bays. One morning we went

exploring in search of an old mining camp mentioned on the US chart near the Amook Narrows.

On a black slate beach at low tide, we found blocks of white quartz that hinted at the possibility of gold. As we were looking at them, a homesteader – the first person we'd seen in ten days – rounded a point on the beach. He was as surprised as we were to see somebody here but took us exploring in the woods behind his small cabin. Almost buried in the lush undergrowth, were the workings of the Amok (one 'o') gold mine, dating from the period 1910 to 1920. There was an embankment built to carry a small-gauge railway, and the collapsed grey timbers of a steam-driven stamp that crushed the quartz before it was assayed. In another location was a sinister-looking entrance to a shaft, that Jim told us went 200 metres into the mountain, and in a third a near-collapsed cabin with a wooden cross nearby. We found a large,

rusty piece of iron that must have come from a stove: it had the word 'Diana' stamped on it, and a bas-relief of Diana the Huntress.

Over tea in his own cabin, Jim – he wore an NRA baseball cap and had an arsenal of rifles on racks – showed us a share certificate from the Amok Mine, dated 1912. Mining operations had ceased in 1920. A caretaker had been left in charge for many years, but eventually – about 1940 – his wage cheques stopped coming, and in anger and frustration he blew up most up the mine workings.

Near Karluk we worked our way into a narrow fjord, then hiked for an hour up a creek to a weir. Half an hour after we arrived, 30 metres below us, the first Kodiak bear arrived: a massive male lumbering up the stream, his head rocking close to the water's surface. He was soon followed by an only marginally smaller female with two cubs. The youngsters played happily, clambering on and off the weir, but were eventually persuaded into the water and shown how to catch their own. Kodiaks are a subspecies of the grizzly: better-fed and larger, often the size of a polar bear. They can be just as aggressive but tend not to be when the salmon are abundant and the living is easy, as it was at this time of year.

The local weather forecasting was good, but conditions change at a frightening speed in Alaska. Most dangerous are the frigid outflow winds that pour from coastal inlets and accelerate at headlands when the atmospheric pressure in the interior is high: they often reach 50 or 60 knots. So from Karluk, we chose our moment carefully to cross the Shelikof Strait to

At anchor, Geographic Harbor

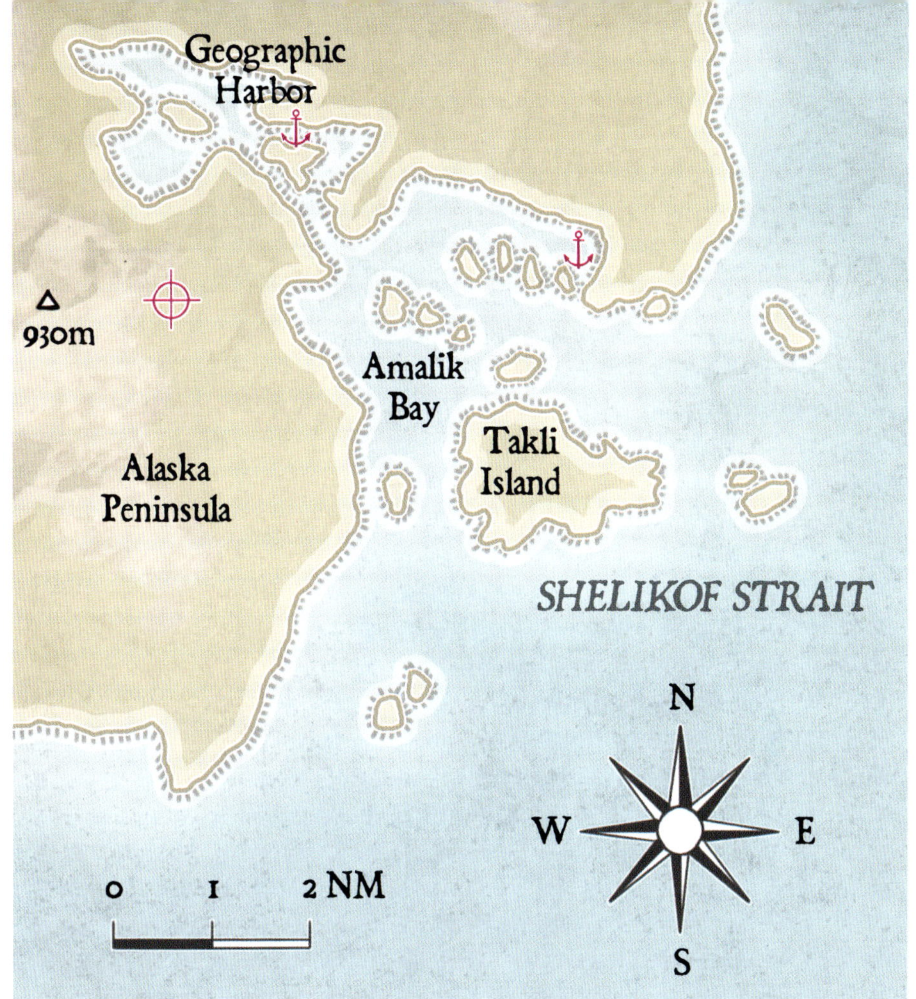

GEOGRAPHIC HARBOR & SURROUNDINGS, ALASKA, USA
58° 05' N 154° 35' W

the Alaska Peninsula. We were rewarded with a 20 knot north-easter on the beam for the entire 32-mile crossing, snow-capped peaks occasionally peeping tantalisingly through the clouds to the west. The mountains on the Peninsula side of Shelikof are higher than on Kodiak, reaching to around 2,500 metres. They are perpetually covered in snow, but what at first sight appear to be large patches of dirty snow on many lower slopes are huge areas of volcanic ash, left over from the massive 1912 eruption of Mount Katmai.

After a long day at sea we wound our way through narrow channels to the emerald green and still waters of Amalik Bay, then deeper into the mountains to a small complex of lagoons known as Geographic Harbor (after a *National Geographic* reporter who came here to report on the Katmai cataclysm).

This is Grizzly City. Over the week we spent at Geographic there was almost invariably a bear in sight on the tideline, turning over rocks, or lumbering up into the salmonberry patches above. Big males, with their distinctive hump,

Bald eagle

would eye us quietly for a minute or so but other than that take no notice of us. One swam by *Bosun Bird* blithely, only 20 metres off our bows. If there were no bears around, sea otters would back-stroke over and just hang out, often with a pup fidgeting on their chest.

At Kukak, a little way up the coast, we found another calm anchorage off the rusting, nearly overgrown ruins of an old cannery, with small islands all around. We explored by dinghy and on foot. There were more grizzlies far in the distance, and fresh tracks on the beaches. There's a tragic story associated with Kukak. Self-described bear enthusiast and film-maker Timothy Treadwell spent 13 summers here and claimed that the local bears – many of which he named – had come to respect and trust him; he even played with cubs. It all went wrong one day in October 2003. An animal known to rangers as Bear 141 killed Treadwell and his girlfriend, eating most of their remains. The episode – the first ever such fatality in Katmai National Park – was inadvertently recorded by Treadwell himself. His last words are a screamed

'Come out here… I'm being killed out here!' German film director Werner Herzog used hours of Treadwell's own film footage to describe his life and death in the 2005 documentary *Grizzly Man*.

We hauled out for our first Alaskan winter at Fuller's Boatyard on Kodiak, in a wooden cradle we had to build ourselves; they weren't accustomed to blocking sailboats. One September day, as I was walking around *Bosun Bird*, fingering a possible osmosis blister on the now-exposed hull, Jenny beckoned me over to the other side of the yard, where some men were adjusting blocks under a black-hulled steel crabber.

'It's *Time Bandit*!' she exclaimed.

This was one of the stars of *The Deadliest Catch*. It had made the national headlines when its engineer had turned up dead in a hotel room in Homer, Alaska. One of the crew was complaining of a two-degree list as the yard workers rammed wedges under the hull.

Crusty Bill Fuller, supervising the operation, was unimpressed. 'F***ing Reality prima donnas,' we heard him mutter.

Humpback whales off Kodiak

IF YOU GO…

For information on entry formalities to the USA see Chapter 5, page 46.

Notes specific to Alaska: Vessels approaching from the south will most likely choose to enter at Ketchikan. Kodiak and Valdez are classed as Ports of Entry but do not have staff on hand; phone in as indicated. The only port of entry in the Aleutians is Dutch Harbor; the US Navy was formerly present at Adak and the Coastguard at Attu, but both have long since withdrawn. There is talk of a military return to Adak.

GETTING THERE

Under sail, Kodiak and Geographic Harbor are best reached from the south (Hawaii) or south-west (Japan and the Aleutians); access from Southeast Alaska is a hard upwind beat. Kodiak is served by flights from Anchorage and by the Alaska State Ferry system; floatplanes can be chartered in Kodiak to visit Geographic and other locations on the Alaska Peninsula.

DISTANCES

Tokyo to Kodiak, 3,000 miles; Hilo (Hawaii) to Kodiak, 2,300 miles; Kodiak (Chiniak Bay) to Geographic Harbor, 107 miles; Kodiak to Anchorage, 250 miles.

WEATHER

Westerly winds predominate, but frequent low-pressure systems bring strong southeasterlies, usually at 2 to 3-day intervals. The year-round climate range is on average between −2°C and 17°C; harbours do not freeze over, but there are occasional heavy snowfalls. With an active local fishing fleet and the US's largest Coastguard station at Kodiak, weather forecasting here is good.

ANCHORAGES

Geographic Harbor, GPS 58°06'.369N 154°33'.684W, depth 16 metres; Amalik Bay 58°05'.373N 154°28'.831W, depth 18 metres; Kukak (Aguligik Island), GPS 58°18'.952N 154°11'.439W, depth 14 metres.

GENERAL

Kodiak (pop. 5,400) offers most services, including chandlery and diesel maintenance, but groceries can only be found at Walmart, 5 kilometres out of town. Visitors are usually encouraged to moor at St Paul Harbor; for longer-term moorage the St Herman Harbor – less convenient/accessible – is another option. See **www.city.kodiak.ak.us/ ph/page/marina-information**. The three remote anchorages listed above fall within the Katmai National Park and Preserve; see **www.nps.gov/katm/index.htm**.

CHARTS

USA (NOAA) 16576G/165760G, Shelikof Strait-Cape Nukshak to Dakavak Bay; USA (NOAA) 16603/16603OG, Kukak Bay-Alaska Peninsula.

GRIZZLY BEAR AT GEOGRAPHIC HARBOR

NELLIE'S REST, PRINCE WILLIAM SOUND, ALASKA

USA

The *US Coast Pilot*, describing the south-western approach to Prince William Sound, was sober:

The wind among the Barren Islands is often twice as strong as it is a few miles away and the seas are often three times higher, attaining speeds of 100 knots and heights of 30 feet respectively.

We were steering north-east, and it was midnight off the Barrens. At 60 degrees north in early July the sun never sets: the jagged islands were bathed in an eerie golden glow. We were reaching in a chilly but manageable 15 knots of wind, leaving a straight phosphorescent trail in the black ocean. The favourable forecast was holding.

Then there was a sudden hard roll to starboard. The rhythmic rustle of our bow wave turned to a splash. The boat juddered, we lurched back the other way and the mainsail backed. Briefly we were at a standstill. A smooth, black oblong shape was receding slowly beneath the water, with an audible sigh and a smell of rotting fish. We'd grazed a sleeping humpback whale.

Prince William, which we reached without apparent damage two days later, was named not for the current heir to the British throne but after the third son of King George III, at a time when Captain Cook was running short of more obvious people to honour. A massive rectangular-

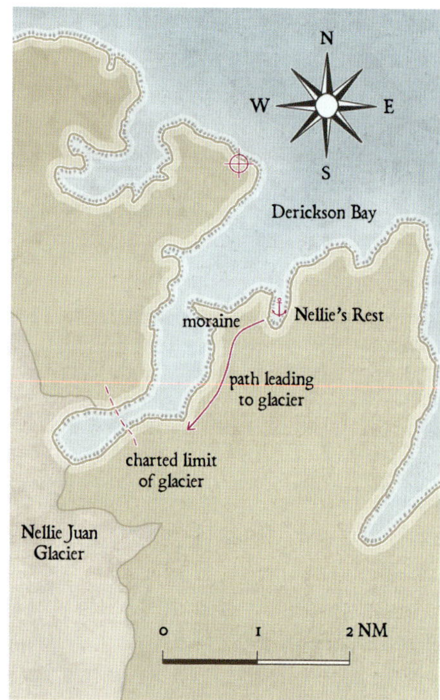

NELLIE'S REST, ALASKA, USA
60° 30' N 148° 20' W

shaped inlet at the head of the Gulf of Alaska, protected from the Gulf's stormy waters by a screen of high barrier islands, it is fed by over a hundred named glaciers. This makes for spectacular and protected cruising.

There are plenty of underwater rocks to watch out for. Cook's sailing master on HMS *Resolution*, the later infamous William Bligh, discovered one the hard way; it is now marked by a small metal beacon. We heard more about Bligh Reef when we called in for replenishment at Valdez. The only must-see stop in this rough-and-ready community is an unlikely one: a dark and smoky dive with carpet on its walls, known as the Pipeline Club (this being the southern terminus of the Alaska pipeline). Here, at 9pm one March night in 1989, Captain Joseph Hazelwood had a last drink before taking the *Exxon Valdez* to the open sea, with a million barrels of crude oil on board. Three hours later the vessel diverted to avoid ice calving from the Columbia Glacier. She struck Bligh Reef. Much of Hazelwood's cargo promptly drained into the ocean; tens of thousands of birds and mammals were fouled; it was alleged that the captain was drunk in command.

With a smirk, the barman pointed out to us the favourite drink on the cocktail list at the Pipeline: 'Tanqueray on the Rocks'.

We were blessed with uncharacteristically fine weather as we explored the deeply indented coastline: hot, cloudless days with little wind. Most days on the VHF we'd hear commercial fishermen talking, trying to trick each other into saying how the day's trolling was going. On weekends a small flotilla of sports fishermen with their runabouts would be on the water, too. They weren't always well prepared; we would eavesdrop on the US Coastguard orchestrating rescues for boats that had run out of gas or had mechanical issues. The recreational boats had cute names – *Ciao Baby*, *Bonecrusher*, *Saltwater Addiction* – that distinguished them from

The Barren Islands at midnight

the working fishing vessels: *Icy Cape*, *Akatan Lady*.

Tiny Whittier, where the sports fishers are based, is at the head of dark and steep-sided Passage Canal, overlooked by several glaciers. The settlement was established in the Second World War by the US Army when a sustained Japanese attack on mainland Alaska looked possible. Shrouded in cloud most of the year and all but surrounded by near-vertical granite peaks – deterrents to bombing – this was a rare ice-free location accessible to ocean-going ships. Once a rail tunnel was bored under the Portage Glacier in 1942, it was linked directly to Anchorage.

In the Cold War Whittier saw a new lease of life as a secret army base. Two monolithic buildings were erected to house hundreds of servicemen: the 14-storey Begich Tower and the even

larger Buckner Building. The military are long gone and Whittier's 200 or so permanent residents now all live on two floors of Begich, which has its own post office, shops and gym and which is linked to the few other buildings in town by tunnels. The Buckner complex is a post-apocalyptic ruin, half-engulfed by the rainforest.

The glaciers are the great attraction of Prince William. For a few days, we diverted into a complex of fjords called Port Nellie Juan, anchoring in a well sheltered and aptly named bay: Nellie's Rest. Here the water was emerald green – a function of glacial sediment in suspension – and a few bergy bits would float idly in and out with the tide. Doing the washing-up was absolutely chilling.

Using the nautical chart for guidance, we bush-whacked from Nellie's Rest through dense rainforest to emerge at

In Passage Canal, approaching Whittier

the terminal moraine of the Nellie Juan glacier. We edged around the bay on foot until we could see its face: 2 kilometres wide, 70 metres high, composed of craggy and ethereal blue ice. All along the beach were great chunks of ice stranded by the tide. Some were clear as gin and were beautifully stippled by weeks or months of erosion, others had the same bluish tinge as the glacier face. They were incongruous, stranded in lush knee-high grass. On the more hospitable floes in the bay, harbour seals lolled as if sun-bathing, but would have to shuffle off when a calving berg sent a meter-high wave their way. You could watch for hours.

Chilling and inhospitable as the waters at the foot of the glacier seemed, the stream over and through the moraine was choked with thrashing salmon, desperate to return to the very spot where they had hatched three or four years earlier, now to spawn then die.

The Columbia was the second great glacier we inspected close-up. So rapidly is it retreating that the number of bergs

Prince William Sound, Alaska, USA
60° 14' N 146° 55' W

it generates can clog the waters for many miles around. We quizzed local boats for up-to-date advice before we edged our way into Glacier Passage and then to a nook in Heather Bay, the very place where our 1970s paper chart showed the face to be. There were a few house-sized pieces we needed to steer around; for smaller ones we used the boathook for fending off. We recalled *The Rime of the Ancient Mariner* in these silent and ice-beset seas, but there was no albatross to be seen. From Heather Bay, the face was a day's walk, so far had the glacier receded in 40 years.

When autumnal lows swept in from the Aleutians, threatening winds of 40 to 60 knots, we made for the third and last settlement in the Sound, where we would haul out for the duration of another Alaskan winter.

With a population of 2,000, Cordova (pron. Cor-DOE-ver) is snugly located on a narrow, shallow inlet, with high mountains all around. We tied up in the crowded fishing harbour just as dozens of salmon fishing boats were also decommissioning and readying for the winter. The walkways were busy with bearded young men carting duffel bags ashore in wheelbarrows, a few holding earnest and occasionally profane conversations by mobile phone with patient (or not so patient…) girlfriends and wives in the Lower 48.

Over at the boatyard, Glenn the Travelift driver confided that he had not hauled many sailboats. But his pride was piqued when we mentioned that Bill, back in Kodiak, had twice taken us out without any problems. He measured us carefully, Googled our profile and gave precise instructions – to the minute –

Exxon Valdez

DISPLACEMENT: 240,000 TONS
CAPACITY: 1.48 MILLION BARRELS
ESTIMATED SPILL: 260,000-755,000 BARRELS

about when to arrive so as to make the most of high tide.

All went well. As Glenn pressure-washed *Bosun Bird*'s bottom, we said how impressed we were with his professionalism to his buddy Jerry, who'd be renting us the space to winter over. Jerry nodded absently. He walked around, pondered our long keel and thoughtfully contemplated the near-bare patch where we'd grazed the humpback. He looked preoccupied.

'Thing is,' he eventually confessed, 'I kinda wish I hadn't agreed to do this. Fishing boats, see, they sit nice and squat, know what I mean?' And he pointed over to *Lucky Lady*.

We looked back at him questioningly.

'Three years ago, that's the last time I did a sailboat. See, we got this 140-knot williwaw one day. Lifted the darn boat clean off the blocks. A write-off. I only just finished paying the guy off.'

Happily – tied down to lead blocks that Jerry had salvaged from the keel of the unfortunate flying sailboat – *Bosun Bird* was still waiting for us, intact, next spring.

IF YOU GO...

For information on entry formalities to the USA see Chapter 5, page 46. For notes specific to Alaska see Chapter 9, page 71.

. . . .

GETTING THERE

Under sail, Prince William Sound is best approached from the south-west or south. From the nearest sheltered waters in Southeast Alaska it is a 400-mile beat against prevailing westerlies, with Yakutat as a possible intermediate stop; depressions might bring more favourable winds for such an itinerary, but often at gale force and with heavy rain. Ferries link the three towns in the Sound (Cordova, Valdez and Whittier); Valdez is accessible by road, Whittier by road and (in summer) train; Cordova has no road access.

DISTANCES

Hilo (Hawaii) to Hinchinbrook Entrance, PWS: 2,500 miles; Kodiak to Hinchinbrook Entrance, 230 miles; Hinchinbrook Entrance to Nellie's Rest, 60 miles; Nellie's Rest to Whittier, 25 miles; Nellie's Rest to Cordova: 110 miles.

WEATHER

In summer, lows pass south of the Sound every two to three days, and the prevailing fair-weather westerlies shift to south-easterly, with rain. Wind speeds inside the Sound are typically well below those experienced in the open waters of the Gulf of Alaska to the south. But there are many local effects. Inlets with glaciers at their head often generate strong outflow winds 24 hours a day; these can build to great strength in Passage Canal (the approach to Whittier). Intercontinental air routes pass over the Sound; local sailors find jet contrails are a useful guide to upcoming weather:

- no contrail = stable weather for 2+ days;
- fast dispersal into wide, fuzzy lines = an unfavourable change in 20 hours or less.

ANCHORAGES

Nellie's Rest, GPS 60°28'.469N 148°19'.186W, depth 12 metres; Heather Bay (Emerald Cove), GPS 60°57'.244N 147°01'.457W, depth 10 metres; Heather Bay (Dalli Bay), GPS 60°58'.339N 147°02'.114W, depth 14 metres.

GENERAL

Whittier (pop. 270) has a marina (**www.cliffsidemarina.org**) used largely by sports fishermen from Anchorage, to which the village is linked by a road/rail tunnel; fuel and water; two small stores. Valdez (pop. 4,000) has a two-basin boat harbour (**www.valdezak.gov/146/Harbor**), a Safeway and many boat-related services. Cordova (pop. 2,600) has a large marina (**www.cityofcordova.net/port-and-harbor/**), a Travelift and a small grocery.

CHARTS

USA (NOAA) 16700, Prince William Sound; USA (NOAA) 16705 – PWS, Western Part (for Nellie's Rest); USA (NOAA) 16713/167130G, Naked Island to Columbia Bay (for Heather Bay).

REFERENCE

Lethcoe, Jim and Nancy. *Cruising Guide to Prince William Sound (6th edn)*. Chugiak, Alaska, USA: Prince William Sound Books, 2022.

KLIUCHEVOI BAY, ALASKA

USA

The harbourmaster at Sitka, Alaska's old Russian capital in Southeast Alaska, welcomed us when we checked in but handed us a leaflet that blared 'Warning!'

Over the past couple of years there had been a lamentably high incidence of inebriated crew of fishing boats falling into the frigid harbour waters on late weekend nights (and promptly drowning). Guests of the marina were advised to 'use the buddy system when walking back to their vessels at nights'. The leaflet went on to refer enigmatically to 'the sealion issue'. Steller's sealions, which can be very large and aggressive, periodically hauled out on the fishing harbour floats, it seemed. This was recognised as inconvenient, but marina patrons were formally warned that it was an offence physically to persuade the creatures to move on. Specifically, it was

Mount Edgecumbe, Sitka

not permitted to direct high-pressure hoses at them.

We survived these unexpected hazards and enjoyed our fourth and final Alaska winter here. The New Archangel dancers gave shows in the town's opulent performing arts centre (funded by oil money), there were sundry historic buildings to visit, and there was the Running of the Boots Festival. This is held to mark (or celebrate, in the minds of many locals) the departure of the last cruise ship of the season. It is a race through the streets for which all participants are required to wear Sitka's official footwear: Xtratuf brand fishing boots.

One chilly day in March the whole town turned out to witness the Governor of Alaska and various other dignitaries mark the 150th anniversary of the Alaska Purchase, by which the US acquired all of Russian Alaska for US$7.2 million. That evening we mentioned to Ted, a Tlingit friend we'd made at the library, that we'd been at the ceremony.

'Yes, I heard about it,' and he smiled sadly. 'I didn't go. Everyone jokes about what a great deal the US got. But y'know what? It was never the Russians' to sell. It was ours. It always has been.'

Long winter layovers are always a good opportunity to whittle down our eternal list of boat jobs. My top priority for some time had been the stress-inducing tendency of the engine to signal, on start-up, that the oil pressure was low, by means of a flashing yellow light and insistent beeping. The engine manual indicated that immediate shutdown was in order. By trial and error, I had found that if I hand-cranked vigorously, with the engine's

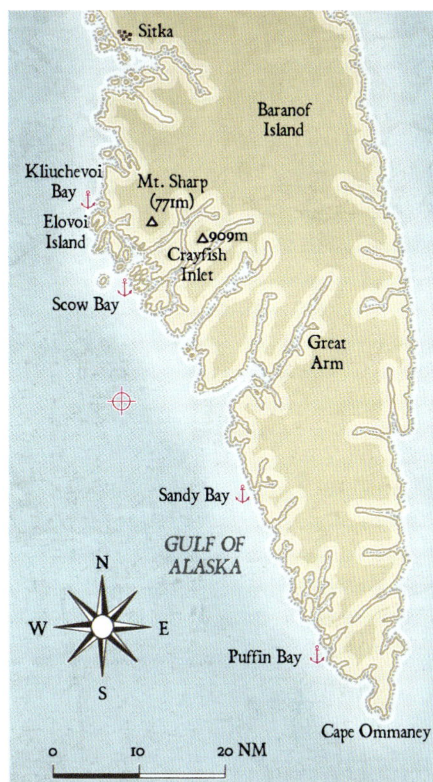

Baranof Island, Alaska, USA
56° 36' N 135° 18' W

decompression levers off, I could achieve a head of pressure and the engine would run well enough. But each time I was having to crank for longer and longer. It was getting exhausting. A better solution was needed.

I am no mechanic, but it seemed to me that the oil pump could be at fault.

'No, those pumps never fail,' was the unanimous verdict of Facebook and everyone else I buttonholed.

'Try the oil pressure relief valve. It's probably stuck… It's got a little spring in it. Just stretch it out…' suggested Sam, an affable Aussie on the only other foreign yacht in town.

The valve in question was difficult to access. You had to disconnect the batteries, take off the alternator and starter motor, carefully extract and stretch the tiny spring, then reverse the operation; it took two hours. But after several exercises of disassembly and reassembly – stretching the spring more vigorously each time – the problem went away. I took pleasure in crossing 'oil pressure' off the to-do list. We bought Sam a drink and had a couple more ourselves to celebrate.

We pulled out of our winter berth one sunny spring morning and motored under the suspension bridge that joins Sitka to Japonski Island. It was against a dazzling backdrop of snowy peaks, the ocean a brilliant blue, the ubiquitous humpback whales puffing steam as we passed. The forecast was good. We'd got used to the US Coastguard's continuous broadcasts on the VHF. Since last season they'd been automated, with a computer reading the written text. But there were a few glitches, we noticed. The frequently repeated phrase 'ocean entrances' was read as a transitive verb, rather than a geographical

ST MICHAEL'S CATHEDRAL, SITKA

description of the points at which internal channels meet the open sea. And the automatic reader was still having issues with odd names, spelling them out staccato fashion and letter by letter – Y-A-K-U-T-A-T – when flummoxed.

One finger on the chart, we weaved our way through a maze of small islands and zigged past some lurking rocks into Kliuchevoi Bay, one of dozens in the region named after the first Russian explorers. From here, a short boardwalk led to the Goddard Hot Springs, a favourite winter destination of Sitka-ites with runabouts, and long known to the Tlingit.

There were two wooden cabins with open picture windows looking out onto the ocean, each with a large stainless tub into which extremely hot water bubbled endlessly. The trick was to discover exactly how much cold you needed to add so as to make the temperature tolerable. Unlike in Japan, the convention here was to remain at least partly clothed. It was just as well that we knew this, because as we were getting out after a two-hour

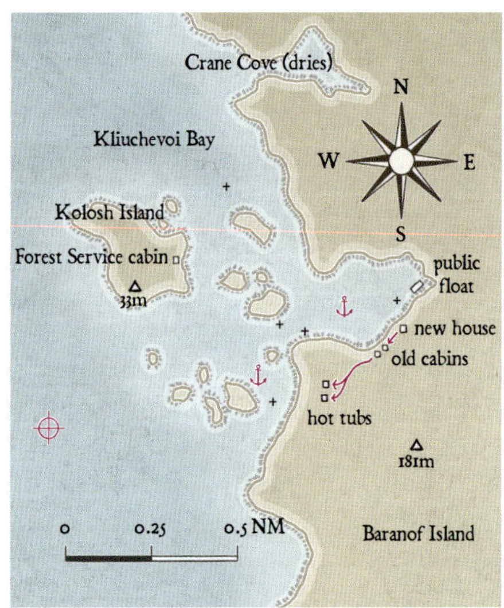

KLIUCHEVOI BAY
56° 50' N 135° 23'.7 W

soak, a clutch of energetic young male 'Coasties' from the large Coastguard base in Sitka arrived with a launch crammed with Budweiser six-packs, bent on an afternoon revel. They were good-natured, not too rowdy and wished us well as they roared off after a couple of hours.

We were alone now. From the tubs you could look one way up into the forest, the other towards the Fuji-like outline of Mount Edgecumbe. We could have lingered for days, but we had Miles to Go.

We made short runs in the open ocean, down the west coast of wild Baranof Island to the uninspiringly named Scow Bay, then Sandy Bay and finally Puffin Bay. Swell and foam piled up frighteningly as we approached each anchorage – as they do all along the outer coastline of Southeast Alaska – but inside all was still. These steep shorelines have never been logged; wherever we put the hook down you could not have told that humans had ever passed this way. A downside of the isolation was that the Coastguard's VHF transmissions failed to reach into the bays, so we found ourselves relying on our Iridium satellite phone in order to obtain the texts of weather updates.

The next major waypoint was Cape Ommaney, the southernmost point of Baranof. It looked as though it would be a fast passage south from our refuge at Puffin, with a forecast of 20 to 25 knots of wind in a favourable direction. Up at dawn, we clambered into our harnesses and foul weather gear, slid the right charts into the slicker and checked via a quick Iridium download that the forecast still held. It did.

'Looks good. Let's have breakfast underway,' I said as I reached for the ignition key. The engine roared into life. And on came the yellow light, immediately, along with that nearly forgotten beeping. 'Bugger.'

'We'll be here a while, I suppose,' Jenny eventually said quietly. 'I'll put the kettle on.'

Puffin Bay, Baranof Island

IF YOU GO…

For information on entry formalities to the USA see Chapter 5, page 46. For notes specific to Alaska see Chapter 9, page 71.

GETTING THERE

Under sail, Kliuchevoi is best approached in settled westerly weather from Sitka to the north. There is no overland access. The western coast of Baranof Island, on which the bay lies, is exposed and rugged; there are good anchorages, but Chatham Strait – inside Baranof – allows for easier, more protected passages. Sitka is served by the Alaska State Ferry and frequent flights to/ from Juneau, Anchorage and Seattle; it has no road access.

DISTANCES

Kliuchevoi to Sitka, 15 miles.

WEATHER

Air temperatures range from a winter average of 1°C to 14°C in August; rain is frequent all year. Summer winds are predominantly from the west; in winter, stormy and wet weather from the south-east prevails. Wind speeds off the headlands on this coast are often 5 or 10 knots higher than elsewhere. In settled weather, inflow winds often start mid-morning and peak late afternoon.

ANCHORAGES

Kliuchevoi Bay, GPS 56°50'.318N 135°22'.346W; depth 11 metres; the entrance is narrow and rock-encumbered, requiring a careful watch. Local fishing boats often anchor off the springs at GPS 56°50'.13N 135°22'.81W, in view of the hot tubs; depth 16 metres; this is more exposed.

GENERAL

Sitka (pop. 8,400) lies along both sides of a narrow navigable channel between Baranof Island and the much smaller Japonski Island. Settled in 1799 by Russian trader Alexander Baranov (Baranof is the anglicised spelling of his name), it was known as New Archangel under Russian rule and there are reminders of that period, including the Russian Bishop's House and St Michael's Orthodox Cathedral. There are five small-boat basins; visitors are usually assigned to Eliason Harbor. All marine services are available, haul-out is possible at Halibut Point Marine, at the north end of town by the cruise ship terminal. Cruise ships visit, but not to the same extent as Ketchikan.

CHARTS

USA (NOAA) 17327, Sitka Harbor and approaches; Sitka Harbor; USA (NOAA) 17326, Baranof Island – Crawfish Inlet to Sitka (available as a 20-page 'booklet chart').

REFERENCE

Hemingway-Douglass, Don and Réanne. *Exploring Southeast Alaska (3rd edn).* Anacortes, USA: Fine Edge, 2007.

On Baranof Island's west coast

SUMMERS BAY, ALISON SOUND, BRITISH COLUMBIA

CANADA

If you want to sail any great distance in British Columbia, you have to get used to negotiating the tidal rapids that are formed where constrictions occur between the islands that line the coast. They can run frighteningly fast: Seymour Narrows, which is relatively wide and used by cruise ships headed from Vancouver to Alaska, reaches 15 knots on spring tides.

The favoured technique is the same in every case. Approach the constriction against the last of the adverse tidal current, aiming to arrive at the midpoint of the narrows at predicted slack (which may not necessarily coincide with high/ low tide). Then, hopefully, you will be washed out of the other side as the current, after a short calm period, reverses and gathers speed. If your timing is good and everything goes to plan, you wonder what the fuss was about. But return overland when things are at full spate and

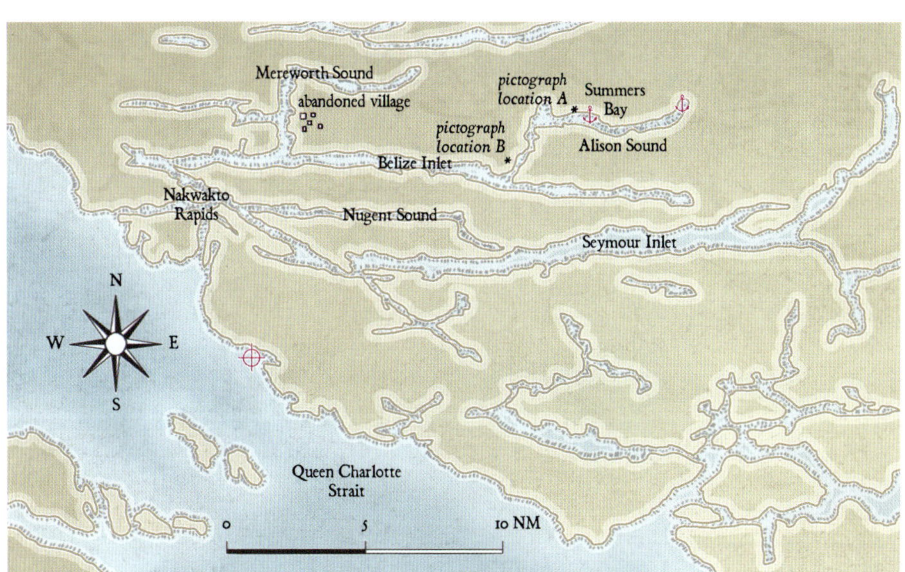

SUMMERS **B**AY, **A**LISON **S**OUND, BC, **C**ANADA
50° 59' N 127° 29'.5 W

you may see logs the size of telephone poles being tossed clear into the air, deep whirlpools moving slowly up and down, and standing waves of 1.5 metres.

One summer, we decided to make for the intriguingly shaped and hardly visited Belize and Seymour Inlets, deeply cut into the mainland 250 miles to the north-west of Vancouver.

Our itinerary took us first through the potentially formidable Yuculta rapids. Here the chart indicates a travelling whirlpool called The Devil's Throat, which has been known to sink commercial fishing vessels. Then we were into a maze of islands known as the Broughtons, where grizzly and black bears roam the shorelines while orcas ply the narrow waterways.

We spent a day anchored off the abandoned indigenous village of Mimkwamlis, on Village Island. Here there still stand the massive supporting poles of an old longhouse, and – almost indistinguishable from fallen logs – moss-encrusted remains of two totems, the more eerie and evocative for their abandonment. Hughina Harold wrote

Remains of a Long House, Mimkwamlis

Totem Poles and Tea[2] about the years she spent here as a nurse in 1935–37, hosted by two dour British missionary women. She describes her arrival, aboard the government's *Black Raven*:

The whole place was deathly still, a stillness punctuated only by the odd wisp of smoke pluming from one of the tin chimneys… The backdrop for this drab cluster of houses and totems was the forest, its trees – thick dark and impenetrable – reaching into the very sky… My heart sank.

Hughina came to love the place. But in another Canadian classic called *The Curve*

---

2 Harold, Hughina. *Totem Poles and Tea*. Victoria, Canada: Heritage House Publishing, 2006.

of Time[3], Capi Blanchet, who came with her children aboard their motor cruiser *Caprice* one summer day in the 1920s, recounts that she also found Village Island eerie. They went ashore when the islanders were nearly all out fishing.

> *…when we landed, no chief came down with greetings, no one sang the song of welcome, only a great black wooden figure, standing waist high in the nettles up on the bank, welcomed us with outstretched arms. It was Dsonoqua, of Indian folklore, who runs whistling through the woods, calling to the little Indian children so that she can catch them and carry them off in her basket to devour them.*

Working our way onwards, we had a choice of two approaches to Nakwakto Rapids, which guard access to Seymour and Belize Inlets. Slingsby Channel, which is 4 miles long and which runs west–east off Queen Charlotte Strait, is ostensibly the most straightforward: it is quite wide and unobstructed. But the current runs up to 9 knots and should there be any swell at all in the Strait (which here is exposed to the open Pacific), then the effects of a strong ebb meeting ocean swells can be severe indeed. Much safer is the shorter Schooner Channel, which runs south to north for 2 miles; this is narrow and should not be negotiated in poor visibility, but the current reaches only 3 or 4 knots and there are anchorages at either end that are in still water. We waited in Allison Harbour (once a Union Steamship call, but long since uninhabited) for the last hour of the flood (ie north-going current) to make a careful but uneventful transit of Schooner. Then we anchored again, with a sternline out, within sight of Nakwakto.

For years, these rapids were featured in the *Guinness Book of World Records* as the fastest navigable reversing rapids in the world, with recorded speeds up to 18.5 knots. The Canadian Hydrographic Service these days assesses that the normal maximum is a mere 14.5 knots, which places Nakwakto neck-and-neck with Seymour and Skookumchuck (on the Sunshine Coast, closer to Vancouver).

---

3 Blanchet, Muriel Wylie. *The Curve of Time*. Vancouver, Canada: Whitecap Books, 2011.

Approaching Nakwakto Rapids

Blanchet, before she took *Caprice* through here, met a tugboat captain who had mistimed his passage by 20 minutes and spent a whole night stuck in the rapids, being battered from one rock to another, first into, then out of the narrows. His stern had been crushed, the propeller rendered inoperative, and a few hours later the bows took similar damage. He dourly advised Blanchet to go home, or at least to observe things for a day before committing herself:

The next morning found us watching that fearsome roaring hole in action. Turret Rock (in the centre of the channel) was not breasting the current but bracing itself against it on its tail. It was hard to tell whether our mound was trembling, or it was just the motion of the rushing water. Probably the air was in motion from so much turbulence…

Caprice makes it through, within the advertised slack period of six minutes. But Capi's son Peter shrewdly asks his mother: 'You were scared too, weren't you mummy?'

'I winked at him. "Weren't we sillies!"'

Beyond the gateway of Nakwakto there are 115 miles of major waterways, with sundry off-shoots, each with a different name. We turned left and spent our first week meandering up Belize Inlet and into Alison Sound.

Near-sheer granite walls rose on either side as we ghosted into Alison. To port and 5 metres above sea level was a well-preserved pictograph, painted in red ochre. It showed three canoes, in the largest of which was a standing figure holding a rifle; the men were confronting a three-masted sailing vessel; orcas frolicked around. The pictograph, we learned, depicted the Royal Navy's shelling of the Nak'waxda'xw (Nakwaktok) settlement at Village Cove (in nearby Mereworth Sound) in 1869, in

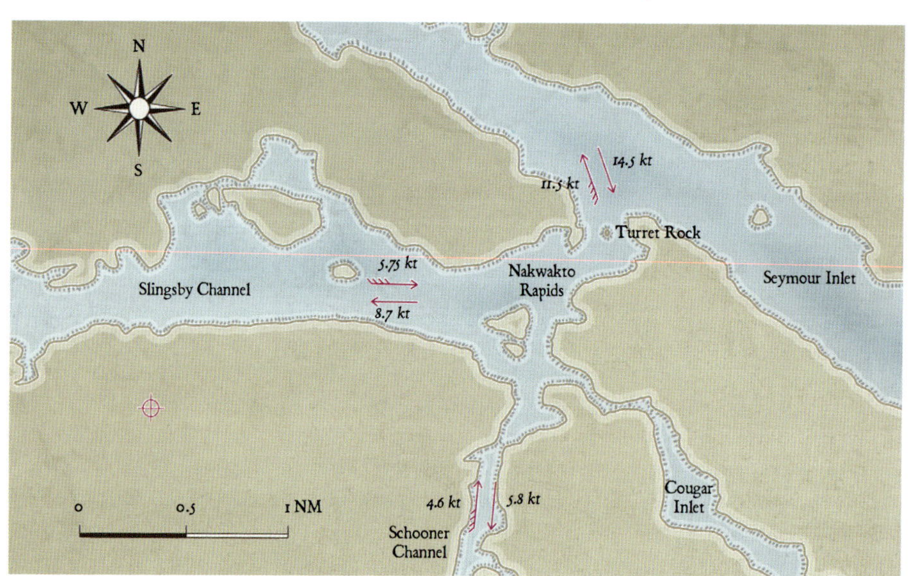

Nakwakto Rapids
51° 05' N 127° 33'.3 W

At anchor, Summers Bay

which many villagers were killed. Further inside, 1 mile east of a lovely anchorage at Summers Bay, was another well-preserved pictograph. This one showed six canoes, each with gun-toting warriors, again facing off against a single larger vessel. Other pictographs in Belize Inlet were easier to date: the fishing vessel or tug *Blue Wave* had considerately added *16/10/44* to their annotation, just above the water level.

The sense of isolation in these inlets is palpable, exacerbated by the lack of VHF weather reception. Here the water is tannin-coloured and barely tastes of salt, this on account of heavy seasonal run-off but also of the small exchange of salt water with the outside. You feel you are on a lake far inland.

The two most scenic anchorages in Alison are at the head of the Sound and in Summers Bay, on its north shore. Both are steeply shelving. As we usually do in such locations, we dropped anchor, then backed towards into the beach, holding ourselves stern-to by means of lines. This minimises the chances of the anchor freeing itself on the steep underwater slope as and when outflow winds blow at night.

In the space of two weeks inside Nakwakto – at the peak of summer and the cruising season – we saw one power boat, two sailboats, and one tug with its tow. This while in Desolation Sound, 150 miles to the south-east, you'd be lucky to share an anchorage in July or August with fewer than a dozen boats.

The rapids? They were just as flat going out as they were when we were coming in. But, like Capi Blanchet, I was still nervous.

IF YOU GO…

ENTRY FORMALITIES

Citizens of most countries need either a Visitor ('Temporary Resident') Visa or an Electronic Travel Authorisation to visit Canada; US citizens require only a valid passport.

There are approximately 25 Telephone Reporting Sites (TRS-M) where foreign yachts may check into BC if arriving from abroad. The skipper (only) should land and call toll free to 1-888-226-7277, from the indicated phone. If no further verification is required, you will be given a report number. For the full list of TRS-M sites see **www.cbsa-asfc.gc.ca/do-rb/services/trsm-sdtm-eng.html** and filter by Province. For an overview of yacht entry regulations, including penalties for non-compliance, see **www.cbsa-asfc.gc.ca/travel-voyage/pb-pp-eng.html**. Note that there is no designated reporting site in Haida Gwaii; vessels arriving from Southeast Alaska must first check in at Prince Rupert.

GETTING THERE

Alison Sound is off Belize Inlet. Belize and Seymour Inlets are both accessed via the Nakwakto Rapids (GPS 51° 05'.898N 127° 30'.335W). Current tables should be used to calculate the time of slack water (which does not necessarily coincide with high/low water), see **www.tides.gc.ca/en/current-predictions-station**. The rapids are most safely approached from open water (Queen Charlotte Strait) through the 2-mile-long Schooner Channel (rather than Slingsby Channel), at each end of which there is an anchorage; currents in Schooner reach 4 to 6 knots.

In Belize Inlet

Pictograph at the entrance to Alison Sound

DISTANCES

Vancouver to Nakwakto, 225 miles; Port McNeil to Nakwakto, 43 miles; Nakwakto to Summers Bay, 25 miles.

WEATHER

In BC's coastal inlets, the summer weather pattern has inflow winds starting mid-morning, dying in the evening; then outflow winds starting around midnight and dying in the early morning. A high-pressure area over the mainland (as occurs in winter) spells sustained outflow winds. Belize and Seymour are close enough to the open Pacific (Queen Charlotte Strait) to be affected by fronts that pass every few days, bringing south-east to south-west winds. VHF weather reports may be difficult to access inside the inlets.

ANCHORAGES

Summers Bay, GPS 51°10'.215N 127°01'.473W; depth 22 metres; stern-tie. Head of Alison Sound, GPS 51°11'.165N 126° 55'.215W; depth 11 metres; stern-tie.

GENERAL

The two clearest pictographs can be found near Summers Bay at GPS 51° 10'.323N 127° 02'.110W (Location A) and at the entrance of Alison Sound: GPS 51° 07'.48N; 127° 09'.02W (Location B). There are no permanent residents within these inlets, but sporadic logging operations may be under way. In Mereworth Sound (Village Cove) are the remains of an old native village; nothing should be removed; the extent of the Indian Reserve (marked I.R.) is indicated on Chart 3552.

CHARTS

CHS 3921, Fish Egg Inlet and/et Allison Harbour; CHS 3552, Seymour Inlet and/et Belize Inlet. Note spelling difference: Allison Harbour vs Alison Sound.

REFERENCES

(1) Hemingway-Douglass, Don and Réanne. *Exploring the North Coast of British Columbia (3rd edn)*. Anacortes, USA: Fine Edge, 2008.

(2) Chappell, John. *Cruising Beyond Desolation Sound*. Vancouver, Canada: Gordon Soules Publishers, 1987.

ROSE HARBOUR AND S'G̱ANG GWAAY, HAIDA GWAII, BRITISH COLUMBIA

CANADA

The Spanish navigator Juan Pérez was the first European to sight the archipelago of Haida Gwaii, 100 miles off the coast of North America in latitude 54 north, in 1774. But fog and strong currents deterred him from landing. Thirteen years later George Dixon, an English fur trader, came along in the *Queen Charlotte*, named after the consort of King George III; Dixon made a rough survey and called the islands after his vessel.

The name – often abbreviated to The Charlottes – stuck for 200 years. But

A quiet morning east of Moresby Island

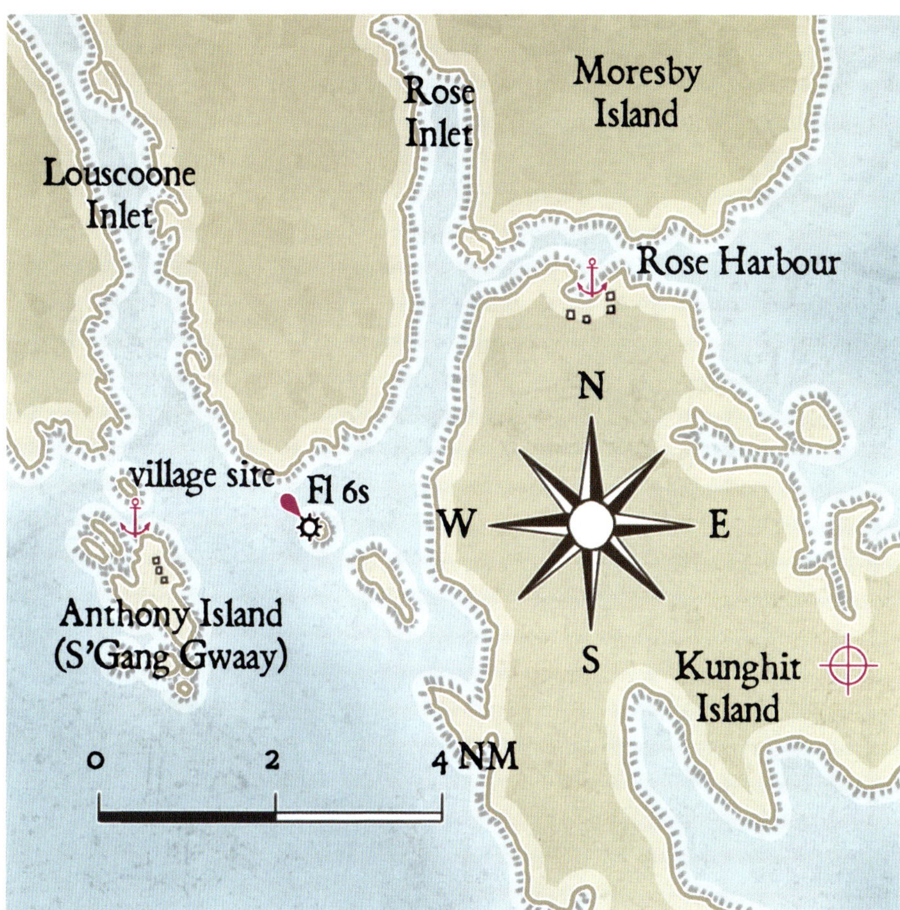

ROSE HARBOUR & S'GANG GWAAY, HAIDA GWAII, BC, CANADA
52° 05' N 131° W

there had been people here for 13,000 years before Pérez and Dixon showed up. Numbering maybe 10,000 at their peak, the Haida had a rich, artistic culture, lived in coastal villages and traded up and down the coast in their ocean-going canoes. For them the islands had always been Haida Gwaii (Islands of the People) or, more poetically but elaborately, The Islands at the Edge of the World.

The white men – traders, then missionaries – brought pestilence, alcohol, firearms and forced assimilation. The population declined vertiginously to a few hundred. But in the late 1960s a modest renaissance began. The Haida raised the first new totem in over a hundred years; the Haida language was made mandatory at local elementary schools; and leaders successfully confronted loggers and the federal government to block further pillage of the islands' great stands of spruce and cedar.

June 2010 was another landmark date. In a solemn but slightly tongue-in-cheek ceremony in Victoria, elders of the Haida nation politely presented to the Premier

Ruins of a Long House, S'G̱ang Gwaay

of British Columbia a cedar bentwood box, containing a slip of paper. On it was written 'The Queen Charlotte Islands.' 'You gave us this name,' they said. 'We hereby return it to you and reclaim our own name: Haida Gwaii.'

The passage up the coast from southern BC is long and intricate. It took us five weeks to arrive at a launch-pad near Prince Rupert from which to make the 70-mile open water crossing of Hecate Strait to the archipelago. It's wise to be patient here. When strong winds from either of the two prevailing directions – north-west and south-east – oppose the fast tidal currents that flow through the shallow strait, dangerous seas quickly rise.

But the forecast was good. All we had to face on our overnight passage was zigzagging crabbing boats laying their traps across our path; a couple of brightly lit cruise ships edging carefully through the only deep-water channel; and sloppy seas where spring tides converged from opposite directions.

We arrived shortly after sunrise at the small, well-protected fishing harbour of Sandspit, at the mouth of the inlet that separates the two major islands of Haida Gwaii. We parked *Bosun Bird* and rented a car to explore the larger of the two (Graham), on which there are few sailboat-friendly anchorages.

Gaw and Skidegate (pron. SKIDDY-gut) are the two modern Haida villages, with many totems to admire, but the tiny inland logging community of Port Clements also has a tale to tell. Close by, there once stood a unique 200-year-old tree, the Golden Spruce, a beautiful genetic freak. In a shocking act of eco-terrorism in 1997, a young ex-logger turned environmentalist felled it, hoping to draw attention to the indiscriminate logging then going on. The gesture backfired – the tree was sacred to the Haida – and the perpetrator was arrested then bailed, a court date set. He never made it to court in Masset, disappearing for ever with his kayak into a wintry Hecate Strait. Many locals believe he faked his own death. Today you can see a graft from the tree stump, but it is doubtful it will grow again to full size.

Sailing south from Sandspit and into the Gwaii Haanas National Park that includes the southern third of the island group, we were in a landscape of steep-sided granite-topped mountains on whose summits snow lingers in July; mirror-still inner channels; anchorages with plunging wooded sides; and tidal flats at their head where the deer come to graze every evening. At Crescent Harbour a Haida Gwaii black bear, hungry after the long winter, rummaged along the beach, turning over rocks in the hope of finding something tasty. At Thurston Harbour a dozen raccoons foraged at low tide, washing their dainty forepaws as they stood up to look at us. Oystercatchers peeped, loons wailed hauntingly, and ravens and eagles – both of them sacred to the Haida – called raucously to us from the treetops.

There are several abandoned villages; all can be visited with permission from the Watchmen who take care of the sites in summer. But counterintuitively, few have convenient anchorages. The Haida travelled by canoe, valuing shingle beaches with gentle slopes and – above all – a good view to the open water, whence their enemies were likely to come. The finest of all the sites – S'G̲ang Gwaay, also known as Ninstints – has an anchorage close to it that is acceptable in southerlies, but the prevailing summer winds are from the north-west and

sometimes strong. So we anchored *Bosun Bird* securely off the abandoned whaling station at more distant Rose Harbour, and rode over by dinghy.

S'G̲ang Waay was once a village of 300 people who lived in great cedar longhouses above the beach. Before each longhouse stood a tall heraldic memorial pole, by which any visitor would know the exact lineage and importance of its inhabitants. By the water's edge were shorter mortuary poles, similarly carved with images of real or mythical creatures, but topped with an aperture into which a bentwood cedar box had been inserted, containing the remains of the illustrious deceased.

The memorial poles have long ago fallen or been taken away to museums. But the mortuary poles remain. Some tilt at crazy angles; one lies on the ground where it fell ten years ago; some have cracked; others have grass or weeds growing in the bentwood-box aperture. There is no sign of the red, black and blue that once adorned them. The woods – cleared when this was a vibrant village

At anchor, Moresby Island

– have grown back and seem ready to swallow up the site.

This is an evocative place. David, our Haida guide, tells us the story of every pole, and the myths he learned in his childhood at Gaw. Central to many stories is Raven, the Trickster. It was Raven who, walking on the beach one day, came across a clamshell, pecked at it, and released the first humans. It was Raven who, tired of always bumping into things in the darkness that covered the world, stole the sun from the box in which it had been locked up; escaped through the smoke-hole in the roof of the longhouse (thus covering himself with soot); and set the sun free.

Here on a pole, with his large ears and prominent cheeks, is Bear; here is Sea-Wolf (half bear, half orca); here is Orca with his great fin; and Beaver, who even has a stick to gnaw on. On one pole are the remains of a small copper shield. This means that here was buried a chief, whose status was measured not by the extent of his wealth, but by how many shields or other trading goods he gave away at ceremonial occasions ('potlatches'). The mortuary poles will, by decree from the elders, not be raised again when they fall, neither will they be in any way restored.

David tells the old myths with passion and enthusiasm, as if they were undisputed fact. For a few moments, you suspend disbelief: after all, why not? Then he brings us back to earth. Picking up a wavy strand of kelp from the beach he mentions that somewhere he has a few drops of Italian blood, and says to the inscrutable Japanese tourists who have arrived by floatplane and who are making

Mortuary pole at S'Gang Gwaay

up our group: 'See? This is what I use to make Haida lasagne.'

Back at Rose Harbour, with the wind set fair in the north-west and the sun setting behind Cape St James, we set our Aries windvane and make a fast overnight run back to the mainland. Three weeks later, as we are tying up at our home marina in southern BC, it is still high summer. But in the Islands on the Edge of the World, autumn is coming.

'West coast of Haida Gwaii,' says the pert automated female voice on VHF Weather One, whom we call Georgia. 'Storm warning: winds southeasterly 50 to 65 knots, backing to southerly; seas 8 to 10 metres.'

IF YOU GO…

For information on entry formalities to Canada, and to BC in particular, see Chapter 12, page 88.

Note that there is no designated reporting site in Haida Gwaii; vessels arriving from Southeast Alaska must first check in at Prince Rupert.

GETTING THERE

The shortest approach to Haida Gwaii by sea is from Browning Entrance, at the north end of Banks Island, to Sandspit. BC Ferries offers service to Skidegate from Prince Rupert three times weekly (eight hours) and a frequent link between the two principal islands, Moresby and Graham. There are flights from Vancouver to Sandspit and Masset.

DISTANCES

Browning entrance to Sandspit, 55 miles; Sandspit to Rose Harbour, 130 miles; Rose Harbour to S'G̱ang Gwaay, 7 miles; Rose Harbour to Millbrook Cove (mainland BC), 137 miles.

WEATHER

The further north you go before crossing Hecate Strait, the more chance you have of a beam reach (south-east or north-west winds). In summer more lows brush this area than Vancouver Island; a front can be expected every three to four days. Hecate Strait is shallow and subject to strong currents that set up notoriously heavy seas when the wind is contrary; monitor VHF reports from North and South Hecate weather buoys, as well as Bonilla Island light and Sandspit. The west coast of the archipelago is subject to wilder weather than the east and offers fewer opportunities for shelter.

ANCHORAGE

There is a cove on the north-west side of S'G̱ang Gwaay (Anthony Island), where tour boats tie up, but it is shallow, rock-infested, open to the north-west and marginal except in calm or south-easterly weather. Rose Harbour (Houston Stewart Channel) is better protected. The National Parks maintain a pink mooring buoy here that may be used with permission (VHF Ch 06) or anchor close by at GPS 52°09'.013N, 131°05'.197W; depth 13 metres.

GENERAL

The population of Haida Gwaii is 4,500, of whom 500 claim Haida ancestry. Sandspit, Skidegate and Queen Charlotte City are located on Skidegate Inlet, a narrow channel that separates the two principal islands, crossed by ferry. Masset, on the north coast of Graham Island, has many totem poles.

HAIDA RAVEN

There are floats available to visiting yachts at Sandspit and Queen Charlotte City; fuel and other basic services at Queen Charlotte City; car rental at Sandspit airport. Rose Harbour has the only permanent population within the park (three houses). Companies offer guided sailboat and kayak expeditions in the Gwaii Haanas National Park.

CHARTS

CHS 3855, Houston Stewart Channel; CHS 3825, Cape St James to/à Houston Stewart Channel (includes S'Gang Gwaay/Anthony Island).

REFERENCE

Hemingway-Douglass, Don and Réanne. *Exploring the North Coast of British Columbia (3rd edn)*. Anacortes, USA: Fine Edge, 2008.

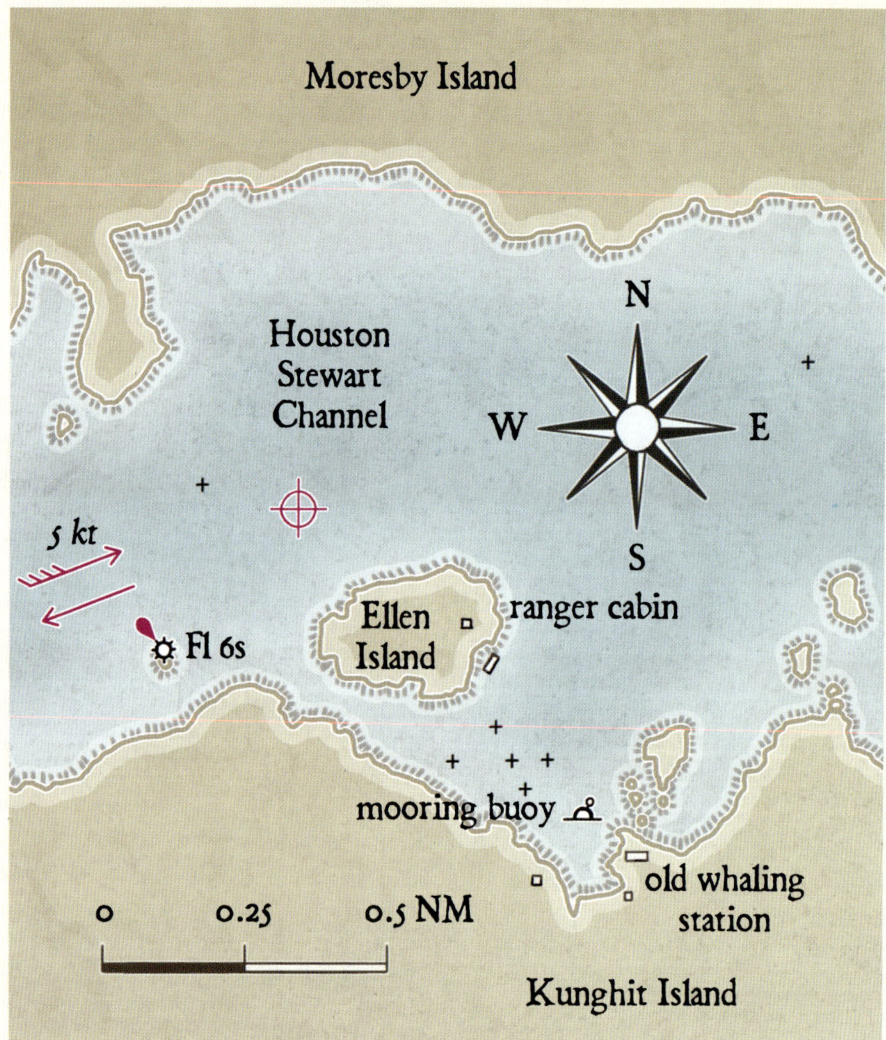

DETAIL: ROSE HARBOUR
52° 09'.5 N 131° 06' W

HOLLYWOOD PASSAGE, BUNSBY ISLANDS, BRITISH COLUMBIA

CANADA

O n the wild and wet west coast of Vancouver Island, there's a 600-metre-high, heavily forested protuberance that juts 12 miles into the Pacific. Winds off the point are commonly double those found inshore, but Captain Cook seems only to have considered the promontory a minor inconvenience when he was sailing north-west in 1778. The best name he could come up with here was 'Woody Point.'

Eighty years later, ace naval hydrographer Captain GH Richards decided this was less than useful – there is no land here that is not woody – and that the landmark deserved more respect. It has since been known as Cape Cook. The steep off-lying rock at its western tip is Solander Island, after Cook's naturalist companion.

The first time we rounded the Cape, back in 1984, we had to weave our way through dozens of salmon trollers as we

Sea otters, Bunsby Islands

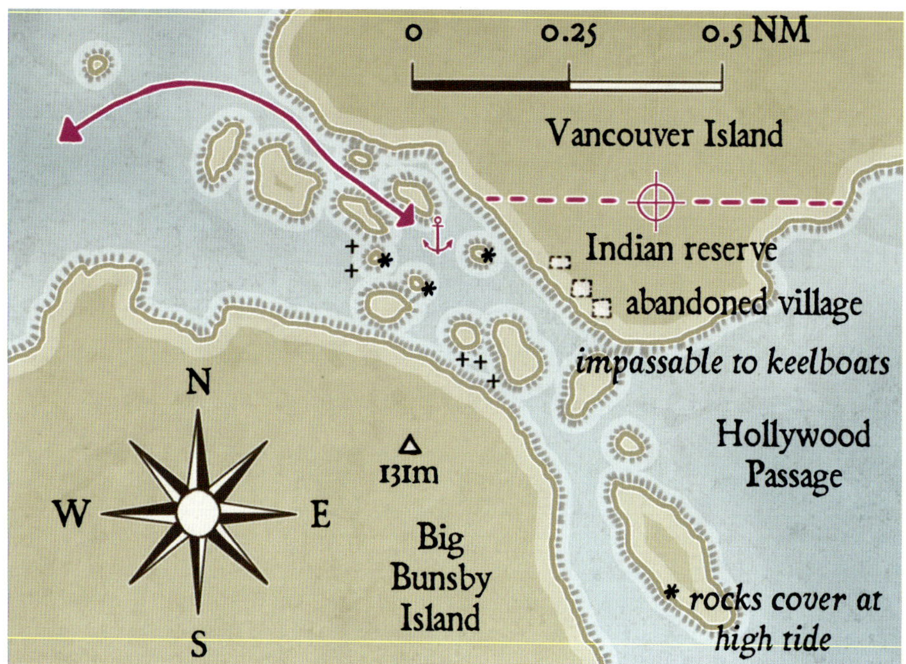

HOLLYWOOD PASSAGE, BC, CANADA
⊕ 50° 07'.1 N 127° 30' W

gybed first one way, then the other in brisk following winds. But the fishermen have all gone, for there are few salmon left. This time – southbound in 2022 – there was not a single vessel to be seen as, under the cliffs of Solander, we powered around over an oil-calm sea, then ghosted east in five knots of wind to look for shelter for the night.

The anchor clattered down at another place with historic resonance: Columbia Cove. This little nook owes its name to the fact that American sea captain Robert Gray anchored here a decade after Cook passed by, aboard the *Columbia*, accompanied by the *Margaret* and the *Adventure*. Gray was the first American to circumnavigate the world; the name of his ship lives on in both the great river of the same name and in Canada's westernmost province. But the

cove had silted up noticeably since we were here in the eighties, and its head was now too shallow for us. It was almost impossible to see how Gray's three large ships had ever squeezed in.

If you believe Canadian writer Samuel Bawlf (a one-time resident of our home island, Salt Spring), Cook and Gray were far from being the first white men to cruise these waters. Bawlf – in *The Secret Voyage of Sir Francis Drake*[4] – suggests that the legendary English buccaneer made landfall at Cape Cook in 1579, sailing north from Mexico, and that he founded New Albion hereabouts.

It is true that there exists a significant and puzzling gap in Drake's own narrative of his round-the-world voyage. It is also true that the search for a navigable Northwest Passage connecting the Pacific to the Atlantic was the holy

---

4 Bawlf, Samuel. *The Secret Voyage of Sir Francis Drake*. Vancouver, Canada: Douglas & McIntyre, 2004.

grail of explorers of the time (and later). Discovery of such a Passage would have been a diplomatic, political and commercial coup of the first order for Drake and his patron, Queen Elizabeth I. It would have been well worth concealing from Great Power rivals, at least for a short while.

But the evidence Bawlf presents for this spot as Drake's northern landfall (rather than the much more likely Drake's Bay, 600 miles to the south) is tenuous. The theory depends on a rudimentary standalone drawing Drake made of a rectangle of land that Bawlf says is Cape Cook; it is not attached to a coastline. By the sketch is a latitude notation that the author says has been deliberately falsified. Things get more fantastic as Bawlf develops successively more elaborate hypotheses on this foundation. One academic critique of the book begins aptly: 'This remarkable voyage left the present reviewer in a state of advanced incredulity.'

Equally sceptical, but nonetheless appreciative of the wild scenery, we made our way over from Columbia Cove to the Bunsby Islands, in sight to the south, and spent half a day poking around.

According to Georgia – the automated voice on the VHF weather channel – some strong winds were coming our way and we needed 360-degree shelter. Unusually for Canadian waters, our chart was not good. Soundings were scant in the bays that held promise and were represented in fathoms (not metres), an indication that our survey was possibly that undertaken by Captain Richards himself in 1862. But, after scrutiny under the magnifying glass, there looked to be protected space in a pale-blue-coloured narrow passage between the Bunsbys and Vancouver Island. We hung around until it was low tide – when, hopefully, any dangerous rocks would show themselves – and motored in at dead slow. After making a wide circle in a large pool, all the while eyeing the depth sounder, we returned to the centre of the circle to drop anchor.

The mountains on every side disappeared at 500 metres into cloud. That evening, we watched as whitecaps picked up at either extremity of the channel. The clouds were lower now and scudding. But inside, the water's surface was black and still, rippled only occasionally as a slight puff of wind found its way in. It was fortunate that we had come in at low water. At high, a number of menacing sharp rocks slid just below the surface and became invisible. And it was a good thing we had not attempted to plot a route relying on either the electronic or the paper chart: both were at variance with reality by a hundred metres or more. As you'd expect from older surveys, the latitude was good, the longitude not so much.

Outside and as forecast, it blew hard for two days. We spent the

14

View from the cockpit, Columbia Cove

At anchor in Hollywood Passage

time exploring by dinghy, picking salmonberries, beachcombing. At the south-eastern end of our pool, you could tell by differences in the vegetation that there had once been human settlement here. When we landed, we found a few rotting posts driven into the beach at the high tide level. On the beach and in the woods behind were shards of old pottery and glass. We knew from past experience that the forest reclaims everything in BC at great speed, so it was hard to tell how long the place had been abandoned. But we found the broken, square base of a whisky bottle made of black glass. Stamped on it, you could make out 'Walker – Kilmarnock'. Later I found that this design was in use in the 1930s.

Down the coast at the little village of Walter's Cove, the home of the Checleseht First Nation, we asked around. At the coffee shop (Java the Hut) we found someone who knew the place:

'Nobody goes there anymore, but I've heard the elders talk,' he said. 'The name? Hollywood, I think. I dunno why… Maybe they once made a movie there?'

A search of the provincial archives in Victoria revealed only this, from a report dated 1955:

On the Vancouver Island side of Hollywood Pass are the remains of an Indian settlement known locally as Hollywood Village. It had been unoccupied for at least two years at the time of our visit… Two carved wooden figures in human form were entirely overgrown by salmonberry and other underbrush; they, too, were in an advanced stage of decay, beyond being salvaged.

A misty morning on the government dock at Walter's Cove (Kyuquot)

IF YOU GO...

For information on entry formalities to Canada, and to BC in particular, see Chapter 12, page 88.

GETTING THERE

The rounding of Cape Cook should be undertaken with a favourable forecast; there is an automatic weather reporting station on Solander Island, which reports the current windspeed/direction at the Cape. The approach to Hollywood Passage is between the 'mainland' (Vancouver Island) and a clutch of small islands to the south-west (the Bunsbys). Narrow, rock-strewn and inaccurately charted, it is best attempted at low tide and in good visibility. Columbia Cove does not provide shelter as good as the chart indicates; silting now limits access to the Cove's head. Walter's Cove (Kyuquot) is only accessible by boat or floatplane.

DISTANCES

Winter Harbour (Quatsino Sound) to Hollywood Passage, 45 miles; Hollywood Passage to Walter's Cove (Kyuquot), 10 miles.

WEATHER

The prevailing summer winds are from the north-west, interspersed every three to four days with a day or two of southeasterlies. South of Cape Cook the weather is often markedly better (ie lighter winds) than to the north; weather forecasters use the Cape as a dividing point. Off Vancouver Island's five great Sounds, in fair weather inflow winds blow during the day, outflow at night; there are often turbulent seas where outgoing current meets incoming swells. Fog is frequent starting in late July.

ANCHORAGES

Columbia Cove, GPS 50°08'.271N 127°41'.531W, depth 6 metres. Hollywood Passage, GPS 50° 07'.044N 127° 30'.497W, depth 14 metres. There are isolated rocks in the Hollywood pool that only show at half- to low tide. Enter from the north-west end of the passage; the other end is foul.

GENERAL

Most of the Bunsby Islands are within a Marine Provincial Park; there are no facilities. Extirpated in BC by 1920, sea otters from Alaska were transplanted to the Bunsbys between 1969 and 1972 and may now be found all along the west coast of Vancouver Island. Winter Harbour and Walter's Cove each have a small shop with limited supplies, open for a few hours most days in summer. Fuel and moorage are available in both locations.

CHART

Chart CHS 3683 – Checleset Bay (in fathoms/feet).

REFERENCES

(1) Hemingway-Douglass, Don and Réanne. *Exploring Vancouver Island's West Coast (2nd edn)*. Anacortes, USA: Fine Edge,1999.

(2) Yeadon-Jones, Anne and Laurence. *The West Coast of Vancouver Island (2nd edn)*. Madeira Park, Canada: Harbour Publishing, 2017.

(3) Watmough, Don. *Pacific Yachting's Cruising Guide to British Columbia Vol. IV: West Coast of Vancouver Island*. Everett, USA: Evergreen Pacific, 1993.

SAN MIGUEL ISLAND, CALIFORNIA

USA

Cruising offshore, there's always the Next Big Obstacle to worry about. All summer, as we readied *Tarka the Otter* for her first offshore passage – 800 miles, from Victoria to San Francisco – we'd worried about how we would cope. There'd be the likely hard beat out of the Strait of Juan de Fuca and into the gale that sits almost permanently off the Washington coast, both to be weathered with self-steering gear that we'd not yet tested. As for

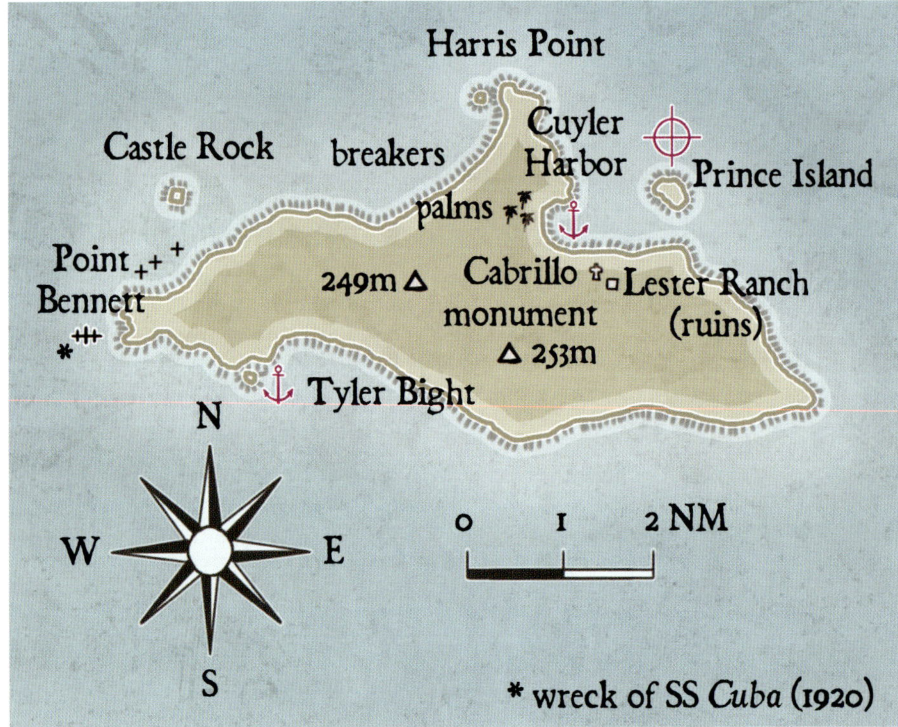

SAN MIGUEL ISLAND, CALIFORNIA, USA
34° 04' N 120° 20' W

celestial navigation, we'd practised at sea
with John on *Jacaranda*, under his careful
supervision. But we'd never actually taken
a sun sight from the deck of our own
boat when our lives depended on it.

Sailing unscathed under the Golden
Gate Bridge, ten days out, would turn
out to be the memory of a lifetime.
But it seemed that within hours we
were fretting over the next challenge:
rounding Point Conception, known
reverently to California sailors as the
Cape Horn of the Pacific. Ever the
pedant, I pointed out to Jenny that
the real Cape Horn was actually half
in the Pacific anyway. But even sober
authorities such as the *US Coast Pilot*
warn that this is an especially windy
place. Richard Henry Dana, whose *Two
Years Before the Mast* (1840) we'd been
reading as we sailed south, had certainly
found it so. He recounts a rounding in
the brig *Pilgrim*: 'Everything was in
confusion on deck; the little vessel was
tearing through the water as if she had
lost her wits, the seas flying over her and
the masts leaning over at a wide angle.'

We decided to leave our anchorage
in San Luis Obispo Bay before dawn,
in order to reach Conception before the
afternoon gale set in. As the sun rose,
huge gantries were silhouetted against
the brightening sky to port: the launch
pads at Vandenberg Air Force Base,
a testing centre for intercontinental
ballistic missiles. A laconic VHF
exchange confirmed that we were being
watched. To starboard, there were
more framework towers: oil rigs with
helicopters buzzing between them.

*The first time offshore in our own boat: off
the coast of Washington*

Northern elephant seals at Point Bennett

The wind began to build. Soon we had two reefs in the main and were down to the No. 2 jib. But it steadied at 25 knots, the seas at no more than a metre. Then we were past the stubby white lighthouse on the Point and surging into its lee at an exhilarating 7 knots. We worked our way in through kelp beds and dropped the anchor in a roadstead known locally as Cojo anchorage. The seas stayed calm, but it never blew below 20 knots that night: the halyards clanked, the mast shivered. I woke in sudden alarm at 02:00 to a great roaring noise only to realise it was a freight train passing the head of the bay.

Next morning, instead of following the east-trending coastline, we kept on south. It was another fast sail – 25 miles – to Cuyler Harbor on San Miguel, the westernmost of California's Channel Islands. In San Francisco we'd picked up Brian Fagan's definitive cruising guide to these waters. Jenny now read to me the operative section: 'Do not visit San Miguel until you have had considerable experience cruising in the Channel and of heavy weather sailing.'

I wasn't sure if our sail down Northern California covered this. Probably not. But the weather was forecast to be stable for the next couple of days. The island looked enticingly deserted and barren as we dropped the anchor at the west end of Cuyler, in the lee of Harris Point. We knew there was a National Park ranger station somewhere, but from here there was no sign of habitation: just a sandy trail leading up from a long white beach, through dunes to a scrub-covered plateau. Reassuringly, there were two local fishing boats swinging at anchor; less so, we could see the wreck of a third in heavy surf at the eastern end of the bay. But no yachts. Who would have thought, just a hundred miles from Los Angeles, you could find such a wild place?

We landed by three tall, incongruous palm trees and spent the rest of our first day beachcombing. Legend has it that the trees were planted here, fully grown, at the orders of producer Irving Thalberg, for location filming of *Mutiny on the Bounty*. The movie, starring Clark Gable and Charles Laughton, won the 1935 Oscar for Best Picture. More reliably, it is known that he used the usually heavy seas off San Miguel to film maritime sequences using the *Baby Bounty*, an 18-foot exact replica of the full-sized ship, big enough for two men to steer it from concealed positions. The men lost control in strong winds and it was two days before they were found, miles away. Thalberg had refused to call in the Coastguard because he wanted to keep this trick secret.

Next day, we radioed to the resident ranger, who came down from his cabin to meet us: unaccompanied walks in the island's interior were not allowed on account of unexploded ordnance left over from when this was a navy bombing range. Above the beach he showed us a lichen-encrusted monument to João Rodrigues Cabrillo. Sailing from the south, on behalf of the Spanish crown, Cabrillo had spent a week in Cuyler in October 1542 with his flotilla of three ships, one of which was the *San Miguel*. The next few weeks he spent exploring the other Channel Islands. Cabrillo somehow contracted gangrene and he came back here to die in January 1543.

At Tyler Cove, on the southern shore, we paused as the ranger took out his binoculars to note the name of the solitary yacht anchored there in the lee: 'Should'a radioed in,' he commented. We walked for another two hours until Point Bennett, the western extremity of San Miguel came into view. We sat eating our sandwiches and studied the rocks below us, from where you could hear raucous barking.

'Northern fur seals,' the ranger commented. 'Doing well. They've only been here since the 1960s. A few of the first ones had tags from the Pribilofs, up in the Bering…'

On a patch of sand were 30 or 40 much larger and less active northern elephant seals (cousins of the Isla Guadalupe population); one would occasionally raise its head to look around, but otherwise they were somnolent.

As we walked home in the late afternoon to *Tarka*, our guide told us stories of the Chumash people, who had colonised San Miguel as long as 13,000 years ago. More recently, starting in the 1860s, the San Miguel Island Company had run up to 3,000 sheep. The last ones

Approaching the Golden Gate at sunrise

The monument to Cabrillo, above Cuyler Harbor

hills into the bay. Our kerosene anchor light blew out and wouldn't relight. We sheered first one way, then the other; the inflatable dinghy flipped up onto *Tarka*'s deck with a bang and fell back into the water. We got up, hauled it in and deflated it. In the morning the wind was down, but we decided we'd probably pushed our luck as far as was wise. It was time to move on to the next Big Challenge: the famously crowded anchorages of Catalina Island and the reportedly expensive, unfriendly marinas of Southern California.

Much later, we came across TC Boyle's haunting novel *San Miguel*.[5] Loosely based on fact, it tells the stories of three pioneer women – Marantha, Edith and Elise – starting in 1888. We read of those 'elephant seals stretched out on the beach like enormous stuffed sausages…' A major character kills himself by jumping off Harris Point. The women are tough, but the island and its weather always win out. Marantha's first night ashore sets a gothic tone:

> *The wind kept up all night, just as the boy had said it would. It was furious, unrelenting. She'd never experienced anything like it, not even the hurricane that had come raging up the eastern seaboard to uproot the big weeping willow … of the house she'd grown up in. Every time she thought the wind was dying, it seemed to come back all the more furiously…*

were taken off the island by the end of the Second World War, but you could still see the effects of over-grazing. Then there'd been the period when the navy took over. San Miguel had been a National Park since 1972.

It blew hard again that night, katabatic gusts rushing noisily down the

We could relate to Marantha.

---

5   Boyle, TC. *San Miguel*. London, UK: Penguin, 2013.

IF YOU GO...

For information on entry formalities to the USA see Chapter 5, page 46.

Yachts require a permit to visit San Miguel. Overnight anchorages are restricted to Cuyler Harbor and Tyler Bight. The only authorised landing site is Cuyler. Permits can be obtained at a self-registration station on the beach. Visitors may explore the beach, Nidever Canyon, the Cabrillo Monument and the Lester Ranch site unescorted but have to be escorted beyond the ranger station. No off-trail hiking is permitted. To arrange an escorted walk, see **www.nps.gov/chis/ planyourvisit/san-miguel-things-to-do.htm**.

GETTING THERE

San Miguel is most easily reached under sail from the north or west. If approaching from the other Channel Islands or the Los Angeles area, an early start is advisable: strong westerlies pick up around noon. Island Packer Cruises run a launch service from Ventura (three hours; July to October) **www. islandpackers.com/trips/san-miguel-island-smi/**; overnight camping is possible.

DISTANCES

Cojo anchorage to Cuyler Harbor, 24 miles; Cuyler to Becher Bay (Santa Rosa Island), 19 miles; Cuyler to Ventura, 55 miles.

WEATHER

North-west winds prevail in summer and are stronger off Point Conception and San Miguel than elsewhere. Starting in September there is a risk of Santa Ana winds, powerful north-easters that can blow out of a clear sky for 2 to 3 days when there is abnormally high pressure over the continent. Fog is common from May to July.

ANCHORAGE

GPS 34°03'.235N 120°21'.382W, depth 11 metres. Land at the west end of the beach. Exposed/ dangerous in winds between north and east.

GENERAL

No services are available. The ranger station is often unstaffed out of season and exploring inland is not then permitted. As well as the sea lions, fur seals and elephant seals at Point Bennett, it is interesting to visit the Caliche Forest, a large area of petrified trees.

CHARTS

USA (NOAA) 18727, San Miguel Passage; Cuyler Harbor.

REFERENCES

(1) Fagan, Brian. *Cruising Guide to Central and Southern California: Golden Gate to Ensenada, Mexico.* Camden, USA: International Marine/Ragged Mountain Press, 2001.

(2) Fagan, Brian. *California Coastal Passages.* San Francisco, USA: Capra Press, 1981.

POINT CONCEPTION LIGHTHOUSE

PART II

SOUTH PACIFIC

CALETA BRECKNOCK, TIERRA DEL FUEGO

CHILE

We had an unexpected problem when the time came for us to leave our snug berth at Puerto Williams, the little naval town on the south shore of the Beagle Channel that had been our haven for the winter. The heavy mooring lines that had held us tight against the inside of the *Micalvi*, an old military supply ship that serves as a Yacht Club, were frozen rigid and their knots defied undoing. Faced with persistent engine-starting problems in these waters, we'd bought a small propane torch to heat our air intake: this was now judiciously employed to thaw the bowlines out.

Out in the 3-mile-wide Channel, punctiliously toeing the international border between Chile and Argentina, a grey navy gunboat – the *Piloto Sibbald* – passed us from astern. The skipper hailed us politely on the VHF in impeccable

CAPE HORN & ROUTES FROM THE ATLANTIC TO THE PACIFIC
⊕ 55° 59' S 67° 16' W

Battened down for the winter at Puerto Williams (Beagle Channel)

English. After noting down our details, he inquired: 'And are they still serving cream teas at the Empress Hotel?'

It turned out that he had once made a courtesy call, on a much larger Chilean vessel, to the Canadian Forces base at Esquimalt, Victoria. The stately Empress is one of the city's landmarks.

As we made our way slowly west against the prevailing winds, we had to relearn our anchoring techniques. Sheer rock walls all around the boat in these latitudes do not, contrary to what one might think, spell quiet, windless anchorages. They are likely instead to be generators of williwaws or – as they are called in Spanish – *rachas*. Powerful gusts of short duration and unpredictable direction unique to Patagonia, these sweep down steep rock faces, create visible depressions in the surface of the water, then bounce back upwards.

The trick is to find a moderate rock wall or a barrier of trees between you and the wind (but check to see if the trees are healthy and vertical: if stunted and bent it means this is a bad place). Then, having dropped the anchor, reverse up to the wall or the trees as close as you dare. Next row at least two lines ashore to hold the boat's stern in position, preferably four. If you can edge in close enough, the worst of the williwaws will pass you by at the level of your mast-top.

Getting that initial line secured is easier said than done. First, we would need to pump up and launch our dinghy on deck while under way (no towing the dinghy in these rough waters), which blocked the skipper's view. Once we were anchored with the transom facing unnaturally into the wind, Jenny would scramble over the side into the inflatable, with one 100-metre line attached to her waist, another in a cloth bag. While I tried to hold the boat in position, usually in reverse, she would row hurriedly to shore, identify a suitable tree, boulder or shrub, secure the dinghy, climb out and tie the line on. Repeat three times, with an accompaniment of shouting and gesticulation over the wind and the noise

Previous pages: Sighting Cape Roggeveen, Easter Island

of the engine: 'No, not that tree there, the one higher up, to the left…', or: 'That's the end of the line; wait while I tie another one on…'

Hardy fishermen work these waters year-round. At Caleta Olla, at the eastern end of the Beagle's north-western arm, two men rowed over and offered us as much *centolla* (king crab) as we could eat. Disconcertingly, when we pointed out the individual crab we'd like, which was slowly crawling about in the bottom of their launch, one of them picked it up and calmly pulled the eight legs off, one by one. Depositing the legs in the bucket we'd proffered, he threw the body back in the water. The men would never accept any money. But we'd been primed by a more experienced yachtie.

'If you insist, there are three things they'll take,' and he smiled in anticipation. 'Pornography, wine or cigarettes.'

We had none of the former on board, and it seemed unwise to offer wine: the crew would probably appreciate it, but their skipper might not be pleased.

So, although we don't smoke and don't greatly appreciate being with smokers, cigarettes seemed the lesser of the three evils. We'd stocked up with 20 or so packs of Belmont; they went down well.

After Olla, you are in glacier alley. All along the north shore, great walls of blue-white ice drop to the level of the black channel, their source often lost in the overcast skies. Somewhere up in those clouds was the peak of Monte Darwin, second highest on Tierra del Fuego; we had seen it once from the air, when flying by Twin Otter from Puerto Williams to Punta Arenas, but we never saw it from sea level.

At Seno Pia we crept over a 2-metre-deep shelf (a sunken moraine) and made for Caleta Beaulieu, but the inlet was choked with large pieces of ice that moved back and forth with the tide; we had to back out. On the Beagle's south shore, we spent days tied up in snug Caleta Julia, four lines to shore and an anchor down, as *rachas* heeled us over to one side and the other. Tramping over the peaty hills one foggy morning, we

The mountains of Tierra del Fuego, from the Beagle Channel

were startled by the whoosh of a pair of Andean condors.

It wasn't all wind and waves. In Canal O'Brien the water was black and utterly still. But by now, as we moved closer to the western tip of Tierra del Fuego and the full force of the gales of the Southern Ocean, the vegetation was becoming more sparse. The predominant colours were the grey of smooth granite and the russet yellow of grass that spends much of the year under snow.

A major test, we knew, would be the rounding of the Brecknock Peninsula, the far western tip of Tierra del Fuego. This is as wild a place as can be. Gloomy and almost bare mountains are perpetually snow-capped, their lower slopes exposed to the full fury of the greybeards of the ocean. A few dwarf shrubs survive close to sea level. But they all point east like flags in a stiff breeze, blown that way by the perpetual westerly winds. The nearest human settlements are a one-family Chilean naval outpost at Timbales, 140 miles east, and Fairway Lighthouse, 150 miles to the north-west.

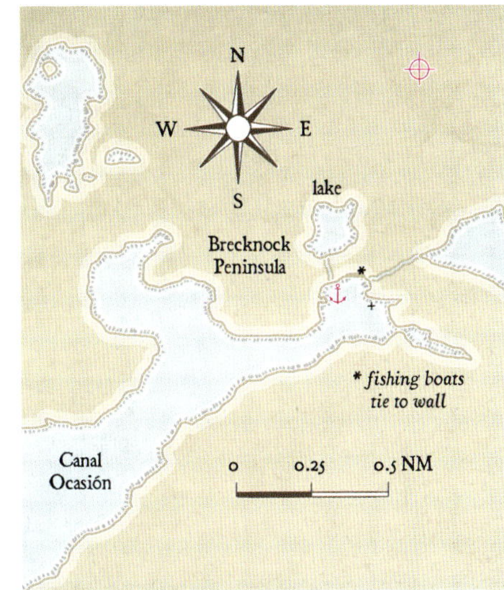

Caleta Brecknock, Tierra del Fuego, Chile
⊕ 54° 32' S 71° 54' W

Here in Caleta Brecknock, tied to the shore in a spider's web of nylon lines in an imposing rock cirque like something from *Lord of the Rings*, we first experienced the full extent of the worst weather in the world, hitherto only imagined from the cosiness of armchairs. For nine days gale and storm-force gusts whipped at us from all directions, rocking us one way then another, making our rigging howl and our mooring lines strain. In the bay, only metres away from our bows, the water was churned into a white frenzy. The crackly navy forecast on the SSB radio warned of seas of 14 metres in nearby Brecknock Channel. The sea-state report from the Evangelistas lighthouse, at the Pacific entrance to the Strait of Magellan, was '*montañoso*' (mountainous). The barometer descended unimaginably. One day the synoptic chart that we received by satellite phone was indicating a low of 934 millibars 200 miles to the south of us. A yacht anchored in Ushuaia reported that his instrument was reading 'G' (the needle was on the G in 'Made in Germany,' he clarified).

We read Dostoyevsky (slowly) and ventured out in lulls to clear snow off the decks, to check the lines or to make forays up the mountain before the snow and sleet closed in again. Most days, wrapped in our warmest clothes, we played two or three games of Scrabble. Jenny complained when I hit a winning streak, and threatened not to play anymore. We agreed that she'd be given an extra letter until the results became more balanced.

When the storm finally passed it was a day we will long remember. The snow was falling noiselessly onto utterly still waters as we worked to undo our web of lines and hoist the dinghy on board. You could see the flakes dissolve greasily on the surface. Then the sky began to clear. As Jenny used a dustpan and brush to clear the decks, it was with a sense of joy that I unrolled the genoa and felt *Bosun Bird* heel to the light wind and gather speed.

The full splendour of the Darwin Range rose dazzlingly white out of what was now a deep blue, sparkling sea.

Caleta Brecknock after a fresh snowfall

IF YOU GO...

ENTRY FORMALITIES

For most nationalities, a 90-day visa is issued upon entry to Chile; this can be extended once, or you can restart the clock by crossing to Argentina and back. Customs (*aduana*) will grant the yacht entry for one year; this can be extended (in country) once only.

For onward internal travel, a *zarpe* – a combined clearance and passage plan – must be obtained from the navy (*armada*), which has a presence in all significant ports. Underway, you must check in twice daily with them. If you have only a VHF radio it is acceptable to check in, instead, with all lighthouses and *alcamares* (small naval detachments) that you pass, as well as with other vessels. If you have an HF/SSB radio, you may find the twice-daily scramble to call in (in Spanish) intimidating; the navy may in this case accept position reports by email.

Yachts are liable to inspections to check for safety equipment, the state of their engine and – occasionally – that the relevant charts are being carried. In the latter regard, an alternative to buying the large quantity of individual charts required for travel within the Chilean channels is to obtain an older edition of the *Atlas Hidrográfico de Chile*, a large book which includes – at a reduced scale – every single possible chart; use with a good magnifying glass. Charts are not easily available in Puerto Williams. South of the Golfo de Penas, longitude readings on the paper charts may be up to two miles out; night-time navigation is to be avoided when possible.

There may be a small charge for light and buoy fees; vessels entering Chile at Arica or Iquique have sometimes been charged additional fees.

Weather forecasts are broadcast twice daily

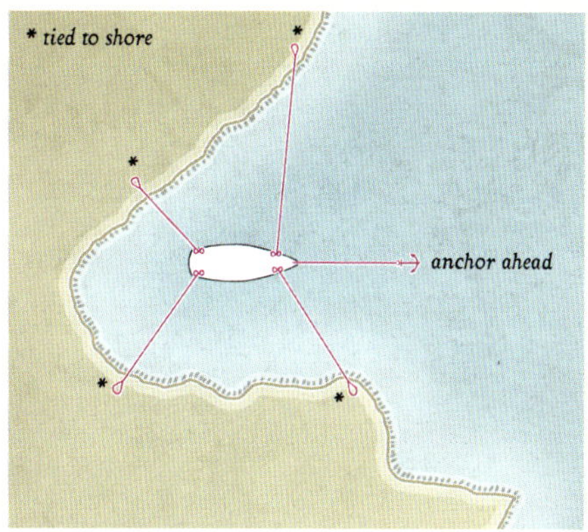

ANCHORING AT CALETA BRECKNOCK

in Spanish by coast radio stations on 2738 and 4146 kHz. South of Puerto Montt they are also available on VHF, retransmitted by a*rmada* and a*lcamar* stations.

Note that (a) If planning to cruise the Chilean channels from Ushuaia (Argentina), you must first proceed east to Puerto Williams for check-in to Chile; there are no Ports of Entry between Puerto Williams and Puerto Montt, 1200 miles to the north; (b) Only Chilean-flagged vessels are permitted to pass through Canal Murray, otherwise the safest and shortest route to Cape Horn.

For entry at Puerto Williams, call on VHF Ch 16 for directions where to tie up, likely at the *Micalvi*. Do not make a prior landing at any other location. Chilean officials are highly efficient and vigilant. In southern waters in particular, infractions of the rules will be reported by fishing boats and/or detected by the navy. The frontier with Argentina is considered sensitive; in 1978 the two countries nearly went to war over three islands at the eastern entrance of the Beagle.

GETTING THERE

Under sail, the Beagle Channel can be approached down the coast of Argentine Patagonia with favourable winds as far as

Cabo San Diego, after which the vessel will necessarily turn into the prevailing westerlies. Approaching down the coast of Chile, the outer coastline is a poorly charted and ironbound lee shore; it is preferrable to follow the inner channels, where the winds will be lighter and usually favourable. Few sailboats choose to transit the Strait of Magellan: its eastern half is low and bleak and, while Punta Arenas has all services, there is no sheltered anchorage for small boats.

There is a weekly ferry from Punta Arenas to Puerto Williams, that passes along many of the channels described above; 300 miles/32 hours; see **www.tabsa.cl/rutas/parenas-pwilliams**. DAP offers one daily flight between the two towns; in summer, tourist companies offer boat trips to Puerto Williams from Ushuaia (Argentina).

DISTANCES

Puerto Williams to Caleta Brecknock, 203 miles; Caleta Brecknock to Puerto Edén, 456 miles.

WEATHER

Westerlies prevail throughout the year but are strongest in summer. Late autumn or early spring are the best times for a northbound passage. From May to September some anchorages south of 50 degrees are liable to icing, especially those with freshwater streams and/or close to glacier faces. Average high temperatures are 14°C in January, 4°C in July. Rainfall is heavy, but less so east of the longitude of Cabo Froward (71° 20'W). It can snow any month. If sailing north, maximum advantage should be taken of rare easterlies.

ANCHORAGE

Caleta Brecknock, GPS 54°32'.68S, 71°54'.63W; anchor in 12 metres, lie in 8 metres. Four shorelines.

GENERAL

Puerto Williams (pop. 2,800), is a navy town, but tourism is playing an ever greater role. The Silversea cruise line bases its ships here and a large new wharf is under construction (2023). There is a small supermarket, a restaurant and a hotel. Yachts tie up at the half-beached *Micalvi*; this is well sheltered, especially if your draught permits you to go inside; showers and, in summer, a bar. There is fine hiking in the Dientes del Navarino range behind the town. Northbound, there are no further settlements until Puerto Edén (see next chapter).

CHART

SHOAC 12711, Canal Ocasión, Caleta Burnt, Ancha y Paso Aguirre.

REFERENCES

(1) Rolfo, Mariolina and Ardrizzi, Giorgio ('The Italians'). *Patagonia and Tierra del Fuego, Nautical Guide (3rd edn)*. Rome, Italy: Nutrimenti Mare, 2016.

(2) O'Grady, Andrew. *Chile: Arica Desert to Tierra del Fuego (4th edn)*. St Ives, UK: Imray Laurie, Norie & Wilson, 2019.

(3) Mantellero, Alberto. *Yachtsman's Navigator Guide to the Chilean Channels*. Chile: self-published, 1995 (bilingual English/Spanish).

Andean condor, Caleta Julia

PUERTO EDEN

As we cruised the waters of Chile's far south, we carried with us the luminous but sad book in which Lucas Bridges recounts growing up at Harberton Estancia, on the Beagle Channel, a witness to the disappearance forever of the Ona, Selknam and Yaghan peoples: *Uttermost Part of the Earth*.[6]

Aboard a small schooner rigged with an auxiliary engine, Lucas and his father Thomas would spend months at a time exploring the Channel and the maze of islands to the west. On one voyage, they had on board two Yaghans '…from that rough region round the shores of the Brecknock peninsula. The first was Acualisnan, nicknamed Wapisa, or Whale because of his girth…'. Now, leaving Caleta Brecknock, we followed to the Strait of Magellan a narrow channel that Acualisnan had showed to Thomas and Lucas. It bears his name today.

Many other channels hereabouts are still uncharted. There are often no soundings, and the outlines of some islands are shown only with dotted lines. If you venture here it is called 'sailing on the white', ie on the blank spaces. On one of our older paper charts we found an intriguing notation by a tentatively drawn

6 Bridges, Lucas. *Uttermost Part of the Earth*. London, UK: Hodder & Stoughton, 1948.

At anchor, Puerto Mayne

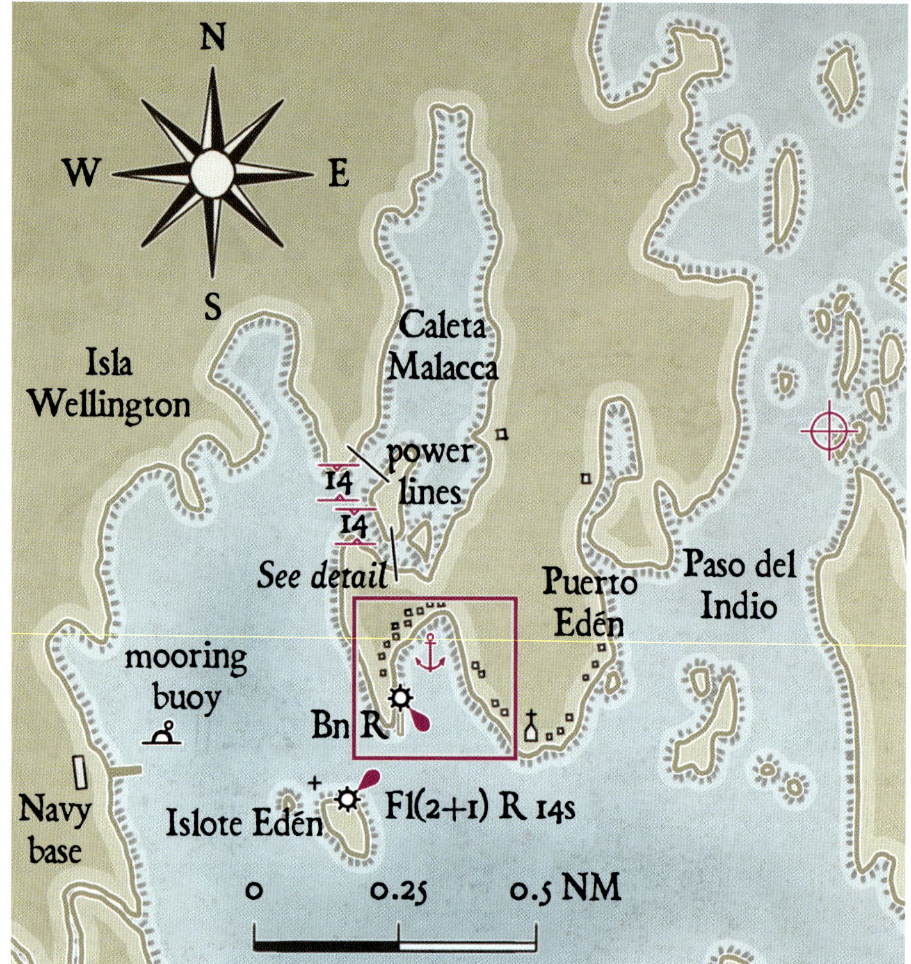

Puerto Edén, Chile
49° 07'.3 S 74° 23'.9 W

'white' bay on Santa Inés Island: Dresden Hort (German for Dresden Haven).

SMS *Dresden* was a light cruiser that was the sole German survivor of the Battle of the Falklands, on 8 December 1914.

Fleeing west from the catastrophe at a boiler-bursting 27 knots, it seeks refuge in the Strait of Magellan. British Consul Charlie Milward spots it off Punta Arenas and alerts the British fleet. For days the British steam up and down the Strait. The *Dresden* is not to be found. Eventually it slips into the little bay on uncharted Santa Inés, sending word to a German businessman residing in Punta Arenas, Albert Pagels, and asking him to arrange for clandestine coaling and re-victualling.

Pagels mobilises the entire German community and leads the resupply mission himself. Milward suspects something. He thinks the *Dresden* must be close and he prevails upon the Chilean authorities to prevent Pagels from making any further sorties. Pagels frustrates him by sometimes leaving harbour aboard a vessel called the *Explorador*, which is owned by the Austro-Hungarian consul and

Running in Force 7, Strait of Magellan

which enjoys diplomatic immunity. In February, the German makes his last visit to Dresden Hort; when he returns, he sends a coded message to Berlin, saying the *Dresden* has broken out, and will rendezvous with a coaler at Juan Fernández Island. The British miss it (for now). Pagels is awarded the Iron Cross.

When we look closely at our chart, we see that an ill-defined point on the western shore of Dresden Hort is labelled Pagels Huk (Pagels Hook).[7]

There are more stories. Sailing up the Strait of Magellan in 1896 aboard *Spray*, Joshua Slocum famously spreads carpet tacks on his decks every time he anchors, to deter boarders. When he sees strangers he goes below and changes clothes before coming up again, so they will think there is more than one person on board. One day, at Mussel Bay, he fights off a party of boarders, led by a locally infamous character called Black Pedro:

'I knew by his Spanish lingo and his full beard that he was the villain … a renegade mongrel and the worst murderer in Tierra del Fuego.'

The Chilean authorities later reprimand him for not having shot Pedro dead.

We had no such dramas as we turned to port from Acualisnan, into the Strait of Magellan. We had a rare easterly with us and roared along at 7 knots, leaving the great headland that is Cape Froward – the most southerly point of the continent – sinking slowly behind us. We passed Mussel Bay, now silent and deserted. We ducked into the shelter of the maze of waterways that is known as the Chilean Channels and saw no one for weeks.

Some days progress was painfully slow. The wind from now on was never in our favour, always from dead ahead. Our engine was not powerful enough to motor

---

7   Dresden Hort is the north-west extremity of Bahía Stokes, at GPS 54° 02'.555S 72° 31'.039W. A comparison of the German chart (#745, Magellanstrasse, Westlicher Teil, dated 1972) with photos from Google Maps/Earth shows how approximate the chart was even at that date.

into anything beyond a light breeze, so we tacked hour after hour, day after day. If we were not handy enough going about at the end of a mile-long board, we'd find ourselves back at the same place on the other side of the channel. One day, the log records, we sailed only 2 miles in ten hours. The *Admiralty Pilot* sums up the scenery: 'The general features of the channels are high and abrupt shores with innumerable peaks and headlands … giving an appearance of gloomy grandeur rarely seen elsewhere.'

Everywhere – on the chart at least – there are reminders of the Royal Navy ships and commanders who first surveyed these waters. Here are Estrecho Collingwood, Paso Farquhar, Paso Tamar and Canal Smyth. There is an Isla Vancouver, an Isla Mayne and other placenames also found in British Columbia, a sailing ground where many of the navigators had cut their teeth. Abra Lecky's Retreat recalls a sea-captain of the generation following Fitzroy. His magnum opus *Lecky's Wrinkles in Practical Navigation* contains such timeless aphorisms as: 'There is nothing so distressing as running ashore, unless there is also doubt as to which continent the shore belongs.'

At Estero Peel, we decided to venture into The White. It wasn't just unsurveyed: it was literally white, dotted with bergy bits from the Amalia Glacier. Legendary hard man, curmudgeon and wit HW (Bill) Tilman was here aboard his Bristol Channel cutter *Mischief*[8] in 1956. He and Charles Marriott landed and made the first recorded crossing of the Patagonian ice cap. He left *Mischief* in the hands of

one WA Proctor. It is significant that we are not told Proctor's first name. There was one disaster after another. Tilman was particularly displeased on his return to find the vessel's engine unusable. At the end of the narrative he drily remarks: 'I will not pretend that at all times throughout the 20,000 mile voyage we were a band of brothers.'

We found that the face of the Amalia had retreated significantly; but the sound was so clogged with ice that we could not get close enough even to see it.

Two months out from Puerto Williams, we came to our first houses: the colourful, ramshackle village of Puerto Edén, built at the head of a horseshoe bay with a boardwalk as its main street. We were reminded of remote outposts on the west coast of Vancouver Island. With a population of 160, everything in the village seemed to be run by Don José, a plump, balding ex-navy man in charge of the government shop.

We were hopeful of buying diesel, but feared there might not be much to be had. There had been a German yacht some distance behind us, stating emphatically on the Patagonian Cruiser's Net that they had reserved 500 litres in Edén. This is when speaking the language comes in handy. Two or three days of idle chit-chat, some flattering remarks about the navy, the exchange of a few stories and jokes – and we raised the question of diesel almost in passing. José laughed when I mentioned the Germans.

'Yes, I got their messages. They can think what they like. *Pero no hay*. There isn't any. But…' and he went on, tapping his nose conspiratorially. 'I think that

---

8   Tilman, HW. *Mischief in Patagonia*. Cambridge, UK: Cambridge University Press, 1957.

for you we can come to *un arreglo*, an arrangement with La CONAF.'

CONAF was the National Parks Agency. They owed Don José a few favours and could part with half a barrel, and at a fair price. 'Just don't say anything to *los amigos alemanes*, OK?'

When we asked if there was anywhere to eat out, our friend put us on to Doña María Vera. We went to call on her and found her living room ankle-deep in what seemed to be a shaggy brown carpet, the furniture upholstered in the same material. It was edible seaweed.

'*Está secando*,' Doña María explained. It's drying.

She cleared a space and we became regular visitors, repaying her in part with a hand-painted signboard in English that advertised fresh bread and laundry service. For buying eggs, she directed us to a lively young man. He in turn passed us on to Señora Lolo, who had a freezer full of chickens; they were so deeply frozen that we had to throw a clump of three or four repeatedly onto the wooden floor so as to break one specimen away.

The weather had been fine for a week now, which meant it was time for a big blow. The VHF forecast agreed. We put out our spare anchor – a CQR – at a 30-degree angle to the main Bruce, lashed down everything in sight and

Jenny, Señora Lolo and Jacinta

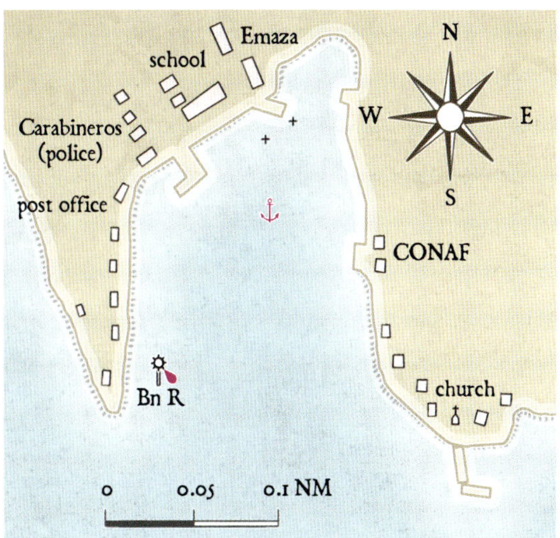

DETAIL: PUERTO EDÉN

retreated below to wait. On the evening navy summary, Evangelistas was this time reporting 50 knots gusting to 75; Cabo Ráper, 100 miles to the north, had 42 knots.

As the night went on, the wind screamed ever more shrilly. There were only 50 metres of open water between our bows and dry land ahead of us, but soon we were swinging violently first one way then the other; water was breaking over the bows. At midnight we had a brief moment of panic when we seemed to lose the two or three lights on shore that were serving as references. Were we dragging? But the GPS said we were holding; the power on shore must have gone out.

Next morning, we learned that the weekly ferry had sought shelter all night at Puerto Riofrio, 6 miles south. Don José said he had looked out for us: 'I thought you were done for.'

We pulled down a couple of casks of Gato Negro red wine. As we were settling up, he added with studied casualness: 'Oh, I thought you might like to know. I had an email. Those Germans. I think they'll be in tomorrow.'

We left that afternoon.

IF YOU GO…

For information on entry formalities and references see Chapter 16, page 115.

GETTING THERE

Under sail, access from the north is easier than from the south; the prevailing northwesterly winds become northerlies in the channels. The NAVIMAG ferry company has two vessels plying between Puerto Montt and Puerto Natales, calling at Puerto Edén; frequency is once every three to four days; duration four days/three nights. See **www.navimag.com/en/explore-patagonia-by-ferry-navimag**.

DISTANCES

Puerto Williams to Puerto Edén, 659 miles; Puerto Edén to Puerto Montt, 659 miles.

WEATHER

North-west winds dominate; the climate is wet (Puerto Edén has some of the highest rainfall figures in the world) but relatively mild. Passage across the Golfo de Penas (Gulf of Sorrows), to the north, can be trying for

SMS *DRESDEN*, LIGHT CRUISER

LENGTH:	388 FEET
CREW:	361
LAUNCHED:	1907
SCUTTLED:	1915

northbound sailors: it is open to the Pacific and heavy seas meeting the tide flowing out of Canal Messier can make for rough conditions; wait in an anchorage at the north end of Messier for a moderate forecast.

ANCHORAGE

Puerto Edén, GPS 49°07'.668S 74°24'.7344W, depth 12 metres. Note: access to the inner anchorage to the north of the village, Caleta Malacca, is under a power line with 14 metres of clearance.

GENERAL

Population 170. There is a government-run shop (Emaza) with basic food supplies; diesel is sometimes available. There is a police (*carabineros*) as well as a navy (*armada*) presence, but this is NOT a port of entry. The village is home to the last living Kawésqa – or Northern Alacaluf – people.

CHARTS

SHOAC 9510, Angostura Inglesa y Paso del Indio; SHOAC 9511, Puertos en el Canal Messier y Paso del Indio.

The waterfront, Puerto Eden

ROBINSON CRUSOE ISLAND (ISLAS JUAN FERNANDEZ)

CHILE

It's always difficult to find good crew prepared to sail offshore. For some reason, people these days resent being shouted at by their captain; having to get up at all hours to respond to emergencies on deck; trying to cook when the boat is swinging around madly; and unclogging the head while underway. Plus, in the case of my partner Jenny, suffering the self-appointed skipper's Bligh delusions and not even getting paid for the pleasure. But it seems it was always like this.

When in 1703 Captain Thomas Stradling recruited a young Scot called Alexander Selkirk as a deckhand aboard his privateer the *Cinque Ports*, it must have been with misgivings. Alex was known to have a 'quarrelsome and unruly disposition' and had been charged for 'indecent conduct in church' in his hometown of Largo, Fife. He participated enthusiastically enough in the rape and

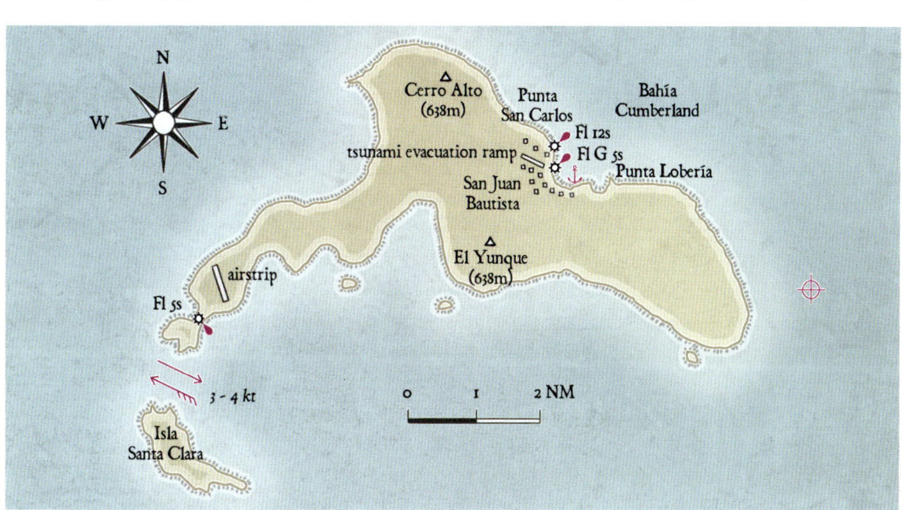

ROBINSON CRUSOE ISLAND, CHILE
33° S 78° 45' W

At anchor, Cumberland Bay

pillage that Stradling approved on the Spanish Main but then, when the ship and crew were recuperating at the lonely island of Más a Tierra ('Closest to Land'), part of the Juan Fernández archipelago off Chile, Selkirk began complaining to Stradling about the seaworthiness of the *Cinque Ports*. Admittedly, the ship had had a rough time of things when rounding Cape Horn. But Stradling was a no-nonsense captain. He immediately put the stroppy Selkirk ashore on the uninhabited island, with a musket, a hatchet, a cooking pot and a Bible. And sailed away.

The castaway had four and a half years to regret his petulance. Two Spanish ships anchored off Más a Tierra during that period, but he dared not approach their crew when they landed to take on water: as far as he knew, Spain was still an enemy. He hid in a tree and came close to being detected when a sailor came over and unbuttoned his britches to urinate. It was not until 1709, with Alex daily scaling the prominent peak now known as El Yunque (The Anvil) to scan for sails, that another privateer, the *Duke*, hove into view and took him on board.

Selkirk's solitary ordeal attracted widespread interest when he arrived back in England, and he became a celebrity. Later, he inspired WS Gilbert (of Gilbert & Sullivan), Charles Dickens, and the poet WM Cowper, whose most famous verse is:

I am monarch of all I survey,
My right there is none to dispute;
From the centre all round to the sea,
I am lord of the fowl and the brute.

A writer who read about Selkirk with particular attention was Daniel Defoe: his *Life and Strange Surprizing Adventures of Robinson Crusoe* (1719) was the result, with Más a Tierra transposed to the Caribbean and Man Friday thrown in. Much, much later (in 1966), with Crusoe having become one of the best-known characters in English literature, the Chilean president renamed the island after him in the hope of attracting tourists.

Like the *Cinque Ports*, we had a rough passage to Robinson Crusoe. Only a day out of Puerto Montt, we were surfing north in winds of 40 knots and 5-metre seas, with three reefs in the main. Jenny was heard to utter rare profanities when she spilled an entire tin of powdered milk on the cabin floor and then, seeking to recover her balance, fell against the control panel and snapped the ignition key off. Later we prised the remains of the key out with a paper clip.

Cumberland Bay, at the head of which lies Robinson Crusoe Island's only settlement – Juan Bautista, population 840 – is more open than you'd hope, and deeper too. As we meandered around looking for a shallow patch Jenny, whose responsibility it is to haul up our 15 kilogram anchor plus 30 metres of chain by means of a manual windlass, grumbled as I read out the changing depths to her. Already she was anticipating hard work when we came to leave. But the location is spectacular, with high cliffs backing the small town, a lush and mountainous interior, and a few traditional green-and-white lobster-fishing boats bobbing at their moorings.

After rowing ashore and checking in with the port captain, we wandered along the quiet and shady waterfront and bumped into a friendly old gentleman who presented to us his card, with a little bow that said: 'Victorio Bettullo Mancilla: Professor and Historian.'

Over coffee, Victorio – who was lonely and admitted that the tourist rush anticipated in 1966 had yet to materialise – explained that the two large and rusting excavators we had seen in the long grass had been landed with a view to improving the island's small airstrip; the problem was that the airstrip is at the other end of the island and there is no road. He filled us in on some of the common but odd island surnames – Green, Schiller, de Roodt and Recabbaren (which is Basque) – and then directed us to a small monument visible along the foreshore.

Here, a plaque commemorates the sinking in Cumberland Bay of the *Dresden* in 1915. After Captain Lüdecke and his crew had given his pursuers the slip in the Fuegian channels, the British

The plaque at Selkirk's lookout

Monument commemorating the sinking of SMS Dresden

intercepted a radio transmission and caught up with the cruiser here. This time there was no escape: warning shots were fired, the captain raised a white flag and then scuttled her before the British could board.

Among the crew members interned by Chile was Wilhelm Canaris, later to be chief of German military intelligence in the Second World War. Some of the crew enjoyed their detention: one returned to the island in 1931 to farm; you can still see the foundations of his stone farmhouse.

'But he was denounced as a Nazi spy in 1943,' said Victorio, 'and we never saw him again.'

Meanwhile, high up on the slopes of El Yunque is Selkirk's lookout, marked by a plaque placed here in 1869 by the crew of HMS *Topaze*. The climb had us puffing after the enforced inactivity of days at sea. It's a windy place with a superb view, but it's hard to imagine that Selkirk actually had the time to trek this high up every day, in search of a sail.

We had our own adventures here. After making a few modest purchases at the Minimarket Crucero Dresden, Jenny put her foot through a section of rotten planking on the shop's exterior deck and sank to mid-thigh level, with a great screech. She incidentally crushed our fresh baguettes. Worse was to come that evening. We rowed over to have a pisco sour (or two) with some old sailing friends – Graham and Avril, aboard *Dreamaway* – who had pulled into Cumberland Bay before us. Jenny fell in as we reboarded our own boat at one o'clock in the morning; she later claimed, unconvincingly, that she had not realised that pisco sours were alcoholic.

Occasionally, I like to remind her of what can happen to 'quarrelsome and unruly' crew members, and of Alexander Selkirk's fate in particular. She has yet to take the hint.

Local lobster boats, Cumberland Bay

IF YOU GO…

For information on entry formalities see Chapter 16, page 115.

GETTING THERE

The island lies 360 miles off the Chilean mainland. At 33°40'S, it is within the belt of the south-east trades, and under sail is most easily approached from the south. There are flights (up to two weekly) by small twin-engine aircraft from Santiago. The airstrip is at the western extremity of the island; passengers are brought to San Juan Bautista by boat.

DISTANCES

Puerto Montt to Robinson Crusoe, 601 miles; Valdivia to Robinson Crusoe, 460 miles; Valparaíso to Robinson Crusoe, 360 miles; Robinson Crusoe to Easter Island, 1,740 miles.

WEATHER

The trades are more southerly than southeasterly in this vicinity; they falter in winter. The climate is subtropical, with summer highs averaging 22°C, winter lows reaching 9°C.

ANCHORAGE

Cumberland Bay, GPS 33°38'.39S 78°49'.54W, depth 20 metres. There are two mooring buoys close by, which may be available. The bay is open to the north-east. Winds from that direction are unusual, but stay attentive to the fishermen, especially if you see them hauling their launches out.

GENERAL

Population 840; lobster fishing is the main occupation. There is a small grocery store but few other services; do not count on fuel availability. Small lodges cater to tourists. There are no immigration officials. This means this cannot be your first port of call in Chile and that if you are sailing from here to another country, you will not be able to obtain departure clearance. Meanwhile, check in and out with the navy (*armada*). A tsunami caused major damage and loss of life in 2010. Eighty-five miles to the west is Isla Alejandro Selkirk, pop. 50. Moorings may be available opposite the former penal colony, halfway down the east coast, but the location is extremely exposed.

CHARTS

SHOAC 5410, Archipiélago de Juan Fernández; 5411, Bahía Cumberland.

REFERENCE

O'Grady, Andrew. *Chile: Arica Desert to Tierra del Fuego (4th edn).* St Ives, UK: Imray Laurie, Norie & Wilson, 2019.

ROBINSON CRUSOE ISLAND
BEARING 226°, 5 NM

EASTER ISLAND

CHILE

Astern, the rugged outline of Robinson Crusoe Island sank slowly beneath the horizon, the near-cloudless sky turning to a hazy purple as dusk overtook us.

At the beginning of long passages, I always feel excited but a little queasy as well. I checked my tether and shuffled backwards in the cockpit to lean out and make an adjustment to our self-steering gear, one eye on the slowly swinging compass. The optimal course was west-north-west, the wind was south-south-east at a gentle 10 knots: the vane liked any wind forward of a run, so we were off to a good start. After supper Jenny ran through with me our evening checklist.

'No need to reef or to pole the jib? Lifejacket on? Tether on? Check the strobe, the rigging knife. Here's the headset, the iPod, there's coffee in the vacuum flask. I'm off to bed. See you at 10:30.'

Most of the stars were out now. I stood up for a look around, bracing myself on the rigid dodger frame. There were no lights to be seen, I didn't expect there to be in this empty corner of the South Pacific. *Bosun Bird* rustled quietly into the darkness, occasionally slapping down a wave that was bigger than the

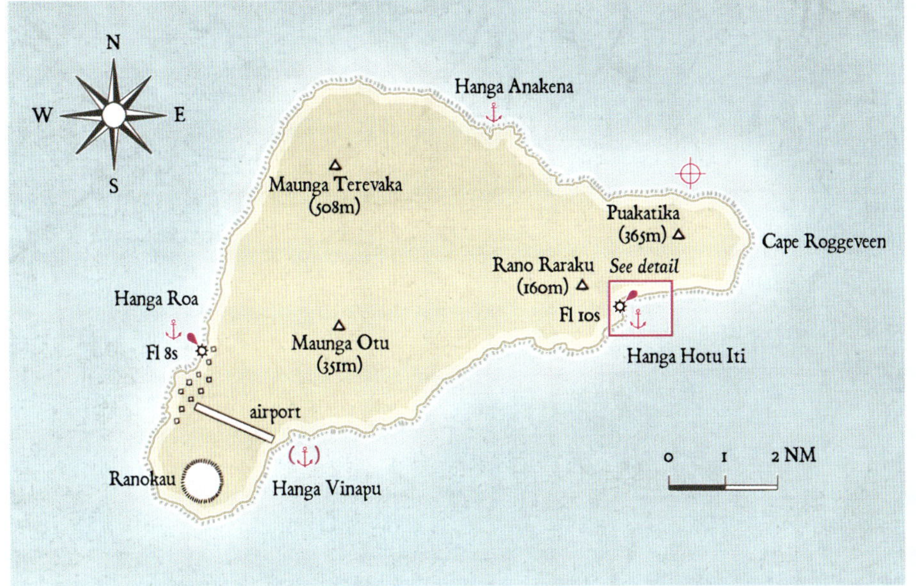

Easter Island – Isla de Pascua – Rapa Nui, Chile
⊕ 27° 05' S 109° 15' W

rest. It would be 1,750 miles to Easter Island, known to the Polynesians as the Navel of the Earth.

Every morning, we studied the grib files we had downloaded to our laptop. We adjusted our course a little to the north so as to avoid the light winds we risked finding at the centre of the South Pacific High. Wolfgang, who ran the Patagonia Cruisers' Net out of Valdivia, told us on the SSB radio that *Ludus Amoris* were behind us, now approaching Robinson Crusoe, *Andiamo* had just left Puerto Montt, and *Dreamaway* were closing on Iquique. Soon we were reading a novel a day; Jenny spent most of her off-watches catching up on our finances.

Steadily the wind picked up. Now, day after day, it was at 25 knots. We put up our downwind running rig: the staysail poled out to one side, the double-reefed main to the other, with a tight preventer. *Bosun Bird* bowls along in these conditions but she rolls heavily. Down below, we jammed our two biggest pink fenders (known as 'the boobs') between the bunk that was marginally more downhill and the cabin table, so that the off-duty crew member would not roll into the gangway when sleeping.

The shoreline at Hanga Roa

Hanga Hotu Iti

Day 17 was 1 April. I took advantage of the date to convince Jenny – briefly – that I could see Easter Island, even though it was still 130 miles distant. But by next morning we really were closing in on the 400-metre cliffs of Cape Roggeveen. I briefly regretted the uncertainty and anticipation of landfalls in the days of celestial navigation, but not for long.

As forecast, the wind had gone northerly. This would make the anchorage off the main settlement at Hanga Roa untenable: it is an open roadstead off a coastline that inclines to the north-east. We plumped for Hanga Hotu Iti, on the south-eastern side of this triangular island.

It was a dream of a setting. At the head of the bay was a row of 15 of those iconic *moai* (the enigmatic standing heads of Easter Island), backed by low, rolling green hills. The warm water was clear and we zigzagged among dark coral heads to find a large patch of white sand and drop our Bruce anchor in 12 metres.

As the sun set, we had a glass of our Chilean box-red to celebrate our arrival.

Next morning Jenny dived on our anchor. Already our chain was working its way around a large coral head, risking becoming jammed. On cue, a small launch zipped out from the one house on shore. Victor, who fished the bay every day, advised us to move to a different corner, where it would be deeper but the bottom would be uniformly sandy. We realised when we tried to get the anchor up that his warning had come none too soon: it took an hour of manoeuvring back and forth to break free and we bent one fluke in the process. As he watched, Victor helpfully detailed for us the number of sailboats that had been wrecked in this bay.

Our new friend adopted us. He saved us the labour of inflating our oar-powered Avon (and a row of half a mile) by running us back and forth in his launch, plied us with strong black coffee in his shack on the beach, and drove us across the island to the 'capital' at Hanga Roa. We were glad we hadn't gone around to Hanga Roa by boat. A half-mile off from the town a couple of sailboats were dipping and rising violently at anchor, with two surf-lines between them and the beach. There is a tiny square artificial harbour – Hanga Piko, about the size of a moderate swimming pool – but there were heavy breakers in the entrance and a swell was working its way in and out, creating a 1-metre rise and fall and an awful sucking sound.

We loaded up on as much fresh fruit as we could (an entire stalk of green bananas) and set off to see the sights.

Ah, those statues. However much you have read about them, however many photos you may have seen, the *moai* do not disappoint. Most thought-provoking of all the sites is the 'nursery': a quarry cut into the hillside, where you can see 6-metre-long monoliths still only half-cut out of the living rock. All around are more heads set at steep angles into the hillside. It is as if one day the order had been given to stop work, and everyone just downed tools.

There are few definitive answers to anything about Easter Island. What do the *moai* mean? How were they raised? How did the first inhabitants get here? How and why did an apparently once thriving population of over 5,000 suddenly collapse? Thor Heyerdahl is among the many who have published their theories: controversially, he postulates that the original settlement was from South America.

Back at Hanga Hotu Iti in the late afternoon, we were alarmed to find that *Bosun Bird* was hardly visible, disappearing

Moai at the head of the bay, Hanga Hotu Iti

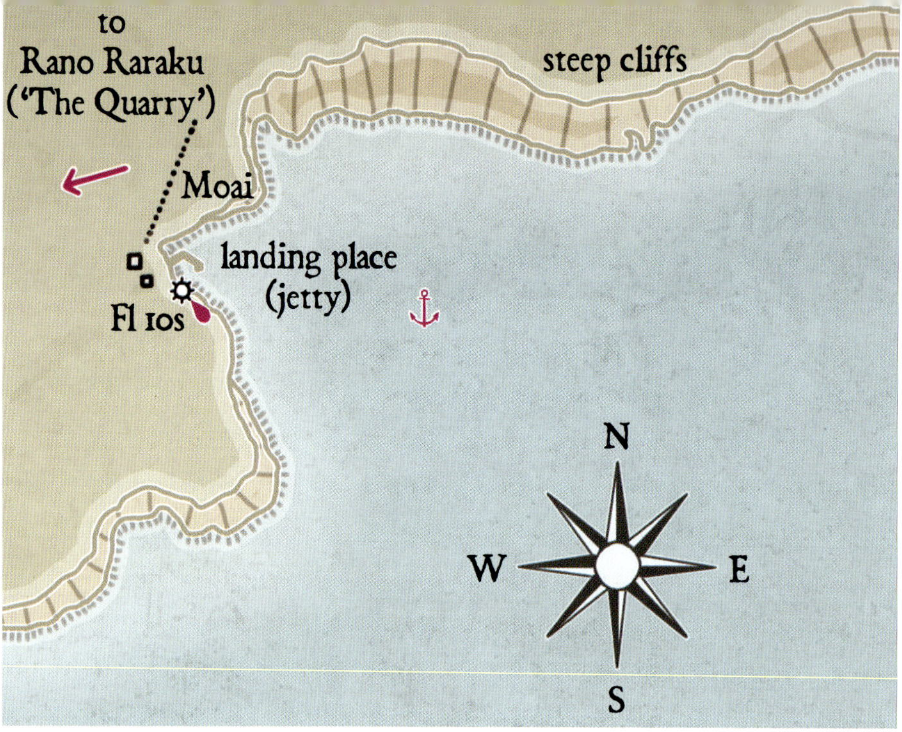

DETAIL: HANGA HOTU ITI

between enormous swells that were now rolling in from some distant storm and breaking thunderously. Victor came to the rescue. He hurried us into his launch with the admonition: '*Es mejor que se vayan … ya!* It's best you leave … now!'

We edged out from his tiny concrete jetty and for several minutes cruised slowly along the beach in front of the breakers, which Victor eyed carefully. Then, 'Hold on!' He gunned the 90hp Yamaha and we headed straight for a roller. We lifted high in the air, seemed to pause there, then crashed down into the calmer water beyond.

We said our quick thank yous to Victor as we boarded, and barely spoke to each other as we frantically readied to leave. There was no wind, but the oily waves were larger by the minute and seemed to be carrying us inshore. I turned on the depth sounder and saw with alarm that we were rising and falling 5 metres; the barograph was in free fall. The anchor came up on sheer adrenaline. I gunned our engine into a now-threatening dusk and we set a course to clear Roggeveen.

Those bananas we bought at Hanga Roa? Well, they were great, but all 90 ripened on the same day.

Victor to the rescue

IF YOU GO…

For information on entry formalities see Chapter 16, page 115.

. . . .

GETTING THERE

Prevailing winds favour an approach from the east in summer, the north in autumn. The lack of all-weather anchorages means that you should not count on being able to land; authorities may require that you always leave a crew member on board if/when you do land. LATAM flies regularly from Santiago (six hours).

DISTANCES

Galápagos to Easter Island, 1,950 miles; Easter Island to Valdivia, 1,945 miles; Easter Island to Papeete, 2,285 miles.

WEATHER

The island is on the north-western edge of the South Pacific High. For Dec/Jan/Feb, south-east winds blow 60 per cent of the time; at other times winds are quite variable and there may be spells of north-west winds. Storms to the south can generate heavy swells that make southern anchorages untenable.

ANCHORAGES

There is no completely safe anchorage. Hanga Hotu Iti, GPS 27°07'.63S 109°16'.11W, depth 16 metres; only tenable in north or west winds; look for a sandy spot, land in the north-west corner. Hanga Roa, GPS 27°08'.60S 109 26°.60'W, depth 20 metres, in line with range on shore; best in south-east winds (off the only town); surf landing. Hanga Piko, GPS (entry) 27°09'.257S 109°26'.442W, very confined, impossible to enter/leave in westerly winds, by permission of the port captain; a pilot may be required. Anakena, GPS 27°04'.3182S

Moai near The Quarry

109°19'.4132W, depth 8 metres; good in anything except north winds; dinghy dock on the east shore.

GENERAL

The port captain (navy/*armada*) is available by VHF Ch 16 to discuss anchoring options; authorities understand that weather may preclude formalities; they will normally come out to yachts at Hanga Roa. Groceries and fuel are available in Hanga Roa.

CHARTS

SHOAC 2510, Isla de Pascua (Rapa Nui); 2513, Fondeaderos en Isla de Pascua (Vinapu and Hotuiti); 2512, Hanga Roa y Hanga Piko; 2511, Hanga La Perouse y Hanga Anakena.

REFERENCES

(1) Hinz, Earl. *Landfalls of Paradise: Cruising Guide to the Pacific Islands (5th edn)*. Hawaii, USA: University of Hawaii Press, 2006.

(2) Clay, Warwick. *South Pacific Anchorages (2nd edn)*. St Ives, UK: Imray, Laurie, Norie and Wilson, 2001.

(3) Wood, Charles and Margo. *Charlie's Charts of Polynesia (8th edn)*. Blue Lake, USA: Paradise Cay Publications, 2021.

AUKENA, ILES GAMBIER

FRENCH POLYNESIA

After a hasty departure from Easter Island we called up the Chilean navy at the settlement, Hanga Roa, to apologise for having neither checked in nor out.

'*No se preocupen. Ningún problema…*' and they kindly read us the latest weather forecast. '*Rachas … chubascos … 30 nudos.*' Squally, gusts to 30 knots.

'I thought we'd put all that behind us, in Patagonia,' Jenny commented grimly.

Three days and many sail-changes later the front was past, the wind nearly all gone. Now we were inching along at 1 knot, getting excited when we crept up to two. The sails were slatting heavily, the surface of the sea glassy. Several days, we went swimming over the side: it was an uneasy feeling so far from land and in water 4 kilometres deep. One afternoon, Jenny was climbing up the ladder on *Bosun Bird*'s transom when there was a disturbance in the water just behind her. It was a 4-metre-long shark of undetermined species, no doubt attracted by her thrashing around.

Out in these expanses of barely travelled ocean, we were seeing the world as it has been for millennia, and as it presumably will be for millennia to come: there can be few other environments on earth so ostensibly untouched. The nights were clear, the stars startling in their sharpness. We saw shooting stars so bright that you almost expected to hear the ocean hiss as they plunged down. One night there was a bright white-and-red light moving west at a speed of at least 500 knots, probably a Santiago to Tahiti flight. I remember listening on the iPod, those nights, to Christopher Cross and 'The Canvas Can Do Miracles'.

A thousand or more miles out, we drifted – for two days – past lonely Pitcairn, a British dependency. This was the final refuge of the mutineers of HMS *Bounty* once Fletcher Christian had taken command, put dour Captain Bligh into his longboat with a few faithful followers and taken on a much better looking and more amusing shipload of young Tahitian women. There was a heavy swell running: we were not inclined to repeat our experiences of Easter Island in the famously marginal Bounty Bay. We sailed on.

After 23 days, the archipelago of the Gambier Islands, the easternmost outliers of French Polynesia, hove into view: ten small but high and lush islands all within or on a large diamond-shaped encircling reef, with three wide entrance passes. We hoisted our Q flag and the French tricolour and motored in through

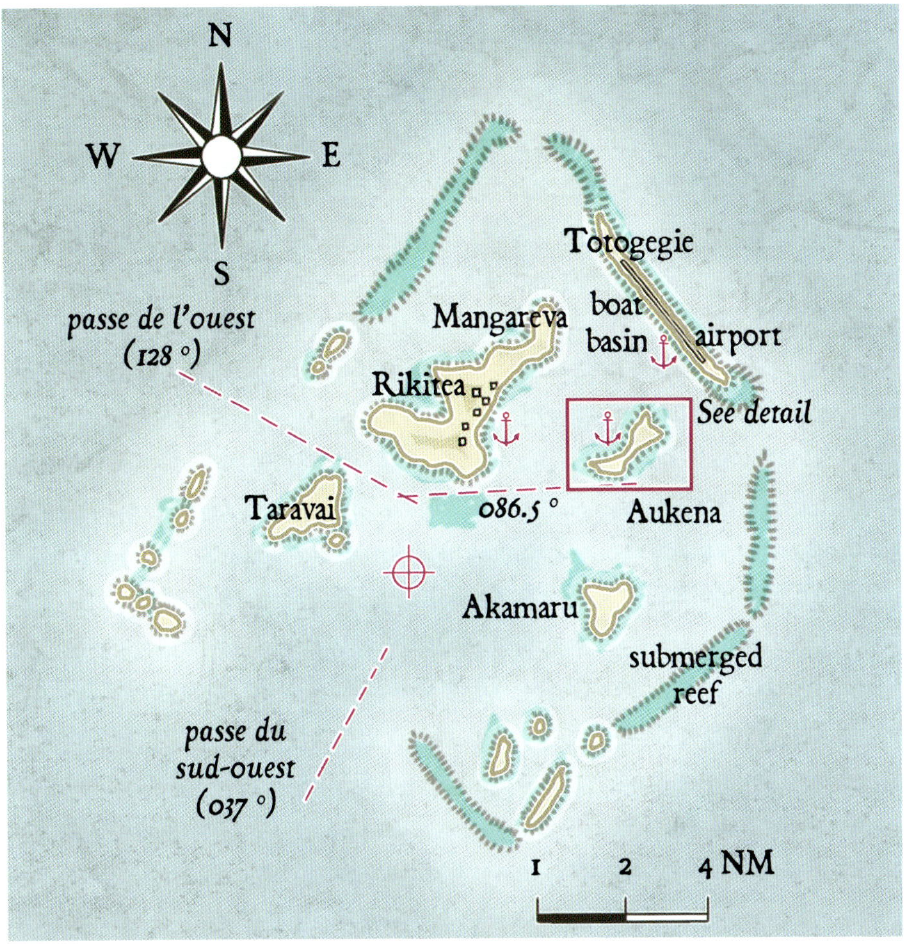

Gambier Islands, French Polynesia
23° 10' S 135° W

the Passe de l'Ouest. Jenny anxiously reminded me that here we were on the European system of marking – the opposite of that used in the Americas, with red buoys now to be left to port – then perched herself on a set of ratlines, where she'd get a better view of the coral heads on the intricate approach to Rikitea, the only significant settlement in the island group.

It took us a while to find a nice, clear sandy spot that would allow us to swing in a full circle without grazing coral. Once the anchor was down, we got the binoculars out. The little village looked quiet from seawards: 20 or 30 whitewashed and red-roofed houses half obscured by vegetation, some larger buildings in plain grey stone and – directly opposite us – a long, dilapidated hangar.

The big shed, we would soon learn, had an interesting past. For nearly a decade (1966–74) this was a fallout shelter, into which French officials would herd the entire population of the island group when they were conducting atmospheric nuclear tests at Mururoa, 130 miles to the west. There was an irrigation system by which potentially radioactive ash would be sluiced off the roof. As international

Eglise Saint Raphaël, Ile Aukena

pressure (and local protests) grew, the tests went underground. But that didn't necessarily mean they were safer. Sailing through the Marquesas in the mid-1980s we'd chatted with some off-duty French military, their tongues loosened by Hinano beer: 'Whenever we had a VIP,' they said laughingly, 'we'd all be told to swim happily in the lagoon. But the rest of the time it was totally forbidden.'

The test programme had now been abandoned in favour of electronic simulations, but Muroroa remained off-limits. In Rikitea the period is remembered with bitterness and sardonic humour. The island's one and only restaurant is called *Pizzatomic* and has as its logo an outline of the island with a fiery red cloud rising behind it.

We checked in with the police. As we were finishing the paperwork we asked the gendarme – a *métropolitain* (ie from mainland France) as they always are – where we might get some fresh fruit. He warned us not to pick fruit anywhere: it all belonged to somebody.

'The problem is this,' he went on, 'You can't buy fruit in any of the shops either; it's assumed you have your own garden. But there are a couple of Chinese shops you might try. I expect you know the saying: we – *les métropolitains* – have the power here, the Polynesians have the land, and the Chinese have the businesses.'

We wondered whether he found it a lonely life here, as one of only a very few Europeans in this small and isolated location. Perhaps deliberately ignoring the first part of my question, he gave a Gallic shrug.

'Oh, you know… The Gambiers are now more connected to civilisation than they were. We have an airstrip now, not like Pitcairn. Did you know that that the islanders learned of both the outbreak of the First World War and of its culmination on the same day? Just imagine that: "We have good news and bad news … which would you like to hear first?"'

At the Chinese shop, there was no fruit. We shelled out instead for some sliced white bread from New Zealand. It was rock-hard from the freezer and cost us US$8 for a small loaf; but we were tired of heating our boat to sauna-like temperatures when we baked our own bread.

We spent a week cruising around the smaller islands within the atoll. They are largely uninhabited, but most have monumental churches and buildings that are out of place in a location so remote and with such a modest population. These date from a dark period: 1834 to about 1870. During this time the Picpus Fathers under Père Honoré Laval established a Catholic gulag, a theocracy with strict rules of clothing, social and moral behaviour known as the Mangarevan Code. The entire Polynesian population of the Gambiers (initially about 5,000, but it soon fell to less than 2,000) worked on church-run labour schemes. The marriageable female population was permanently confined to an enormous convent, the ruins of which we explored. The Cathédrale Saint-Michel at Rikitea is intact; seating 1,200 persons, it is the largest church in the South Pacific.

Off the island of Aukena, we anchored by a deserted palm-backed sandy beach in 5 metres of bright blue sandy-bottomed water, careful to avoid the numerous coral heads. Not only are they unfriendly to fibreglass hulls, but we'd learned the hard way there is a risk that your anchor chain can wind itself inextricably round lumps of coral as the wind shifts and your boat wanders around. On shore we found an old stone well, a complex of now roofless buildings with full-sized trees growing inside them and – quite invisible from seawards so dense was the surrounding vegetation – a white-and-blue-painted chapel, firmly locked with a new padlock. Although most of these churches have not been used in a hundred years, their roofs and walls are still maintained. This one was dedicated to Saint Raphaël. Dating from 1839, it is the oldest in French Polynesia.

We saw nobody for three days. Then one morning, on a path in the forest, we met a man in shorts and a ragged shirt, a machete in one hand, a pair of coconuts in the other. He explained that he came over once in a while from the main island to tend to his *'jardin'*.

'Servez-vous. Help yourselves,' he said to our unspoken question, waving the machete at the coconut, breadfruit and pamplemousse trees all around.

Back at Rikitea there were a couple of boats we knew from Chile: the French *Ch't'imagine* (normally known to the anglophones as *Shitty Machine*; we hoped the owners didn't know that) and *Breakpoint* from Germany, with the much more serious Tom and Tatiana on board. There were several new arrivals – mainly Germans – from Panama and the Galápagos, including a large and professionally crewed mega-yacht from the UK called *Impression*. Her owner flew in for a week's stay and hosted everyone at a posh cocktail party on board, with the uniformed crew serving drinks and canapes from silver trays. The guests were barefoot, in ragged T-shirts and shorts; the topics of conversation were the weather, engines and autopilots.

With ten boats now in the anchorage (more than we had seen in total in two years), the Gambiers were starting to seem crowded. One day an American yacht anchored too close to us. The etiquette is that he should have moved, not us. We ostentatiously put out fenders and stared hard at the miscreant, hands on hips. It didn't work. We took this as a sign. After a final run ashore to get some of that not-so-delicious sliced white bread, we upped anchor ourselves and headed out of the pass.

Ile Aukena from Mangareva

IF YOU GO…

ENTRY FORMALITIES

Citizens of the EU and most Western countries do not require a visa prior to arrival in French Polynesia. EU passport holders may stay as long as they like; others will be granted a 90-day stay, not extendable within French Polynesia.

A non-EU-flagged vessel is granted permission to remain for 24 months, extendable to 27. After this period, import duties apply (7 per cent).

Non-EU passport holders must, within 30 days of arrival, post a bond equivalent to the value of a one-way air ticket to their home country. This is refunded by the gendarmerie of your island of departure.

You will be required to fill in a Declaration of Entry; this can be found online at **www. demarches-simplifiees.fr/commencer/ declaration-unique-plaisance-polynesie-francaise**.

Check-in can be made at any one of the 13 islands where there is a gendarmerie (both the Gambiers and Raivavae have one). The gendarmerie will deal with customs and immigration formalities and will forward your customs declaration to Papeete. Once checked in you may go anywhere, but you must call at a gendarmerie wherever there is one. If leaving from an outer island, you must first make arrangements to do so in Papeete.

GETTING THERE

Prevailing winds mean that the Gambiers are best approached under sail from the east. Air Tahiti flies twice weekly from Papeete (4.5 hours). Mangareva serves as a hub for passenger service aboard the *MV Silver Supporter* to Pitcairn (three days).

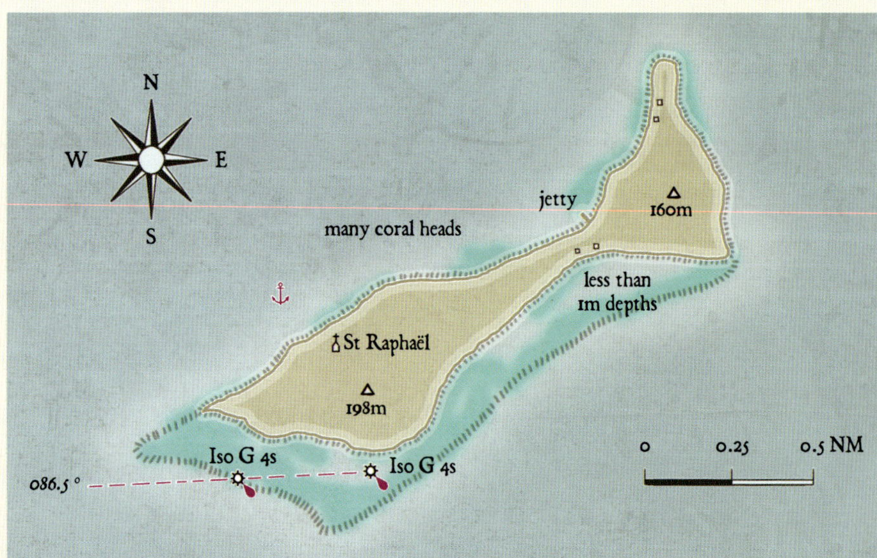

DETAIL: AUKENA

DISTANCES

Easter Island to Iles Gambier, 1,465 miles; Nuku Hiva (Iles Marquises) to Îles Gambier, 920 miles; Iles Gambier to Raivavae, 725 miles; Îles Gambier to Papeete, 880 miles.

WEATHER

The Gambiers are not normally affected by tropical cyclones. The islands lie at the southern edge of the south-east trade wind belt; the trades are strongest from June to September and may be intensified/weakened by highs/lows passing to the south. Fronts bring a wind shift to the north-east.

ANCHORAGES

Aukena, Iles Gambier, GPS 23°07'.89S 134°54'.86W, depth 7 metres among coral heads. Totogegie (for airport), GPS 23°05'.245S 134°53'.27W, depth 15 metres; there is a small boat basin here. Rikitea, GPS 23°06'.85S 134°58'.01W, depth 16 metres.

GENERAL

Overall population 1,450. Gendarmerie; post office; water; basic supplies at Rikitea (pop. 1,100). Google Maps/Earth is useful for plotting a course around the many coral heads that

On the beach at Ile Aukena

CATHÉDRALE DE ST. MICHEL, RIKITEA (1848)

encumber the lagoon; move when the sun is high and behind you for better visibility.

CHARTS

SHOM 6461, Iles Gambier; 6464, Ile Mangareva (Rikitea); 6462, Iles Gambier – Sud.

REFERENCES

(1) Hinz, Earl. *Landfalls of Paradise: Cruising Guide to the Pacific Islands (5th edn)*. Hawaii, USA: University of Hawaii Press, 2006.

(2) Clay, Warwick. *South Pacific Anchorages (2nd edn)*. St Ives, UK: Imray, Laurie, Norie and Wilson, 2001.

(3) Wood, Charles and Margo. *Charlie's Charts of Polynesia (8th edn)*. Blue Lake, USA: Paradise Cay Publications, 2021.

(4) Hawkings, Francis. *The Pacific Crossing Guide (4th edn)*. London, UK: Adlard Coles, 2024.

(5) For a variety of useful cruising-related pdfs for these and adjoining waters see **http://svsoggypaws.com/files/#sw-pacific**.

MOTU HAAMU, RAIVAVAE, ILES AUSTRALES

FRENCH POLYNESIA

At sea as on land, little-visited places are often unfrequented for a reason: they may have few, if any safe anchorages; the climate may be forbidding; the local people hostile; or they may simply not be on the way to anywhere else.

Like the Gambiers, Raivavae (pron. reh-vah-VYE) is part of French Polynesia, one of the group of islands known as the Australs. High and lush, it has an encircling reef that provides safe anchorage, friendly people and low-key authorities. In a word, it closely resembles the far better-known islands of the adjoining Societies: Tahiti, Bora-Bora, Huahine, Raiatea. The only reason this island receives fewer than a dozen yachts a year is that if you are sailing westwards with the trades, coming from

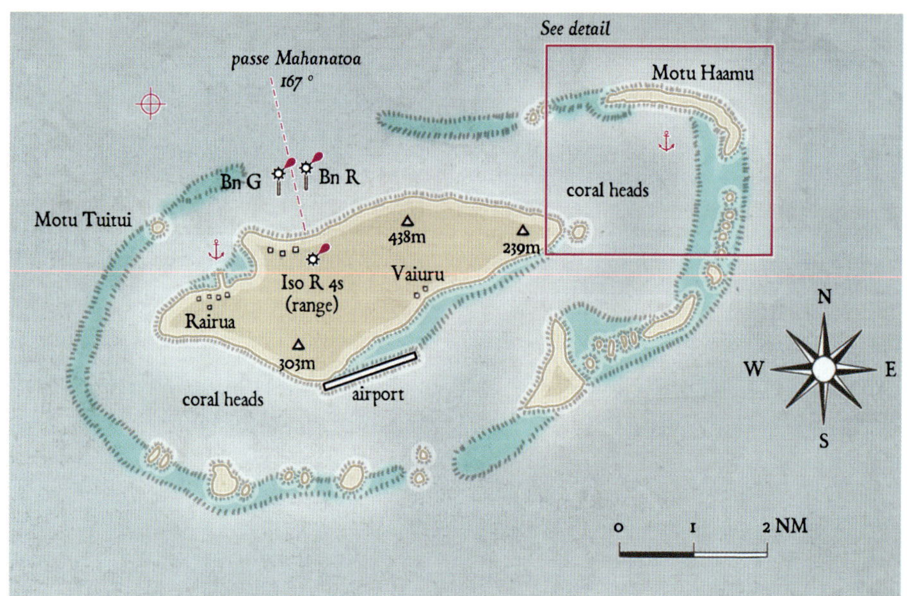

MOTO HAAMU, RAIVAVAE, ILES AUSTRALES, FRENCH POLYNESIA
23° 50' S 147° 42' W

At anchor, Rairua Bay

Panama or North America with the usual three-month visa stamp in your passport, then calling in here means bypassing or skimping on the (understandably) popular Marquesas and Tuamotus.

Shortly after daybreak, we were lining up the range markers that lead vessels in through Raivavae's Passe Mahanatoa, motoring into the flat waters of Rairua Bay and letting our chain out in 10 metres of water. Winding down after a sleepless night over coffee in the cockpit, we followed our arrival ritual: scanning the small village onshore through the binoculars, savouring a faint smell of smoke and rotting mangos on the light offshore breeze. An old-fashioned Renault panel van with corrugated sides – the kind the French call '*un tub*' – trundled along the coast road from the west, paused for two or three minutes and moved on again. By the time we rowed ashore, there had been no further movement. There being no one to ask the way, it was quite by chance that we stumbled on the gendarmerie and asked if we could check in.

'*Mais bien sûr…*', was the warm reaction of the evidently surprised young shorts-clad gendarme. '*Et soyez les bienvenus!*'

Over more coffee, we were introduced to Jean's wife, his deputy and their new kitten Motu. We mentioned how quiet the place seemed, and the Renault van.

'Ah, that would be the *boulanger*, the baker. He drives all the way round the island every morning; you just hail him if you want to buy some bread.'

This small team at the gendarmerie represented three-quarters of the *métropolitains* on this island of 900 people, and we were soon firm friends. One day they came out to *Bosun Bird* for chocolate cake with Earl Grey tea. But after ten minutes, with the boat only shifting ever so slightly as people moved around, Jean had to excuse himself, much to the amusement of the other two.

'*Mal de mer…*' explained his wife with a shrug.

With a pair of bicycles lent to us by the police, it took us two hours to ride all the way around Raivavae. There were two or three tiny shops, but there was little to buy. The only vehicle we ever encountered on Raivavae was '*le tub*', rather eerily travelling first one way around then the other.

The weekly supply ship came in from Rapa, and for a brief period there were a dozen people on the town wharf. Feeling the need to get away from the unaccustomed excitement, we upped anchor and carefully wended our way along a sporadically marked channel, around menacing bommies, to Motu Haamu, 6 miles away on the north-eastern corner of the encircling reef. As at Aukena, it took time to find a patch of clear sand over which to anchor in the lee of the low, wooded island. We tied marker buoys to the most threatening coral heads in the neighbourhood, so that we could easily judge if we were swinging too close.

Ashore, we gathered coconuts, limes and papayas: there were a couple of ruined shacks that indicated that long ago, there had been a settlement on the motu. We burned a few weeks' worth of garbage. We roamed the windward beaches for days. There was flotsam that was exotic and tantalising in its provenance yet depressing in its quantity:

a plastic crate from New Zealand's South Island, part of a dinghy marked 'The Waltons', a buoy marked 'PG Tips', another 'Osprey'.

On the big island, as suggested with enigmatic smiles by our friends at the gendarmerie, we sought out the only other *métropolitain*, a 70-year-old former *légionnaire* who – we were told – lived in a small house close to the range markers.

'*Il est un peu spécial*,' Jean warned us. But he would not be drawn.

We found Edmond. He had a large fruit and vegetable patch, and we were more than happy to load up prior to our departure for Tahiti. But really he wanted to talk. And to show us something.

Propped up on beams under a breadfruit tree was the love of his life: *La Bourrasque* ('Squall'). Edmond had been building this grey-painted 30-foot sloop for years now (to judge from the green mould on the cap rail), using scraps of plywood supplemented with castoff items from passing yachts. To imply any criticism of the lines or seaworthiness of another person's boat is very poor form, so we were duly complimentary. But Edmond would not let up. We noticed a person who might be Mme Edmond, hovering as if to interrupt or offer us a juice; he dismissed her with a peremptory wave of the hand.

At anchor, Motu Haamu

Next day, we picked Edmond up by dinghy and, over tea (again) in *Bosun Bird*'s cockpit, he talked some more. He asked our advice about navigating the cold and windy waters we had recently left (in Patagonia) but didn't wait for an answer. Instead, he launched into a detailed description of his plans to return home (France) via the Roaring Forties, Cape Horn and the Atlantic.

'*Mon idole…*', he commented in a brief parenthesis and with a faraway look, '*C'est Bernard Moitessier … vous le connaissez sans doute…*'

'*Mais oui, naturellement.*'

But before I could go on Edmond was back into a lyrical, emotional recounting of his lifelong dream, the hardships he would face, the romance of the sea and the wind. It took hours for us to winkle out of the old soldier the fact that he had never sailed before.

In our experience, while it is one's duty to point out to dreamers some of the practical obstacles facing their enterprise, it is both useless and cruel to be dismissive. Edmond half-listened when we suggested cautiously that perhaps a trial run downwind to Tahiti might be a good way to start his voyage. He brushed this off impatiently, his hand over his heart.

'*Mais vous ne comprenez pas… C'est le Cap qui m'appelle. Le Cap…* It is Cape Horn that is calling me… It is a call I must answer…'

We took a more practical tack. Repeating my admiration for *La Bourrasque*, I wondered how Edmond intended to extract her from his back garden, carry her across the road and 100 metres of very shallow coral foreshore, and into deep water – this on an island

Edmond and La Bourrasque

where there was no crane, let alone a Travelift.

Edmond nodded sagely. '*Oui, effectivement, c'est un défi…*' A challenge.

But military men are good at plans. It would take 40 men, and he counted them out on his fingers: ten to keep *La Bourrasque* steady, 20 to pull, and the remaining ten to run relays, placing greased palm tree trunks under the boat's keel as she staggered forward.

Months later, Jean filled us in by email. *La Bourrasque* made it into the water, more or less unscathed. Jean and many others were on the quayside soon afterwards when Edmond set off towards the pass, '*to find my destiny*'. After half an hour, the engineless sailboat was still in sight but headed for a reef, with the just-visible Edmond at a loss. The gendarmes stepped in. They hastily launched their RIB, towed him back in and impounded *La Bourrasque* on the grounds of general unseaworthiness.

Edmond did not venture out again. The last we heard he was still selling fresh produce to passing yachties and doing good business.

IF YOU GO…

For information on entry formalities and references see Chapter 20, page 138.

GETTING THERE

Like the Gambiers, Raivavae is best approached from the east. But it is sometimes used as a convenient stop for yachts coming from New Zealand, that have turned north for Tahiti having made their easting further south. Air Tahiti flies from Papeete (two hours) two to three times weekly.

DISTANCES

Auckland (NZ) to Raivavae, 2,100 miles; Iles Gambier to Raivavae, 725 miles; Raivavae to Tubuai, 100 miles; Raivavae to Papeete, 430 miles.

WEATHER

Like other islands in the Australs but unlike the Gambiers, Raivavae is prone to cyclones; these may occur from October to April, with the highest danger from January to March.

Cycling around Raivavae

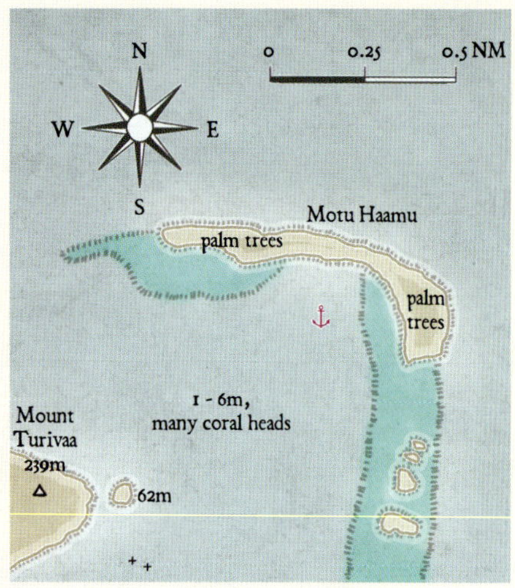

DETAIL: MOTU HAAMU

The prevailing south-east trades are strongest from June to September and are intensified/ weakened by highs/lows passing to the south. Fronts bring a wind shift to the north-east.

ANCHORAGES

Motu Haamu, GPS 23°50'.40S 147°35'.53W, depth 6 metres, many coral heads. Rairua, GPS 23°51'.95S 147°41'.21W, depth 11 metres.

GENERAL

Population 900. Gendarmerie; post office; water; basic supplies. There is range for entry through Passe Mahanatoa, on the north-west side of the island. From Rairua (the main village) to Motu Haamu (6 miles), follow the deepwater channel close to the big island – there are occasional beacons – with careful attention to coral heads; Google Maps/Earth is useful to indicate these.

CHART

SHOM 6207, Ile Raivavae (Vavitu).

AITUTAKI

COOK ISLANDS

When cruisers start talking about Tahiti and the Society Islands, the common refrain echoes Yogi Berra: 'Nobody goes there anymore. It's too crowded.'

No cruising boat should pass this spectacular set of islands by. But it is true that these days you know you're approaching Papeete not so much by the breaking surf on the barrier reef, as by the sun reflecting off the windshields of cars stuck in traffic on the four-lane highway into town. Bora Bora and Moorea – one of the locations for the movie *South Pacific* – prohibit anchoring and charge hefty fees for the use of dodgy mooring buoys; sailing blogs report hostility from the tourist-fatigued locals. And then there are those pesky (to long-term liveaboards, that is…) charter yachts that fill the choicest anchorages in Huahine and Raiatea.

The crowds die away once you move west from Bora Bora.

Cycling on Aitutaki

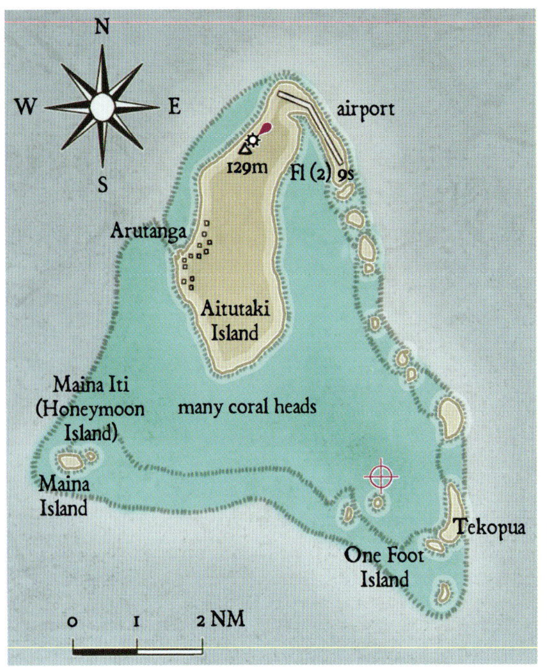

AITUTAKI, COOK ISLANDS
⊕ 18° 55' S 159° 45' W

It also gets windier. It commonly blows 20 to 30 knots for days on end across the long stretch of ocean between the Societies and Samoa, higher in squalls. We took a brief look at Maupiti, only a few hours on from Bora Bora. But there were heavy breakers in the narrow entrance pass. A quick and crackly chat on the VHF with an Australian yacht, whose mast we could see in the anchorage, confirmed what we thought: 'Don't even think about comin' in 'ere, mate; we've been stuck for three days now; you need to wait 'til this swell's gone down…'

We rolled downwind for five days, reefed down and wet, and entered that large island-specked square of ocean labelled 'Cook Islands' on the map. Years earlier, we'd spent an idyllic week at Suvorov Atoll, where New Zealander

Tom Neale had famously lived and written about his desert island dream;[9] we'd not been disappointed. But we find it's usually a mistake to return to places we love. They could still be the same (maybe…) but what's sure is that you're not the same person you were then. So, we looked this time around for new anchorages. Aitutaki seemed to fit the bill. The entrance pass, we knew, was shallow – under 2 metres – but we only draw 1.4 metres; it shouldn't be a problem.

We rounded the island's northern tip at dawn and an hour later were in a lee and off Arutanga Pass, a channel that was blasted through the fringing reef by American Seabees in the Second World War. We soon found that it's all very well to have your tide tables on hand – high water slack was predicted to be at 11am – but if it's been blowing hard for days around atolls such as this, then the lagoons fill up and there is a constant, strong outflow current in passes. With the engine at maximum revs, it took us half an hour to negotiate the kilometre-long Arutanga. We seemed not to graze the white sandy bottom. This was just as well: giving up and turning around was not an attractive option in a channel nowhere more than 10 metres wide.

Once into a very small pool by the shore, we carefully manoeuvred ourselves into a slot between the two other boats present – *Camelot* and the double-ender belonging to the character we knew as Freeloader Bob – and anchored in 2 metres of water, taking lines ashore to hold us in position. You'd think that with 30 metres of chain out in that depth, you'd be fine, just as you'd

9   Neale, Tom. *An Island to Oneself.* New York, USA: Collins, 1956.

think that in the heart of the south-east trades the wind never comes from the west anyway. You'd be wrong on both counts. We spent a large part of our first night on deck in intermittent rain squalls, laying out a second anchor then helping *Camelot* to do the same. Annoyingly, Bob slept through it all and didn't drag an inch.

The population of Aitutaki, which is the second largest of the Cook Islands (after Rarotonga) is 1800, mostly spread very thinly along the road that fringes the main island. Downtown Arutanga consists of two small banks, a post office, a shop and a magnificent church that dates from 1821. The church was first established by John Williams of the London Missionary Society, who was later famously eaten by the Big Nambas of Vanuatu. A shiny black marble monument to him quotes only a verse number: John 3:16[10].

It was a 20-minute walk to Spider's Café, where we had our internet fixes. A little further was Puffy's Beach Bar, where a friendly waiter showed us how to sneak into the weekly tourist-oriented Island Nites for only the price of a beer. And close by the wharf was The Blue Nun, an unlikely name for a discotheque that would twice a week come dramatically and noisily alive; it was unpromisingly located in a large shed once used for banana-packing.

We didn't do too much. One afternoon we went to the final of the island rugby championship where the Tautu Blues came out victorious in a skilful game. Chatting to supporters on the touchline,

we learned that Aitutaki supported nine 15-a-side adult rugby teams.

We attended church twice, largely for the very beautiful hymn-singing, but also because – as the port captain had quietly made clear to us – this is about the only activity allowed on Sundays. The women wore the bright floral Mother Hubbards that missionaries introduced, with straw hats decorated with flowers. Most of the men dressed in impractical white suits, which gave them a less dignified air of ice-cream salesmen. The singing was in Cook Island Maori. But now and again you could recognise a traditional hymn from John Wesley, and even figure out what the words would be in English: '*Tabu, tabu, tabu*', Holy, Holy, Holy.

We rented bikes and rode around the island. One day we climbed to the highest peak – only 130 metres, but you get puffed out after spending so much time immobile on the boat. Another day we chartered a runabout for a cruise inside the lagoon (it was too shallow for our boat) and enjoyed snorkelling in visibility of 30 metres and with abundant fish life. On one of the remoter motus (islets) we found nesting 'bosun birds' (red-tailed tropicbirds) in massive numbers, very tame and apparently helpless, easy prey to the large frigate birds that were cruising ominously. The tails of the bosun birds used to be prized throughout Polynesia for ceremonial purposes.

'Of course, we don't gather the feathers anymore,' said Johnny our boat driver. 'That would be cruel.' There was a pause. Then he added: 'Some people like to eat the birds, though. They are very

---

10 'For God so loved the world that he gave his one and only Son, that whoever believes in him shall not perish but have eternal life.'

Stern-tied at Arutanga, Aitutaki

easy to catch, you see; they just sit there. They taste a bit oily for me.'

Freeloader Bob was meanwhile living up to his ocean-spanning reputation. We dutifully responded to heavy hints he dropped and had him over for dinner and frequent coffee sessions. Usually, Bob would go back to his boat clutching a tube of silicone sealant or a couple of stainless bolts, assuring us: 'I'll pay you back.'

The time came for *Camelot* to leave. This, we knew, might prove interesting. They drew 2 metres and had briefly got stuck coming in at high tide – would they clear the passage this time around, which was set to be the first big tide since their arrival? Unspoken was our fear that if they didn't, they would effectively block the way in or out for anyone else. There was no point in being coy: we got the binoculars out to watch.

Sure enough, halfway out *Camelot* was unmistakeably jammed. We couldn't hear anything, but we could imagine the exchanges that were now taking place between our friends Neil and Jackie. We watched as they tried first to rock the boat free. Then arms were pointed, instructions given. The boom was pushed out to one side, the dinghy launched. A halyard was led down from the mast and Jackie set off across the shallows, in an attempt to pull the top of the mast over and thus lift the keel. It seemed to be working. But then *Camelot* slewed around. Now she was blocking the channel at 90 degrees. More hand waving, surely some cursing. Neil must be yelling to tow the bows back into line … and yes! This time we could hear cheering: *Camelot* was free.

Jenny was pensive as we watched our friends sail out to the open sea: 'I'm thinking there's a good reason why Aitutaki doesn't get so many visitors.'

IF YOU GO…

ENTRY FORMALITIES

Most nationalities are granted a visa for the Cook Islands for 31 days; NZ passport holders are given 90 days; extensions may be granted, but only in Rarotonga. Visiting yachts are required to notify Cook Islands customs authorities (who also handle immigration) with full details, 48 hours in advance of their anticipated arrival: fax +682 29465, email **customs.craft@cookislands.gov.ck**. On arrival they will be issued with a Temporary Import Entry (TIE) authorisation, valid for 12 months.

Arutanga (Aitutaki) is a port of entry (POE). Neither Palmerston nor Suvorov are POE, but they host officials; prior permission to visit should be requested at your first POE. Significant fees apply, including a NZ$2.30 per metre per day 'port fee' charge for yachts and a NZ$71.77 pp departure tax. Avoid arriving on a Sunday; landing may be prohibited and/or heavy additional fees may apply.

For full details on formalities see **www.mfem. gov.ck/customs/arrival-and-departure- information-for-marine-crafts**.

On arrival at both Aitutaki and Palmerston, call on VHF Ch 16.

GETTING THERE

Under sail, Aitutaki is best approached from the east; for most yachts, their previous port of call will have been Bora Bora (Society Islands). There are direct flights from Australia, New Zealand, French Polynesia and Hawaii (USA) to Rarotonga, from where there are daily flights to Aitutaki.

DISTANCES

Bora Bora (Societies) to Aitutaki, 420 miles; Rarotonga to Aitutaki, 140 miles; Aitutaki to Palmerston, 205 miles.

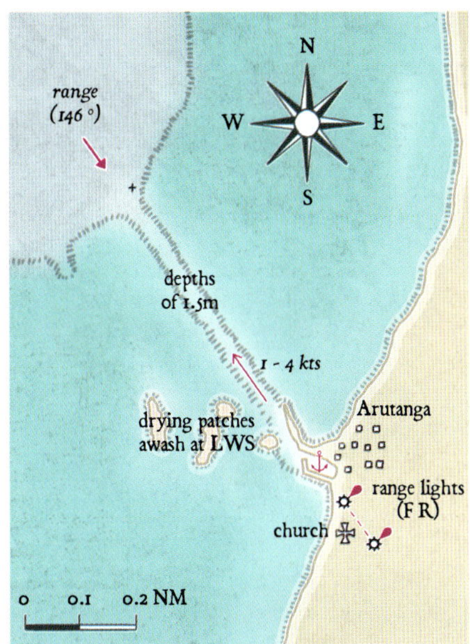

ARUTANGA, AITUTAKI

WEATHER

All of the Cook Islands are prone to cyclones, which are most likely between November and April. Yachts are discouraged during these months; there are no anchorages/moorings in the islands safe in such conditions. Aitutaki and Palmerston are firmly within the south-east trade wind belt; winds are strongest and more easterly in the southern winter. However, temporary reversals of the trades occur with the passage of depressions to the south. There is a westerly set of about 1 knot through the Cooks.

ANCHORAGE

Arutanga, GPS 18°51'.907S 159°48'.028W, depth 2 metres, stern tie in a small coral-free pool south of the concrete pier. With permission it is possible to tie to the pier. Deeper-draught vessels sometimes anchor off the entrance pass; this is marginal. There is a range through the long pass, which is straight with a sand bottom but which may be as shallow as 1.6 metres halfway through. There are some battered marker beacons.

GENERAL

Limited supplies are available at Arutanga. Exploration of the extensive lagoon is possible by dinghy; there are small resorts on some of the outer islands.

CHARTS

(NZ) CK142, Plans of the Cook Islands – Southern Sheet; USA (DMA) 83425, Islands and Anchorages in Cook Islands (for Aitutaki).

REFERENCES

(1) Hinz, Earl. *Landfalls of Paradise: Cruising Guide to the Pacific Islands (5th edn).* Hawaii, USA: University of Hawaii Press, 2006.

(2) Clay, Warwick. *South Pacific Anchorages (2nd edn).* St Ives, UK: Imray, Laurie, Norie and Wilson, 2001.

(3) Wood, Charles and Margo. *Charlie's Charts of Polynesia (8th edn).* Blue Lake, USA: Paradise Cay Publications, 2021.

(4) Hawkings, Francis. *The Pacific Crossing Guide (4th edn).* London, UK: Adlard Coles, 2024.

FROM THE LOG OF HMS BOUNTY, 1789

APRIL:	LEAVES TAHITI
APRIL 11-23:	AITUTAKI
APRIL 28:	MUTINY (OFF TONGA)

For a variety of useful cruising-related pdfs for the Cooks and adjoining waters see **http://svsoggypaws.com/files/#sw-pacific**. Also see **https://cookislandspocketguide.com/sailing-guide-to-rarotonga-the-cook-islands-tips-for-yachting/** and **www.bbc.com/news/magazine-25430383** (December 2013).

The entry pass, Aitutaki

PALMERSTON ATOLL

COOK ISLANDS

It was 200 miles from Aitutaki to Palmerston, another of the Cook Islands, and we were off the atoll's southern edge at sunrise in less than two days.

'Remember the night we spent off Suvorov, all those years ago?' said Jenny. 'Up all night, hove to, listening for breakers… Thank God for GPS.'

A classic coral atoll has land that rises maybe a metre or two above sea level, sometimes with palm trees that could add another 20 metres. From the deck of a sailboat and in good visibility you might see breakers on a reef at 2 miles (much less at night), palms at 7 miles. These distances were within our margin of error when we used to navigate by the sun and the stars in the 1980s. GPS made landfalls today a lot less stressful.

But there is still one caveat in the GPS era. In the South Pacific, small islands far from the shipping lanes may well be charted in the wrong position.

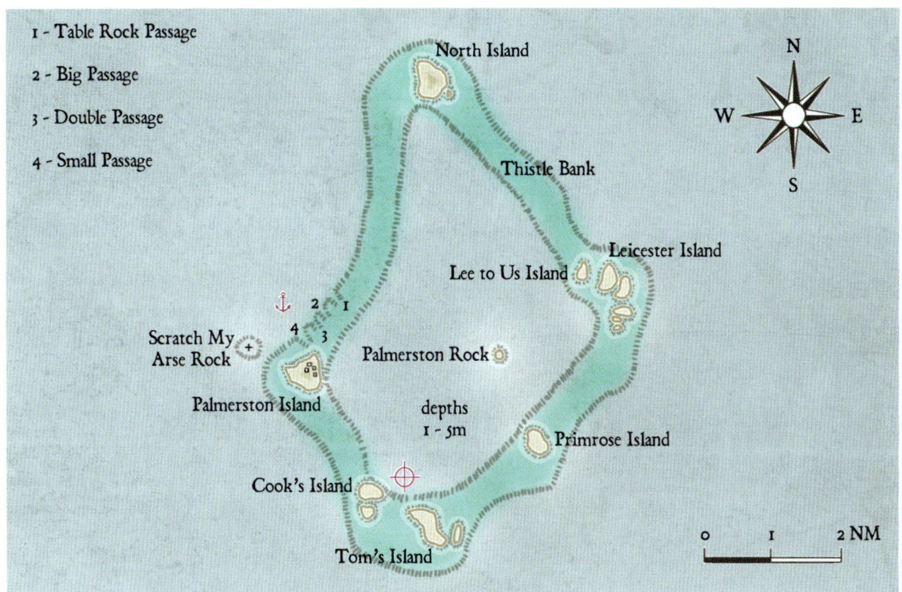

PALMERSTON ATOLL, COOK ISLANDS
18° 05' S 163° 10' W

Because it was easier in the days of celestial navigation to estimate latitude accurately (it requires only a sextant and an almanac, no timepiece), it is almost always the longitude that is incorrect. So, as we approached Palmerston in the night, we remained at a latitude that we knew would keep us short of land, rather than heading straight in.

Palmerston is about 10 x 6 kilometres, with half a dozen motus (islets), one of them inhabited, sprinkled around the atoll's rim. The inner lagoon is shallow and strewn with dangerous coral heads. We knew in advance that visiting boats must anchor on the outside, on the western edge where the reef offers protection from the prevailing easterlies.

The recommended site is precarious: the bottom is coral and the reef drops off very quickly, leaving only a very narrow shelf on which to anchor. And if the wind shifts much from the usual easterlies you need to get out immediately. To ease the situation, half a dozen mooring buoys, tied to coral heads with chain, have been placed. But even so, yachts have been lost here. We knew our stay might necessarily be short. But we were very curious.

The population of Palmerston, we would soon learn, was about 50, including 23 children, and they nearly all descended from a colourful 19th-century sea captain called William Marsters, who arrived here in 1863 with three Polynesian wives. Marsters was born Masters, but either he preferred the alternative spelling or his descendants, recalling his rolling Gloucestershire accent, added a gratuitous R. He devised strict land ownership and inter-marriage rules for his many children, and these prevail still. The 2-kilometre-long island is divided into three segments, each occupied by the descendants of William and – respectively – one of his three wives. Each family is known by the Polynesian clan name of the original wives from Tongareva (now known

Bosun Bird *moored off Palmerston, from inside the atoll*

as Penrhyn): Tepou, Akakaingaro and Matavia.

There is no airstrip and the supply ship comes in from Rarotonga only once every few months. Families take it in turn to host the crew of visiting yachts and treat it as a competitive sport. We'd barely tied up when the first launch was heading out of the small pass by the main island to greet us. Tere Marsters introduced himself in a friendly manner as Island Secretary. Within a few minutes he'd summoned a second launch, crammed to the gunwales with portly officials in colourful Hawaiian shirts, who checked our passports and our clearance from Aitutaki, and joined in the welcome. Tere smiled as they went through our paperwork.

'There are 15 of us who work for the government, one way or another… That's half the adult population of Palmerston.'

In his launch, Tere ran us in through a little channel marked as Boat Passage on our chart. It zigzagged, was never more than 20 centimetres deep, and there was a 6-knot outgoing current running: it was no place for our oar-driven inflatable, let alone *Bosun Bird*. We stepped out on a white sand beach and followed Tere through the woods to his home, where we were expected for lunch. It wasn't exactly a free lunch – we'd been warned back in Aitutaki to take items that might be in short supply, such as sugar and flour – but his wife Yvonne welcomed us warmly and we lingered chatting over marinated parrotfish and papaya.

Our host hadn't spent all his life here. He'd lived a few years in Rarotonga, then Australia, where he'd met Yvonne. He'd also served as a pastor. He added, matter-of-factly: 'It was a good job you didn't come in on a Sunday. We don't allow any activities at all on the Lord's Day.'

It took us time to figure out that when Tere and Yvonne mentioned 'Father', they were talking neither about their parents nor – as I thought for a moment – God. Father was William Marsters, dead in 1899 but still the patriarch of Palmerston. It was Father who had laid down that English, rather than Cook Island Maori (preferred in Rarotonga), should be the language of the island and it was Father who had made respect for the British monarchy a tenet of island life. But it seemed the old man had a ribald sense of humour, too. The best place to catch parrotfish, Tere told us, was named by Father: 'Scratch my Arse Rock.'

We spent the rest of the day strolling around the tiny island, which was covered almost entirely in coconut palms but with some very ancient mahoganies at its centre. There was an airy one-room school, where the children followed ACE, an American (Christian) correspondence scheme. The honour roll of teachers went back to 1945, with at least half bearing the name Marsters. Tere showed us the small, modern island church, financed by the Marsters community overseas.

'We stick together, wherever we find ourselves,' he commented. 'The guys in Melbourne even have their own rugby team – every single member is called Marsters.'

Elderly resident, Palmerston Island

There was one building remaining from Father's time, constructed with timbers from a wrecked sailing ship. Back in those days, the unlit and poorly charted atoll was a ship's graveyard, which meant good building timber and sudden windfalls of supplies for the residents. The church bell was from another such wreck, the *Thistle*; a reef on the windward side of the atoll bears the same name.

We paid a visit to one of the other three families. Our guide was careful, as we stood at the line of small white rocks that delineated the border of his land with the other families, to ask their permission before stepping over it. An old and cheery lady was busy cleaning fish. Parrotfish fillets, we learned, were the island's only export. Although their flesh fetched a good price, it was a precarious business, with the ship coming so infrequently, and having limited freezing capacity. We asked if there was any prospect of an airstrip being built. Tere cut us off rather peremptorily. Later and in private, he confessed to us that the matter was highly political. Rarotonga had offered the necessary funds but one of the three island families would have to give up one of 'their' motus for this to happen. 'It's not resolved,' he said shortly. Nor would the islanders accept visits from cruise ships, but for other reasons: 'Can you imagine it? A thousand people here…We'd be like animals in a zoo. No sir, no way.'

We chatted about the weather. Cyclones pass here quite often. Tere recounted that the previous year it had blown so hard that he was about to give the traditional and time-honoured order to people to lash themselves to the biggest mahogany lest they be washed away. But the storm had veered away at the last minute.

As we sat back on *Bosun Bird*, with the sun going down, we reflected that this was an utterly beautiful place, far removed from the world's worries and troubles, and that the Marsters clearly knew they had something special. This, at last, was utopia in the South Pacific.

Or was it?

There was that all-pervasiveness of religion; the cult-like deference to 'Father'; the rigidity of those rules designed to pre-empt … incest; those lines of white rocks that indicated borders that must not be crossed. We'd detected, in the formalities around our arrival and in contact with the second family, hints of jealousy that the Secretary may have pulled rank to 'bag' these new arrivals for himself. We were sad when, next morning, a forecast for westerlies meant that we would have to leave and not be able to spend any more time getting to know Palmerston. There was material here for a PhD in anthropology, I thought, a novel at least. But would it be a novel with a happy ending?

Much later, as I write these words, I see the population of Palmerston has halved, to 25.

IF YOU GO…

For information on entry formalities, weather, charts and references see Chapter 22, page 149.

GETTING THERE

Under sail, Palmerston is best approached from the east. Once every few months, there are cargo ships from Rarotonga that take passengers. Some small cruise ships now call.

DISTANCES

Aitutaki to Palmerston, 205 miles; Rarotonga to Palmerston, 270 miles; Palmerston to Suvorov, 295 miles.

ANCHORAGE

There are six mooring buoys (not necessarily reliable) in 20 metres+, at GPS 18°02'.7078S 163°11'.5683W. Do not land or enter the lagoon without prior permission; authorities are reachable on VHF Ch 16. Safe only in easterly winds.

GENERAL

There are no supplies available. Bring staples (flour, sugar etc) to exchange for hospitality. The islanders are welcoming, but the entire atoll should be considered as private property; undertake no activities without prior permission. Maintain a low profile on Sundays.

View across the atoll from Palmerston Island

NIUATOPUTAPU

TONGA

Sometimes the elements just go against you, and you have to abandon your resolution to Never Go Back. Hoping to stop at tiny Niue on our 2010 voyage west, strong winds and heavy seas drove instead into superior shelter in the Vavau group of Tonga, which we'd visited in 1986.

Vavau has long been a popular destination for cruisers. It has a cyclone hole and is a convenient last stop en route to New Zealand (or first stop on the way north). The Moorings yacht charter company has had a base here for 40 years, and their free *Cruising Guide to the Kingdom of Tonga* is a book even the long-distance yachties carry – to the point at which people call the anchorages by their number key rather than their correct Tongan name.

But now the expat scene was more institutionalised. There were yacht races every weekend and cruisers' happy hours at Tonga Bob's Taco Place or The Giggling Whale. Touts toured the anchorage in their dinghies offering 'genuine' island feasts, all the while bad-mouthing their competitors. The ramshackle old movie theatre on stilts over the water, where we'd watched *The Hills Have Eyes* and the residents of Neiafu had screamed in genuine terror, was long gone. So was that symbol of the old South Seas, Morris Hedstrom Traders. Today's cruisers watched DVDs over margaritas on their boats, the locals at home. Somehow, I doubted anyone screamed anymore, even at *The Hills Have Eyes – 2*.

We tried not to be disappointed. And the islands were still lovely. We were gratified as we sailed the outer edges of Vavau to find that humpback whales, which had not been seen in

these waters for a century or more, were back. But we were itching for somewhere new. After perusing the charts and checking in with the weather forecasts (which had changed for the better in quality and frequency) we decided to set sail for the country's northernmost outlier: Niuatoputapu.

We'd found the tendency of Vavau cruisers lazily to say 'Let's head for Number 27' rather than trying to get their tongue around Luaa Fuleheu, insulting to Tongan culture. So we practised saying 'newer-topu-TAPu' before visiting the authorities for our clearance papers. We were rewarded with a gentle smile and: 'Thank you for not saying "New Potatoes". It's a joke we're a bit tired of.'

It was a fast 180-mile reach. We had a photocopied fragment of an out-of-print Admiralty chart of the island, which was frustratingly faded in places. A previous owner had written by hand: 'Two range markers – white triangles.' Slightly to our surprise these were in place, along with a freshly painted set of port and starboard beacons that led into a pool, with the bulk of the 150-metre-high island to our south-east and protective reefs in all other directions.

There were two other yachts in. *Tauhara* waved, *Kalalua* shouted over some directions, and we rowed ashore to walk to check in. Mistakenly, we found ourselves calling in first at the island prison. The jovial uniformed superintendent pointed to a group of three or four men squatting and chatting in an adjoining yard, separated from the dirt street by a stretch of chicken wire: 'They send us their criminals from Tongatapu,' he said, referring to Tonga's most populated island, far to the south. 'That one's in for murder; the others are just thieves.'

There was one shop for all three island villages; it was in a corrugated-iron shack at Hihifo and was, as usual, Chinese owned. The only item to be bought was corned beef from New Zealand, the extra fatty version that is popular in the islands. 'You see,' said the shopkeeper as we contemplated his near-empty shelves in some disappointment. 'There is normally a ship once every three or four months, but the ship, she sank.' And he shrugged. 'Maybe next year?'

There was one local export, we learned, and it was under the supervision of the same enterprising Chinese

Inside the lagoon, Niuatoputapu;
Tafahi in the background

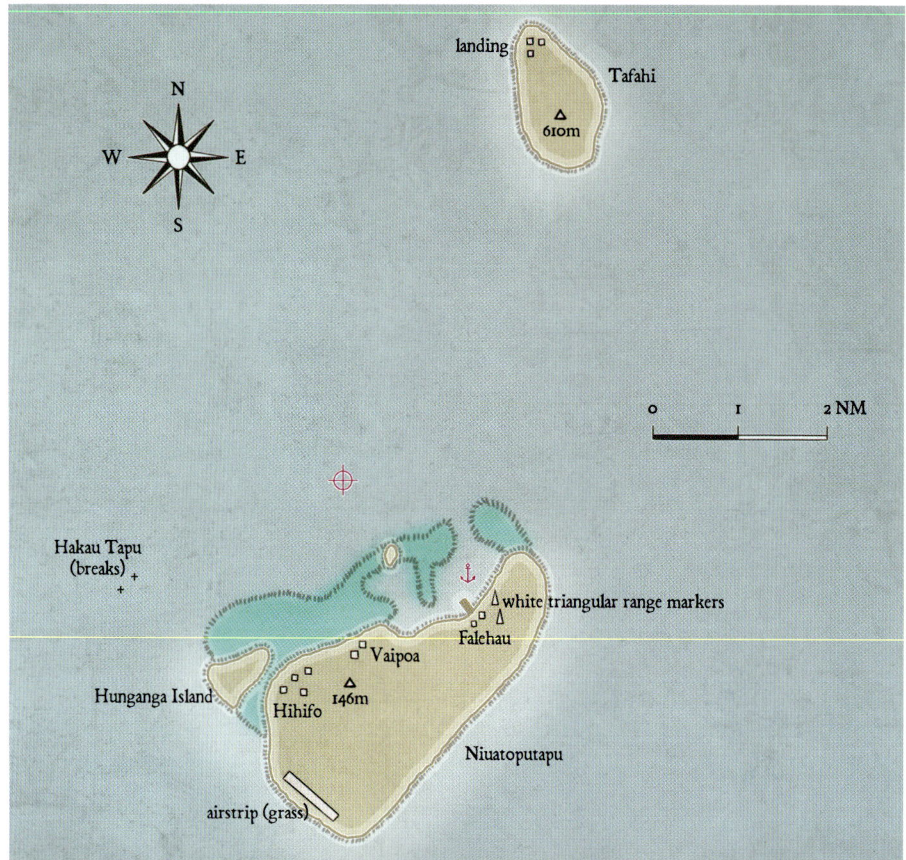

Niuatoputapu & Tafahi, Tonga
15° 55′ S 173° 47′ W

shopkeeper: the (to us) revolting looking Bêche de Mer (sea slug), which grows abundantly in the lagoon and is prized as an aphrodisiac in China. We made friends with the same group of men that we'd pass every day, boiling up dozens of the creatures in a vast and foul-smelling vat on the beach fronting the lagoon.

One day we explored Niuatoputapu's long windward beach, where the surf pounded. Indulging our usual pastime, we found a battered plastic crate with 'Lima, Peru' moulded into it and a soft-drink bottle with a label I recognised from Chile. Another day we bushwhacked to the top of the island. We'd had to ask where the beginning of the path was.

'You can't miss it,' said a local. 'You'll see a dead pig, hanging up by the side of the road.'

The pig was very dead indeed. I thought of *Lord of the Flies* and wondered why it was hanging there.

One morning Nico, whom we'd got to know over the sea slug cooker, took us over in his fishing launch to meet his mum and dad on Tafahi, a spectacular 600-metre-high standalone volcanic island 5 miles to the north. It was a bumpy, wet ride but we reeled in a couple of mahi mahi without even slowing down. We left them thrashing around in the bottom of the boat as we hauled the boat up on a sandy beach on the island's west side. On Tafahi 50 people lived in a village perched precariously about a quarter of the way up the mountain. They survived on fishing and – above all – cultivation of the much sought-after kava root. On account of the semi-sacred associations of kava, we learned, this was a men-only activity.

While we explored up the volcano, Nico's mother retrieved and cooked our mahi mahi in a traditional umu (an oven consisting of a pit lined with hot stones). Our last, soggy packets of Chilean Belmont-brand cigarettes, which we'd been keeping for such an occasion, were gratefully received. But it was embarrassing to be laden down with even more gifts in return – in this case a stalk of 100 bananas.

'Drop it in the sea,' said Nico as we made our way back to the main island. 'In case of spiders.'

By now, there were two more other boats in the anchorage and Nico's wife Sia organised a roast for all five yachts at her house. We all brought cake and soft drinks and the party went on well into the night. It was difficult to be sure in the dark, but I had a feeling the main attraction was that well-aged pig.

One of the boats that had joined us was a Hallberg-Rassy 46, skippered by John and Amanda. Thirty-five years earlier, John had written and self-published a book called *Log of the Mahina*[11], in which he recounted his adventures in the South Pacific as a young man on his first boat, an Albin

11 Neal, John. *Log of the Mahina*. Seattle, USA: Pacific Intl Publishing Company, 1993.

Falehau

The village, Tafahi

Vega 27. This had been an inspiration to us, giving us the confidence to buy a Vega ourselves: *Tarka the Otter*. John and his partner now had a full-time business offering seminars and taking paying passengers/crew on 'cruise and learn' expeditions all around the world on their new, larger and much more comfortable *Mahina Tiare.*

We didn't have much chance to speak to them at the party, and they kindly invited us on board for coffee and pizza next morning.

As we rowed back to *Bosun Bird* an hour later, Jenny and I agreed we'd sensed a slight awkwardness on board. John had inspired us as a free spirit, who – on the basis of nine months sailing in Puget Sound on a 20-footer – had bought his cheap, production boat and simply set off one morning in 1974, lured by the classic dream of the South Seas. By his own admission, he knew next to nothing about offshore sailing; he'd taken classes on celestial navigation but had never done the homework. He lived on a shoestring. But when we expressed our admiration for John's story, in front of his clients on *Mahina Tiare*, he batted away our compliments in evident embarrassment. And he seemed anxious, too, when we tried to enquire politely of the guests if they had offshore sailing plans of their own.

'They've got a good business model,' Jenny eventually commented. 'John's experienced, knowledgeable and I'm sure he's a good teacher. Amanda too. But the thing is … it's "Do what I say", not "Do what I did", isn't it? Otherwise, they'd have no clients.'

IF YOU GO…

ENTRY FORMALITIES

Visas valid for 30 days are granted on arrival in Tonga to most nationalities; they may be extended upon application to the Department of Immigration in Nukualofa.

Yachts must file an Advance Notice of Arrival (ANOA) form with no less than 24 hours' notice, to **info@customs.gov.to**, or fax 676-24124. To download this form, see **www.revenue.gov.to/customs-forms**. Onward clearance (a Local Movement Report) is required for each island group within the Kingdom. Call on VHF Ch 16 an hour before arrival at each port for detailed instructions regarding clearance. Niuatoputapu and Neiafu (Vavau) are both ports of entry.

GETTING THERE

Under sail, the prevailing south-east trades mean that Niuatoputapu can easily be approached from Samoa, Vavau (Tonga) or the Cook Islands. There are occasional ferries from Vavau to Niuatoputapu but no regular air service. There exist two yacht charter companies in Vavau (Sunsail and The Moorings); charter vessels are restricted to the Vavau archipelago.

DISTANCES

Vavau to Niuatoputapu, 180 miles; Apia (Samoa) to Niuatoputapu, 190 miles; Aitutaki (Cook Islands) to Niuatoputapu, 815 miles; Niuatoputapu to Savusavu (Fiji), 430 miles.

WEATHER

An average of one tropical cyclone strikes the Tonga group annually; the peak cyclone season is January/February. The natural harbour at Neiafu is well protected, but boats have nevertheless been lost in powerful storms. The prevailing south-east trade winds are strongest from May to November; they sometimes bring rain for up to three days; as and when the wind shifts to north of east, it brings sunshine.

ANCHORAGES

Niuatoputapu, GPS 15°56'.356S 173°46'.059W; depth 11 metres. Land at the pier at Falehau and undergo formalities in the nearby village, but the main village is Hihifo, 3.5 kilometres to the west. Well protected from all seas (but not cyclone-proof). There is no safe anchorage off Tafahi Island; a dinghy may be landed through a small opening in the fringing reef at GPS 15°50'.5362S 173°45'.3702W. If using the old BA paper chart, add two minutes to the longitude notations.

GENERAL

Most services are available at Neiafu, Vavau, including on-land storage for yachts, see **www.boatyardvavau.com**. Very few supplies are available on Niuatoputapu; there is a freshwater spring. On 29 September 2009 a tsunami inundated 46 per cent of Niuatoputapu, killing nine; the yachts at anchor saw 8 metres of the reef surrounding the anchorage suddenly exposed but survived unscathed.

CHART

(NZ) TO 201 Niuatoputapu Group and Niuafo'ou; replaces BA968, Niuatoputapu and Tafahi.

REFERENCES

(1) Hinz, Earl. *Landfalls of Paradise: Cruising Guide to the Pacific Islands (5th edn)*. Hawaii, USA: University of Hawaii Press, 2006.

(2) Clay, Warwick. *South Pacific Anchorages (2nd edn)*. St Ives, UK: Imray, Laurie, Norie and Wilson, 2001.

APIA

SAMOA

It was 1987 and we were on our first Pacific crossing, aboard *Tarka the Otter*. It had been a rough sail west, with the south-east trade winds frequently interrupted by blustery squalls that brought sou'westers of 25 knots for hours on end. The boat pounded, the rigging shuddered and we were working hard for every mile. It was with relief that in between curtains of spray and rain we sighted the green hills of Tutuila, the principal island of American Samoa.

We wouldn't make it into Pago Pago before dark, so we worked our way into Aoa Bay, on the island's northern shore, hoisted the Stars and Stripes and let the anchor down in delicious calm. After dark we heard the clang of an empty propane tank being struck on shore: villagers were being summoned to church. And soon the faint strains of 'Jesus Thy Blood and Righteousness', in Samoan.

Pago Pago was less bucolic. It's built at the end of an L-shaped inlet rimmed with high mountains that make it a safe harbour and the home base for dozens of deep-sea tuna boats. We motored past a

Yachts and the tuna fleet, Pago Pago harbour

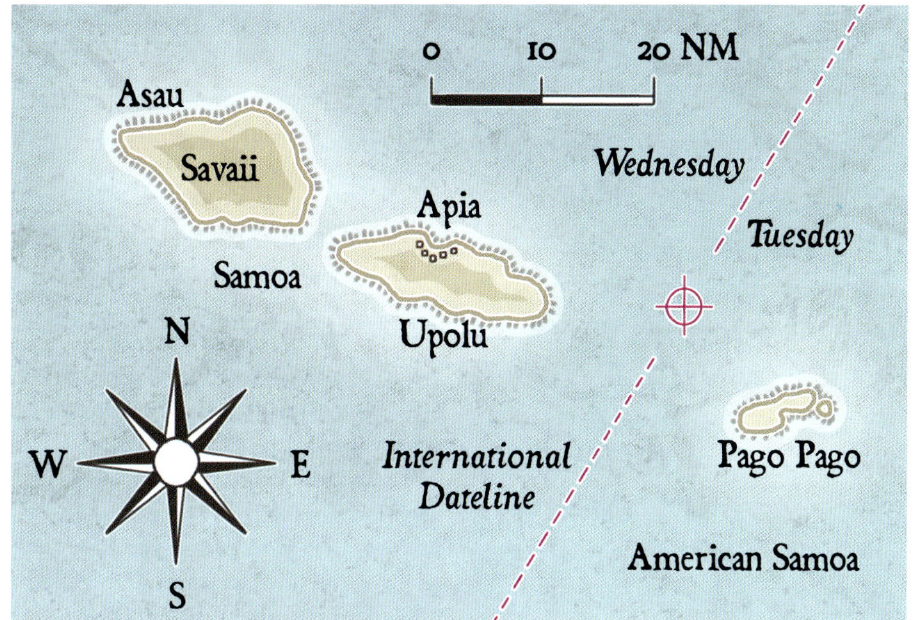

Samoa & American Samoa
⊕ 14° S 171° W

few modern ones that were 60 metres in length with spotter helicopters, but most were like the *Kyushu Maru #42*: rust-streaked, listing, cluttered with gear, a man in his underpants stringing laundry up on the bridge. The water smelled of spilled diesel and rotting fish. As we searched for a place to anchor, we waved at Jeff and Mary aboard *Companion.* We'd last seen them in Bora Bora. They were leaning over their bows with a boathook, trying to disentangle the putrefying remains of some dead animal from their anchor chain.

At least it wasn't a human cadaver. Somerset Maugham's story *Rain* is set here. It's about the puritanical Reverend Davidson, who makes it his mission to reform prostitute Sadie Thompson, and whose body is found one morning 'half in the water and half out, a dreadful object … the throat was cut from ear to ear.' Exactly what has happened and why is never made clear. But the climate plays a part in creating an atmosphere of doom: 'The rain was unmerciful and terrible; you felt in it the malignancy of the primitive powers of nature. It did not pour, it flowed.'

We took a free tour (in the rain) of Starkist Samoa, home of Charlie the Tuna. We accepted a case of complimentary tins with hesitation. We'd seen a man hosing down the cannery's forecourt, which was littered with fish bones, scraps and cigarette ends; there were rainbow-streaked puddles of oil. Gesturing at the mess, he'd cheerfully told us, 'None of this is wasted.'

Then we looked for Sadie's house. Maugham had described it thus:

A frame house of two storeys, with broad verandas on both floors and a roof of corrugated iron… On the ground floor, the owner (a half-caste named Horn) had a store where he sold canned goods and cottons.

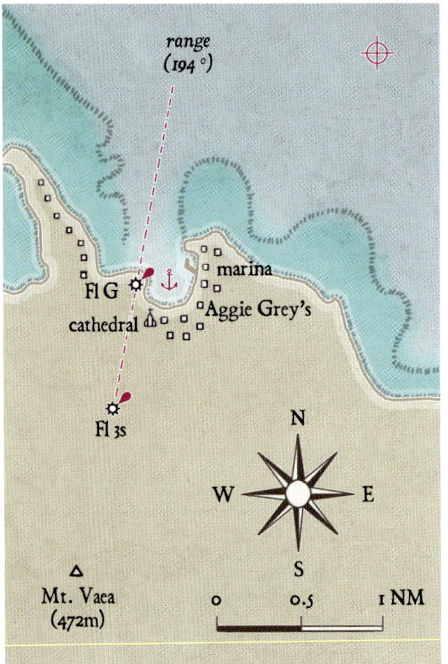

APIA, SAMOA
⊕ 13° 48' S 171° 44' W

We found a shop in a back street called Sadie Thompson's Mart that fitted the bill. But the man behind the counter seemed not to understand our questions. He grew impatient with us and snapped: 'You wanna buy sump'n or not?'

Samoa itself (the independent country, that is, not the US territory) is 80 miles and a whole world away. Apia, the capital, is located on a north-facing bay and is more exposed than you might wish, but safe enough most of the time. Here was *Edelweiss*, whose skipper had shed his wife, two children and a crew member since we last saw him in the Marquesas. Our nearest neighbour was a large ferrocement ketch with rusty patches where rebars were sticking through the cement. A clumsy, hand-daubed name on the stern read *Roving Stone*; vessel and crew were better known on the cruising circuit as *Roving Stoned*.

Our first objective was something I'd been looking forward to for many months: a long, hot trek up Mount Vaea, behind Apia. Here, in a clearing and on a whitewashed stone plinth, is Robert Louis Stevenson's tomb.

Stevenson had seen the mountain from his home at Vailima, far below, which he and his American wife Fanny had bought soon after their arrival in Samoa aboard the chartered schooner *Casco*, in 1889. Only 39, he had been diagnosed as terminally ill with consumption. Five years on he had embarked on a new novel: *Weir of Hermiston*. The last words in the unfinished manuscript are '…a wilful convulsion of brute nature.' That is what he died of while making the mayonnaise for dinner on 3 December 1894.

Stevenson's famous epitaph is inscribed on a blackened bronze plaque:

Under the wide and starry sky,
Dig the grave and let me lie;
Glad did I live and gladly die,
And I laid me down with a will.

This be the verse you grave for me,
Here he lies where he longed to be.
Home is the sailor, home from the sea,
And the hunter, home from the hill.

The grave was freshly if sloppily whitewashed, and someone had placed on it a single bright red hibiscus bloom.

At the time of our visit, you couldn't go into the writer's old house at Vailima. A magnificent low and rambling two-storey building with white clapboard walls and a pale blue roof, it was in use as the residence of the governor (ie head of state). But we obtained a permit to visit the grounds. It was a soft, rainy day,

Apia from Mount Vaea

the manicured gardens were dripping. The guard at the gate told us that the governor was away, so we peered in from the verandas. The rooms looked dusty, with white sheets over much of the furniture, sepia photographs on the walls.

Sailing around in Samoa was not really an option. There were bays that might give shelter, but in order to anchor you needed advance permission from the local chief, to whom a gift must also be presented. A story was doing the rounds of a Canadian yacht that had failed to observe this custom and had (literally) been stoned. So, we took the local bus to the western end of the main island, Upolo, and there caught a landing-craft ferry for the 12-mile crossing to Savaii.

As we rattled through a succession of seaside villages, schoolchildren in immaculate uniforms got on and off. The houses were novel to us but practical: large, oval structures with straw roofs, and walls made of pandanus blinds that could be raised or lowered according to the weather conditions. We found ourselves looking straight into people's daily lives: a couple in bed, a lady doing the cooking, some small children on their knees watching TV. That night, at the guesthouse in the little village of Sale'aula, to which a polite young man in a green lava-lave and school blazer with an enamel badge that read 'Prefect' had escorted us, we couldn't see how to manage those pull-down walls. We undressed very carefully in the dark.

Next day, we were invited to a game of kirikiti. It was recognisably the English game but played with a bat with three sides. The same polite schoolboy caught up with us and explained some local rules. In an official fixture, for example, it was normal and acceptable to

Evening cricket match, Savaii

pay the other side so that you could field more players than them. If you half-closed your eyes, you could hear the click of the bat, the cries of encouragement and the applause and think you were on a village green in England.

There was time for some more South Seas nostalgia before we moved on. The half-English, half-Samoan Aggie Grey founded a hotel in Apia in 1933. She played hostess to Hollywood stars from Dorothy Lamour to Marlon Brando and became a close friend of American writer James Michener. She and her sister Mary Croudace are widely believed to have been models for his Bloody Mary, one of the chief characters of *Tales of the South Pacific*. There Aggie was, at the end of the hotel bar, sun-freckled and wrinkled with her trademark red hibiscus behind one ear, telling a funny story that involved a lot of gesticulation. She gave us a brief smile and interrupted herself to say 'welcome'.

Next morning, we were getting ready to haul up our anchor when in came *Companion*, happily having got rid of the dead pig from their anchor chain. We shouted our plans as they did circles around us.

'But you can't go yet!', called Mary. 'Just one more day; we've got a surprise for you! Come around this evening!'

It was the wedding of Prince Andrew and Sarah Ferguson, on Jeff and Mary's tiny portable TV. We honestly weren't interested; we'd left the UK years earlier and only desultorily followed royal news. It was a long evening. Our hosts fortunately interpreted our prolonged silence as sheer emotion.

Taiwanese fishing boat, Pago Pago

IF YOU GO…

ENTRY FORMALITIES

Most nationalities are granted 60-day visas for Samoa. Apia is the only port of entry/exit. Contact Samoa Port Authority 48 hours in advance at email: **portmaster@spasamoa. ws** or **spa@spasamoa.ws**. On arrival contact the Apia harbourmaster on VHF Ch16. Local chiefs are now more welcoming to yachts, but a cruising permit is required to visit other locations besides Apia; obtainable from the 5th Floor, Government Building, Apia. Officials check yachts in Asau Bay (Savaii), a favoured departure point, to see if they have a permit.

GETTING THERE

Under sail, Apia is best approached from the east, ie along Upolo island's north coast. It can be reached by air from Australia, New Zealand, American Samoa and Hawaii. There is a weekly ferry from Pago Pago.

DISTANCES

Pago Pago to Apia, 90 miles; Apia to Neiafu (Vavau, Tonga), 370 miles; Apia to Savusavu (Fiji), 600 miles.

WEATHER

On average, one tropical cyclone per year strikes Samoa; the season is November to April. The south-east trades prevail, but short spells of westerlies bring rain and squalls.

ANCHORAGE

Apia, GPS 13°49'.7657S 171°45'.7426W, depth 8 metres. Fees apply for anchoring. There is a small marina in the north-east corner of the bay ('The Edge'). The bay is exposed to the north. Pago Pago would be preferrable – but far from secure – in a cyclone.

GENERAL

The country was known until 1997 as Western Samoa. In 2011, Samoa 'moved' west across the dateline, partly in recognition of its strong ties to New Zealand (now in the same time zone); Tuesday in American Samoa is thus Wednesday in Samoa. Society is conservative but welcoming; most visitors find the country more relaxed than American Samoa, closer to old Polynesia. Most supplies and services are available at Apia.

CHARTS

(NZ) WS 311/312: Approaches to Apia; Apia Harbour. US (DMA) 83476, Harbors on Upolu.

REFERENCES

(1) Hinz, Earl. *Landfalls of Paradise: Cruising Guide to the Pacific Islands (5th edn)*. Hawaii, USA: University of Hawaii Press, 2006.

(2) Clay, Warwick. *South Pacific Anchorages (2nd edn)*. St Ives, UK: Imray, Laurie, Norie and Wilson, 2001.

(3) Hawkings, Francis. *The Pacific Crossing Guide (4th edn)*. London, UK: Adlard Coles, 2024.

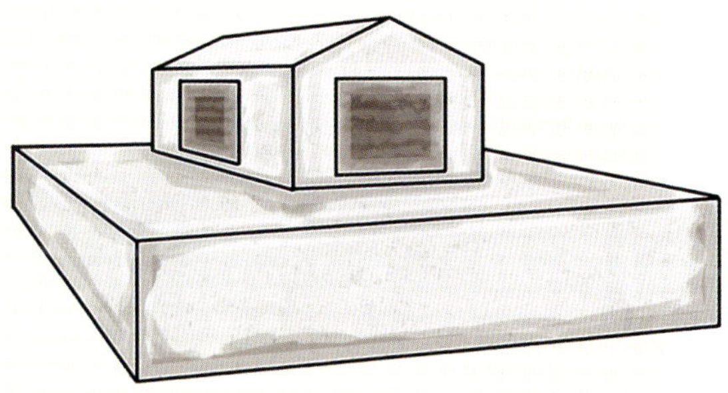

ROBERT LOUIS STEVENSON'S TOMB, MOUNT VAEA

KAVALA BAY, KANDAVU

FIJI

North Astrolabe Reef forms an almost perfect circle 6 kilometres in diameter, with a small rock called Solo, dead centre, on which sits a prominent 32-metre-high lighthouse painted in red and white hoops. We'd been able clearly to see the lighthouse all day as we reached south from Fiji's capital, Suva. The challenge was to find that encircling reef, which nowhere rises above sea level, and through which there is one narrow pass.

We jilled round under sail for half an hour as the sun sank, until we had the lighthouse on the right compass bearing, and then began to edge forward slowly. Jenny spotted a beacon: a single downward-pointing triangle on a skewed steel pole. Was it red, or green? Impossible to tell. Mostly it was rusty and stained with bird droppings; we decided it must be a port-hand marker. The depth sounder went from 'no bottom' to 15 metres in 10 seconds. We crept slowly into the lagoon.

There was no lee behind Solo rock. So we anchored in shallow but open water with no other land to be seen except a couple of tiny islands 7 or 8 miles to the south. It felt as though we were in mid ocean. As the tide rose, the little protection the reef offered diminished, and a chop began to be felt. The night was an uneasy one.

We were happy next day to move on to North Astrolabe's big brother, the Great Astrolabe Reef. Named after the ship of French explorer Jules Dumont D'Urville who surveyed these waters in 1828, it encloses the large hilly island of Japan-shaped Kandavu and a multitude of smaller ones. You can hide from the wind

At anchor inside the Great Astrolabe Reef

behind any of these if you don't trust the protection of those invisible sea-level reefs.

En route, we rehearsed what we knew would be expected next. At the first inhabited island within the Great Astrolabe, Ndravuni, a clutch of giggling children led us by hand, up from the beach to the village and the open-sided hut where the chief was sitting chatting with a few elders. We slid in unobtrusively and sat down cross-legged; it's rude to address the chief from a standing-up position. Jenny unwrapped the package we'd brought with us: a few pages of an old *Fiji Times* around some dirty roots that looked like ginger. This was highly prized kava we'd purchased in the Suva market. She carefully laid it out in front of us on the dirt floor and we waited. The children hung around outside, whispering to each other.

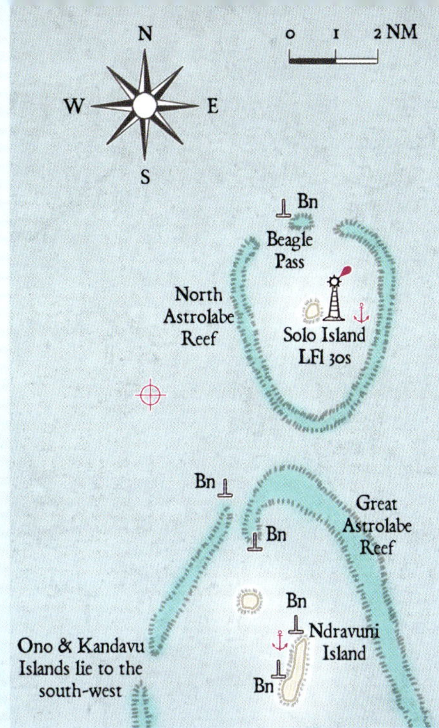

North & Great Astrolabe Reefs, Fiji
⊕ 18° 40' S 178° 30' E

Approaching Solo Island, North Astrolabe Reef

After a time – there seemed to be a little indifference in the air – the kava master took the roots and, chanting all the time, began to pound them in the village's large four-legged kava bowl: the tanoa. He then placed the powder in a muslin bag, filled the bowl with water and swirled the bag around in it. A few more old men filtered in and in a desultory manner the kava ceremony began. A string made of coconut fibres, with intertwined cowrie shells, was laid out, pointing towards us. A single half-coconut shell of the muddy brew was passed to me, then Jenny. As the guests of honour, we each clapped once, downed it in one go, and everyone else clapped three times.

The cup went slowly around the circle. The effect was a mild tingling of the tongue and lips, and it seemed that a somnolence took hold. At sunset and to quiet nods we slipped away, our legs aching but now authorised to anchor at will in the neighbourhood. The ceremony is known as Sevusevu and is de rigueur for visitors to any of Fiji's outer islands.

Day by day, we meandered from one empty anchorage to the next, picking up shells, snorkelling in the clear water, cooking on small fires on the beach at night. The sun would go down, the moon came up and all you could hear was the lapping of waves and the crackling of the fire. The only artificial light to be seen was the small kerosene lantern hanging in our rigging, 50 metres offshore.

After a week, we moved on to the main island – Kandavu – and a bay cut deep into its north shore: Kavala. There was a village at the head of the bay and once the local children in their dugouts had spotted us, the Herald – the chief's foreman, whose symbol of office is a large conch shell – adopted us. We had his whole family on board for cake (evidently a novelty) and then were invited to a traditional meal at Sireli and Maraia's home in the village. The main dish was freshwater shrimps cooked in garlic and coconut milk, taro and cassava in coconut milk and tea (of the coconut variety, of course). As well as the last of our kava, we presented a few tins of Charlie the Tuna, which were reverently placed on an upper shelf. We suspect they are still there, kept as heirlooms.

After dark, the four-man village band assembled. While they tuned up, out came the kava bowl. The Sevusevu was more informal this time. As he brewed up, the kava master entertained us with stories of the years he had spent crewing on Korean fishing boats, the guitarists began strumming and soon the party was in full swing. There was no segregation of the sexes here, as there had been at Ndravuni. The old ladies of the village taught us all the traditional dance steps, one of them gleefully chanting the only English word she knew – 'Disco! Disco!'

In between songs, we talked Fijian politics with Sireli. There'd been a military coup a few months earlier, by which a hitherto unknown colonel in the army, Sitiveni Rambuka, an ethnic Fijian, had seized power. This was in reaction to the election earlier in the year of an IndoFijian-dominated government. The back-story was an old and contentious one. Asians had been imported to Fiji by the British to work sugarcane plantations, starting in the 1880s. The indenture system was terminated in 1916, but most of the labourers chose to stay. They had since prospered and, by the mid-1980s,

were about to outnumber ethnic Fijians. There were very few IndoFijians on Kandavu, but Sireli left us in no doubt where he stood.

'Our country has been taken over. These Indians, who have not been here so long, are running everything. We Fijians have nothing now, just our land. Our chiefs have no power. We call him Steve Rambo, Colonel Steve Rambo. I say good luck to him…'

We mentioned that we'd called in at Ndravuni. Sireli nodded thoughtfully, and didn't seem surprised when I said we'd found the chief and his elders polite but a little distant.

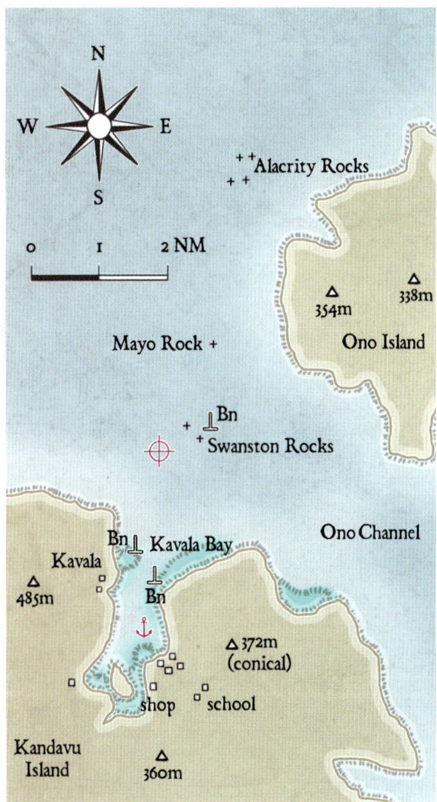

Kavala Bay, Kandavu Island, Fiji
18° 56' S 178° 25' E

At anchor off Kavala

'Yes,' and he hesitated. 'You see, they get ships on that island, cruise ships. The ship must pay to land passengers. They are not so interested when a small yacht comes and just brings kava. I cannot blame them. But here? No ships. And yachts … you are the first we have seen in a long time.'

It was 2am when Sireli finally led us back to the water's edge and our dinghy. He'd written his name for us on a slip of paper and now gave it to us, so we could send him prints of the photos we'd taken. With a flashlight, I examined it: 'Sireli Kawa Number Two, Solotavui, Nakaselaka, Kadavu, Fiji Islands.'

'Why Number Two?'

'Number One is my elder brother, in another village. If you do not write this, he will get the photographs.'

I could see him smiling in the dark.

'But I am the Herald. This is more important than being the Big Brother.'

Village boy and dugout, Kavala Bay

Maraia and Sireli

IF YOU GO…

ENTRY FORMALITIES

Passport holders from most Western countries are granted a 4-month visa for Fiji.

Yachts must file an Advance Notification/Inward (C2-C) form, no less than 48 hours before arrival, available on the Fiji Revenue and Customs Service site, at **www.frcs.org.fj/our-services/customs/yachts-and-vessels**. This requires a photo of your vessel and a scan of the captain's passport. The form (and/or inquiries) should be sent to **yachtsreport@frcs.org.fj**.

For internal travel, cruising permits are mandatory; they are issued by the *iTaukei Affairs* Board, which has offices in Suva, Savusavu and Lautoka, or can be obtained through marinas; weekly location reports must be made by phone, VHF or email to **yachtsreport@frcs.org.fj**. The permit serves as a Letter of Introduction (in Fijian); it must be supplemented by a Coastal Clearance from customs. See **www.fijimarinas.com/itaukei-affairs-board-cruising-permits**. If you do not have an AIS transponder, you can expect extra scrutiny.

Ports of entry are Suva, Levuka, Savusavu, Wairiki (Taveuni Island), Lautoka, Rotuma and the Vuda Point and Port Denarau marinas. Vessels proceeding from the east should not stop in the Lau Group before clearing in. Outward clearance requires 48 hours' notice. Substantial additional costs are levied for weekend arrivals. The complete menu of possible forms required is on the website of the Port Denarau Marina: **www.denaraumarina.com/forms-and-documents**.

GETTING THERE

Arrival at any ports of entry will involve passing outlying reefs and small islands;

Kava roots, ready for the Sevusevu ceremony

particular vigilance is required as some of these may be as far as 2 miles from their charted positions. The prevailing south-east trades mean that approach under sail is best made from the east, but many yachts make the annual trip to/from New Zealand. The sail between Kandavu and Suva is normally a reach. Fiji's Nadi airport has many international connections.

DISTANCES

Suva to Kavala Bay, 53 miles; Lautoka to Kavala Bay, 130 miles; Bay of Islands (NZ) to Suva, 1,050 miles.

WEATHER

Fiji receives one to three cyclones annually; the peak season is November to April. For the rest of the year, south-easterly trade winds prevail. Daytime sea breezes may affect waters west of Viti Levu between Nadi and Lautoka. The Vuda Point Marina (Viti Levu) has cyclone pits (trenches on land into which vessels are lowered); see **www.vudamarina. com.fj/facilities-services**.

ANCHORAGE

Kavala Bay, GPS 18°58'.4832S 178°25'.5858E, depth 20 metres. Call at Ndravuni for permission/Sevusevu before visiting small islands in the area; anchor at GPS 18°45'.5111S 178°31'.1026E, depth 8 metres.

GENERAL

Kandavu is also spelled Kadavu, and Ndravuni may be spelled Dravuni. Some supplies are available at Vunisea, on the isthmus that nearly divides Kandavu in two; airport; police. Buy kava in Suva for Sevusevu. Sitiveni Rambuka was (democratically) elected as prime minister in 1992 and again in 2022.

CHARTS

BA 745, Kadavu to Suva Harbour. Fiji Hydrographic Service: F9 Kadavu-Western Portion; F10 Kadavu-Northern Portion; F11 Plans in Kadavu.

REFERENCES

(1) Calder, Michael. *A Yachtsman's Fiji: A Navigator's Notebook (3rd edn)*. Sydney, Australia: The Cruising Classroom, free online via **http://svsoggypaws.com/ files/#sw-pacific**, 2011.

(2) Cregeen, Phil. *Migrant Cruising Notes – Fiji (3rd edn)*. Auckland, NZ: South Pacific Cruising Services, 1996.

(3) Hinz, Earl. *Landfalls of Paradise: Cruising Guide to the Pacific Islands (5th edn)*. Hawaii, USA: University of Hawaii Press, 2006.

(4) Clay, Warwick. *South Pacific Anchorages (2nd edn)*. St Ives, UK: Imray, Laurie, Norie and Wilson, 2001.

LIGHTHOUSE ON SOLO ISLAND, BUILT 1888

PORT RESOLUTION, TANNA

VANUATU

We'd taken a beating in a gale on the passage north from New Zealand's Bay of Islands, and never found the trade winds that are supposed to predominate north of 30 degrees. So we were happy to find a haven off the southernmost island of Vanuatu: Aneityum. 'Surveyed by Captain Denham, HMS *Herald*, 1853,' we read on our Admiralty chart.

We anchored in a pool off the south-western edge of the high, volcanic island, protected from the swell by a horseshoe reef, most of it awash but with a stretch covered by palms: Inyeug Islet. Over on the main island we could see the straw huts of a small village, with smoke rising above the treetops. At night all was dark.

Aneityum was not an officially designated port of entry, so we could not

Rolling around below the Yasur volcano

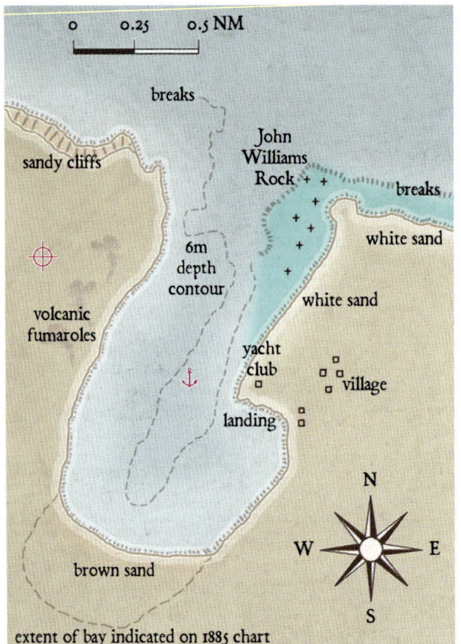

DETAIL: PORT RESOLUTION
19° 31'.3 S 169° 29'.3 E

go ashore. But we spent two peaceful days here, drying out from our wet and lumpy passage, swimming in the lagoon and trading with the friendly youths who came to visit us in their dugouts. Two batteries and a tin of tuna bought us eight enormous pamplemousses and a hand of 30 bananas.

'I guess not too much happens here,' I hazarded to one of the boys.

He shrugged. 'You'd be surprised. Once every few weeks we get a cruise ship, from Auckland, I think. Eight hundred, a thousand people, mebbe, all on that little beach.' He gestured at Inyeug. 'Course, they don't call it that. It's "Mystery Island" now.' And he laughed.

From Aneityum, it was an overnight sail to the next island north, Tanna. I got Jenny up in the middle of the night. Although the sky was clear, we could hear thunder. Should we reef down? Together in the cockpit, we looked forwards. Every few minutes there

would be deep rumbles and red-and-white flashes on the horizon. We soon realised this must be no thunderstorm, but Tanna's Yasur volcano, spectacularly active ever since Captain Cook became the first European to see it.

As we drew closer the scene was apocalyptic with red-orange molten lava being shot high into the night sky, the sound of explosions reaching us seconds later. When dawn came up and the lava was no longer visible, we could set our course on thick black smoke belching from the 800-metre-high cone.

We anchored in Port Resolution, a U-shaped cove open to the north, on the windward side of the island. Cook landed here in August 1774, remarking on the 'vast quantities of fire and smoak' the volcano threw up and complaining of the ash that fell everywhere. He stayed nearly two weeks, taking on water and firewood and – after some initial tension and a few warning shots – established a good relationship with the local people.

In a typical misunderstanding, Georg Forster, the ship's naturalist, asked one man the name of the island, all the while pointing downwards. The man replied 'Tanna', which means 'earth'; the real name was Ipari. In further conversation: 'They gave us to understand in such a manner which admitted of no doubt that they eat human flesh, they began the subject themselves by asking us if we did.'

There was no need for *Bosun Bird* to make a show of force. The Port Resolution community had nominated one person to be the lead contact with yachts, in this case a friendly young Melanesian called Stanley. Once we'd landed, he made arrangements for Jenny to ride to the other side of the island next day, to officially clear into Vanuatu, and gave us the lowdown on Tanna. The community had set aside one building as the Port Resolution Yacht Club: it was festooned with the flags of yachts from up to 30 years ago, and served meals, even Tusker beer. Frustratingly, though, until Jenny came back from the settlement of Lenakel, we had no local currency to take advantage of this.

A visit to the rim of the volcano was pretty much obligatory, Stanley thought, even though there were plenty of vents steaming all around Port Resolution. A bumpy one-hour trip in the back of a pickup, as dusk came down, delivered us to within a few minutes' walk of Yasur's rim.

'You see over dere?', asked Stanley, pointing along the crater edge to a small promontory 50 metres or so away. 'Well last year dere was some yachties from France, I tink. Standin' dere. An' guess what?'

We looked at him expectantly.

'One of dem, he was hit by dose hot rocks,' said Stanley with satisfaction. 'Splat. Dead.'

The earth shook. Every few minutes streams of red lava streaked up directly in front of us. As darkness fell, the glow from deep inside the crater lit the underside of the clouds above.

We drove downhill again, to Sulphur Bay. This tiny community to the north-west of Port Resolution is the home of the John Frum movement. Frum was a mysterious person who appeared from the sea in 1936 to some kava drinkers, and said he was related to the God of the Volcano. In a six-part TV broadcast made in 1960 by BBC legend David Attenborough, a Tanna man described him:

''E look like you. 'E got white face. 'E tall man. 'E live 'long South America.'

The significance of the name is not clear. Does it signify he was 'From America' or just from anywhere but

Yasur by night

Running north in rolly seas, from Port Resolution

Tanna? And there are differing versions of what happened next. One has Frum preaching that if the Tanna-ese renounced Western society, including money and Christianity, then the white people would leave and there would be prosperity for all. Certainly, a movement thousands-strong grew up, much to the alarm of the colonial authorities. Men quit their work on plantations and took their children out of schools; entire congregations left their churches; people moved into the forests and new rituals took place.

Then, a few years on, nearby Espiritu Santo Island became the principal base for the massive Allied effort to dislodge the Japanese from the Pacific islands: 250,000 American troops passed through Santo in only two years. They brought with them affluence: Coca-Cola, cigarettes, refrigerators, electric fans, earth movers. Many of the men were Black, which was astounding to the people of Santo (and the many men from Tanna who went there as local labour),

who had hitherto associated material wealth only with white men. The African Americans also brought their own music: rollicking gospel and guitars.

In some manner, for the people of Tanna, all this seemed to fit with the prophecies of John Frum. The movement adopted the American flag, held military parades in imitation of the Americans (but with wooden guns), took on their music. In the 1950s a parallel but smaller cult took hold on the island, involving veneration of Prince Philip, the husband of Queen Elizabeth; some said he was the brother of John Frum.

Now, every Friday night representatives from John Frum communities all over Tanna – 'companies', as they are known in militaristic terms – assembled at Sulphur Bay for 12 hours of music and singing, from dawn to dusk.

In a straw-roofed shelter and under the light of a single bulb lit by a car battery, we sat as the celebrations got underway. A group of men with guitars, one with a drum, were formally summoned out of the dark by rhythmic stick beating. They formed a scrum outside the open-sided hut and then shuffled in. Women followed them, and a circle was formed on the big pandanus mat on the ground. There began a session of rousing songs in Tanna-ese. It sounded just like gospel singing. The old man sitting beside us told us that it was, but that the songs had the aim of summoning John Frum back.

Around the hut, in the darkness of the tropical forest but with Yasur rumbling eerily in quiet moments, many of the rest of the community jived and moved to the songs. After the set of ten songs was over, there was a pause, more beating of the stick, and another 'company', this time from the community of Port Resolution, took over.

There is no definitive version of what John Frum is about. For example, were the red crosses we saw on buildings in John Frum communities just an adaptation of the Christian cross, or do they date from the Second World War, when the Red Cross itself was another supplier of free goods? The Vanuatu government of today is ambivalent, but uncomfortable about the movement's militaristic overtones and its fascination with the USA. There are other cargo cults in the Pacific, notably in Papua New Guinea, but John Frum is unique to Tanna.

The night at Sulphur Bay was oddly moving. These were communities where radio, let alone TV, were still unknown: the weekly music sessions brought people together in a traditional, ancient way that we suspected survives in few other places in the modern world. And

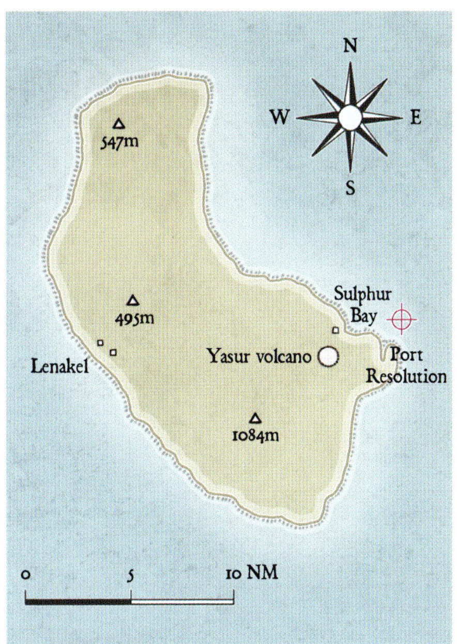

Tanna, Vanatu
⊕ 19° 30' S 169° 30' E

as our headlights picked out our route back, through tunnels of lush jungle and gargantuan banyan trees, the volcano rumbled on.

'If I'd grown up here,' said Jenny, 'I'd have no problem in believing a god lived in the volcano. And if someone turned up and said I could have wealth like the Americans, then I think I'd give them a hearing.'

At Port Resolution, the rollers coming into the bay were starting to make things uncomfortable, to a point at which I began to feel seasick at anchor. More worryingly, strong north-east winds were forecast and the bay is open to the north. We'd only been here two days, but it was time to get out. We sailed on from Tanna, into a 30-hour-rainstorm that felt as if we had firehoses trained on us. It was a fittingly apocalyptic coda to our time Under the Volcano.

IF YOU GO…

ENTRY FORMALITIES

Passport holders of most nationalities are granted a visa for three months upon arrival in Vanuatu.

Yachts must file notice of their arrival (see https://customsinlandrevenue.gov.vu/index.php/customs/forms-2) no less than 24 hours in advance, email to **CustomsBorder@vanuatu.gov.vu.**

Upon entry, an Interisland Cruising Permit valid for six months is issued; the form is available at the customs website (see above). Ports of entry are Lenakel (Tanna), Port Vila (Efate), Luganville (Espiritu Santo) and Sola (Vanua Lava). It may be acceptable to check in at Port Resolution or Aneityum, but only if this has been requested well in advance; extra fees are applicable. Similarly, when checking out at Luganville, permission may be given to visit northern islands on your way out. Extra fees apply for weekend arrivals. Lenakel and Sola are both poor anchorages.

GETTING THERE

The alignment of the islands relative to the trade winds means that Vanuatu is easily approached under sail from New Zealand or points to the east; it also means that islands are best visited from south to north; reaching Tanna from Port Vila is likely to be a hard beat. There are international air connections between Port Vila (and occasionally Luganville) and Australia, New Zealand, Fiji and New Caledonia. Air Vanuatu flies to over 20 domestic destinations. Ferries and cargo boats ply between the islands.

Calling John Frum at Sulphur Bay

DISTANCES

Bay of Islands (NZ) to Port Resolution, 1,073 miles; Aneityum to Port Resolution, 50 miles; Suva (Fiji) to Port Resolution, 515 miles; Port Resolution to Port Vila (Efate), 132 miles.

WEATHER

Vanuatu receives more cyclones that most island groups in the Pacific, usually at least three annually. The peak cyclone season is from December until the end of March. Although Port Vila is sometimes seen as a safe cyclone hole, 30 out of 50 boats on moorings were lost when Cyclone Pam hit the harbour in March 2015. At other times of the year, the south-east trades prevail; they can be gusty between islands and may wrap around headlands with increased intensity.

ANCHORAGES

Port Resolution, Tanna, GPS 19°31'.476S 169°29'.718E, depth 5 metres; the anchorage is often rolly and shoals well before its head; give the eastern entrance point a wide berth; unsafe in a northerly. Aneityum, GPS 20°14.611S 169° 46.236E, depth 11 metres.

GENERAL

Charts are from old surveys and are rarely GPS-compliant, making close-in navigation at night ill-advised. Most supplies are available in Port Vila and/or Luganville; elsewhere there are only very small shops with a few tinned goods. For trading for fruit/vegetables, take a supply of staples (rice, sugar, flour, corned beef tins), plus second-hand clothing, notebooks, pencils and pens, fishing line and hooks, reading glasses and old magazines. There is an increasing tendency to charge for visits/festivals, including access to Yasur volcano; be sure to have Vatu on

The village at Port Resolution, Yasur volcano behind

hand as there are no money-changing facilities outside of Port Vila/Luganville.

CHARTS

BA 1642 of Port Resolution (from a sketch made in 1885) has been deleted, its number reassigned. In the event of obtaining a copy, compare it with Google Earth/Maps: the head of the bay has silted considerably. No new chart has been produced. For Tanna (overall) the best is (USA) DMA/NGA 82580, Erromango to Anatom. For Aneityum: BA 1581, Islands and Anchorages in Southern Vanuatu.

REFERENCES

(1) Clay, Warwick. *South Pacific Anchorages (2nd edn)*. St Ives, UK: Imray, Laurie, Norie and Wilson, 2001.

(2) Cregeen, Phil. *Migrant Cruising Notes – Vanuatu (2nd edn)*. Auckland, NZ: South Pacific Cruising Services, 1995.

(3) Hinz, Earl. *Landfalls of Paradise: Cruising Guide to the Pacific Islands (5th edn)*. Hawaii, USA: University of Hawaii Press, 2006.

(4) (E-guide) **https://cruising-vanuatu. rocketcruisingguides.com**.

PORT HAVANNAH, EFATE

VANUATU

Port Vila, Vanuatu's laid-back capital, has a few reminders of the confused colonial period when these islands were known as the New Hebrides, and Britain and France ruled jointly under an arrangement known formally as The Condominium. More informally it was known as pandemonium.

In those days, an accused criminal could take his pick of two court systems – English common law or French civil law – and serve his sentence in a French prison or an English one. For a period, there was also a Joint Court. It had three judges: English, French and Spanish, the latter appointed by the King of Spain. This fell into disuse in 1939 when the Spanish judge died and there was no longer a King in Spain to appoint a successor. There were two police forces, two health services, two education systems and two currencies.

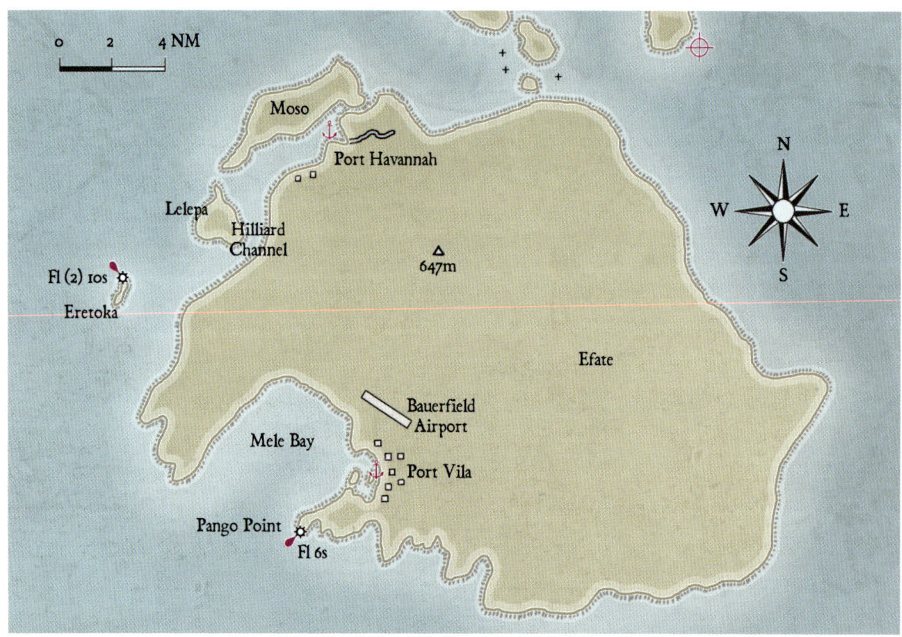

PORT HAVANNAH, EFATE, VANUATU
⊕ 17° 30' S 168° 30' E

PORT HAVANNAH, EFATE
28
VANUATU

Today, the most tangible reminders of past French influence in Port Vila were some classy French restaurants, one of which offered bat in a red wine sauce; French baguettes; a chain of supermarkets called Au Bon Marché. Elsewhere in the islands we'd find more subtle traces of the French presence. The islands where (by mutual agreement) French missionaries had been given licence remained Catholic and French was still spoken. But where the Presbyterians or Anglicans had sway, you'd find English.

At the time of independence (1980), the New Hebrides' split personality led to violence: the 12-week-long Coconut War. A charismatic, bearded figure called Jimmy Stevens, who claimed Scottish and Tongan descent and had 23 wives, led an uprising on Espiritu Santo Island against independence plans. He feared they would spell domination by a socialist Anglo elite embodied in the country's first prime minister, Father Walter Lini. Stevens had the backing of French planters, of the libertarian Phoenix Foundation (USA) and, it was learned later, of the French government. The rebellion fizzled out after Stevens' son was killed in a shootout. But an important lesson was learned. Neither English nor French was made the official language of Vanuatu: rather, it would be Bislama. Forty years on, while English and French are common (this on top of an estimated 145 other native languages), Bislama has become the lingua franca that binds the country together. Later, we'd contrast the relative unity of Vanuatu with the fragmented Solomons, where English remains the official language.

There are many amusing myths about Bislama. Often quoted is the supposed translation of the word helicopter: 'Mixmaster blong Jesus Christ'. Another is the phrase for a piano: 'black fala box we igat black teeth, hemi gat white teeth, you faetem hard I singout'. Disappointingly, these are fabrications. But there is no lack of real colourful and expressive terms: 'bagarup' means broken (from buggered

At anchor, Port Havannah

up), while 'man wiwi' is a Frenchman (a man who says 'oui, oui'); a bra is a 'basket blong titi'. The country's national anthem is 'Yumi, Yumi, Yumi' (You-Me, You-Me, You-Me).

A walk down Port Vila's main street and a scan of street signs and ads taught us that Bislama is an effective and flexible medium of communication: 'Rejista besfren blong yu, pem 1 minit nomo, ol nara minits oli fri' exhorted the Smile mobile phone service provider.

There were linguistic reminders in the capital not just of colonial days but of the massive American presence here in the Second World War. The main districts of town are known as Numbawan, Numbatwo and Numbatree because those were the names of the three US radar stations. 'Numbawan' has also come to mean 'great' or 'fantastic' in Bislama (conversely you could say of a place that is a dump or of a person that you don't like, 'it/they're numbaten').

In all cruising grounds, you find boats and their crew suffering from inertia and gathering weed on their real or metaphorical waterlines for years on end. One of our neighbours in Port Vila's anchorage was a middle-aged American on a sturdy double-ended fibreglass boat with the telltale growth trailing in the water. He rowed over and we talked.

'Dave's the name. Yeah, been here a while. I'm looking for crew, in fact.'

He went on to explain:

'Sailed here with my wife. Took us two years; living the dream. A year ago we went up the islands, headed for the Solomons. Then … then she came down with what seemed like malaria. But it wouldn't go away. It kept coming back. I spoke with a couple of the other boats on the net. One of them recommended a herbal remedy he'd found on the internet. It took me a couple of weeks, but I finally got some shipped in. She took it. And she died. Almost right away.'

Not everyone's dream turns out. A boat can then become a massive encumbrance, something it can be hard to walk away from.

Restocked and replenished, we started north through the rest of Vanuatu. First stop was just around the corner on Efate Island: the vast lake-like Port Havannah. Named after a Royal Navy ship that explored these waters between 1849 and 1850, this became a key part of Naval Operating Base Efate, which the USA began to consolidate in March 1942 as part of its strategy to retake the offensive in the Pacific. Out of range of Japanese bombers in the Solomons and New Guinea, Havannah was the assembly point for the fleet that fought the Battle of the Coral Sea in May 1942. This was the first ever engagement between opposing aircraft carriers and the first naval battle in which neither fleet saw the other.

Now Havannah was deserted. But on shore all around there were overgrown, decaying remnants of those days. There was an abandoned fighter airstrip in the jungle behind the bay. Imagine those great but now deserted expanses of cracked concrete in Yorkshire and Lincolnshire, where the Lancasters and Flying Fortresses took off to bomb Europe, but in a tropical setting. A few ruined structures had been all but engulfed by kudzu, the fast-growing creeper that the Americans introduced so as to camouflage installations. By the water were the concrete ramps and

Ernest at the World War Two museum, Port Havannah

installations that were built to service a fleet of 14 Catalina flying boats. These were the first aircraft to take the fight to the enemy, with a bombing raid on the Japanese in Guadalcanal in June 1942. Rusting iron pipes led down from springs in the interior of the island to the water's edge: these were used to replenish the US battle fleet.

In a shack under the palm trees, an eccentric and enthusiastic local man called Ernest maintained a museum of war memorabilia. There were bent propeller blades from P38s, unidentifiable scraps of aluminium fuselage, old jeep radiators and rusting carburettors. Ernest called us over with a smile and a self-mocking American accent: 'Welcome, mah frens! On de yott? Yass, welcome indeed! Come right in, ya'll! An' where y'all from? Now you jus' take a look at this … ain't it sumpin'?'

Some of his items were even for sale. 'Now you just look at these, if you will!' and he pointed to rows of old-style Coke bottles rescued from the mud of Port Havannah. 'See here … San Francisco, 1943; Cincinnati 1944… Special price for you, my fren!'

Ernest told us to make sure, when we sailed up the island chain, to go diving at Million Dollar Point, near Luganville. Chuckling, he told us the story of how at the end of the war, rather than ship back to the US the vast fleet of heavy equipment and vehicles that had built up over four years, the commanding American general offered it to the colonial authorities at a knock-down price. The French and British governors slyly calculated that if they refused the offer, the Americans would leave it all anyway.

'Dey was wrong,' chortled Ernest. 'De Americans bulldozed de whole damned lot into de water… You can see it still!'

At Havannah we took up the pattern of daily shopping that would now be with us for months. Most mornings, a few dugouts would pull up alongside, offering coconuts, tomatoes, snake beans, a variety of spinach known unappetisingly as 'slimy cabbage', pawpaws. After some chitchat, we would ask the standard question, 'Do you want money or to trade?' Trading usually involved, on our part, staples not available far from shops – sugar, flour – and items such as school exercise books, pens, fishhooks. But sometimes, you just had to say no: 'OK, I'll give you three pens and exercise book for two coconuts.'

'Make dat four pens, mon…'

'Sorry, no more pens. How about an AA battery?'

'No, no… You got an iPod? Dat be good.'

People often asked for reading matter. Once we exchanged a one-year-old copy of *The Economist* for two large mud crabs. It was possible to place orders; people were on their way to or from their 'gardens' (vegetable plots), which could be some distance from their homes, so they could easily pick a few more of some particular item on our shopping list.

One evening as we sat in the cockpit pondering how to cook those snake beans, we paused to watch the sun setting behind the palms. The water was mirror-still; you could hear a few bullfrogs cranking up on shore; somewhere a surfacing turtle wheezed. It was difficult to imagine that this was the place where America began the long, bloody campaign of the Pacific. Right where we sat at anchor, so had the most powerful warships of the age.

Floating salesman, Port Havannah

IF YOU GO…

For information on entry formalities, getting there, weather, general and references, see Chapter 27, page 180.

DISTANCES

Port Vila to Port Havannah, 28 miles; Port Havannah to Revolieu Bay (Epi Island), 56 miles.

ANCHORAGE

Port Havannah, GPS 17°33'.128S 168°16'.830E, depth 14 metres.

Remains of a wartime airfield, Port Havannah

CHARTS

BA 1494, Vanuatu, Efate and Plans; (USA) DMA/NGA 82571, Efate Island.

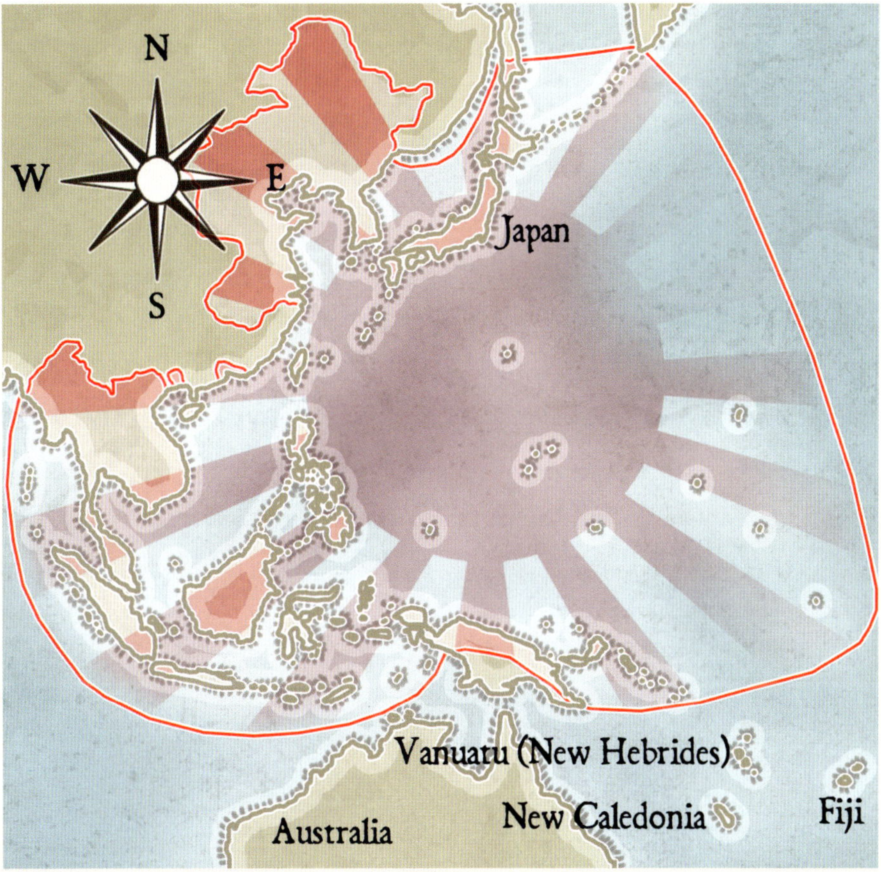

MAXIMUM EXTENT OF THE JAPANESE EMPIRE, 1942

TWIN WATERFALL BAY, BANKS ISLANDS

VANUATU

We'd sailed overnight to Gaua, in the Banks Islands, and anchored in water so still and clear that you could see the chain snaking over black sand, 12 metres below. After a pancake breakfast, Jenny was reading in the cabin, and I was snoozing in the cockpit, in the shade of the dodger. Then, from below, came a very quiet, tense: 'Nick, I need help. Now. But move very slowly.'

I peered down the companionway, cautiously. Jenny was holding her paperback almost up to her face, while a snake – a metre long, silver with black hoops – was slowly sliding across her bare thighs, moving its small head from side to side in curiosity. It then curled up at the head of her bunk, on a pillow.

She got up very carefully and moved quietly out into the cockpit. We were incredulous. How had it got in? Up the outlet of the marine toilet? That was an interesting if frightening prospect to contemplate, but not possible: there was a pump in the way. Up into the galley sink? No, the plug hole was obstructed. It had to have been up one of the two cockpit drains. With the help of a boathook and keeping a respectful distance – we later found out that this species of sea snake

is venomous – we cajoled our stowaway into a bucket, and returned it to its natural habitat, hearts beating a little faster than they had been.

When we landed later that day, our feeling of slight unease was not relieved. Six months earlier the villages on the downwind side of the island had been evacuated for fear of noxious gases and the possible violent eruption of Gaua volcano. In the woods behind a spring and propped up against tree trunks, were half a dozen tam tams: 2-metre-tall slit

Tam tam at Gaua

wooden drums, intricately carved. They were covered in bright green moss and looked to be rotting. A stylised face – a vertical nose and two bulbous eyes on stalks – stared at us through the greenery.

I was reminded of abandoned native villages we'd visited in British Columbia, where old and decaying totems would lie half buried in the undergrowth. The place was sinister. The drums had clearly been here for many years, but why had they been abandoned? Were we breaking some taboo just by being here?

We moved north again, to Vureas Bay on Vanua Lava Island, and anchored off a long black-sand beach, backed by seaward-leaning palms. It wasn't the most tranquil of places in the gusty trade winds we were now experiencing. There would be half an hour of calm, then a sequence of 30-knot 'bullets' would send us reeling, circling our anchor. In between gusts, the water was just as clear as at Gaua, and after a couple of days I could see that our wandering about had unravelled several metres of our three-strand anchor line. We hauled it in and cut out the section of frayed rope. I spent two hours relearning long-forgotten splicing skills with the help of diagrams in our cruising bible, Eric Hiscock's *Cruising Under Sail*.[12]

We'd timed our arrival in accordance with news we'd picked up on the cruisers' grapevine. On shore Chief Godfrey, his wife Veronica and his committee of elders welcomed us and the crews of the few other yachts in the bay to a long-planned four-day village festival of traditional dance, music-making and magic. A troupe of young men who had

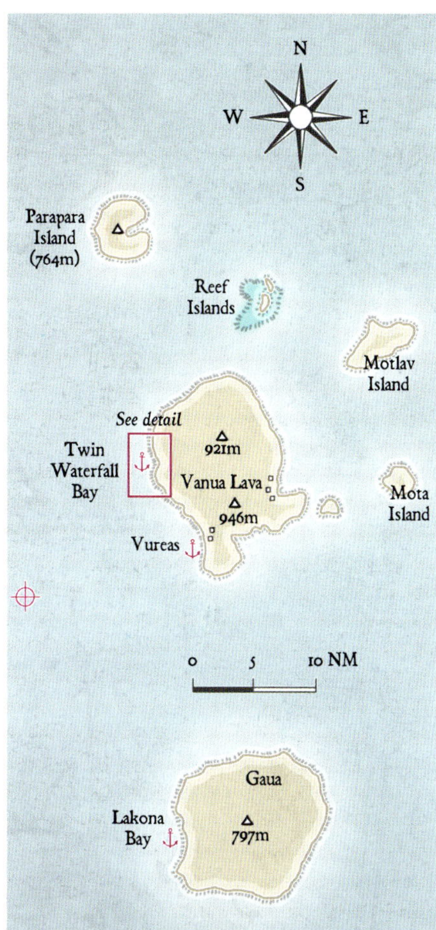

Banks Islands, Vanuatu
14° S 167° 12' E

been living in seclusion for a month, as tradition demands, performed dances in a specially constructed locale behind the beach. Some set pieces had only recently been rescued from the village's collective memory; others were felt to have such power that we were not allowed to photograph them. Especially colourful was the Snake Dance, for which the men had daubed themselves in lime and ashes in imitation of the same species of sea snake with which Jenny was involuntarily familiar.

12 Hiscock, Eric. *Cruising Under Sail.* London, UK: Adlard Coles, 1991.

How 'genuine' was it all? Many villagers still believed in the old ways but it had taken the stimulus of outside visitors (and the US$10 we each contributed to the festivities) to bring them together and relearn their past. It seemed to us touch-and-go whether in 20 years' time the dances would still be remembered, though. It is not tourism that will destroy true traditional culture in these islands, for physical access remains extremely difficult. But, for better or for worse, mobile phones have arrived; there is a (laudable and) growing belief in the importance of education; and the concept of electoral and representative democracy is undermining older, more traditional leadership structures. Not for the first time, we were finding parallels with the challenges facing the indigenous people of our home in British Columbia, as they seek to maintain their pride and their identity in the face of encroachment by the modern world.

Our last port of call in Vanuatu was lovely Twin Waterfall Bay, also on Vanua Lava. Here we were the sole visitors. We were touchingly welcomed by all the inhabitants of the village with their special 'Welcome' song to the tune of 'God Save the Queen'. The women and girls then ushered us over to the deep, cool pool at the foot of the falls from which the bay takes its name. They lined up waist-deep in the water and launched into a sequence of rhythmic water-slapping, from which a discernible tune (or beat) gradually emerged, among gales of laughter and horseplay. The men watched in amusement: 'You see, these ladies, when they say they are doing the laundry, they are just having a party!' joked one.

From Esau, Chief Karely's brother-in-law, we commissioned the carving

Sea-snake in the cockpit

Water music, Twin Waterfall Bay

of a Laplap knife in rosewood. It was ready in less than a day, his only tools an old hacksaw blade, a nail and a piece of glass. When we asked how much we owed him, he just asked to look at what we had to spare, then picked out some D batteries, a 2 kilogram bag of rice and a surplus file from our toolbox. And, after some contemplation, a month-old copy of the *Vanuatu Daily Post*.

Esau walked with a peculiar hunch. We didn't want to ask, but he explained anyway: 'One year ago, I fell very ill. I was in my bed, all my bones ached, I was too tired to get up. Only a few weeks ago did I start to walk again…'

Had he consulted a doctor?

'Oh yes, the kastom doctor. Our traditional doctor. There is no modern doctor on this island. He says I may not go into the sea for exactly five years. It is one year now. I am getting better, I think.'

Karely spent an evening on board *Bosun Bird* with us. He was well informed about the history of the Banks Islands and told us that some visiting archaeologists had recently found obsidian arrowheads from the Lapita culture, dating from maybe 1000 BCE.

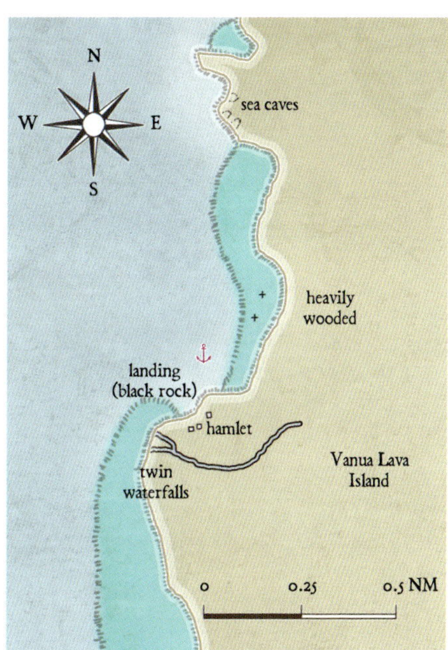

DETAIL: TWIN WATERFALL BAY, VANUA LAVA

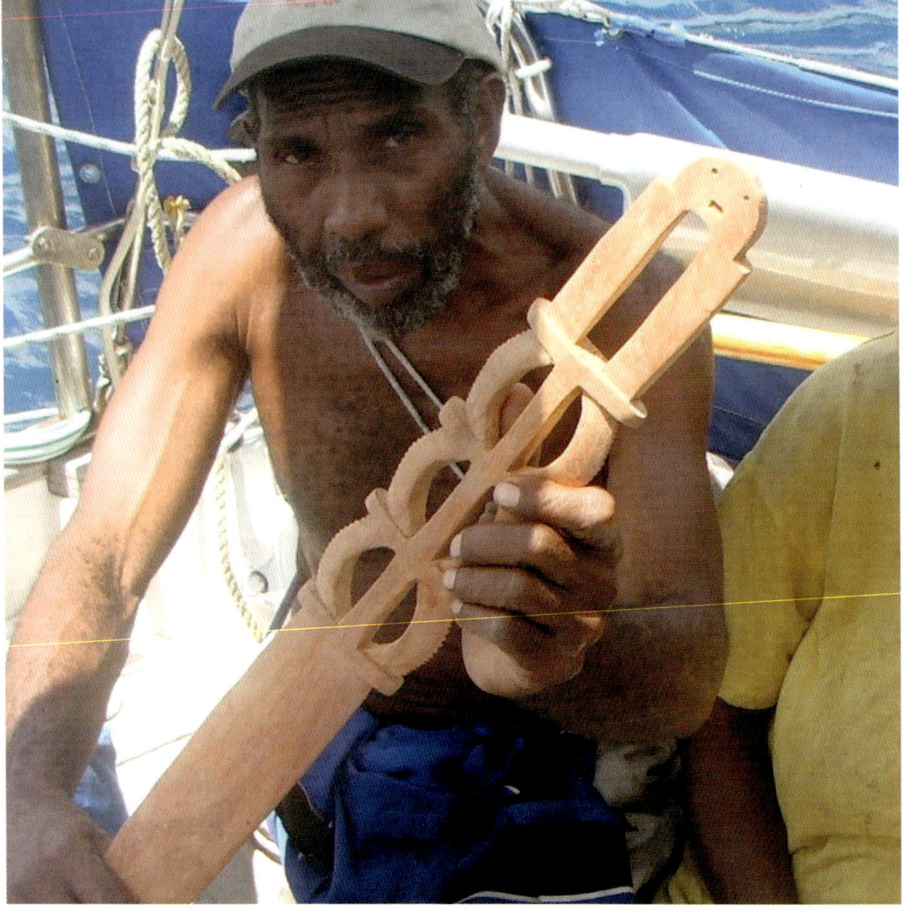

Esau and the laplap knife

Like Chief Godfrey and the people of Vureas Bay, he was one of about 2000 Vurës speakers on Vanua Lava.

'But there are three or four other languages on this island alone,' he said. 'Lemerig, for example, in a village with that name. I think that is finished now, there is nobody left. And Vera'a, yes, there are still many speakers of this. For how long, though? In the schools, you see, it is only English and Bislama, pidgin that is. Maybe this is the same on all the islands in Vanuatu. All those languages, but so many are gone now.'

Karely seemed to us an honest man of great charm and intelligence. These days he was earnestly wondering whether he should enter political life. He asked our advice.

'I want to do something for my people. I think there are many corrupt politicians in this country; I have heard they are selling passports to criminals, just to get money.' Then, in an aside: 'Tell me, is it really true that a Black man is president of America?'

We could only encourage him. As the Banks Islands sank into the gloom and we set a course for the Solomons, Jenny and I agreed on one thing. Vanuatu was what we had always hoped the Pacific would be. It had just taken us 25 years and 15,000 miles of meanderings through Polynesia and half of Melanesia to find it.

IF YOU GO...

For information on entry formalities, getting there, weather, general and references, see Chapter 27, page 180.

DISTANCES

Port Vila (Efate) to Twin Waterfall Bay, 260 miles; Luganville (Santo) to Twin Waterfall Bay, 120 miles; Twin Waterfall Bay to Vanikoro (Solomons), 172 miles.

ANCHORAGES

Twin Waterfall Bay, GPS 13°49'.632S 167°22'.899E, depth 14 metres; this is by the more southerly of the two waterfalls marked on the chart and is just north of the westernmost point of the island. Vureas, Vanua Lava, GPS 13° 55'.5855S, 167° 26'.779E, depth 13 metres. Lakona, Gaua, GPS 14°18'.758S 167°25'.845E, depth 12 metres.

CHART

(USA) DMA/NGA 82534, Banks Islands.

At anchor, Twin Waterfall Bay

"

PORT MARY,
SANTA ANA ISLAND

SOLOMON ISLANDS

It was an overnight sail north-west from the last outposts of Vanuatu – the Torres Islands – to the first of the Solomons: Vanikoro.

Although we had only come 100 miles and were still in Melanesia, it was obvious we were in a new land. The dugouts here were single-hull, not the Polynesian-inspired outriggers of Vanuatu. And when their paddlers opened their mouth, they were stained red as if by blood. Betel nut, not kava, is the narcotic of preference in the Solomons. The people were noticeably less shy: within minutes of our anchoring at Vanikoro, dugouts were heading for us from the nearest village, 3 or 4 kilometres away. Fishing techniques here were new as well: one woman proudly showed us the tethered heron she used as an assistant.

Vanikoro was the setting of a tragedy that in the annals of French exploration held the same morbid fascination as Franklin's doomed expedition to seek Canada's Northwest Passage: *'le mystère Lapérouse'*. Jean François de Galaup, Comte de Lapérouse was, like his contemporary James Cook, a naval officer turned explorer. An epic expedition that began in 1785 saw him taking *L'Astrolabe* and *La Boussole* past Cape Horn, around the Pacific in a long anticlockwise circuit to Australia. The ships left Botany Bay again in March 1788, with the intention of returning to France by June 1789, via the Cape of Good Hope. They disappeared. Only in 2008 was it ascertained that both had been wrecked on Vanikoro's reefs.

At Basilisk Harbour on Utupua, the next island north from Vanikoro, the local pastor came out to greet us. He recalled meeting the French investigative team that had come to the islands. Then, pondering more recent deaths at sea, he asked us:

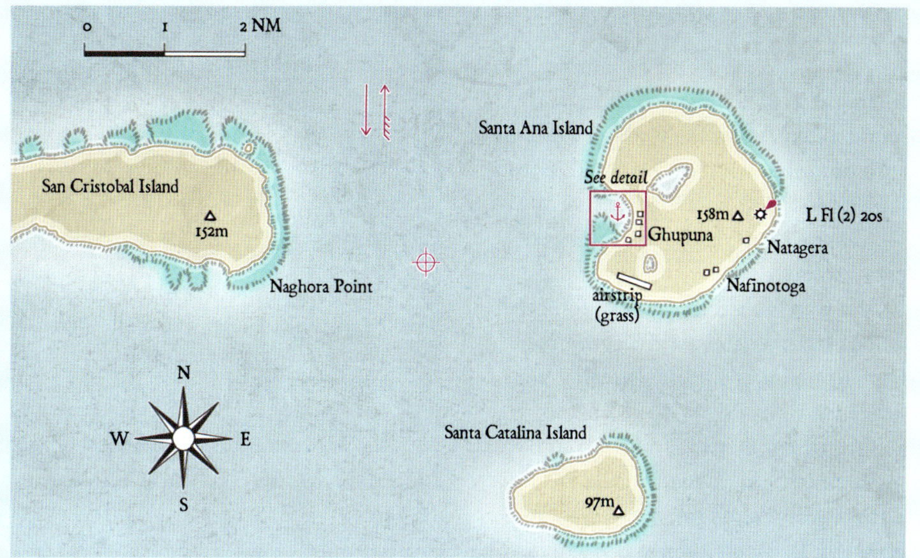

Santa Ana Island (Owa Rafa), Solomon Islands
⊕ 10° 50'.5 S 162° 14'.7 E

'You heard about that Swiss yacht that came here?'

'No…'

'Well, they anchored right here, man and wife, just like you. He wasn't too sure about the anchor, see. So, he decided to dive in and check it. His wife, she was watching.'

We waited for the pastor to go on.

'Well, the crocs, they ate him, didn't they? He still had his mask on when they found his head. His wife, his widow, she sent money, we built a school. She's been back. What was left of him is buried in the village. Don't go swimming here.'

There were no officials to check in with at Utupua or Vanikoro. We'd have to go to the main island of Temotu's province, called Santa Cruz (or Ndende; the big islands in the Solomons all have two names), another 80 miles on. Here Titus, who had worked on American fishing boats and who knew Hawaii, Guam and Pohnpei, assured us:

'Yeah, we got customs, we got immigration, we got an ATM: dere's everythin' you could want in town.'

Titus' estimation was optimistic. In Lata there was a large and new-looking sign informing us of the opening hours for customs and immigration. But it had been six years since officers had been posted here. The local policeman was sanguine: he took our details and said he'd fax them on to Honiara. Having walked an hour to get here, we thought

At anchor, Vanikoro

we might as well buy something and found Titus' ATM. As we were fiddling with our card, a passerby warned us away, tapping his nose knowingly:

'Dat machine, he no good; he take your card, but see, he got no cash…'

We were able to buy a few Solomon dollars from a shop. At the counter, to our surprise, was a florid, heavily built white man.

'Yup, the only white man in the province of Santa Cruz,' he said. 'And I don't reckon there's too many more, white Solomon Islanders I mean, anywhere…'

Ross's life story was unusual.

'I came out here from England with my mum and dad and my twin brother Ben, on a Brixham trawler called the *Arthur Rodgers*. 1948 it was. We stayed on. We've a place on the Reef Islands, Pigeon Island, a few miles offshore from here.'

It rang a bell with me. Years ago, I'd read a non-fiction work called *Faraway*[13] by Lucy Irvine. It was the saga of Tom Hepworth, his wife (a former *Vogue* model), the children and their life on a South Sea island. Irvine had been commissioned by Diana Hepworth to write the family story after Tom's death in 1994, with full access to his private letters and diaries (most of which Diana, unwisely, had not read). Irvine spent a year at Pigeon. The book is a thorough debunking of 'paradise' but also a cruel exposé of a dysfunctional family. I didn't mention it to Ross.

We chatted instead about mutual acquaintances who'd come through by yacht. Then Ross recalled with us some of Santa Cruz Island's interesting history. When the Spaniards were exploring Peru

---

13 Irvine, Lucy. *Faraway*. London, UK: Corgi, 2000.

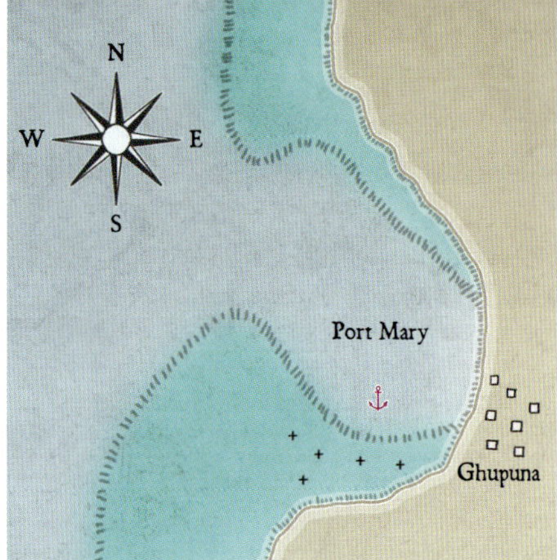

DETAIL: PORT MARY, SANTA ANA

in the early 16th century, one of the most pressing questions was the source of the gold used by the Incas in their fabulous ornamentation. In one of the great con-tricks of history, the conquistadors were told that it came from islands over the horizon. Alvaro de Mendaña was a sea captain who took the Incas at their word. He sailed the width of the entire Pacific before stumbling in 1567 on Santa Cruz where, imagining that this must at least be the site of King Solomon's mines, he gave the islands their modern name. There was no gold.

'There's no trace of any settlement,' said Ross. 'But there's an awful lot of chiefs whose names begin with M. They say that's Mendaña's influence. Can't say I'm convinced myself.'

From Santa Cruz it was two days' sail west to the main grouping of the Solomons. We stopped first at tiny Santa Ana Island, anchoring in Port Mary just off the main village, Ghupuna. This was a beautiful, peaceful anchorage, with the high green mountains of larger San Cristobal Island as a backdrop over our stern. On shore Amos, the designated yacht greeter, took us to meet Chief John and our social round began. There was Amos' sister Monica, who would bring us fresh megapode eggs every day; Stewart who liked to talk world politics; Stacey who took our bread orders; Leonard the woodcarver with whom we bargained (fruitlessly) every day for an exquisite but expensive miniature canoe; Katie who took all our laundry.

And there was a whole family with a fascinating pedigree who adopted us. Heinrich Kuper was a German trader who came to the Solomons in 1912. He married into tribal royalty on Santa Ana. An old photo on the wall of the family home showed him in shirt and tie, towering 50 centimetres over his ornately beaded wife Kafagamurirongo on the day of their wedding. As two world wars came and went, the family anglicised their names. Son Geoffrey Kuper, by then living on Santa Isabel Island, was a leading light among the legendary coast-watchers who clandestinely assisted Allied troops from 1942 onwards.

Geoffrey's widow Clara, daughter Greta and son Henry, now lived on Santa Ana. We spent several lazy afternoons while Greta and her mother reminisced. She'd pull out one old photo after another, as we sat on wicker chairs in her airy front room.

'See this? These are grade-taking ceremonies in the village from 1943, I think. Of course, I wasn't born then, but even Mum wasn't allowed to watch. No women were allowed… That's a canoe being carved, for the Royal Ontario Museum. And this one?' she said with a smile and then answered herself. 'It's Mum with the Queen. 1974, maybe.'

'February,' Clara chimed in, nodding in reminiscence. 'Star Harbour.'

Not quite all of the old ways had been forgotten. At Natagera on the weather coast of the island there was a well-maintained 'kastom' (traditional) house that was used for ceremonies and where the remains of chiefs and elders were buried. The current chief showed me around with a gaggle of giggling children in tow, while Jenny waited patiently outside – it was taboo for women to enter, he explained.

The chiefs' remains were placed in miniature war canoes, 2 metres long and suspended from the rafters. Skulls and bones of lesser elders were encased in baskets or simply piled up on a large altar. There was one rotting cardboard box full of bones that had once held packages of chicken-flavoured instant noodles. Looking up into the rafters, our friend complained:

'That's where I should be buried. But of course, the church won't let me.'

Monica brings us megapode eggs

IF YOU GO…

ENTRY FORMALITIES

Most visitors to the Solomons do not require a visa and are granted, on arrival, a Free Permit valid for 90 days; see **https://solomons.gov. sb/tourism-solomons/essential-services/ how-to-get-a-visa**.

Yachts must complete a Maritime Movement Checklist, available at **www.customs.gov. sb/content.jsf?c=202210**, and submit it to Solomon Island Customs at least three working days in advance of arrival; email: **SI_ CustomsMaritimeClearances@sig.gov.sb**.

Ports of Entry are Honiara (Guadalcanal), Noro (New Georgia Island) and Taro (Taro Island, off the north-west tip of Choiseul Island, the site of an airstrip). Temporary entry clearance may be granted at Lata (Santa Cruz/Ndende Island). Vessels approaching from the east or south of the Solomons should note that it is illegal to land prior to obtaining permission at Lata. Vessels hoping to clear in/out of the Solomons at Gizo often club together and pay for officials to travel by launch from Noro.

There is a steep levy for aids to navigation: in 2023 this was USD $34.75 per metre of boat length, with a scheduled annual 7.5 per cent rise. There is also a (smaller) Pollution Levy. Overtime fees apply to weekend arrivals. For fee schedules see **https://solomons.gov.sb/wp-content/uploads/2023/01/Gaz-No.-326-Sup-No.-225-Friday-23rd-December-2022-1.pdf**

GETTING THERE

Under sail and in winter, the island is most easily approached from the south-east. Approach from the north-west is easier in summer (but this is also cyclone season). Santa Ana is served by Solomon Airlines.

With Greta and her mother (Clara Kuoer)

At anchor, Santa Ana

DISTANCES

Torres Islands (Vanuatu) to Santa Ana, 433 miles; Graciosa Bay (Santa Cruz Island) to Santa Ana, 206 miles; Santa Ana to Honiara, 192 miles.

WEATHER

The south-eastern end of the island chain is prone to cyclones from November through April, on average two per year. Otherwise during that period, north-westerlies prevail. From May through October the south-east trades are dominant; in high summer (July/August) the South Pacific Convergence Zone may reach into the more northerly islands, bringing rain and squalls.

ANCHORAGES

Port Mary, Santa Ana, GPS 10°50'.210S 162°27'.087E, depth 20 metres. The island is also known as Owa Rafa. Vanikoro, GPS 11°40'.184S 166°55'.823E, depth 22 metres. Utupua (Basilisk Harbour), GPS 11°15'.441S 166°31'.166E, depth 17 metres.

GENERAL

Overall population 700,000 (Honiara 90,000; Gizo 7,000). Supplies are available in Honiara and Gizo but in few other places. For yacht services, including haul-out, Liapari Marina (Vella Lavella Island, 12 miles north of Gizo), is a good option. Detailed charting is poor; for Marovo and Vonavona lagoons in particular, Google Maps/Earth is more useful. The common wisdom is that Honiara and the island of Malaita are the least secure areas to visit.

CHART

SLB 304, Solomon Islands – Indispensable Strait.

REFERENCES

(1) Sieling, Dirk. *Solomon Islands Cruising Guide.* Auckland, NZ: Island Cruising Press, 2009.

(2) Clay, Warwick. *South Pacific Anchorages (2nd edn).* St Ives, UK: Imray, Laurie, Norie and Wilson, 2001.

(3) Hinz, Earl. *Landfalls of Paradise: Cruising Guide to the Pacific Islands (5th edn).* Hawaii, USA: University of Hawaii Press, 2006. For a useful overview of an extensive 2019 cruise in the Solomons, including GPS positions for 30+ anchorages, see **http://hackingfamily.com/Cruise_Info/Pacific/CruisingSolomons.htm**. Also see this author's notes at **www.bosunbird.com/solomon-islands-for-cruisers/**.

LOLA ISLAND, VONAVONA LAGOON

SOLOMON ISLANDS

Cruising is not always about sunshine, peaceful anchorages and trading with friendly, hospitable local people. The Solomons are the most beautiful island group we have ever visited, but as we sailed on from Santa Ana we occasionally felt an edginess, a feeling of threat that we have never experienced in other islands. And one night we had the most frightening single experience of our 70,000 miles offshore.

Relations between the different ethnicities in the Solomons have long been difficult. After the US regained the principal island – Guadalcanal – from Japan in 1943, thousands of people migrated to it from the island of Malaita, attracted by work opportunities. Over the years there were spats between Guales (natives of Guadalcanal) and the newcomers. These erupted into open violence and lawlessness in 1998. The police fractured on ethnic lines and in 2003 the governor of the Solomons asked for an international force (the Regional Assistance Mission to the Solomon Islands – RAMSI) to intervene and serve as police. Clashes abated, but it was not until 2013 that RAMSI withdrew. The height of the violence – between

approximately 1999 and 2004 – is recalled as The Tension.

Next to the eastern tip of Guadalcanal, where a maze of islands and waterways forms Marau Sound, we anchored off a plush but underutilised resort called Tavanipupu. The local chief, Justin, explained to us that the resort was one of the few such places that had not been sacked and/or burned during The Tension. But the region had still seen trouble. Justin and the villagers in his care were from Malaita historically. For a year they had been besieged on their small island while 'weathercoast people' (Guales) ran rampant with heavy weapons throughout the Sound. Other stresses still existed today, we soon realised. There were issues between the villagers and the resort management, largely arising from what the white manager, whom Justin called pam-AY-ler, euphemistically described to us as 'differing work ethics'. On top of all this, as a pastor, Justin wanted us to know what he thought about neighbours of other religious persuasions:

'You can't trust those Roman boys,' he said pointing across the bay. 'You just be careful now.'

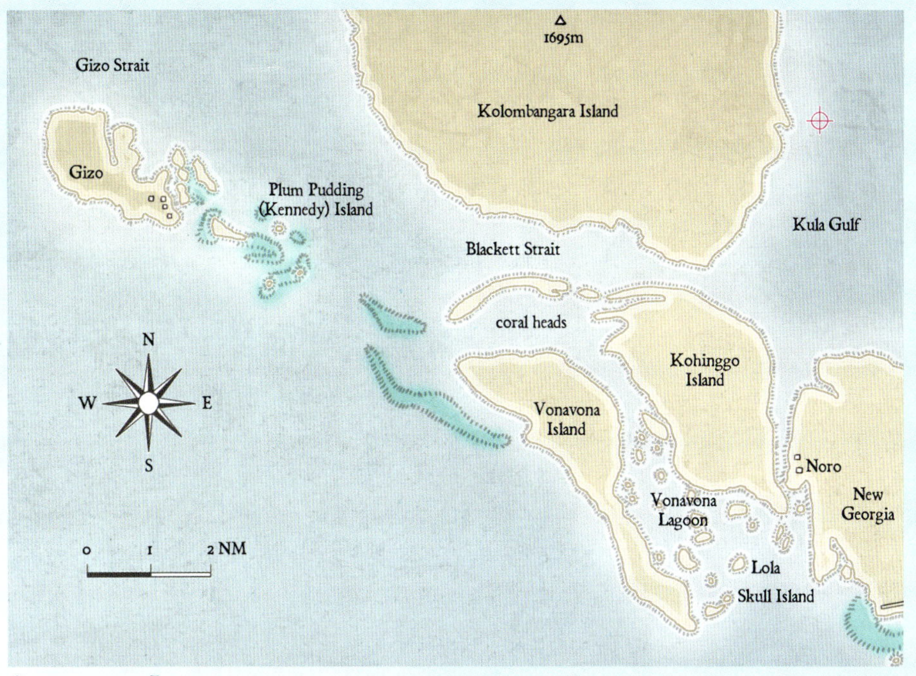

SOLOMON ISLANDS, NORTH-WESTERN PORTION
⊕ 8° 03' S 157° 13' E

Things were no more relaxed in Honiara, where a stop to complete formalities was obligatory. There is a yacht club at Point Cruz, but the denizens of the bar were jaded expatriate Australians who had nothing good to say about their home. The town was indeed unattractive – concrete and tin shanties thrown up after the Second World War – and crime was high. There had recently been anti-Chinese riots that had seen many small businesses burned down. The last straw for us came when we came back to *Bosun Bird* – stern-tied to the breakwater – and found our neighbours on *Ma Ohi* had been robbed while they were out for breakfast. They had locked the boat up, but thieves had ingeniously used a fishing rod, poked through a small porthole in the side, to extract an iPod and other valuables.

As soon as we could, we moved on again. The most popular area for cruising is the Marovo Lagoon and the adjacent island of New Georgia. We spent three weeks moving from island to island, all in clear and well-protected waters. Marovo is home to many wood carvers and – with judicious bargaining – some exceptionally beautiful pieces can be

Plum Pudding (Kennedy) Island

Intricate navigation in Vonavona Lagoon

obtained. The most well-known carver enjoyed the name John Wayne, but we soon learned that he had dozens of capable rivals. They were nearly all Seventh Day Adventists, having been converted by an Australian trader in 1948. SDA'ers may not eat products of the sea that do not have scales, so this was also a good location to find lobster; there was no lack of 'backsliders' prepared to take diving commissions.

We were starting by now to feel better about the Solomons. Then one day we anchored in a tranquil bay east of Matikuri Island. We traded willingly but sensed something awry when one young man in particular kept coming back, with nothing to trade. He asked us our names. When we asked his in return, he just parroted mine: 'Nick.'

Late that night, lying in the starboard bunk, I must have been having a nightmare. Jenny called across to me: 'Wake up!' I shook myself and lay back. As I did so, I became conscious that there was a figure, standing stock still in the dark, between our bunks, right by my head. I couldn't be sure – I was only looking out of the corner of my eye – but he seemed to be holding something in his right hand. I thought I must still be dreaming. My heat began pounding. Ludicrously, I was inhibited for a moment by my nakedness.

Possessed only of adrenalin and without thinking any further, I leapt up, shouting obscenities, and violently shoved the figure – he was quite slight – up out of the companionway and into the cockpit. He fell into the dugout that was tied alongside. I kept yelling at him as he paddled away into the darkness. It was the young man who had called himself Nick; I saw now that he had been holding a machete.

It wasn't clear to us whether he had been intent on violence, theft or maybe just 'peeping'. In the morning, a couple of other islanders came around to check we were OK – they must have heard the shouting. They were sympathetic and confirmed that Nick was really named Piasi and that he was slightly disturbed. We tried to resist paranoia. Years earlier, we'd seen too many yachts in the Caribbean (mainly American) project pre-emptive hostility to young men – 'boat boys' who offered their services at every anchorage – only to find that this became self-fulfilling.

From Marovo we sailed into the shallow, complex waters of the Vonavona Lagoon. There is no good chart here and the water in many places is barely 2 metres deep, so we needed to be on our toes with sunlight behind us (so as to see looming reefs). At Lola Island we found some much-needed peace.

There was a tiny resort with just six thatched bungalows, where Joe (the expat American owner) and AJ (barman) welcomed us warmly. Unlike Pamela at Tavanipupu, Joe was on good terms with all his neighbours, and trading took place in the spirit we'd enjoyed at Santa Ana. With the permission of the local 'kastom' chiefs, he directed us over to nearby Skull Island. In the open or under tiny makeshift rock shelters were hundreds of skulls, some of them of local chiefs but many the result of the head-hunting wars that bedevilled this part of the Solomons prior to the arrival of the missionaries: a fascinating but sinister scene.

In idle hours at Lola, we sipped cold SolBrews in the company of AJ, read

Skull Island, Vonavona Lagoon

years-old *New Yorker* magazines and watched sunsets over the lagoon. There were no other yachts, no guests.

Largely restored, we sailed on to Gizo, the Solomons' second town. Here, just as at Santa Ana, we were adopted, this time by Lawrie Wickham. He was the owner of the bar that doubled as an informal yacht club: the PT109. The name of the bar is an echo of one of the most famous episodes in Solomons history.

One dark night in August 1943 a young American naval lieutenant had been on patrol with his Motor Torpedo Boat, the PT109, in nearby Blackett Strait. He was rammed by a Japanese destroyer running at full speed and with no lights – the so-called Tokyo Express that resupplied isolated Japanese outposts every night, from Rabaul. Lt John F Kennedy, whose back had been injured in the ramming, led the surviving crew on a four-hour swim to Plum Pudding Island at the entrance to Gizo harbour. It was several days – and more swims – before Kennedy was able to alert coast-watchers and orchestrate a rescue. He was awarded medals for his bravery. The rest, as they say, is history.

Once or twice a day in the anchorage, in lieu of traders offering us snake beans or papayas, there'd be a young man with a clear plastic folder, brandishing a much-fingered typewritten letter and offering it for sale. It would be a 'thank you' letter to the bearer's grandfather or some other relative, personally signed. The letter would be dated plausibly – 1944 – but the juxtaposition of the date with the imposing letterhead (The White House) was less convincing, not to speak of the shaky signature.

Lawrie – a member of Parliament – was sorry to hear about our trials in the Marovo lagoon. And he didn't seem surprised when we added that half of the other 12 yachts at anchor here in Gizo had experienced something similar in the Solomons.

'That's too bad,' he sighed. 'That's more yachts than we've had here for years. I'd been hoping that with The Tension now behind us, tourism might start to pick up again. Looks like we've still got some work to do. Just a moment, though…'

And he fumbled under the bar counter. 'Here. Try this.'

It was a large black can of Mortein, an Australian-made insecticide.

'Good at about 2 metres,' he went on. 'I always keep one handy. Works wonders. The bad guy'll be left staggering around unable to see for at least two hours, which should be enough for the cops to pick him up…'

Trading in the Marovo Lagoon

IF YOU GO…

For entry formalities, weather and references see Chapter 30, pages 198 and 199.

GETTING THERE

The island lies within well-protected waters, but navigation is intricate, best conducted under power and, in the absence of useful charts, using Google Maps/Earth. There are a few channel markers. Zipola Habu lodge is served by launch from Noro or Munda.

DISTANCES

Gizo to Lola Island, 26 miles; Lola Island to Honiara, 255 miles.

ANCHORAGE

GPS 08°18'.383S 157°09'.817E, depth 11 metres.

Trading for a carving, Marovo Lagoon

CHARTS

SLB 302, Solomon Islands – Choiseul Island to New Georgia Island; SLB 103, Solomon Islands – Plans in the New Georgia Group.

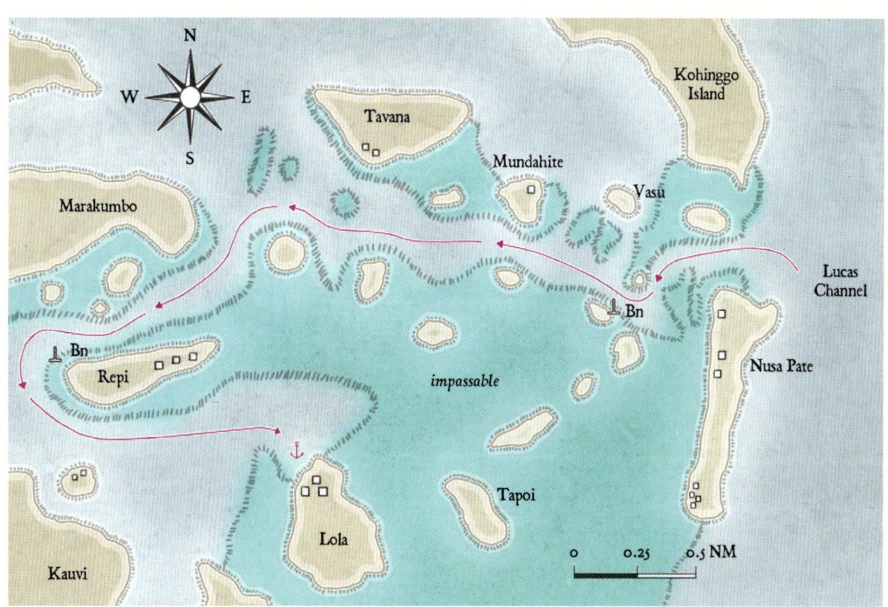

DETAIL: LOLA ISLAND, VONAVONA LAGOON

MIDDLE PERCY ISLAND, QUEENSLAND

AUSTRALIA

Hunkered down in 1987 for the cyclone season with 20 other foreign cruising yachts on the Brisbane River, it sometimes seemed we were living scenes from *Neighbours*, the legendary Australian TV soap opera that was just then taking off.

The English couple on one boat, tied to a pair of pilings just upstream, had been married at 16, built their own boat, then sailed off into the sunset with Skipper the cat. But now, a few thousand miles on, the husband had run off with his mother-in-law, who was pregnant and living in Canberra, the wife had taken up with a single-hander elsewhere on the moorings, the cat was about to be put down and the boat was up for sale.

More serious and shockingly, a young woman called Lillian, described callously in the *Brisbane Courier Mail* as 'a heroin addict and prostitute', disappeared from a blue and white ketch called the *Maria Elena*, and was later found drowned, her body washed up by the Customs House. The police found reason to deem her death suspicious (the Customs House was upstream from the *Maria Elena*) and closely interrogated the men on board with whom she had been seen. But no arrest was ever made.

Meanwhile there'd been a drug raid on another boat. The police had found nothing, but her captain had since then

Tied up on pilings at the Botanical Gardens, Brisbane

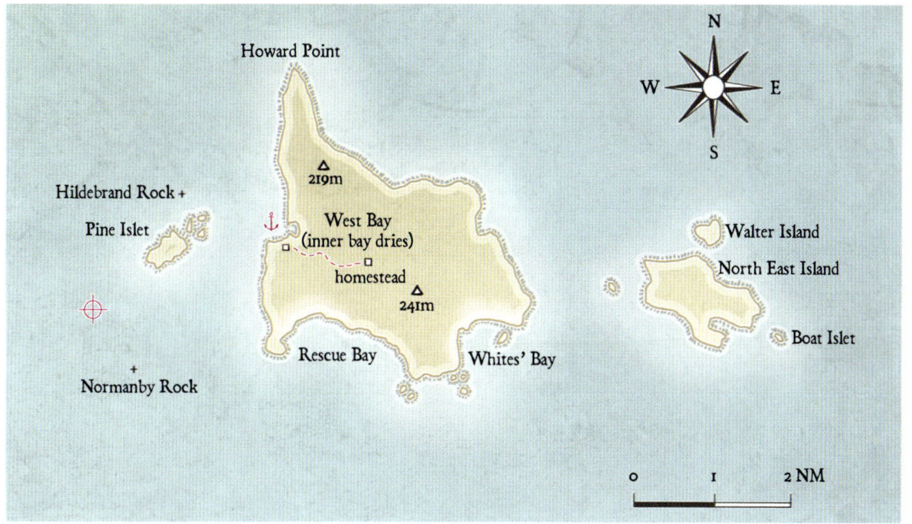

Middle Percy Island, Queensland, Australia
21° 40' S 150° 12' E

been eyeing everyone aggressively, trying to decide who had fingered him. Also pending was the matter of the young Japanese couple who had called in at Brisbane en route to the start of the Melbourne–Osaka ocean race. Coming back to their boat on their first evening in Australia, they'd followed a trail of fresh blood to their dinghy and found it awash in the stuff, smeared with handprints. Police divers had found a brand-new bicycle in the water below the dock; it now looked as though the couple might not make it to the start line in time.

Intriguing as these unfinished stories were, we were happy – once the seasonal threat of cyclones had passed – to head downriver under the Story Bridge and turn north up the coast of Queensland. After a short and rough spell of open water, we were soon inside the protection of the Great Barrier Reef and at the start of what we'd later see as the best thousand miles of our sailing careers.

Every day the wind was from astern, at a perfect 10–20 knots; the seas were never higher than a metre, the water warm and the sunshine unfailing. Every night there was a choice of anchorage, usually behind one of the high islands that form a chain between the reef and the mainland. Only in the Whitsunday Islands – a popular place for chartering – did we see more than the occasional other yacht. The sole downside was those ocean-living critters that gloomy Australians like to warn you about and that give you second thoughts about swimming: box jellyfish, stonefish and (in the north) saltwater crocodiles.

An early favourite anchorage on our progress north was Middle Percy Island, one of a larger group off Mackay that was first described and named by Captain Cook as he sailed this way in 1770.

A Canadian family called the Whites had bought the lease of Middle Percy in the 1920s, then sold it in 1964 to Englishman Andrew Martin. The Whites had built a homestead on top of the island and had welcomed the few yachts that passed their way, installing a telephone line in a shed so that cruisers could call up the hill to alert them. Andy continued this

In the shed on the beach, Middle Percy

tradition, adding an A-frame structure by the beach where he sold produce.

The shed and A-frame today were now crammed with nameplates left by hundreds of yachts. We were thrilled to find a triangular zinc plate daubed with red paint and the legend: '*Trekka. 27/7/58*'. John Guzzwell, a hero of ours, had built his 20-foot yawl in a rented shack behind a fish and chip shop in Victoria (British Columbia) and we'd seen it in Victoria's Maritime Museum. No boat that small had ever circumnavigated at that time, and his book – *Trekka Round the World*[14] – was a perennial bestseller in sailing circles. Here too was a plaque left by Eric and Susan Hiscock a year or two before; like *Trekka*, *Wanderer III* and the exploits of her crew inspired cruisers all over the world during the 1970s and 80s.

We dialled Andy on the phone and, at his invitation, trudged up the hill. Every so often were little signs: 'Tired yet?' or 'Not far now!' Andy was gardening in his purple underpants but invited us into his ramshackle home to sample what he called his Rocket Juice. It was potent; twice as we sat in the cool, bottles exploded in the cellar below with loud pops. Pinned to the walls were a few curling black-and-white photographs. They were intriguing. One was of Andy's schoolmates at Eton; another showed him with team members, competing in the Modern Pentathlon at the 1948 Olympic Games in London. The Rocket Juice prompted a number of related and interesting stories, but their details inexplicably remain hazy to me.

The deal was – as it had been with the Whites – that in return for a few drinks, you helped out on the farm. So (with headaches) we set off in Andy's 1950s Land Rover, which he started by holding two wires together, and worked on bush clearance. We didn't really get that much done. Andy introduced us to two of his friends who had interrupted us: a pet wallaby who came up and nuzzled our knees in turn, and an emu who, Andy said, was always getting into trouble chasing female yachties down on the beach.

---

14 Guzzwell, John. *Trekka Round the World*. London, UK: Adlard Coles, 1963.

As we sailed on next day, we could see the blur of Mackay on the mainland coast, in the distance. We often thought of the old Etonian on his island hilltop, but I didn't have cause to think of Mackay again until 30 years later. We were in the habit in the 1980s of occasionally dropping messages overboard in bottles. An entry in our log, made a few months before our visit to Middle Percy and just after we had departed Fiji, bound for Australia, reads: *'The wind moderated to force 4 from the East; we averaged slightly over 4 knots. At 20° 41' South, 174° 01' East, the captain put a message in the Chivas Regal bottle…'*

We were disappointed but not surprised when we never heard back from these sporadic message-drops. Over the years, as it dawned on us that the ocean already had enough debris floating around, we ended the practice. But whenever we spent an hour or two wandering along some windward beach, I always kept an eye open for the glint of a glass bottle and – hopefully – a piece of paper inside.

Then in 2018 came an email from Cathy in Australia. By the miracle of Google she had traced the former owners of *Tarka the Otter* and had an interesting tale to tell. While Cathy had been helping her 106-year-old grandmother Eileen move into an assisted-living facility, Eileen had pulled out an old scrapbook and told her the story of how one day – 4 September 1987, to be precise – she had been walking along McEwan's beach, near Mackay, and had found a glass bottle with a message inside it.

In under a year, our long-forgotten Chivas Regal had drifted 1,650 miles, washing over or dodging countless reefs around New Caledonia, and even

surmounting the Great Barrier Reef. The message was soggy and barely legible. Eileen could make out the name of its senders and the sailing vessel but the contact details were not readable. Eileen had tried in vain to find us, going so far as to write to 'The Canadian Sailing Yacht *Tarka*, Canada', but (unsurprisingly) the letter had been returned to her.

We wrote back immediately; Eileen was just as thrilled as we were. A little later, Cathy emailed to tell us that her grandmother had died in April 2019, just a few weeks short of her 107th birthday. She added: 'I am so pleased I was able to make contact with you all late last year and (Eileen) was able to enjoy the knowledge that her efforts from all those years ago had eventually paid off. I couldn't wipe the smile from her face when she read your messages.'

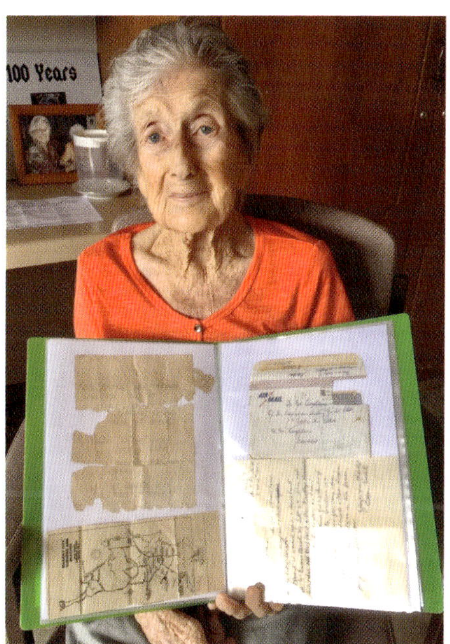

Eileen and the remains of our Message in a Bottle (2018)

IF YOU GO…

ENTRY FORMALITIES

New Zealand passport holders are granted a visa upon arrival in Australia, but all other nationalities must apply in advance. If you know you will need to stay for more than three months, seek a Visitor Visa/Subclass 600, which allows up to a 12-month stay. See **https://immi.homeaffairs.gov.au/visas/ getting-a-visa/visa-listing**

Yachts are required to give notice of their arrival at least 96 hours in advance. Full details should be sent to **yachtreport@ homeaffairs.gov.au**; fax +61 2 6275 5078; tel +61 2 6246 1325. Ports of entry in Queensland are Brisbane, Bundaberg, Cairns, Gladstone, Mackay, Southport (Gold Coast), Thursday Island, Townsville and Weipa. No landing may be made prior to clearance; there is aerial vigilance, notably in northern Queensland. On arrival you will be asked to fill in a Small Craft Arrival Report and an Incoming Passenger Card.

You can expect rigorous biosecurity checks, including an inspection of ships' stores. Boats with extensive woodwork will be inspected for weevils; an extra charge is incurred for the inspectors' time. Vessels with a pet must remain at a mid-water mooring and keep the animal secure on board for the duration of their stay in Australia. Pets may only be imported/permitted to land under strict (and costly) conditions: **www. agriculture.gov.au/biosecurity-trade/cats-dogs**. Firearms must be declared and will have to be handed over, to be delivered back to you at your port of departure.

Once you have entered, a Control Permit (ie a cruising permit) is issued to the captain of the vessel. Control Permits may be issued for a period of 12 months or the length of the captain's visa, whichever is less. Extensions may be granted on application, to a maximum of three years (after which the vessel must be imported).

Requirements are summarised on the web page of the Australian Border Force (ABF) at **www.abf.gov.au/entering-and-leaving-australia/entering-and-leaving-by-sea/ yachts-and-pleasure-craft**.

DISTANCES

Manly (Brisbane) to Middle Percy, 460 miles; Middle Percy to Cairns, 437 miles; Middle Percy to Cooktown, 573 miles.

GETTING THERE

The passage north from Brisbane to Cape York involves an initial 190 miles in open water, after which the Great Barrier Reef offers protection; this is a brisk downwind sail all the way in winter. On the mainland, it is now possible to drive all the way to Cape York, but much of the road north of Cairns is unpaved and impassable in the rainy season.

WEATHER

On average, four tropical cyclones per year strike Queensland. The entire coastline – including Brisbane – is vulnerable, but many yachts nevertheless choose to spend the season on the Brisbane River. Mangroves near Cairns are a popular refuge when a cyclone is forecast in north Queensland and evacuation of city marinas is mandated. For a map showing historic cyclone tracks, see **www. ausstormscience.com/tropical-cyclones/ historic-tropical-cyclones/**. The cyclone season normally runs from November to April; the south-east trade winds become established in May.

ANCHORAGE

West Bay, GPS 21°39'.1265S 150°14'.6089E,
depth 8 metres; can be rolly.

GENERAL

Andy Martin left Middle Percy in 1996,
suffering from schizophrenia; he died in
Mackay in 2003. Following years of legal
wrangling, most of the island is now a National
Park. Andy's cousin Cate Radclyffe holds a
lease of 50 hectares, including the homestead
and land extending down to the anchorage at
West Bay; yachts remain welcome.

CHART

Aus 823, Percy Isles to Mackay.

REFERENCE

Lucas, Alan. *Cruising the Coral Coast (10th
edn)*. Gosford, Australia: Alan Lucas Cruising
Guides, 2019.

On Great Keppel Island

LIZARD ISLAND, QUEENSLAND

AUSTRALIA

Andy Martin (see Chapter 33) was only one of dozens of people who had over the years come to the sunny islands off Queensland to find their utopia. On Dunk Island is a memorial to writer Edmund Banfield (1852–1923). It is engraved with an epigram from Thoreau:

> *If a man does not keep pace with his companions, perhaps it us because he hears a different drummer. Let him step to the music which he hears.*

Banfield and his deaf wife Bertha came to Dunk in 1897, Edmund having been diagnosed – as Robert Louis Stevenson had been – with terminal tuberculosis. With the help of an Aboriginal Australian called Tom, they built a homestead and lived a solitary life, sustaining themselves by the fruit trees and vegetables they planted, with a few goats and cows for milk and meat. Edmund had sufficient leisure and education to study and record (Thoreau-like) the natural history of the island: *Confessions of a Beachcomber*[15] was his first and remains his most well-known book. Elegiac in tone, it is notable for its sympathetic retelling of Aboriginal Australian myths and discussion of questions such as the meaning of Aboriginal message sticks.

Starting in the 1950s Dunk became a high-end resort and was graced by

15 Banfield, Edmund. *Confessions of a Beachcomber*. London, UK: Unwin, 1908.

Cooktown, Queensland

luminaries including Sean Connery and Henry Ford II. A large part of the island was still an exclusive resort today, and we were informed it was off-limits to us; we doubted The Beachcomber would have approved.

North of Cairns we sailed into emptier waters. But place names on the chart – Cape Tribulation, Hope Islets – reminded us of earlier navigators. Here James Cook, taking HMS *Endeavour* around the world, suffered the second-greatest setback of his entire naval career.[16] A sounding taken in the bows just before 11 at night on 11 June 1770, had indicated a depth of 17 fathoms. But as Cook records in his blunt and eccentrically capitalised style:

16 The greatest was, of course, his murder in Hawaii in February 1779…

Watson's Bay, Lizard Island

*…before the Man at the lead could
heave another cast the Ship Struck
and stuck fast.*

They had hit a reef at a bad time, just before high tide. Officers and men worked frantically all night to lighten ship:

*We throw'd over board our guns Iron
and stone ballast Casks, Hoops staves
oil jars, decay'd stores.*

The ship had sustained heavy damage, but the men hauled her off what is now known as Endeavour Reef and – with 4 feet of water in the hold, the ship taking on 15 inches every hour – sailed her very slowly and carefully into the mouth of a large river on the mainland. Here they were able to beach the vessel safely and undertake repairs.

We came into Cooktown, where the *Endeavour* had been careened, after one our fastest sails ever – 62 miles in ten hours – then spent a further two hours edging up and down the sandbank-encumbered Endeavour River, looking for a place to anchor where we wouldn't obstruct the large prawn-fishing boats that were coming in and out. On shore, we explored the museum – which has an anchor rescued from the reef – and signed the Yachties' Register. Just as at Middle Percy, there were names that had echoes for us, including *Jacaranda*, aboard which John Fox had given us our first offshore experience a few years earlier.

Cooktown had a certain faded grandeur. There were many stately late 19th-century buildings, recalling the town's past as a supply centre for a gold rush at the Palmer Goldfields. The amount of money that the miners had to spend also accounted for the number of 'hotels' (Aussie-speak for pubs) that still lined the main street. Parked outside one we saw a battered VW camper. Inside, a stereotypically hippie-looking man called Billy and his kaftan-wearing partner Julie were nursing a pair of Fosters tinnies, looking disconsolate.

'Hey man!' Billy called, brightening up visibly. 'C'mon over!'

Billy spoke in an accent and with vocabulary that tried to sound American but remained touchingly Australian; Julie made no such effort and seemed amused as Billy tried to keep it up. We exchanged stories. They were headed in their van to the Daintree ('or at least as far as we can'). This expanse of tropical jungle in Cooktown's hinterland was seen as Australia's last frontier; it was now home

Anna running wing-on-wing astern of us, off the Queensland coast

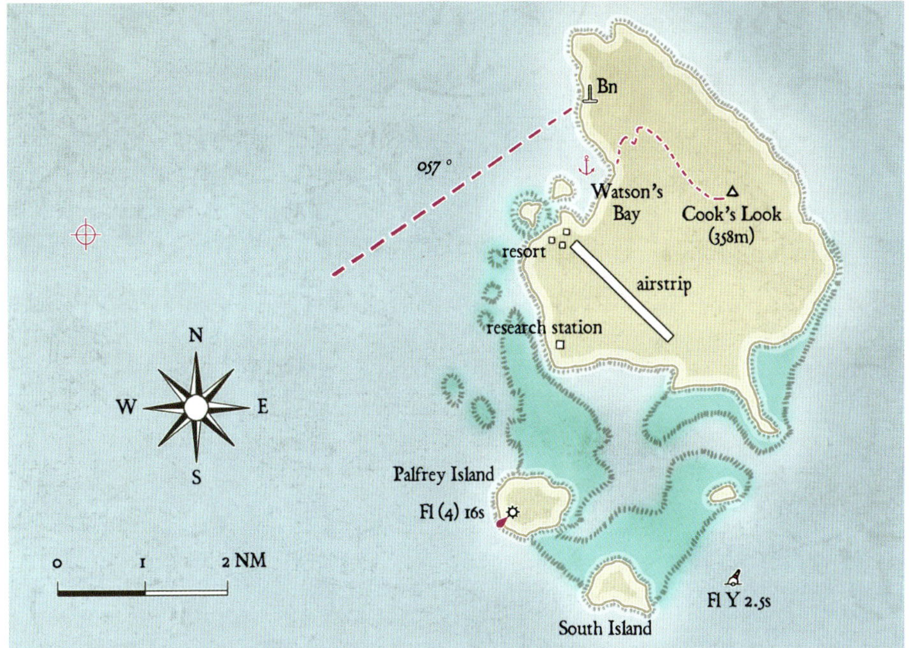

Lizard Island, Queensland, Australia
⊕ 14° 40' S 145° 24' E

to dozens of hippie communes. They'd brought their two young children along – 'Hey f*ck, Jules, where are they, anyway?' – but their main preoccupation right now was the radiator of their VW's engine. The track from Cooktown into the rainforest was notoriously muddy and littered with abandoned vehicles. 'Bummer,' was the glum reaction when I said that although we knew something about diesels, ours was sea-water-cooled. So we wouldn't be able to help them out on their last leg. Then a resigned, 'Another frostie, mate?'

High above Cooktown by the lighthouse, we watched a sailboat running into the river mouth. It was one we'd seen once or twice before: Dutch-registered *Anna*, with Wim and Karin aboard. Painted grey and yellow and made of steel, she was – like *Trekka* – just 20 feet in length, the only boat smaller than ours that we'd seen in months. As a rule, we don't like to

'buddy boat'. Agreeing to sail in company means one or the other of you is always having to slow down or speed up for the other's sake, you feel you have to go to the same places, and sometimes you make decisions that you wouldn't have if you were sailing alone. We never set up anything with *Anna*, but it turned out over the next few months that we sailed at similar speeds, were equally conservative and shared the same idea of what was the ideal anchorage. So, more by accident than design, we found ourselves in their company on and off all the way up the Cape York peninsula and across the Indian Ocean to Durban.

Wim and Karin's story was of a maritime Romeo and Juliet, recounted to us over cockpit drinks when we found ourselves as the only yachts at Lizard Island, near the outer reef and two days on from Cooktown. Karin, Swedish and tanned with short blonde hair, had been crewing on her parents' much larger boat when Wim, taller, a little older and then single-handing, asked for her help in transiting the Panama Canal. Since then, she'd never left *Anna*. Her parents weren't comfortable with the situation and were still out there on their own boat. Every so often a letter would catch up with Karin (this was before email), imploring her to come 'home'. Wim, of course, was not cast favourably in these letters. We tried to stay above the fray – we were earnestly consulted for our opinions – but what was clear was that the two of them were very happy together.

Together we explored Lizard from the anchorage in Watson's Bay. High up on a hill was a rock called Cook's Look, where we were able to tell Wim and Karin about Cook's disaster and its sequel. The story is that with the *Endeavour* ship-shape again, her captain decided it would be better to sail clear of the reef system into open water. Lizard – which has the highest land for many miles, at 360 metres – was the spot he chose for a reconnaissance. The visibility was hazy that day, but he concluded that: '…there appear'd to be several breaks or Partitions' in the outer reef.

The *Endeavour* broke out a couple of days later. In the meantime, Cook had noted 'Lizards, and these seemed to be Pretty plenty', and given the island the name it now bears. You can see the pass he used to escape (it is marked 'Cook's Passage' on the nautical chart) and there are many of those reptiles still around, hissing quietly to warn you of their presence. Known properly as yellow-spotted monitors, they are not small – we saw several over a metre in length – but they behaved to us timidly.

Behind our anchorage at Watson's Bay was a welcome freshwater shower, and we poked around a ruined stone hut on the beach. This had associations at odds with the tranquillity of this place. In 1879 Captain Robert Watson, a harvester of Bêche de Mer for the Chinese market, set up home here with his wife Mary, two Chinese servants and their baby son Ferrier. He was away one day when a group of Aboriginal Australian men arrived from the mainland and killed one of the servants, Ah Leung. Although they then withdrew, Mrs Watson was fearful of another attack. With the baby and the other servant she fled the island in an iron tub used for boiling up the sea slugs.

The tub drifted not to the mainland, but downwind to Howick Island. There was no water here; all three died nine days later. Mrs Watson's diary survived, and she became a national heroine, the patron saint of European women pioneers. A public drinking fountain in Cooktown now commemorates her, with the inscription:

> *Five Fearful Days Beneath*
> *The Scorching Glare*
> *Her Babe She Nursed*
> *God Knows The Pangs That*
> *Woman Had to Bear,*
> *Whose Last Sad Entry Showed*
> *A Mother's Care,*
> *Then – 'Near Dead With Thirst.'*

The immediate consequence of the tragedy was one all-too-familiar to us from Canadian pioneer history. Mounted police and native troopers shot 150 Aboriginal men in retaliation, none of whom – it was later surmised – had been involved in the killing on Lizard.

IF YOU GO...

For entry formalities, getting there, weather and references see Chapter 32, pages 210 and 211.

DISTANCES

Manly (Brisbane) to Lizard Island, 1,090 miles; Cooktown to Lizard Island, 57 miles; Lizard Island to Mt Adolphus Island (Cape York), 355 miles.

ANCHORAGES

Watson's Bay, GPS 14°39'.579S 145°27'.040E, depth 8 metres; anchoring is only permitted in the north-east part of the bay; see the National Parks map (link below) for limits. Cooktown, GPS 15°27'.703S 145°14'.937E, depth 4 metres.

GENERAL

Most of Lizard Island is a National Park; see **www.parks.des.qld.gov.au/parks/lizard-island/about**. There is a research station, a small luxury hotel and an airstrip; there is no scheduled transport service from the mainland. No supplies are available; the bar at the hotel may occasionally be open to non-guests.

CHARTS

Aus 832, Cape Flattery to Barrow Point. For Cooktown, see Aus 270, Plans in Queensland, Sheet 2 (now withdrawn; no replacement announced).

View west over Watson's Bay and the resort

POSSESSION ISLAND, ENDEAVOUR STRAIT, QUEENSLAND

AUSTRALIA

Day after day, we'd be up at sunrise as we ran north inside the Barrier Reef. Often the wind was so steady from the south and the anchorages clear in the downwind direction, that we'd sail the anchor out then set the main and jib for a dead run. *Anna* might be half an hour ahead, or an hour behind.

When I look at the charts today, I recall that we tried to stay out of the marked shipping channel. There was a steady flow of ore freighters (and a few smelly sheep carriers), bound for Asia and the Gulf. But it meant we had to be on our toes navigationally. Every 4 or 5 miles, I see the sets of pencilled lines running from marked reefs to starboard or to headlands

Anna and Tarka anchored in the lee of Cape Melville

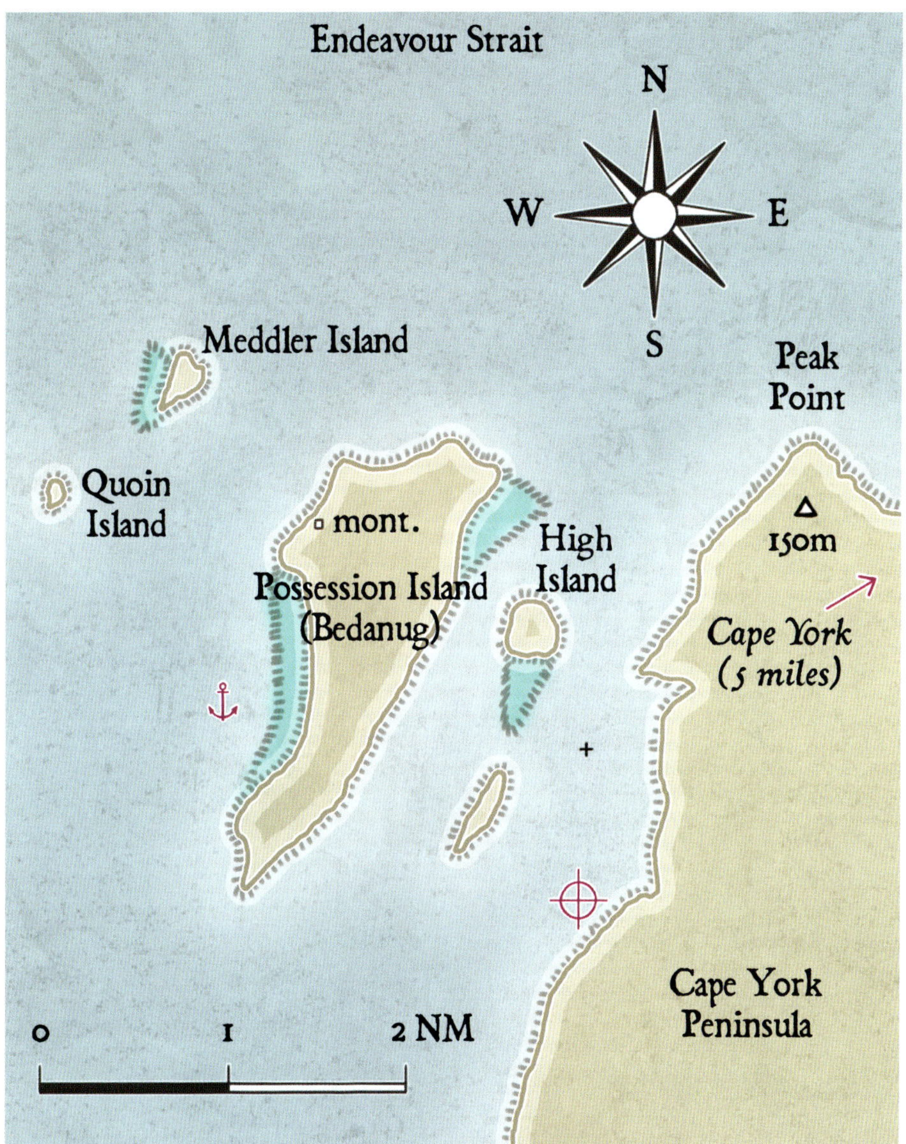

Possession Island, Queensland, Australia
10° 45′ S 142° 25′ E

to port as we constantly recalculated our position with running fixes. GPS will have made things easier these days, but not entirely so. Those reefs that squeeze in tightly from the starboard side remain imperfectly charted and many are so low that they won't show up on radar.

Our first day out of Lizard, we are buzzed by the Coastwatch aircraft. They don't try to speak to us, but from now on we'll see them every two or three days. One day, they make repeated low passes and I wave back. Months later, we write – on the off-chance – to the federal police in Canberra and they send us a colour photograph of *Tarka* taken that day. The first night, we anchor in the lee of tiny, low Coquet Island. The halyards clank noisily all night: as in many anchorages along this coast, we have good shelter from the seas but little from the unceasing wind. There's an air of gloom here, enhanced by the fact that just a mile over our stern is Howick Island, where Mrs Watson and her companions died.

We anchor early one afternoon behind Cape Melville. It's a beautiful but wild spot. We're reminded of how exposed we are when we find the 'Mont.' marked on the chart, behind a wide expanse of beach. A white marble stone commemorates pearl fishers lost in a 'dreadful hurricane' on 3 March 1899: Cyclone Mahina. Eleven men are named along with their vessels. Then, if you kneel down, you see '…and over 300 coloured men drowned'. Walking back, we cross emu tracks on the beach and find a brown booby perched tranquilly on our boom, apparently awaiting our return.

Next day, we pull into Owen Channel, in the Flinders Group. This anchorage has more protection, and we find a moored barge that supplies the prawn fishing fleet. Jenny rows over to pick up a couple of cardboard casks of Australian red, and we venture ashore again. Carved into the face of a sandstone boulder in letters 40 centimetres high is the legend 'HMS Dart – 1899' and a survey mark. Starting in 1883, *Dart* spent nearly 20 years undertaking hydrographic work in the western Pacific. The mark doubles as an indicator of a waterhole, of which

A visitor (brown booby), off the Cape York peninsula

we take advantage to fill our tanks. In a meadow behind the well, we find some graves marked with whitewashed sticks. The men on the barge think there was a military camp here in the First World War but, they say, those could just as well be Aboriginal Australian graves.

The navigable channel between the reef and the mainland starts to narrow now. On the VHF, we talk to *Pacific Trader*, coming up close behind us, to make sure they've seen us. In a moment of freak radio reception, we pick up a 'Man Overboard' Mayday call, from Weipa, which is 220 kilometres away (as

the crow flies) and over the other side
of the Cape York peninsula. At Hannah
and Night islands, there are three or four
prawn fishers at anchor when we come
in, but they leave soon after dark. Usually,
it's just *Anna* and ourselves.

At Night Island, I run my finger
over the next day's route. To the north-
east of us is Bligh Reef and, just below
it, Bligh Boat Entrance. Following the
infamous mutiny aboard HMS *Bounty*,
Captain William Bligh was cast adrift
near Tonga on 28 April 1789, along with
18 crew members loyal to him. He knew
the nearest settlement where he might
find Europeans was at Kupang on the
island of Timor (Indonesia), 3,500 miles
away: a grim prospect. Eking out their
rations, the men passed first through
the uncharted reef-strewn waters of the
Fiji group but – fearful of rumours of
cannibalism – dared not land. A month
on, the Great Barrier Reef was sighted.
Bligh spied a gap, and they sailed
through it into relatively calm waters. The
same afternoon, 20 miles to the north-
west, they landed at a small island just off
the mainland, where the men found fresh
water, oysters and berries.

Bligh made it safely to Kupang and
his voyage is regarded as one of the
greatest small boat voyages of all time.
He still had some explaining to do,
though. His first letter from Kupang
to his wife goes straight to the point:
'Know then, my own Dear Betsey, I have
lost the *Bounty*…'

On to Margaret Bay, then Bushy
Islet, which rises barely 50 centimetres
above high water and has only three or
four bonsai-like mangroves to justify the
name. From Bushy, we once more sail
our anchor out in silence, hoping not to
wake *Anna*, but by the time we have our
mainsail boomed out there she is, her
sails silhouetted dramatically against the
rising sun.

Every day we are running at 6, even
7 knots, setting up a rooster tail behind
the white fibreglass paddle of our self-
steering gear. Our Walker Log – a steel
and black plastic impeller towed on a
10-metre line behind us – is also zipping
through the water, leaving a trail of
bubbles… until it isn't. Noticing that the
dial on the Log has not advanced in an
hour, we pull the rotor in to find its short
steel leader has been bitten right through,
presumably by a shark.

We reach the latitude of Cape York
on midwinter's day – 21 June – and sail
into Blackwood Bay, on the lee side of
Mount Adolphus Island. The wind is in
the east. Over our stern to the west as we
lie at anchor we have, for the first time
in many months, not the continent but
open water. Beyond the horizon is the
Arafura Sea, the Timor Sea… and then
the Indian Ocean.

Cape York is not spectacular. There
is a squat white structure on top of
tiny Eborac Island that we can hardly
see in the dim light of dawn as we
coast by 3 miles offshore. The surface

Leaving Bushy Islet with Anna, at sunrise

Termite mound, Possession Island

of the sea is strangely turbulent: the Admiralty chart – 'Adolphus Channel to Harvey Rocks' – shows that the current runs at 3 knots here. Once we're past, we're on to a new chart, one we've been anticipating for months: 'Endeavour Strait – East'. I scan it quickly. It's sobering that there is no sounding above 10 fathoms for 20 miles all around, and there are huge patches of pale blue (under 5 fathoms). We pass a small, white-painted rectangular monument on shore and anchor just to the west of Possession Island.

We spend two quiet days at Possession. There is a mile of white sandy beach to explore, strange red termite hills inland and everywhere the shallow ocean seems more than usually blue. There are animal tracks on shore: might this be a wallaby with a trailing tail, or perhaps another monitor lizard waddling along?

Cook landed here on 22 August 1770, and – looking west – soon sensed the importance of the moment:

We could see no land, so that we were in great hopes that we had at last found a passage into the Indian Seas.

He hoisted the 'English Coulers' (again that spelling…) on the hill and claimed in the name of His Majesty King George the Third the whole east coast of Australia (while graciously ceding the already-explored west coast to 'the Dutch Navigators').

We walk to the monument. Oddly, it's just a whitewashed cement block, with no inscription or plaque. Later, reading up, we deduce it's been vandalised. Even back in the 1980s there are plenty of people who (understandably) aren't happy about Cook's claim. Not least the proud but historically abused Torres Strait Islanders, whose home is just over the northern horizon on Thursday Island.

We can't say we're particularly disappointed the plaque is gone. For we're just as happy to be here as Cook must have been.

IF YOU GO…

For entry formalities, getting there, weather and references see Chapter 32, pages 210 and 211.

DISTANCES

Manly (Brisbane) to Possession Island, 1,463 miles; Thursday Island to Possession Island, 14 miles; Possession Island to Nhulunbuy (Gove), 363 miles.

ANCHORAGE

Possession Island, GPS 10°43'.8559S 142°23'.1845E, depth 8 metres. Expect surveillance (maritime and/or aerial) from Thursday Island.

GENERAL

The island, which is uninhabited, is central to the Possession Island National Park. In 2001, the territorial rights of the Kaurareg people to this and other nearby islands were recognised; the aboriginal name is Bedanug.

CHARTS

Aus 292, Wyborn Reef to Twin Island; Aus 294, Endeavour Strait.

At Possession Island

PART III

INDIAN OCEAN AND AFRICA

CHRISTMAS ISLAND

AUSTRALIA

Sailing west across the Gulf of Carpentaria at a good clip and 100 miles offshore, we were surprised to see a big, waterlogged tree trunk in the water ahead of us, rolling with the chop. Then it seemed to see us, flicked its tail and dived. It was a 6-metre saltwater crocodile.

Later, over beers at the Gove Yacht Club, on the west side of the Gulf, the talk was all of 'salties'. A story was told in all earnestness of a crocodile climbing up the sugar-scoop transom of a local yacht, and into the cockpit. But we had a feeling that the influence of the Yacht Club's main sponsor – 'Victoria Bitter: for a Hard-Earned Thirst' – was in play.

The Yacht Club was really a drinking club for workers at the bauxite mine. Conveyors by the side of the red-dust roads rumbled day and night, bringing ore to the silos at the port; occasionally a massive earth-moving truck, its wheels taller than a man, came past. We were in Arnhem Land, a vast expanse of mangroves and low jungle, where 70 per

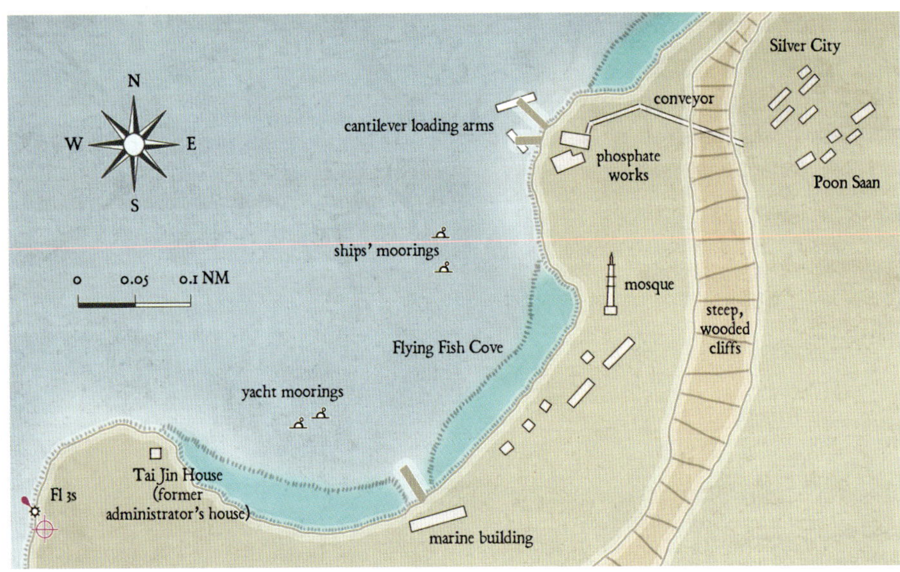

CHRISTMAS ISLAND, AUSTRALIA
10° 25'.8 S 105° 39'.7 E

Flying Fish Cove

cent of the population are Aboriginal or Torres Strait Islander people. But the workers at the mine and the shopkeepers at the company town were all white. The town was properly known as Nhulunbuy; at the Yacht Club they hadn't yet got around to using the Aboriginal Australian name.

We moved on. Day after day for 16 days, we had runs of 100 miles or more. Entertainment was sparse: Australian Rules Football commentary or Indonesian chat shows in Bahasa Indonesia on the radio. There were no more crocs, but most days we'd find a few flying fish on deck, dolphins rode with us for hours on end. We saw a pair of Vietnamese fishing boats one day: we were happy they made no move towards us, as there'd been rumours of pirate activities in these waters.

Flying Fish Cove, the only tenable anchorage on Christmas Island and the site of the small settlement, is not everything you might hope for in a cove. It's a bay entirely open to the north and west, and there's almost always sufficient swell to make landing a challenge. Two enormous khaki-coloured cantilevered arms reach far out over the water: the swell is so persistent that ships cannot tie up, and these are necessary for the loading of freighters that call in regularly. They come to take on phosphate, which is derived from the deep layers of guano that have been deposited here over millennia by seabirds, and which has been mined since 1899.

There were three other yachts in. They watched us with politely concealed concern as we meandered around looking for a space to anchor: the bottom here is coral and while there was a good lee from the prevailing easterlies, the swell meant everyone was wandering about

Previous pages: Sailing past Table Bay, Cape Town, South Africa

Loading phosphate, Flying Fish Cove

unpredictably. Once securely moored, we twice dumped the inflatable in heavy surf while trying to land at the rocky beach. We chickened out and used the jetty where large ship-tending barges are taken in and out.

There were no yachts permanently based here – cyclones make Flying Fish Cove untenable for half the year – but the Christmas Island Boat Club prospered as a watering hole. A key to the bar circulated among whoever was visiting at the time, or you could get one from Stubbie, the club secretary. The routine was to help yourself and leave cash in a tin on the counter. Or you could take a ten-minute walk into Poon Saan (Cantonese for 'Halfway up the Hill'), where there was an arcade of little Chinese stalls and shops (ginseng, ceramic cats, noodles) that were open when their owners clocked off from their jobs at the mine.

The phosphate excavations were originally undertaken with indentured labour from the British colony of Malaya (including Singapore) and China. Asian people still made up most of the population on Christmas, living quite separate lives from the white civil servants and mine executives from mainland Australia. We made friends with a Nepali called Sam who, with his Gurkha background, was able to bridge the two worlds.

'The Aussies and the others… they don't mix at all,' he explained. 'Each community goes its own way, even though there's no rules like there used to be.'

Sam took us one night to one of the Australian 'messes'. These are direct descendants of colonial-era chummeries: informal clubs where single men gather in the evening to eat, drink, play snooker and – these days – watch DVDs. The Chinese people had their own clubs, the Malays too.

The tacit truce between the races hadn't always held. Out beyond Tai Jin, the old administrator's mansion, was a naval gun of the Second World War vintage. It was once fired in anger when a Japanese submarine surfaced in the Cove, but there is a grimmer story than that. In March 1942 the garrison, which was made up largely of Indian troops sympathetic to nationalist leaders at home, mutinied. A British officer and four NCOs were executed here, the rest of the Europeans locked up. The Indians handed the island over to the Japanese when they landed at the end of the month.

It takes a lot of birds to make all the guano on Christmas. We spent long days walking along the clifftops, where noddies, boobies, tropicbirds and frigatebirds roost in huge, noisy numbers. Inland we were lucky enough to spot a couple of endemic Abbott's boobies. This endangered species nests in high treetops, but there are fewer and fewer tall trees as the mining operations (which literally peel away the surface of the island) encroach on the last big stands.

Down in the anchorage, it was our turn to be nonchalantly vigilant when another boat came in: *Salty Dog*, made of rust-streaked steel and registered in Darwin. The captain dropped his anchor randomly and quickly – or so it seemed to us – and was then seen rowing ashore with two crew.

'Hmm,' said Jenny, scrutinising the boat through our binoculars. 'I don't think much of that anchoring technique. And he's flying his Australian ensign from the spreaders, not the stern, where anyone knows it should be. Fishy, I'd say. Stolen, maybe?'

I didn't give *Salty Dog*'s flag etiquette a second thought. But that evening, as we sat with skipper, crew and everybody else in the Boat Club bar, I went out on the porch to tend the barbecue. There was a clearer view of the bay here than from inside. *Salty Dog* was unmistakeably drifting on to the beach, her anchor rode slack, likely chafed through. I raised the alarm. Within ten minutes, half the population of the island was down at the jetty. Advice flew in four languages; the harbourmaster was summoned. *Salty Dog*'s captain dived in fully clothed, clambered aboard his vessel with difficulty and immediately started

Brown booby & chick

West across the Gulf of Carpentaria

the engine. But he let a line become entangled in the propeller, the engine stalled and soon the boat was bouncing on the bottom.

By now it was getting dark. Floodlights were switched on and, under the direction of the harbourmaster, a barge was lowered. Thanks to its 1,000hp engine, *Salty Dog* was unceremoniously dragged seawards and attached to a ship-sized buoy, taking with it a few pieces of the jetty with which its rigging had become entangled. The captain shouted his thanks, saying he'd come ashore in the morning to settle any costs due from the rescue. The rest of us – including *Salty Dog*'s two crew – retired once more to the bar to recover from the excitement. The lights went off.

Rowing back to *Tarka* late that night, we assumed *Salty Dog* had re-anchored further out; it was no longer on the buoy. But next morning when we came ashore, there were the crew, still in the Boat Club where they'd spent the entire night.

'The bastard!' said one of them, and he gestured seawards, where there was no sign of *Salty Dog* at all. 'He's just effed off, hasn't he! He's got our money, our clothes, everything.'

Eventually, the two disconsolate young men headed into town, to find the harbourmaster and explain, and to beg for the $400 each that it would cost them to fly back to the mainland.

'See, I was right,' Jenny said after we'd wished them luck. 'I knew there was something funny about that boat.'

The effect of phosphate mining

IF YOU GO…

ENTRY FORMALITIES

If arriving at either Christmas or Cocos Keeling from outside Australia, see text following Chapter 32. For immigration purposes yachts travelling to either island from the Australian mainland are deemed to have not left Australia if their arrival at the islands is within 30 days of departure from the continent (the same applies if travelling in the reverse direction). Persons on board must ensure that their visa covers the period of their stay as well as travel time between the mainland and the islands. Department of Home Affairs and Department of Agriculture clearances are still required on both arrival and departure at/from both islands.

In advance of arrival at Christmas, call Port Control on VHF Ch 16 for mooring instructions; four or more mooring buoys are now available (fees apply); anchoring is not normally allowed. For regulations regarding movement within Flying Fish Cove, see **www.christmas.net.au/christmas-island-welcomes-the-return-of-yachts/**.

For Cocos, call Cocos Police on VHF Ch 20 when 12 miles out; there is surveillance. Anchor at Direction Island; do not land; call police again and they will likely send a single person from West Island to complete all formalities. There is a harbour fee of Aus$10 daily/Aus$50 per week. For further details see **https://cocoskeelingislands.com.au/travel-info/sailing-to-cocos/**.

GETTING THERE

Under sail, both islands are best approached from points to the east. Virgin Australia flies twice weekly to both Christmas and Cocos from Perth; sometimes

Flying fish on deck

there is direct service between Christmas and Jakarta (Altitude Airways).

WEATHER

Both islands are affected by cyclones two to three times a year; the peak season is November to April. From May to October the south-east trade winds prevail, blowing strongest from July to October. In the rainy period, especially from January to March, the wind – cyclones excepted – is weaker and more variable, often out of the north-west. Although shelter from moderate westerlies and/or northerlies can be found at Cocos, there is no such protection at Christmas.

DISTANCES

Nhulunbuy to Christmas, 1,937 miles; Darwin to Christmas, 1,480 miles; Perth to Christmas, 1,400 miles; Christmas to Cocos Keeling, 540 miles.

ANCHORAGE

Select a mooring buoy as directed by the harbourmaster at approximately GPS 10°25′.70S, 105°40′.08E. Harbourmaster office, showers and washrooms are all at the Marine Building at the head of the jetty.

GENERAL

Population 1,700. Basic supplies are available. The island is increasingly popular as a dive site; visitors also come to see the annual migration of red crabs (beginning of the wet season). For an overview, see **www.christmas.net.au**. Phosphate mining continues, but the current lease ends in 2034 and operations are scaling down. A detention centre for asylum seekers was built in 2001; it closed in 2018 but reopened as a quarantine facility at the beginning of the Covid-19 pandemic.

CHARTS

Aus 920, Plans in Christmas Island; Aus 608, Christmas Island.

REFERENCES

(1) Heikell, Rod. *Indian Ocean Cruising Guide: A Yachtsman's Handbook for the Red Sea, Indian Ocean and Southeast Asia (2nd edn)*. St Ives, UK: Imray, Laurie, Norie and Wilson, 2007.

(2) Lucas, Alan. *Red Sea & Indian Ocean Cruising Guide*. St Ives, UK: Imray, Laurie, Norie and Wilson, 1985. Both volumes may be difficult to obtain, except second-hand.

Yachts at anchor, Flying Fish Cove

COCOS KEELING ATOLL

AUSTRALIA

Sailing south-west from Christmas Island, I'd been reading Dougal Robertson's inspirational *Survive the Savage Sea*[17], and was feeling inadequate. Robertson, his crew and family – six people in all – spent 38 days adrift in their life raft and dinghy, after losing their schooner *Lucette* when it was holed by a pod of orcas. They'd survived above all by fishing.

We were two years out from Canada and we'd caught hardly anything; in fact we'd given up, finding it more profitable to obtain our fish by trading. But now, having lost two expensive trailing logs to sharks, we figured the fish must be biting, and we really ought to learn this basic survival technique. So we read up on lures, depth and speed and – zipping along at 5 knots – tossed a line over. Within half an hour we were feeling elated: we had a 5-kilogram tuna flapping around on a hook in the cockpit, snapping at our bare toes. I whacked

17 Robertson, Dougal. *Survive the Savage Sea*. London, UK: Elek, 1973.

Direction Island (Cocos Keeling) from five miles away

it repeatedly with the winch handle, spattering blood everywhere, and that night we ate as much as we could. On we sailed, confident now that our tested skills would allow us to survive any orca attack or worse.

With the log out of action, we were having to estimate our speed by looking over the side; sun sights allowed us a more-or-less accurate confirmation of our position only once a day, each late afternoon. Then, four days out and using our small hand-held radio direction finder, we were able to find the null of the morse signal from the Cocos Keeling airstrip (ie the bearing at which the signal faded). This gave us a critical line of position as a complement to our sun sights. Next day, Direction Island – on the rim of the atoll – hove into view on schedule.

On hand in the cockpit, we had the grey-and-blue Admiralty Chart 2510 ('Approaches to Cocos or Keeling Islands') with, in the top right-hand corner, an evocative notation: '*Surveyed by Capt. Robert Fitzroy RN, 1836*'.

When the *Beagle* arrived here on 1 April 1836, it had only been 11 years since a Scottish sea captain called John Clunies-Ross had landed at the then-uninhabited atoll, raised the Union Jack and left again, intending to come back and settle later. But a Mr Hare – whom Darwin describes as 'a worthless character' – now arrived with similar intentions and a harem of 40 Malay women. When Clunies-Ross returned

with his own wife, mother-in-law and eight pioneer sailors, a state of war set in between the rivals. Hare's wives steadily deserted him in favour of the sailors and bit by bit his territory shrank until he was on a tiny fragment still known as Prison Island. Once all the women had forsaken him for the sailors, Hare gave up and fled to Sumatra.

Clunies-Ross imported indentured Malays to harvest copra on the largest of the islands, and – while the British, then the Australian flags flew – he and his descendants ran the atoll as a quasi-independent feudal kingdom. For many years workers were paid in Clunies-Ross's own scrip, the Cocos rupee, which could only be redeemed at the company store. The Australian government grew increasingly uncomfortable with this and ordered a referendum on governance in 1984, to be supervised by the UN. John Clunies-Ross campaigned for independence, but nearly all 261 islanders voted for full integration with Australia. The atoll, along with Christmas, is now administered from Canberra as part of the Australian Indian Ocean Territories.

Joshua Slocum called in here aboard the *Spray* in 1897, and later wrote: 'if there is a paradise on this earth it is Keeling.' Idyllic it is. Palm-covered Direction Island gave us a perfect lee from the strong trade winds; there was a dazzling white sand beach on the inner side to explore, miles of rugged outer coastline for beachcombing; and some of the world's clearest diving in

the lagoon. This is the jumping-off point for the crossing of the Indian Ocean, a rendezvous whether you are headed north-west for Suez or south-west to the Cape of Good Hope, so there was also a good assortment of cruisers in the anchorage.

First, we caught up with Wim and Karin aboard *Anna*. They were anxious to buttonhole us, explaining to us that *Thor*, with Lars and Françoise, had just come in too. The *Thors* were friends of Karin's parents and were in radio contact with them; Karin was sure they would try to persuade her to leave Wim and fly home or continue with *Thor* instead; we were enlisted as moral support. Meanwhile *Moonlight* was an Australian boat we hadn't met before. They beckoned us over the first evening at cocktail time. Standing up to board from our dinghy, I realised that Pete and Janice were both stark naked.

'Hop in. We go clothes-free here – hope you're OK with that…'

I hesitated, blushed and looked down at Jenny. She just grimaced back at me silently. I mumbled something apologetic and we backed off.

There were two more Aussie boats rafted up to each other, each with a couple on board, each with two teenage boys. I won't repeat their real names but will call the adults Bob and Carol, Ted and Alice. They were all good company and we spent hours chatting or exploring the beaches. One day the teenagers rowed around the anchorage to announce that in the evening there would be hermit crab races on the beach: we were each to find a crab in its shell, on which they'd mark a number, and to show up at six. The trick, we belatedly realised, was to adopt your crab well before the race and accustom it to being in your hand, moving around. The boys knew this, but ours simply stayed in their shells and only emerged once the shouting was over.

The Clunies-Ross family and their employees – known as Cocos Malays – all lived on Home Island, a mile south of Direction, on the eastern rim of the atoll. We'd occasionally see their lateen-rigged wooden fishing boats scudding across the lagoon. The word was that the current political situation (lingering tension between the family and the local community) meant that visitors to the village weren't welcome, but we could instead go shopping on West Island, on the far side of the lagoon.

Well, it wasn't really shopping. The arrangement was that you placed a food order – fresh veggies and all – by VHF radio with the sole shop. The order would then be transmitted to Perth, 1,580 miles away. Someone at the airline office would go to the supermarket, your order would be boxed up and it would come in on the once-a-week flight – with no freight charge. We clubbed together to pay for the launch that would take us through the intricate channel to West Island and made a day of it. As well as the shop, there was the radio station to visit

Yachts at anchor in the lee of Direction Island, Cocos Keeling

On shore at Direction Island

('VKW – Voice of the Cocos Islands'), the airport terminal ('Cocos Island – Altitude 10 feet'), and the golf course: nine holes up one side of the runway, and nine back the other side. The shopkeeper also directed us to some well-tended grave markers: they commemorate the crews of flying boats that were based here in the Second World War and who were lost in action.

On the windward beach of Direction Island, we were particularly interested by a cluster of decaying brick structures and pieces of thick, rusting cable. Right up until the 1970s, a trans-oceanic cable surfaced and then re-entered the sea here: our Victoria-based sailing hero John Guzzwell mentions the warm reception he was given by the Cable and Wireless staff in 1958. In 1915 the relay station came to the attention of the German surface raider, SMS *Emden* (sistership of the *Dresden*). They sent a party ashore to destroy the installations, but the staff managed to alert Australia. HMAS *Sydney* was immediately despatched and surprised the *Emden*,

which was ill-advisedly loitering in the vicinity. This was Australia's first ever naval victory. The remains of the *Emden* could still be seen on North Keeling, and her anchor was on display at the West Island post office.

Day by day, in dribs and drabs, the yachts at anchor dispersed. It seemed to blow unrelentingly hard. We'd set the date: 20 August. We were as ready as we'd ever be. I was nervous; we knew that the Indian Ocean would be our roughest sailing yet. Everyone honked their horns or beat on their saucepans as we motored out and hoisted the main.

The fishing? Well, we fished all the way round the rest of the world. We caught one more fish; and that was when we were already in sight of Victoria. And why the coyness over the real names of Bob and Carol, Ted and Alice? We saw them again. In fact, we tied up right behind them in Durban, South Africa. But it was the oddest thing. We had to go back to our logbook to check. Now it was definitely Bob and Alice, Ted and Carol.

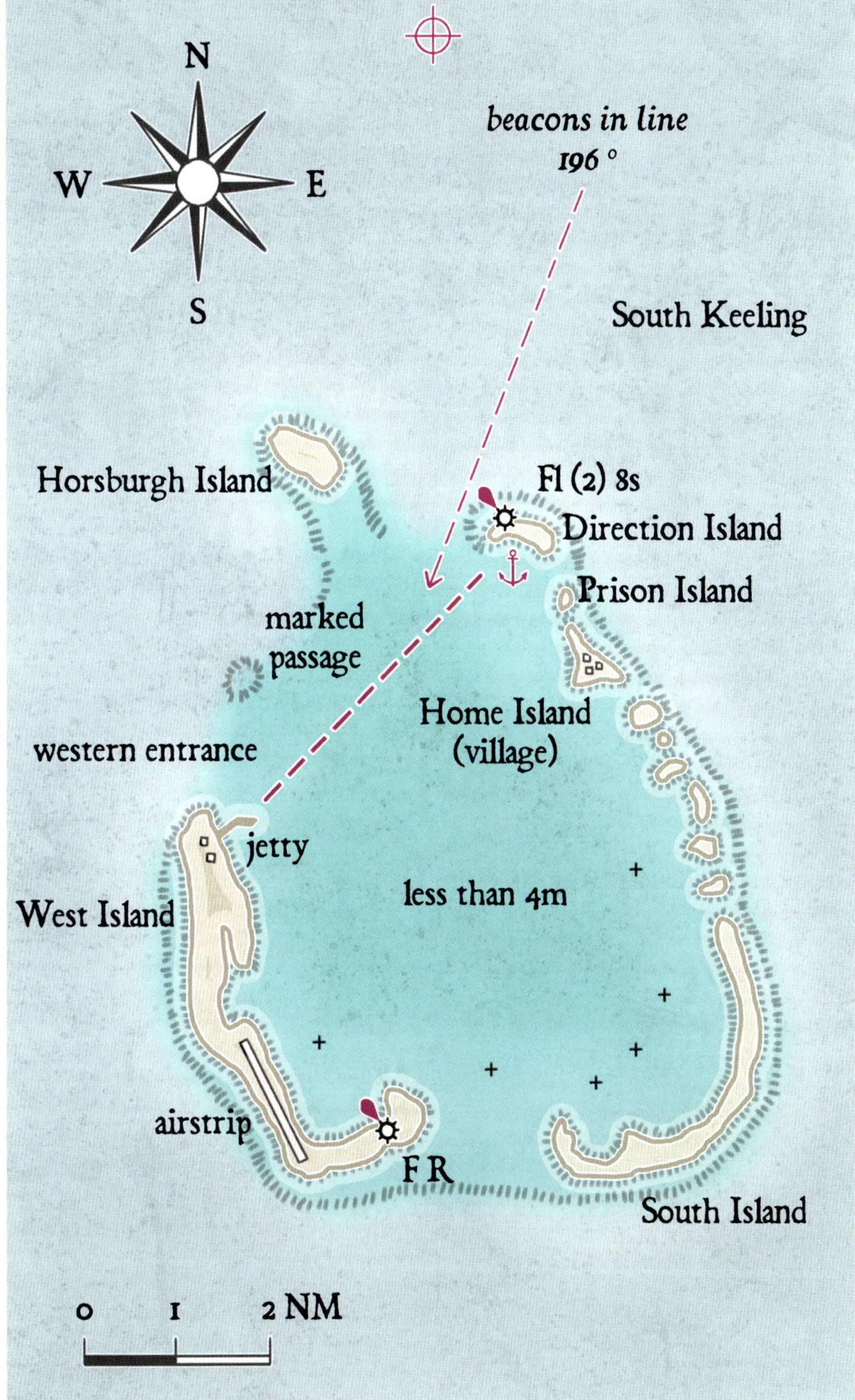

Cocos Keeling Atoll, Australia
12° S 96° 52' E

IF YOU GO...

If arriving at Christmas or Cocos Keeling from outside Australia see Chapter 32, page 210 for formalities. For getting to Cocos Keeling, formalities specific to Cocos Keeling, weather and references, see Chapter 35, pages 231 and 232.

DISTANCES

Perth to Cocos Keeling, 1,580 miles; Christmas Island to Cocos Keeling, 540 miles; Cocos Keeling to Rodrigues, 2,010 miles; Cocos Keeling to Chagos archipelago, 1,520 miles.

ANCHORAGE

Direction Island. If instructed, moor first to the yellow quarantine buoy, otherwise GPS 12°05'.4727S 96°52'.992E, depth 6 metres. For details of permitted anchorage areas and navigation rules within the atoll, see **https://www.transport.wa.gov.au/mediaFiles/marine/MAC_G_Boating_CocosIsland.pdf**

GENERAL

Population 600. The atoll is known as Cocos, Keeling or (more popularly) Cocos Keeling. Enter Port Refuge (west of Direction Island), on a range; night entry is inadvisable. Rain-caught fresh water is usually available on Direction Island. For other supplies (including fuel) make arrangements on West Island. There is a marked channel across the atoll to West Island but the jetty is exposed. With advance permission it may be possible to anchor off Home Island (location of the Malay village; some small shops); dress conservatively in the village. There is a ferry between the three main islands. Superb diving throughout; there is a dive shop on West Island.

CHARTS

Aus 606, Approaches to Cocos (Keeling) Islands; Aus 607, Cocos (Keeling) Islands, South Keeling. These charts may not be fully GPS-aligned.

The golf course, West Island (the length of the airport runway)

RODRIGUES ISLAND

MAURITIUS

Out cruising, there comes a point when things have been going so well, for so long, that a sense of doom starts to creep up on you: you are sure that an out-of-season cyclone will materialise, you'll hit a semi-submerged container and hole the boat, or you will start showing all the symptoms of acute appendicitis. It's just not possible that your luck will hold.

It happened west of Cocos Keeling.

The first few days were as windy as we'd feared: an unrelenting force 6 or 7 that had us constantly fretting whether we needed to take in another reef or change down the headsail. Our Navik windvane was coping well. But all the same, we set our course so as to tack downwind and hopefully avoid a damaging accidental gybe. Then suddenly, one morning, it wasn't coping at all. From below, I sensed we had changed course. A glance out through the companionway confirmed this: the light fibreglass vane was flopped over all the way, no longer aligned with the wind, and the gear was making no attempt to put us back on course. With one foot on the tiller to avoid a gybe, I peered over the transom. There was just a stainless-steel stub trailing in the water, the white paddle completely gone, presumably the result of a failed weld.

When you're daysailing, hand-steering for a few hours is no hardship. In fact, trimming the sails and feeling the tiller respond to your grip is half the fun. It's a different story day after day, 24 hours a day. With just one spare hand to hold plate and spoon, even eating can be tricky, not to speak of attending to calls of nature. So out came Eric Hiscock and his *Cruising Under Sail.* From diagrams, we began to figure out a way to make *Tarka* self-steer without our constant attention. The key component would be a short length of something strong but elastic: the surgical tubing we had on board for trading to spear-gun fishermen served admirably. We still needed to weave a cat's cradle of lines back and forth across the cockpit, but after a few hours we had an arrangement that required only the odd corrective nudge. It served us through our halfway-around-the-world celebration and the remaining 1,700 miles to Rodrigues.

We could only find two written accounts of sailboats having visited this remote island, which is a dependency of the larger and much more populous Mauritius. Nearly all our companions at Cocos Keeling had been bound not for South Africa and the Cape of Good Hope, but the Red Sea and the

Mediterranean. The first account was by Joshua Slocum in 1897. He had happened to come into Port Mathurin, the capital, shortly after the local Abbé had preached a sermon warning of the coming of the Antichrist. The population assembled en masse to watch the *Spray* approach, running fast before a gale, and cried out: 'May the Lord help us, it is he, and he is come in a boat!'

Twenty-six years later Harry Pidgeon, aboard his 34-foot yawl *Islander*, called in. Much of his description of Rodrigues is taken up with a bizarre story of one Thomas, 'who was subject to mental derangement' and stole the undeveloped rolls of photographs Pidgeon had taken on the earlier stages of his circumnavigation. Thomas apologised, saying he had mistaken the visitor for a German, handed them back 'and then demonstrated his affection…with a kiss'. The one useful piece of information that we were able to glean from both accounts was that there was a narrow, reef-strewn entrance and that there was little space to swing at anchor. Our chart was dated 1874, 'Surveyed by Officers of HMS *Shearwater*' and our Admiralty Pilot was apparently of the same era, noting that 'the huts of the natives may be observed on shore'.

Our welcoming crowd wasn't as large as Slocum's. But there were a hundred or more people on the dockside in greeting as we edged in, and a man in a blue uniform waved at us imperiously, indicating we should tie up, not anchor. It was clear that we were the biggest thing to happen in at least a week. For the first few days of our stay we were the only vessel in port. Never, even at dead of night, were there less than half a dozen onlookers on the wall, studying and commenting on our every movement:

'Il lit un livre!'
'Elle fait la cuisine!'

The population was 90 per cent Black people, descended from African enslaved people, plus a few persons of Indian descent (from Mauritius) and the usual handful of Chinese storekeepers. The cost of living seemed very cheap, so we ate out regularly at either of Port Mathurin's two restaurants, the *Restaurant du Port* (friendly but downwind from a public urinal) and the *Snack Victoria*. At the *Victoria*, the owner went through a nightly ritual of asking us what we would like, before eventually stating there was only 'min' available (Chinese noodles laced with chilli). The theme of conversations with the enthusiastic locals who had followed us up from the port was usually on the lines of 'Rodrigues bon, Maurice mal', with hammed-up renditions of the dozens of sly pickpockets we would need to dodge when we went on to the Big Island.

One night we were handed a little brochure, proclaiming: '*Sans Henri, vous n'êtes pas à Rodrigues! Henri est très connu à*

Rodrigues! So we engaged Henri for a tour of the island. We walked together to the government offices, where we obtained an impressive document permitting us to visit the famous Caverne Patate. It was signed: 'Your obedient servant, MP Prudence' and a postscript read: 'You are kindly reminded that you may not take away any produce of the caves.'

Then we set off in Henri's Land Rover, ending up in the middle of a field. Two young Black boys were sitting on a dry-stone wall, apparently expecting us. Henri stripped down to his underwear and prepared our torches: sacks soaked in kerosene and wrapped over the end of sticks. As we went into the caverns, the boys silently lit the way, stopping occasionally and gravely indicating outstanding calcite formations. Harry

Pidgeon had been given the same tour. His guide's torches were of burning palm leaves: 'I was concerned lest the palm leaves give out, but my guide had the same idea, and made his exit in time.' Our torches seemed to give off a lot more smoke than light, so we weren't sorry to come out into the light, either. We bounced off again with Henri, leaving the two boys alone again in the field.

The island roads were numerous but in very poor condition. Every so often we'd come across a repair gang, each equipped with a shovel or two, the men gathered around a pile of gravel. Henri explained that if you were unemployed, you must work a certain amount of hours per week for the highways department before you could collect your welfare cheque. We had lunch at a

Traditional sailing boat inside the reef, Rodrigues

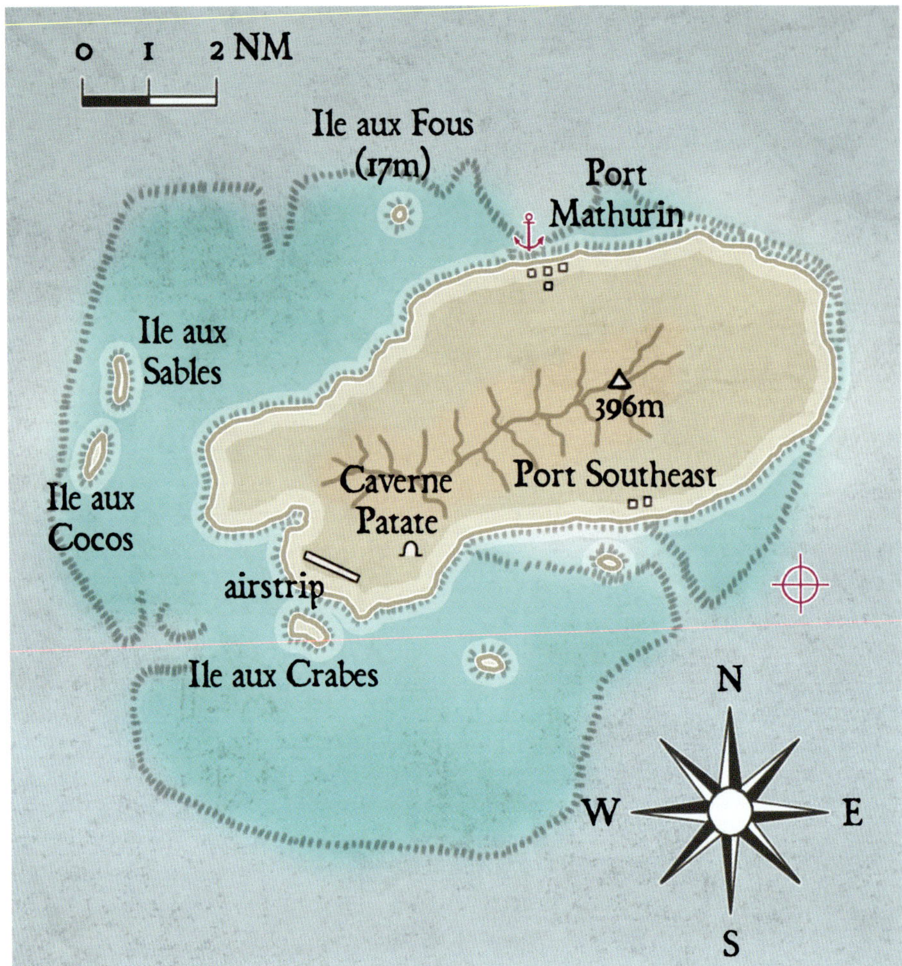

RODRIGUES ISLAND, MAURITIUS
⊕ 19° 45' S 63° 30' E

small square concrete hut with a faded signboard reading: *Restaurant Night Club Mediterranée*. There was a mural inside, with the French Riviera by night and the Anglo-French Concorde taking off. Lunch was goat sausages dipped in liquefied garlic, washed down with a bottled Guinness. We still have Henri's card, pasted in the log:

Henri Meunier
Organisateur de vos excursions
L'homme à tous faire
Plongeur professional

Tous près du Cinéma Métro
Rue Victoria, Port Mathurin

There had just been general elections, and we were invited to a public rally to celebrate the election of the island's two MPs, both from a Rodrigues independence party, the OPR. The rally was held in a large field in the middle of the island, to which everybody could come on foot. There were numerous beer tents, stalls serving samosas and a local band specialising in the local dance: the Sega, rhythmic and highly erotic, with every refrain ending in '*Mon Doudou*' (Creole for 'My Darling'.) As the only white faces here, both MPs made beelines for us, impressing the crowd of onlookers by speaking to us neither in Creole, nor in French but in urbane English. They gave us our cards, but insisted we use their respective first names: Serge and Zita.

For our last call on the island, we took the Boeing Express (an open-sided jalopy) up the hill behind town to meet with Mr B Koonsur of the Meteorological Office. He wrote out by hand a detailed weather forecast for us and was generally most helpful. But as we were leaving, he did shyly suggest we leave him '*un p'tit souv'nir*' for his services. We wonder if he is still wearing his little British Columbia pin, and whether it was what he had in mind.

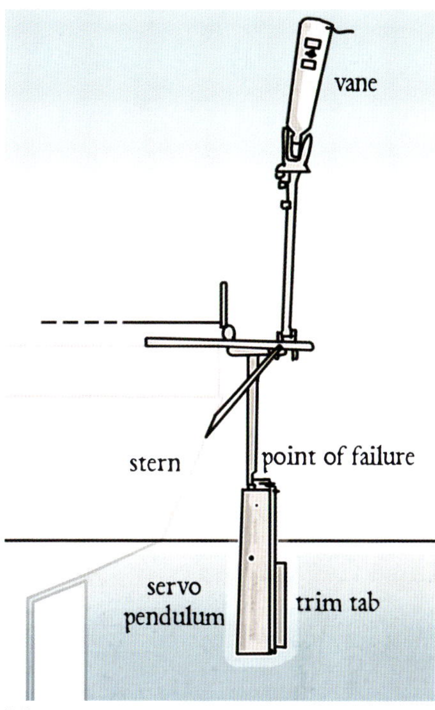

NAVIK SELF-STEERING GEAR

Congratulating ourselves after contriving a self-steering system

IF YOU GO...

ENTRY FORMALITIES

Rodrigues (pron. rod-REEG) is a semi-autonomous dependency of Mauritius; most nationalities are granted leave to enter for 90 days. If proceeding onwards to Mauritius, you must here clear out, then in again at Port Louis.

Call Rodrigues Coastguard on VHF Ch 16 immediately prior to arrival; you will be directed to tie up at the wharf, where formalities will be completed; if the wharf is occupied, there is (restricted) space to anchor off. There is a mandatory fee for quarantine clearance.

GETTING THERE

Approach to Rodrigues under sail from anything but an easterly direction may be hard work; vessels sailing from Diego Garcia/Chagos are advised not to steer a rhumb line, but instead head due south until at least 17°S. There are daily flights to/from Mauritius, and a passenger/cargo ship twice a month between the islands.

DISTANCES

Cocos Keeling to Rodrigues, 2,010 miles; Chagos to Rodrigues, 900 miles; Rodrigues to Port Louis (Mauritius), 395 miles.

WEATHER

Tropical cyclones affect both Mauritius and Rodrigues from November to May. South-east trade winds otherwise predominate and reach their strongest in August and September.

ANCHORAGE

The (blasted-out) approach channel to Port Mathurin has a range and is marked with port and starboard-hand beacons but should not be attempted at night. Tie up at the wharf, GPS 19°40'.8239S 63°25'.2442E, or anchor just off it (restricted space). With permission (and care) Port Southeast offers more secluded, secure mooring.

GENERAL

Population 40,000, largely of African descent, of whom 5,000 live in Port Mathurin. Most people speak Rodriguan Creole, but French and English are widely understood. The island has its own elected Regional Assembly and pride is taken in the Rodriguan identity. Most services are available, but the island is far less developed than Mauritius.

CHARTS

Mauritius Hydrographic Service/INHO 2531 (Rodrigues Island); INHO 2504 (Mathurin Harbour); INHO 2505 (approaches to Mathurin Harbour).

REFERENCES

(1) Heikell, Rod. *Indian Ocean Cruising Guide: A Yachtsman's Handbook for the Red Sea, Indian Ocean and Southeast Asia (2nd edn)*. St Ives, UK: Imray, Laurie, Norie and Wilson, 2007.

(2) Lucas, Alan. *Red Sea & Indian Ocean Cruising Guide*. St Ives, UK: Imray, Laurie, Norie and Wilson, 1985. Both volumes may be difficult to obtain, except second-hand.

KRAALBAAI, LANGEBAAN LAGOON

SOUTH AFRICA

It was 1987 and we were halfway into our circumnavigation aboard *Tarka the Otter*. Our African landfall was fraught. The target was Durban, but for the last several days of the passage from the island of La Réunion, we had no sun sights. We were concerned that the powerful Agulhas Current (which sets south-west at up to 6 knots) could sweep us far past our destination without our knowing it. Our last night at sea it blew hard, rained torrentially and our rigging was lit up in green by St Elmo's Fire (a form of lightning). Tankers and freighters passed across our bows in the blackness every few minutes. In the morning the good news was that we picked up an FM radio station which indicated we must indeed be off Durban. The bad news was that on account of the heavy weather the port was reported closed. The harbourmaster took pity on us and despatched a pilot launch to guide us through the harbour entrance, where standing waves had our hearts in our mouths.

South Africa was then a different country. At Durban's Point Yacht Club, a white member cautioned us not to speak

Sailing southwest from Durban

38

Tied up below the Customs shed, East London

to the Black security staff: 'We don't encourage familiarity.' A few metres away a sign warned: 'This Beach is Reserved for Members of the White Race.' Middle-class white South Africans were invariably hospitable and kind to us, anxious to assure us of their liberal credentials. But they seemed unaware of the artificially high standard of living they enjoyed, with huge estates and many servants.

Local yachting gurus Chris and Libby gave their annual talk to the ten-strong foreign yacht fleet on how to negotiate the tricky section of coastline between Durban and Cape Town. When all the right conditions came together, six weeks on, we ventured out once more. We raced south with the help of the Agulhas but, with a southerly buster due, ducked into East London for Christmas. Outside, it blew 70 knots; inside, the customs shed by which we were tied up collapsed. Fortunately, it fell towards the shore and not on top of us, but we then had to crawl in to find the clearance forms we needed to fill out. On the 26th we went to the beach, where everyone was having a good time and wished us a Merry Christmas. Later, members at the local sailing club were aghast: 'But you've been on the Black beach!'

On the peninsula behind Kraalbaai, Langebaan Lagoon

When the time came to move on from South Africa into the Atlantic, we reflected that sailing the Cape coastline had been an ordeal. There were a few artificial ports that were safe enough, but otherwise we'd been ducking behind headlands waiting for a wind change, at which point we needed to leave immediately or risk a lee shore. The bureaucracy was worse than most places too; you had to formally clear in and out of each port, which meant time wasted that you could ill afford. So, when a local sailor recommended a jumping-off point that had 360-degree protection, warm water for swimming and miles of empty dunes and beaches to roam, it seemed almost too good to be true.

Langebaan Lagoon is located in the southern reaches of the best natural harbour in South Africa: Saldanha Bay, 55 miles north of Cape Town. There's an ugly ore terminal in the north, but by the time you have picked your way south a few miles in shallow turquoise waters, with glaringly white sand beaches on all sides, you're in another world.

At the best anchorage – Kraalbaai – there were half a dozen local yachts on moorings, but not a soul in sight. By mid-morning, the landscape all around shimmered. The whitewashed houses of the two or three small fishing villages that sit on the shoreline seemed to float in the sky. At the head of the lagoon was an incongruous pink line at beach level: two or three hundred flamingos wading in the shallows. Once in a while, momentarily disturbed, they would all take flight and move half a mile in a great rosy cloud. We trekked across the peninsula to the wild Atlantic coast. Small herds of gemsbok watched us from a safe distance, their tan coats difficult to make out against the desert scrub; zebra and ostrich were far easier to see. Down on the beach oystercatchers scuttled about in pairs and an abandoned fur seal pup sat forlornly just above the surf line. Just offshore was the battered wreck of a freighter that had literally been broken in half.

It was in a relaxed mode that we finally checked out from South Africa. The customs official at Saldanha, a 'coloured' (in the South African parlance) man in a well-used boiler suit, was dour but wished us well in a thick Afrikaner accent.

Years later, we were back for a much longer stay in the country, based at Cape Town. Initially boatless, we remedied the situation by buying *Bosun Bird* at

Flamingos, Langebaan Lagoon

Richards Bay, on the east coast. Having already sailed the Cape once, we felt no need to repeat that operation so put the boat on a flatbed truck. For two days, while I returned to my office, Jenny rode in the cab by day and slept aboard at night, crossing the continent at 100 kilometres per hour. We launched again at Veldriff, a little way north of Saldanha, on the Berg River.

Sailing on weekends out of Veldriff for two years, we got to know every nook of St Helena Bay, into which the Berg flows. The weather forecasting was good, but if in doubt we'd check the look of Table Mountain as we set off by car for Veldriff early on a Saturday morning. If the tablecloth was on the mountain – ie there were clouds flowing down the north face – then we were in for a hard south-easterly blow. The bay gave us a lee, but I still recall many anxious nights as we swung at anchor, the line rigid in 40 knots of wind, off Stompneus or Paternoster. You might occasionally hear a penguin moo during lulls in the wind and there'd be the ripe, rich smell of pilchards from the fish-packing plants on land. Every time we made it back to our berth unscathed, we congratulated ourselves. It was no wonder that South Africa consistently produced top-notch sailors: there was always too much wind or none.

When the time came to move on once more, we thought why not make a final visit to Langebaan? It did not disappoint. The wreck off 16-Mile Beach was long gone. But the gemsbok were in the hills, the oystercatchers peep-peeped on the beach and the flamingos still soared in great waves above the shimmering water. It was flat calm at night in the lagoon, but you could hear the surf pounding on the outside,

And the man who'd checked us out last time, 20 years before, was still there. He found *Tarka* in his logbook and gave a slightly surprised grunt of interest before turning to the matter at hand.

'You bought this boat in Richards Bay, South Africa, yiss?'

'That's right, but…'

'And how did you say it got here?'

'We put it on a truck, and…'

'So the boat left South African waters, yiss?'

I could see what was coming.

'It says here, every time a boat leaves South African waters,' and he turned the rule book so I could read for myself. 'You must have the authorisation of both customs and immigration, and the same when you re-enter.'

We cajoled, we pleased, we apologised. Fines were threatened, confiscation even; at one point the word 'prison' may have been mentioned. It was a full hour before we emerged with our clearance. As we rowed back to *Bosun Bird*, Jenny commented: 'Langebaan was great. I don't suppose we'll ever be here again. But just in case we are…'

I finished her thought: 'Yes, we'll make sure it's not that guy's shift when we check out.'

IF YOU GO…

Turning north to round the Cape of Good Hope

ENTRY FORMALITIES

Most nationalities are granted a three-month visa on arrival in South Africa, which may be extended once on application to Home Affairs.

Yachts must register online, at least 96 hours before arrival, with the Ocean Sailing Association of Southern Africa, at **www.osasa.org.za**. Ports of entry are Richards Bay, Durban, East London, Port Elizabeth, Mossel Bay, Cape Town and Saldanha (check to see if Saldanha is currently staffed). There is a registration fee of R400. As a good internet connection is needed, it is advisable to register/pay at your last pre-arrival port. three to four days prior to arrival, again notify **info@osasa.org.za** or WhatsApp +27 72 106 3936. Immediately prior to arrival, call Port Operations on VHF Ch 16. As anchoring opportunities in most ports are limited/non-existent, make prior marina bookings.

For coastal passages, you are required to file an Electronic Flight Plan (EFP) – **www.sailingpe.co.za/coastal-passage-plan**. This has the effect of automatically notifying authorities at the points of departure and arrival, meaning in-person clearance is not needed. For international clearance, an EFP is also required, along with a Letter of Good Standing from all marinas/clubs visited, certifying that you owe no money. Customs and immigration must be visited in person; final clearance is given by the Port Authority.

GETTING THERE

Prevailing winds at all times of year mean that, under sail, Saldanha Bay and Langebaan Lagoon are best approached from the south. Langebaan is a 1.5-hour drive from Cape Town. Navigate the lagoon to Kraalbaai with caution on a rising tide. Favour the west shore; the last part of the channel is buoyed. Depths are nowhere more than 6 metres but the bottom is sand. Google Maps/Earth may be as useful as the chart.

DISTANCES

Saldanha to Kraalbaai, 9 miles; Cape Town to Saldanha, 60 miles.

WEATHER

Southerly winds are dominant all year, frequently 20–30 knots in summer.

ANCHORAGE

Kraalbaai, GPS 33°08'.5285S 18°01'.6574E, depth 2 metres.

GENERAL

The Lagoon is entered off Langebaan village (on the east shore). The National Parks Board has divided the Lagoon into sections: the north is open to all boats, the central to sailing vessels, and the southern section (which largely dries) is closed. There is a yacht club at Langebaan (**www.langebaanyc. co.za**);approach via a buoyed channel), a marina at Club Mykonos (**www.clubmykonos. co.za/facilities-services/marina**) with a boatyard, and another yacht club (with moorings) at Saldanha Bay (**www.sbyc.co.za**). There are now houseboats at Kraalbaai; the beach can be popular at weekends.

CHARTS

SAN 1010 (INT 2671) Approaches to Saldanha Bay; SAN 1011 (INT 2673), Entrance to Saldanha Bay.

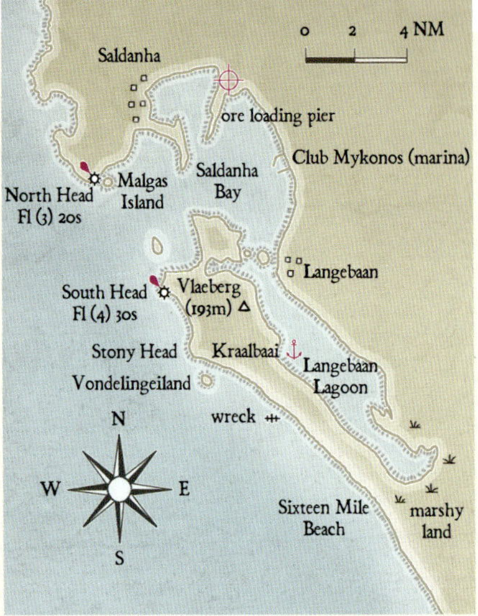

KRAALBAAI, LANGEBAAN LAGOON, SOUTH AFRICA
33° S 18° E

REFERENCES

Royal Cruising Club Pilotage Foundation.
(1) *South Africa to the Caribbean*. Dorset, UK, 2019; free at **https://rccpf.org.uk/pilots/177/ South-Africa-to-the-Caribbean**.
(2) *South West Africa*. Dorset, UK, 2010; free at **https://rccpf.org.uk/Free-Downloads**.

Gemsbok above Kraalbaai

LÜDERITZ

NAMIBIA

Two hundred miles out from South Africa's Saldanha Bay we'd passed the mouth of the Orange River, which marks the border with Namibia. To starboard now was the Skeleton Coast. This is named for the whale and fur seal skeletons that have littered its surf-bound beaches since the days these animals were hunted almost to extinction. But the insistent fog that accompanies the cold Benguela Current makes it a dangerous place for ships as well. More than a thousand wrecks are known, some dating as far back as the late 15th century, when Bartolomeu Dias (Diaz is the anglicised version of his name) and his compatriots were battling their way around the point he called the Cape of Storms.

Late that night, with the boom lightly grazing the surface of the black ocean every time we got into a roll-cycle, I got Jenny up and asked her to call on the VHF. To port was what seemed like a large and very brightly lit oil platform, but it was rocking nearly as much as we were. It showed red and green navigation lights and it seemed to be moving very slowly towards us. Eventually, someone on board responded: they had seen us. But the voice on the radio was curt. The officer would offer no details as to what

he was doing or the nature of his vessel.

Another 200 miles and the wind was up, to a full gale. We were flying our orange storm jib as we ran at six knots in the night. At dawn the panorama was mournful: long, grey foam-flecked rollers with the coast (only 3 or 4 miles away now) obscured by fog. We worried that we'd have to skip Namibia again, just as we had in 1987 when uncertain sun sights and haze had deterred us from a close approach. But over the space of half an hour everything faded away. A watery sun fought through the gloom. Exactly where it was meant to be, the red-and-white Diaz Point light tower emerged. We turned right into the perfect natural harbour of Lüderitz, African penguins honking in greeting.

This was a tenuous-looking place: sharp-edged buildings, some in primary colours, sat among pale brown sand dunes and black rock outcrops; church steeples added a Germanic touch. In the spacious bay, traditional, blue-painted wooden fishing boats lay still on the calm water: *Patience*, *Stormkaap*, *Silver Katonkel*. A handful of flamingos picked their way carefully along one shoreline.

As our anchor chain went down, we noticed that many of the boats had what looked like extra-large plastic hoses –

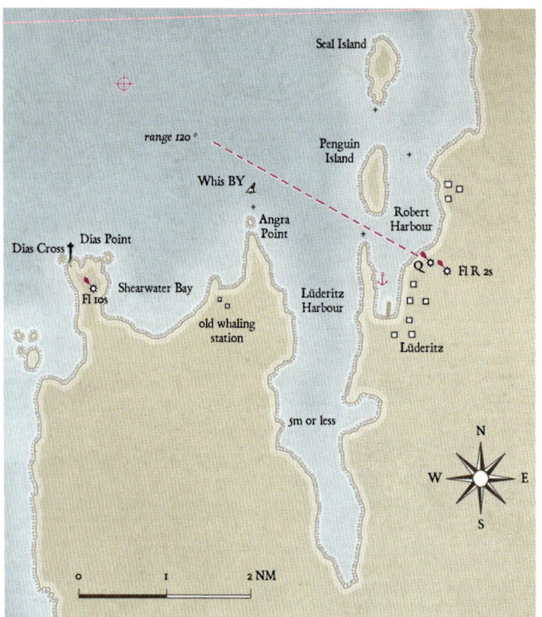

Lüderitz, Namibia
⊕ 26° 36′ S 15° 06′ E

maybe 30 centimetres in diameter, 50 metres in length – snaking out on the water's surface, astern. It dawned that what we had thought was an oil rig was likely larger-scale version of one of these vessels: a dredger. We learned later that they operate at a short distance offshore, and those hoses work like giant vacuum cleaners, sucking up gravel from the ocean floor and sifting it for diamonds. Divers in old-style helmets and lead-soled boots walk on the bottom and guide the hose intakes.

Check-in to Namibia was laid-back. It was a Saturday and a young man hanging around the main wharf advised us to come back on Monday, meanwhile directing us to JJ's Takeaway for the best fish and chips in Lüderitz. This we washed down with German-style beer at the yacht club. The barman was friendly enough, and the club seemed quiet for a weekend. But like many such establishments in southern Africa,

we sensed that this was not a place for the airing of liberal points of view or, indeed, for meeting people of colour. Two men sitting in a corner raised their glasses to us in a toast that was also a clue to their political inclinations: 'Welcome to Southwest!'

It wasn't long before they were telling us about the Good Old Days, the period between 1915 and 1990 when this country was under South African administration and known as Southwest Africa.

'Yah… should been here then, before that bugger Sam got his hands on the place. We're going the way of Zim now, you'll see… they're gonna come after our land, just like Mugabe.'

We doubted that nostalgia for the days of apartheid was widely shared. Nor for the time before when this had been a German colony. European rule was characterised by what many consider the first genocide of the twentieth century: the genocide of the Herero and Nama people. Shark Island (actually a peninsula), which protects the harbour from the west, was the site of a concentration camp in that era.

Lüderitz is at the end of the road, on a 350-kilometre spur off the country's main highway, and is surrounded entirely by desert. For such a remote place, it has a lot of history. First there was Dias himself. Then Bremen merchant Alfred Lüderitz decided money could be made from whaling, sealing and guano deposits, and 'bought' the bay in 1883 from a local Nama chieftain, claiming the hinterland for Germany at the same time. You can still see rusting tanks of an old whaling station at Stormvogel (Shearwater) Bay. The same bay once hosted most of the Russian Grand Fleet,

en route to annihilation at Tsushima in
1905: what a sight that must have been.

And, out in the desert, there's the
ghost town of Kolmannskop.

Namibia's first diamond was found
right here on open ground in 1908. A
few years later, a prosperous German-
looking village had grown up among
the sand dunes, with gabled mansions
for the managers of the diamond field
(which soon became a massive forbidden
area known as the Sperrgebiet),
bunkhouses for the men, a hospital, a
ballroom and theatre.

You can no longer find diamonds at
Kolmannskop just by crawling around on
all fours as they did a hundred years ago:
the active fields are now offshore and
to the south. The town was abandoned
abruptly in 1956 to the dry air and the
shifting dunes. Today, the buildings
are well-preserved but haunting. There
are iron bathtubs full of sand, houses
whose ground floor has been invaded by
the desert. Wooden doors bang in the
ever-present wind, fallen telephone wires
snap like yacht halyards. On a wall in the

Diamond dredger, Lüderitz

working men's quarters is a pin-up style
drawing of a busty blonde, entitled '*Miss
Colman's Kopp*'.

In the Kasino (club), we trod a
creaking stage still set for amateur
theatricals. Downstairs we wandered
alone through a two-lane bowling
alley and a gymnasium equipped with
leather-bound vaulting horses. On the
walls everywhere were black-and-white
photographs of the managerial staff
and of athletic-looking young blonde
men performing in the gym. In the later

Abandoned manager's house at Kolmannskop

Anchored in Menai Creek (Robert Harbour)

photographs – 1914, 1915 – we sensed the distant turmoil of the Great War. A few of the men now wore uniforms; there were patriotic pageants held on the stage; and the formal balls took place under the glaring eye of a double-headed imperial eagle.

We walked out one day to the imposing Diaz Point lighthouse. Nearby was a 3-metre-high black slate replica of the *padrão* – a commemorative marker stone – left by Dias. In search of a sea route to the spice islands, below Africa, he'd rounded this headland on Christmas Day 1487 and entered a complex of bays that he called Angra das Voltas: Bay of Curves. He then left his supply ship here and set off with the two remaining caravels in search of the southern cape that he sensed could not be far off. Heavy sou'easters forced them to sail in a wide arc offshore, and they did not see the headland they named the Cape of Storms (in memory of the hard time they'd had) until they turned around.

In July 1488 the two ships were back here again. The men left behind had had a tough time of it: of the nine crew, only three were still alive and the food supplies had rotted. There was no reliable water source – to this day, the town supply comes by pipeline from hundreds of kilometres inland – and it almost never rained. But Dias' sponsor, King John II of Portugal, was unimpressed by the tales of hardship his navigator told him back in Lisbon. He wanted his traders to be encouraged, not deterred. In an early example of creative rebranding, the Cape of Storms was renamed Good Hope.

Over a final drink at the yacht club, the barman handed us the visitors' book to sign. Flicking to earlier pages, we found old – and braver – friends who'd called in here the year we'd sailed past in a funk (1987): *Malulu* (Australia), *Kaap Bol* (Netherlands), *Pearl* (Canada). There was no such thing as email in those days: sadly, we'd long ago lost contact with them all.

IF YOU GO…

ENTRY FORMALITIES

Most nationalities are granted 90-day visas on arrival in Namibia.

Call Lüderitz Port Control on VHF Channel 16 prior to entering Robert Harbour. You will be directed to an anchorage or mooring on the eastern side of Menai Creek (many yachts report poor holding; a fee may apply if a mooring is taken). Check in (in person) with Port Control (24/7), immigration and customs (west of the yacht club, both open weekdays only). Even if your next port is Walvis Bay, you must formally check out.

In general, yachts find Namibia remarkably relaxed regarding formalities.

GETTING THERE

Prevailing currents and winds mean that approach from the south under sail is easy, but difficult from the north. It is a ten-hour drive or three-hour flight (daily flights) from Windhoek to Lüderitz.

DISTANCES

Cape Town to Lüderitz, 490 miles; Lüderitz to Walvis Bay, 240 miles; Lüderitz to St Helena, 1,365 miles.

WEATHER

From October to March, winds are almost exclusively from the south, reaching their strongest in December and January. Wind speeds are often much higher near Diaz Point than overall. Lüderitz is known as a windy place. Rainfall is very low. The (cold) Benguela Current, which flows north up the coast, means that fog is frequent.

ANCHORAGE

Enter Robert Harbour, then Menai Creek, by a buoyed channel. Anchor east of the channel at GPS 26°38'.4527S 15°09'.4092E, depth 3–4 metres. Land at a long floating dinghy dock in the south-east corner of the bay, or at the shorter one below the yacht club.

GENERAL

Population 20,000. As this is a fishing port, most marine services are available. Hot showers and water are available at the yacht club (which also serves as a bar), for a small fee. Private tour operators will take you to Kolmannskop (permit required) and other locations; car rental is possible. Most visitors find Namibia safer than South Africa.

CHART

SAN 1002 (INT 2631): Approaches to Lüderitz.

REFERENCES

Royal Cruising Club Pilotage Foundation.
(1) *South Africa to the Caribbean*. Dorset, UK, 2019; free at **https://rccpf.org.uk/pilots/177/South-Africa-to-the-Caribbean**.
(2) *South West Africa*. Dorset, UK, 2010; free at **https://rccpf.org.uk/Free-Downloads**.

Remains of the whaling station at Shearwater Bay

ALKWASIR ISLAND, KHARTOUM

SUDAN

When you're living in the middle of the Sahara and the government is an Islamist military dictatorship it can be a challenge to find fun things to do.

The work could be quite interesting. As the sole Canadian diplomat resident in Khartoum (Sudan) I had in 2000 a vicious civil war to report on, that had cost two million lives and had been running for 17 years. And after 9/11 it fell to me to look after journalists who had come to see where Osama bin-Laden had got started. I would show them the chemists' shop where he'd once had an office and we'd go out and meet his ex-cook, who'd tell us how Osama loved Basmati rice and liked to play with small children. For good measure we would throw in a visit to the site of the al-Shifa pharmaceuticals factory that had been destroyed by American cruise missiles in 1998; the custodian would show us a piece of rocket motor on which you could make out the word 'Boeing'.

But the terror-tourism became tedious with repetition. For relaxation there was nothing better than getting out on the river, for Khartoum is located at the junction of the Blue with the White Nile.

Back in the 1920s, when this was a British garrison, it occurred to the colonel of the regiment that a good way of keeping the young officers out of trouble might be to establish a sailing club. The first problem was that there were no boats. Indeed, there was hardly any wood to be had either, the nearest forest being 2,000 kilometres to the south. But there was a large pile of galvanised iron that had had been hauled up laboriously from Cairo in case one of the garrison's old gunboats needed repairs. A reputable yacht designer was commissioned – Morgan Giles – and the result was the Khartoum One Design. This is a steel 18-foot sloop based on a Sharpie, with buoyancy tanks, a retractable centreboard, a Bermuda-rigged mainsail and a jib. Starting in 1932, about 50 were built.

The clubhouse of the Blue Nile Sailing Club (established in 1926) is similarly ironclad: HMS *Melik* ('King' in Arabic). The *Melik* is one of four gunboats that were ferried in pieces past the six cataracts of the Lower Nile. They were reassembled in situ as British forces approached Khartoum

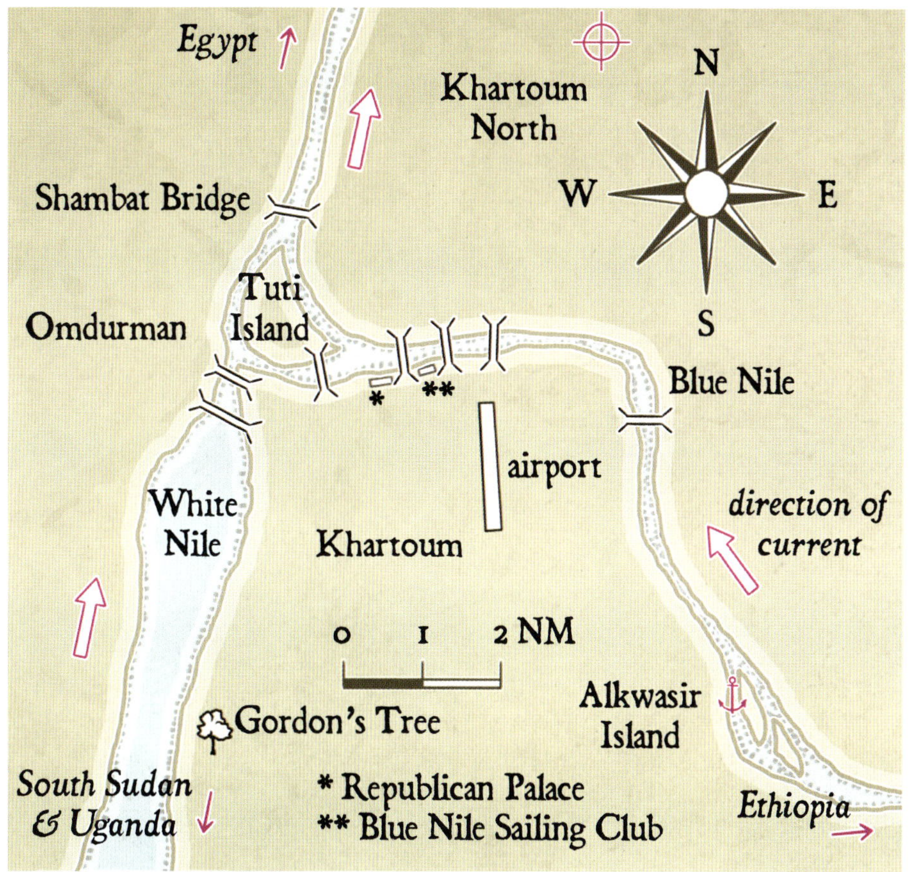

ALKWASIR ISLAND, KHARTOUM, SUDAN
⊕ 15° 40' N 32° 34' E

in 1898, seeking revenge for the earlier killing in the capital of General Charles Gordon by the messianic figure known as the Mahdi. The *Melik* played a part in the Battle of Omdurman, where its deck-mounted machine gun was used to devastating effect, inspiring Hillaire Belloc's short poem:

> *Whatever happens,*
> *We have got*
> *The Maxim Gun*
> *And they have not*

The Khartoum One Design fleet would race twice a week in winter just before sunset, then there would be a longer race on Friday mornings (the Islamic weekend). For the Friday races we would often beat down the Blue Nile to its junction with the White and run back against the current with a usually strong northerly behind us. Jenny and I were a little nervous the first time we took a boat out on our own. The current of 1 to 2 knots would inevitably take us downstream in the direction of Cairo (about 3,000 kilometres and six sets of cataracts) and while the wind would tend to bring us back, late evening calms were not uncommon.

It was also clear that, should we capsize, then righting a heavyweight like the Khartoum might be challenging.

The commodore, a genial and very large man in a flowing white djellabiya that sometimes would catch in his tiller when going about, was nonchalant when we very cautiously inquired if the club had lifejackets: 'No, no, Mr Nicholas, Miss Jenny … do not worry about that. Our Nile is warm.'

But he hesitated.

'There is one thing… If you do capsize, please to do so on the Blue Nile, not the White. You see, there are crocodiles on the White. And… er… do not stand on the bottom of the river. There is, how do you say, bilharzia? It is a worm; it is not good.'

We were generously allocated a boat of our own. The arrangement for temporary residents was that you were welcome to fix up one of the ancient dinghies – being steel they were robust – as long as you bequeathed it once you left. About one-third of the members were expatriates. Our Sudanese fellow-members would offset the cost of rehabilitation by seeking sponsorship – from Pepsi, or maybe the local cooking-oil company – and displaying their logos. We contented ourselves with a sparkling paint job in Canadian colours (red and white), a maple leaf on the bows and the grand name *Canada One.*

Racing around the buoys on weekday evenings was often a robust affair and we rarely did well. In theory the usual racing rules applied, but in reality the terms 'Starboard!' or 'Water!' were taken to mean 'Get out of my way!', and were held to be binding as long as you got in there first.

The club employed two 'boat boys' who filled in as skippers or crew when numbers were short. Farouk was in his eighties, Mohammed Bahar a few years younger but impaired by a severely crooked back. On the race course they were demons. Of course, they knew every eddy, every wind shadow, the location of every sandbank. A common ploy was to lead trusting '*khawajas*' (foreigners) over such a shoal, having surreptitiously hauled up their 1-metre centreboard without our seeing. On one memorable occasion we were thus stranded directly in front of the grand Republican Palace, where Gordon had been speared to death. It was strictly forbidden to loiter around here. The AK47-carrying soldiers who began shouting and gesticulating at us, as Jenny stepped out to lighten ship and move us off the bottom, gave us some cause for concern.

We twice snapped our wooden mast in Chinese gybes but by next

Local fishing boat at sunset; on the Nile, Khartoum

Khartoum One Designs moored at the Blue Nile Sailing Club

race day Farouk had spliced the joint together again, just making the mast a little shorter. Dents resulting from collisions would simply be hammered out. One foreigner took things more seriously. On leave in the UK, he strolled into a venerable sailmaker's on the Solent, anticipating a little quiet one-upmanship.

'I'd like a new mainsail for my dinghy, please.'

'Oh yes sir, what class might that be?'

(Smugly) 'A Khartoum One Design…'

(Coolly) 'Of course sir… Hmmm, I do believe Mr Giles sent us a set of drawings, but I must say I don't think we've cut one of those for a while… 1945 maybe? When do you need it?'

Most clubs have their own historic annual races. One of ours, described in the Club Rule Book, was to Gordon's Tree, long ago felled but once a favourite picnic spot for Kitchener's men following the recovery of Khartoum. The race involved a sharp turn south into the White Nile and there was often turbulence where the waters of the

Racing on the Blue Nile, St Matthew's Cathedral in the background

Blue met the choppier, faster-flowing White. At a skippers' meeting prior to this race we were all asked to take note of the fact that a particularly aggressive hippopotamus had been seen in the grounds of the Hilton, overlooking the junction; he (or she) was 'to be avoided'. Another race involved swimming to and from your dinghy; this favoured the expatriates, as very few locals knew how to swim. But the highlight was the overnighter to Alkwasir, a small uninhabited island 8 miles up the Blue Nile; the name means 'fierce beasts'.

We would set off in the late afternoon and it would be a leisurely run downwind as the sun sank and the call to prayer would be heard from minarets all over Khartoum. There would be blue woodsmoke in the air from the dozens of brick-making kilns that lined the banks. Once away from the city, the only sound was the rhythmic chugging of ancient Lister diesel pumps, taking water from the river to the adjoining fields. As the light faded we'd pull our heavy boats up on the sandy beach of the island. A few people might bring tents, but most of us would sleep out: it never rained in winter.

There'd be a bonfire and then the expats would come into their own, especially the diplomats. As we were among the very few people in the country with legal access to alcohol, there was a quiet expectation that we would bring along the 'tea' (the euphemism for Johnnie Walker Red Label). Once that was exhausted, it would be on to the local homemade '*araki*' (date-based firewater); next morning's long beat home could seem very tedious to some.

It was only on these morning sails back from Alkwasir that we expats could beat our Sudanese friends, in fact. For we were more experienced, you see, when it came to tea drinking.

IF YOU GO...

ENTRY FORMALITIES

Sudan receives few tourists. Nationals of most countries require a visa, which must be obtained in advance. Significant fees apply (USD $154 in 2024) and long delays in processing are common; see **www.sudanembassy.org/entry-visa/** (for North America) or **www.sudanembassy.org. uk/visa-service/** (UK/Europe). A Sudanese sponsor may be required.

At the time of writing (2024) Khartoum was engulfed in heavy fighting between two military factions, all Western embassies had withdrawn their staff and most countries strongly advised against all travel to Sudan.

For sailing on the Nile, arrangements should be made to charter or borrow a boat with the Blue Nile Sailing Club, Nile St, Khartoum (at the foot of the Mek Nimr bridge).

GETTING THERE

From the sailing club, it is 8 miles up the Blue Nile to Alkwasir Island. Although long stretches of the White Nile are navigable, there are major dams downstream from Khartoum at Aswan and Meroe, and rapids at the Third, Fifth and Sixth Cataracts. On the Blue Nile, the Roseires Dam and the new Grand Ethiopian Renaissance Dam (GERD) prevent passage. Khartoum can be reached by air from Middle Eastern/Gulf capitals.

DISTANCES

Blue Nile Sailing Club to Alkwasir Island, 8 miles.

WEATHER

In winter (November to May), winds are reliably from the north, 10 to 20 knots. At other times the current on the Nile is too strong to allow for sailing, the wind too light and high water levels (the annual rise is up to 7 metres) may make it impossible to sail under the city bridges.

ANCHORAGE

Pull your boat on to the beach at the north-west end of Alkwasir: GPS 15°33'.561N 32°36'.162E.

GENERAL

Khartoum is a city of 5 million; the vast majority of Sudanese people are Muslim. Notwithstanding the country's reputation for conflict, ordinary Sudanese people are exceptionally welcoming and hospitable to foreigners. Women should dress conservatively; alcohol is not available and its import is prohibited.

The racing fleet on the beach, Alkwasir Island

PART IV

SOUTH ATLANTIC

ST HELENA ISLAND

BRITISH OVERSEAS TERRITORY

In the 1980s, the passage from South Africa to St Helena had been one of the favourites of our circumnavigation: a brisk start followed by gentle winds, some swimming when becalmed, ever warmer seas. But that was late summer. For our second voyage over the same waters many years later, we were at the tail end of a boisterous winter. For two weeks we saw the sun only sporadically and wore our foul weather gear most of the time. Only when were 60 miles short of our goal did a tropicbird spell off albatrosses, whose home is the subantarctic. Day after day the wind blew at an uncomfortable 25 knots, building swells that had us rolling heavily and dumping dollops of cold water into the cockpit.

The highlight of every day was when we would mark up our position with a small cross on the chart (an enormous one with St Helena at the top, and – at the bottom – Bouvetøya, the remotest island in the world). Low points were getting up for those night watches, usually just as you had found a position in which you could doze off without rolling off your bunk.

SAINT HELENA ISLAND, BRITISH OVERSEAS TERRITORY
15° 54' S 45' W

Approaching St Helena from the southeast

Thirteen days out from Lüderitz we sighted a rugged, sheer mass rising from the ocean in the evening gloom. But we were still 37 miles away, and there was no prospect of making the open roadstead off Jamestown, in the lee of the heavy southeasters, before nightfall. We deliberately slowed down. As night fell, we inched our way closer. There were one or two lights visible. Occasionally one would become suddenly bright then fade: someone out in their car for a Friday night party somewhere, catching us briefly in his headlights from many miles away. When we rounded the north-eastern corner of the island, below angular cliffs aptly named The Barn, we were hardly dazzled by Jamestown: there were a dozen white lights strung out on the shore and a weak navigational aid warning of a reef. A dense black mass filled most of our field of vision to the south.

Getting ready to go ashore in the morning, we could tell that one thing hadn't changed much in the 18 years since our previous visit: the locals' taste in music. Back then, Benny Hill's 'Ernie (The Fastest Milkman in the West)' was the most requested item on Saint FM;

now it was The Notorious Cherry Bombs with their unforgettable hit: 'It's hard to kiss the lips at night that chew your ass out all day long.'

We recalled that in 1988, landing had been a challenge. The 'harbour' is an open roadstead entirely open to the north; for days on end it is subject to rollers generated by distant storms in the North Atlantic. The technique was carefully to back your dinghy into the old stone steps in the eastern corner of the bay, where a set of knotted ropes hung from an overhead beam. As you rose 3 metres with the swell, the idea was to calmly take a rope and step ashore, leaving the dinghy to recede beneath you. There was invariably a gaggle of locals on hand to offer not-so-helpful advice. But now a local man called John, for a daily fee of GBP5, would pick us up and take us back in his longboat, which made a dunking much less likely.

Once checked in, we went for long walks in the hills and along the cliffs; found a Boer War POW camp and cemetery; poked our noses into rural churches; and chatted with the locals, who had an old-style courtesy we had only

Previous pages: Roca Magallanes (right) and the Puerto Deseado inlet, Argentina

The anchorage at Jamestown

encountered in one other place: Ireland. Many Saints had never left home. We wondered where else, today, you would still find people who had never strayed more than 6 kilometres from the place they were born, who had never seen a train or a traffic light nor – until 2016 – an aircraft. One woman we spoke to on the quayside had been once to Cape Town, for two days, she said. But she spent most of her time – when she was not worrying about being robbed – just people watching: 'I wondered where they could all be going, and why they were hurrying so.'

Most of the news was extremely local. Several people separately told us how islanders were aggrieved that the recently appointed governor declined to wear the traditional white uniform and plumed hat to which he was entitled.

In spite of the tiny scale of St Helena – from a mile offshore you can see from one extremity of the island to the other – there was lots to see and do. The hills are rugged and the valleys between them so deep that just getting from one district to another can take hours. One joke has it that none of the cars actually have third and fourth gears, because nowhere is flat enough to allow for them. All around, especially along the coastline, is evidence of the role this place once played in coaling and re-victualling the ships that held the Empire together, and as a combined fortress and prison.

Many of the fortifications were constructed or beefed up on account of that famous one-time resident – Napoleon – who was imprisoned here after his defeat at Waterloo until his death in 1821. But we sensed that the islanders sometimes tire of talking about him. Darwin, who called in near the end of his circumnavigation on the *Beagle* in 1836, expressed surprise at the extent of the fortifications but was also loth to go on too much: 'After the volumes of eloquence which have poured forth on this subject, it is dangerous for me even to mention Napoleon's tomb.'

You can visit The Briars, the small country house overlooking Jamestown

where the famous prisoner spent his first
month or so. But a nicely polished brass
plaque gives equal pride of place to another
temporary resident of this house who
had lodged here several years previously:
Arthur Wellesley, later the Duke of
Wellington. Did Napoleon spot his name
in the Visitors' Book, we wondered?

On a cool and misty plateau in the
centre of the island is the emperor's
longer-term jail, Longwood House,
where the tricolour flies. Here you can see
the billiard table on which he spread his
campaign maps while dictating memoirs
to his secretary, idly rolling an ivory ball
from one side to another; the deep iron
bathtub in which he spent hours soothing
his ulcers and reading; the peepholes he
cut in the shutters to observe his guards.
A plate screwed to the floor marks where
Napoleon's deathbed was. Many visitors
leave flowers.

Our young French guide at Longwood
had no time for Hudson Lowe, the
then-governor, who inhabited the more
salubrious and grander Plantation House.
But he did not believe Napoleon had been
wilfully poisoned by his jailer; the arsenic
found in his hair when he was exhumed
in 1840 and removed to Les Invalides

Jonathan

was most likely a product of the damp
wallpaper, he admitted.

Over at Plantation House, the present
governor was not receiving yachties. This
was unlike a predecessor, who had 'most
royally' entertained Joshua Slocum in 1898,
and whose wife baked 'a great high-decker
fruit cake' that lasted the circumnavigator
as far as Antigua. But we did meet the
other beings with whom the current
incumbent shared his grounds: Jonathan,
David, Myrtle, Fredericka and Speedy. They
are all large Seychelles tortoises. Jonathan
was brought here in 1880, at which time
he was recorded as being 'mature' or, in
tortoise-speak, over 50. We calculated
how old he must now be. Jonathan wasn't
exactly sprinting around the lawn, but the
green paint on his carapace was the same
shade as on the garden fencing, which
suggested a recent escape bid.

Leaving such isolated places, knowing
you will almost certainly never return,
usually makes for a quiet first night at
sea aboard *Bosun Bird*. We wondered if
Slocum felt something of that too:

*…I watched the beacon light at
Plantation House, the governor's
parting signal for the Spray, till the
island faded in the darkness astern
and became one with the night,
and by midnight the light itself had
disappeared below the horizon.*

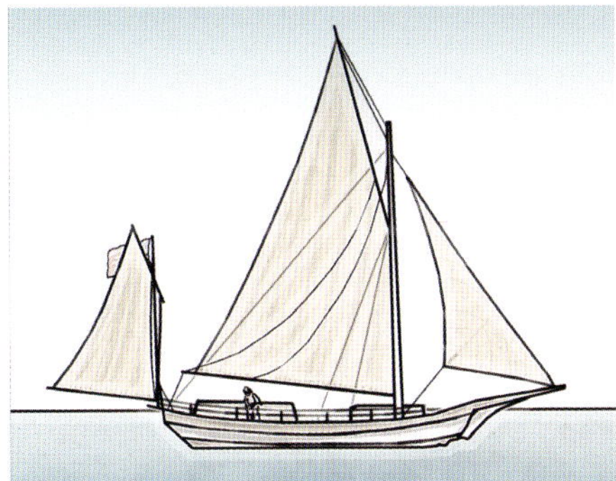

Joshua Slocum's Spray
Saint Helena, April 11-20, 1898

IF YOU GO…

ENTRY FORMALITIES

St Helena is a British Overseas Territory. Most nationalities will be granted leave to enter for up to six months; fee GBP20. UK citizens are not exempt from this fee.

Written clearance from your last port is required, along with proof of health insurance (including evacuation coverage) to a value of GBP175K; it may be purchased on site. Harbour/light dues, GBP35; Pratique GBP5.

The Jamestown harbourmaster requires a minimum of 24 hours' notice of arrival: Harbourmaster: **steve.kirk@sainthelena. gov.sh**; Deputy Harbourmaster: **Nicholas. crowie@sainthelena.gov.sh**; Logistics Co-ordinator: **gene.henry@sainthelena.gov.sh**.

On working days, contact the harbourmaster to arrange for clearance and for mooring buoy allocation on VHF Channel 14; otherwise Channel 16. See **www.sainthelena.gov.sh/ portfolios/safety-security-and-home- affairs/port-control.**

GETTING THERE

The prevailing south-easterly trades mean that under sail St Helena is most easily approached from South Africa or Namibia. An airport opened in 2017; the South African company Airlink operates regular flights to/ from Johannesburg, less frequently to/from Ascension; the airstrip is subject to turbulence and delays/cancellations are common. The Royal Mail Ship *St Helena* has been sold; there is no regular passenger service by sea.

The landing at Jamestown

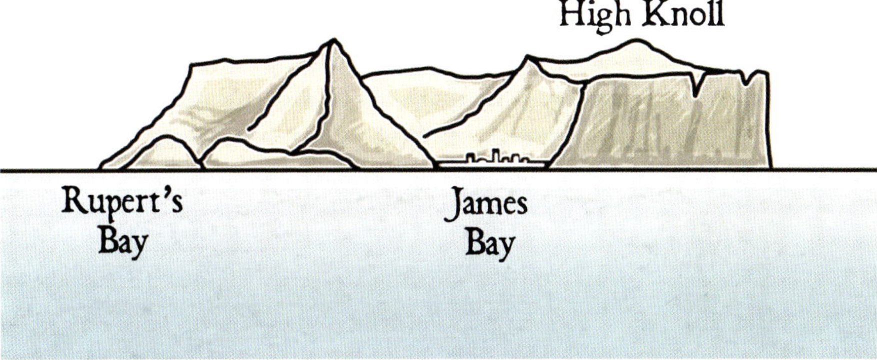

VIEW FROM 2 NM OUT, FROM THE NW

DISTANCES

Cape Town to Jamestown, 1,700 miles; Lüderitz (Namibia) to Jamestown, 1,366 miles; Jamestown to Ascension, 700 miles.

WEATHER

St Helena is firmly within the south-east trade wind belt. There has only ever been one recorded cyclone in the South Atlantic (Catarina, March 2004) but March and August are noticeably rainier than other months. Rollers may occur January through March, usually coinciding with a drop in the Trades; these have constrained plans to build a harbour.

ANCHORAGE

On account of prevailing depths, it is best to take a mooring buoy: there are 18 yellow buoys (max 20 tonnes displacement/50-foot LOA), and five red (50 tonnes/60 feet), located west of the Jamestown harbour; call the harbourmaster for allocation. GBP2 per day. GPS: 15°55'.400S 05°43'.500W. The ferry service (for landing) operates 0400–2000 daily.

GENERAL

Population 5,000, mostly descended from British settlers (in the 1600s) and slaves freed by the Royal Navy in the 19th century; there is a distinctive local accent. The currency is the St Helena Pound, on a par (and interchangeable) with GBP; other major currencies (cash) are accepted but there are no ATMs. The Bank of St Helena makes available a Tourist Card (if arranged in advance) that is good for payment in most island establishments; see **www.sainthelenabank.com/products-and-services/tourist-card**. Yacht haul-out (by crane) is possible. Most supplies are available. Yachties hang out at Anne's Place (in a park, near the library).

CHART

BA 1771, Island of Saint Helena, with approaches to Ascension Island.

REFERENCES

Royal Cruising Club Pilotage Foundation.
(1) *South Africa to the Caribbean*. Dorset, UK, 2019; free at **https://rccpf.org.uk/pilots/177/South-Africa-to-the-Caribbean**.
(2) *South Atlantic Islands*. 2010; free at **https://rccpf.org.uk/Free-Downloads**.

ASCENSION ISLAND

BRITISH OVERSEAS TERRITORY

Before the *Beagle* left St Helena for Ascension in 1836, the locals warned Charles Darwin: 'We know we live on a rock, but the poor people of Ascension live on a cinder.'

And while similarly remote Más a Tierra in the Pacific inspired a classic of world literature – *The Life and Strange Surprizing Adventures of Robinson Crusoe* – Ascension's contribution is *Sodomy Punish'd*, derived from the diary of a Dutch sailor who was cast ashore here for the said crime in 1725.

So, on our first crossing of the South Atlantic in the late 1980s, it was with low expectations that we dropped anchor in the uncomfortably open roadstead of Clarence Bay. We introduced ourselves by VHF radio to the port captain. He spoke with a noticeable American accent; the conversation was terse, but we had our lines rehearsed:

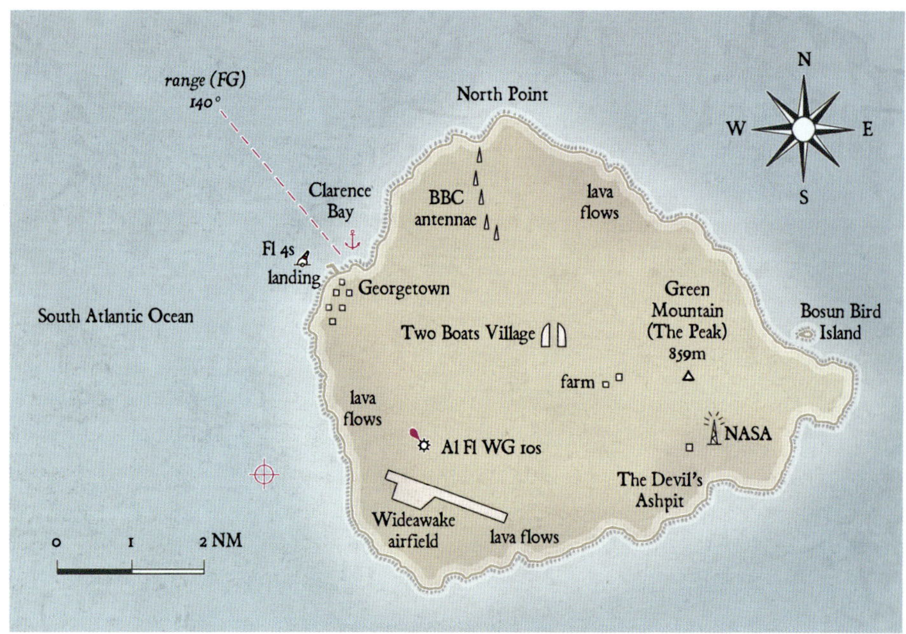

ASCENSION ISLAND, BRITISH OVERSEAS TERRITORY
7° 58' S 26' W

'What is the nature of your distress, Captain?'

'Good morning to you as well. We have an issue with our raw-water pump sir, which I need to work on, and we'd like to take on some fresh water if we may. I believe we are entitled to a 72-hour stay, is that correct?'

There was a long pause. Then reluctant acquiescence and notification that our clock was now running; we were asked to note the exact time in our log.

Ascension has no indigenous inhabitants. It's always been a military outpost; Joshua Slocum on the *Spray* was amused to note in 1898 that the island was then known The Stone Frigate, and that it was technically rated as a Tender to the Royal Navy's South Africa squadron. He records that he took great pleasure in putting ashore, into the navy's care, the goat he had unwisely taken on board in St Helena: it had gnawed at all his lines and eaten his hat and his chart of the West Indies. As on St Helena, Slocum was received in style and taken by a horse and carriage to the house of Captain Blaxland, the commanding officer, 'as if I were a lord of the admiralty and a governor besides'.

Today, Ascension had the Royal Air Force, NASA, the European Space Agency, a BBC World Service relay station, a set of hush-hush listening antennae jointly run (or so it was said) by unnamed British and American intelligence outfits, sundry other British and American military personnel and a surprisingly long airstrip called Wideawake Field (named after an endemic tern). In the 1980s, casual visitors were neither expected nor very welcome.

The same American officer who had spoken to us by radio observed us impassively as we struggled to manhandle our rubber dinghy up a steep flight of 20 steps cut into the pier head – the swell was such that there was no question of leaving it tied up. But he did thaw to tell us, after extracting fees for landing and medical insurance, that the US-run canteen at The Base was currently open. We had better take advantage of it now, as we were required to be back on board every evening by dusk.

A cheeseburger and a Bud, in the fiercely air-conditioned, gloomy and smoke-filled Volcano Club, where American football was showing on TV, made for an odd welcome to this British outpost. Outside, the island was

Clarence Bay, Ascension

Wrestling the dinghy up the steps

as advertised to Darwin: a huge pile of red and black ash and cinders where the equatorial heat made the landscape shimmer and which, as far as we could see, drove everyone indoors. The large golf-ball domes of clandestine purpose and the prefabricated nature of most of the buildings contributed to the feeling that we were on Mars.

But over at the little white church you could have been at any of the old staging posts of the British Empire. Here for example was a marble memorial to Oliver T Lang Esq, RN who, while in command of HMS *Lee* in 1865, 'was killed by a fall from the bridge while coming to an anchor off this island'. A stained-glass window reminded us of a more recent imperial episode: the Falklands/Malvinas conflict of 1982. Ascension was a vital staging post for the fleet steaming into the South Atlantic. It was from Wideawake that Operation

Black Buck was launched: a Vulcan bombing raid on Port Stanley that, at 6,600 miles return, was then the most ambitious such attack ever launched.

In front of a stately cream building that once served as the Royal Marines barracks, was a cricket square, possibly the only ash pitch in the world. We wondered if the evidently large American contingent had ever been persuaded to put an Eleven together.

Our water pump could wait; we had not lied to the port captain, but it had been dripping for two years now. So, for our second day ashore we trudged inland in stultifying heat to Two Boats. On either side of the road into this tiny settlement was a wooden whaleboat standing on its transom; they were placed here by marines in the 19th century, to provide shade for travellers. Passing more white-painted prefabs (still nobody to be seen) the road wound its way high into the cloud that sits permanently on Green Mountain. The landscape changed, the temperature dropped quickly. Now there were green hillsides clad oddly in cracking concrete slabs: a long-disused water catchment system. A well-engineered path – Elliot's Pass – circled the top of the mountain neatly, with tunnels and cuttings. It was built in the 1840s so as to allow sentries to scan the surrounding ocean for approaching ships.

There was a farm up here. It was managed in Slocum's day by one Mr Schank and his sister, from Canada, who 'lived very cosily in a house among the rocks, as snug as conies'. The pigs greeted us enthusiastically and we contemplated the lettuces lustfully. There was nothing for sale to visitors, but we were flabbergasted to find a sign on an oddly shaped whitewashed building with a clock tower, that said 'Red Lion'. Sure enough, it was a pub. We had to bang on a door to find the landlord. It was open on demand, he said, and he was happy enough to draw us a couple of pints of English bitter.

Refreshed, we carried on to the very peak of Green Mountain. Where you might expect to find a crater, was a cool, dark bamboo thicket and a dew pond 5 metres in diameter; to commemorate our ascent we left our names in the logbook provided. As we came down, we could see most of the runway of Wideawake Field. There were military transports parked on the apron; everything seemed wobbly in the heat. In the opposite direction, in a bowl known as the Devil's Ashpit, was another cluster of white buildings: a NASA deep space monitoring station built in the 1960s, used to track early Surveyor missions and the Apollo programme. It's said that Neil Armstrong's 'One small step…' was first picked up here. But when we asked about this back at The Base over yet another cold beer, the young rating behind the bar shook his head:

'Nah, but you know what?'

And he leaned towards us conspiratorially but with a half-smile:

'That whole moon thing was staged, of course. Y'all know that. But they did use Ascension to fake it. All these craters and ash…'

When it came time to leave, and after we had stocked up on Marmite, Sugar Puffs and tinned sponge pudding at the British military store, the port captain came to see us off again. Or, at least, he stood at the pier head, ostentatiously looking at his watch every few minutes as we struggled to launch the dinghy. When we looked back an hour later through the binoculars, the anchor up and our sails set for running, he was still there, watching.

42

Wideawake Field from Green Mountain

IF YOU GO…

ENTRY FORMALITIES

Visitors are now more welcome to visit Ascension than formerly, but all nationalities (including UK) require an e-Visa, issued in advance; fee GBP20, see **www.ascension-visas.com/useful-information** (there is a short list of nationalities NOT eligible for visas). If proceeding from St Helena, the authorities in Jamestown may require seeing your Ascension e-Visa before granting departure clearance.

Medical insurance (including evacuation coverage) is obligatory and is strictly enforced; this can be obtained locally.

Call Ascension Island Radio on VHF Channel 16 when approaching Clarence Bay for instructions. Usually, you will not be boarded but be given appointments with customs and police (for immigration). A GBP15 lights/buoyage fee is payable at customs, and GBP20 per person tourist fee at the police. In working hours, Port Control also monitors VHF Channel 8.

GETTING THERE

The prevailing south-easterly trades mean that under sail Ascension is best approached from St Helena or South Africa. The South African airline AirLink flies once a month to/from St Helena. After several years of suspension, the UK Ministry of Defence has restarted its Airbridge service from the UK to the Falklands via Ascension; seat availability for civilians is restricted.

DISTANCES

St Helena to Ascension, 700 miles; Ascension to Fernando de Noronha (Brazil), 1,100 miles; Ascension to Praia (Cabo Verde), 1,475 miles.

Elliot's Pass, Green Mountain

Jenny practices her batting stance in front of the Royal Marines barracks

WEATHER

The island is in the heart of the south-east trade wind belt. February to May are the hottest and most humid months. As per St Helena, cyclones/hurricanes are all but unknown.

ANCHORAGE

Clarence Bay (off Georgetown, the capital) is the only viable and authorised anchorage; it is open to the north and west, but winds from those quarters are extremely rare. Water visibility is good; it is worth looking around for a sandy patch. There is significant swell. GPS 07°55'.21S 14°24'.79W; depth 14 metres. Land at the pierhead (which has hanging ropes as at St Helena), but the swell means you must haul the dinghy out of the water or anchor it well away. Landing on the beach is both prohibited and dangerous.

GENERAL

Population 700. There is a tourist office inside the sole hotel (The Obsidian). Hitchhiking is easy; car rental is possible but, given the scarcity of vehicles, best arranged in advance. The one shop – Solomon's – usually has produce from the UK and/or South Africa; it may be possible for civilians also to access the NAAFI (UK military) store. The Red Lion on Green Mountain no longer operates as a pub, but the Volcano Club at the US base is open to the public. Between January and May, green turtles come ashore to lay their eggs in Clarence Bay at night; the island is good for birdwatching and diving.

CHART

BA 1691, Ascension Island.

REFERENCES

Royal Cruising Club Pilotage Foundation.
(1) *South Africa to the Caribbean*. Dorset, UK, 2019; free at **https://rccpf.org.uk/pilots/177/ South-Africa-to-the-Caribbean**.
(2) *South Atlantic Islands*. 2010; free at **https:// rccpf.org.uk/Free-Downloads**.

43

FERNANDO DE NORONHA

BRAZIL

The archipelago of Fernando de Noronha lies 220 miles off the north-eastern tip of Brazil, just 4 degrees south of the equator. Jenny spent much of her time on our downwind passage from Ascension rummaging through the bag of coloured spinnaker scraps that we had begged from a sailmaker in South Africa, so as to make a Brazilian courtesy flag. The flag in question has a blue disk with 27 stars (yes, we checked) on a yellow diamond, with an encircling band reading 'Ordem e Progresso' (Order and Progress). While we are punctilious in hoisting such flags (along with the yellow for Q) in advance of arriving in a new country, obtaining them in advance can be challenging.

Fernando is distinguished by a massive thumb-shaped mountain, on top of which sits a rotating aero-beacon so high and powerful that we could see it from 30 miles away. Our arrival in Santo Antônio bay, at the east end of the main island, was a relaxed affair in contrast to Ascension. The police came out to visit us in their launch, bade us

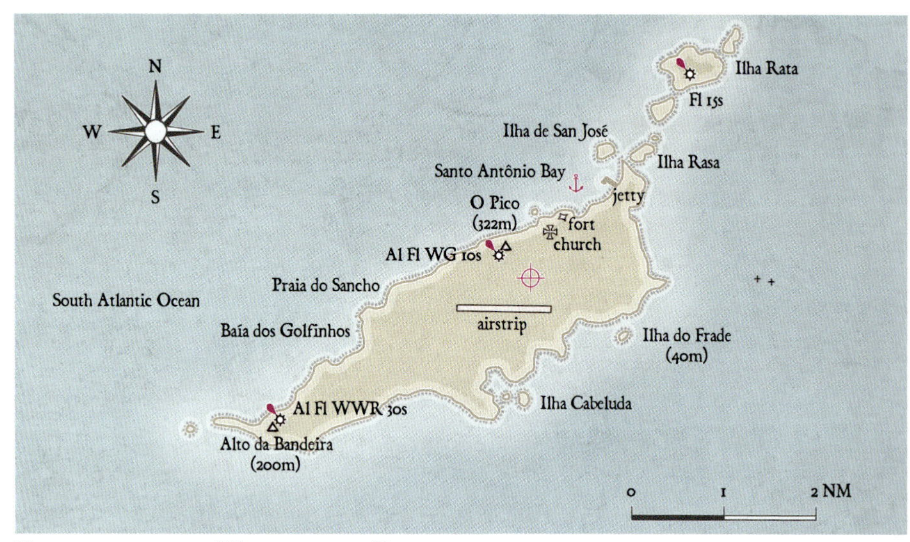

FERNANDO DE NORONHA, BRAZIL
3° 51' S 32° 25' W

O Pico, Fernando de Noronha

a warm welcome and warned that the immigration officer was currently taking his siesta. This should not stop us going ashore, they said; they rattled off a list of suggested things for us to do, of which (speaking Spanish but no Portuguese) we understood a fraction.

One recommendation – this had been rubbed in with much gesticulation and many thumbs up – was to climb O Pico, which sounded straightforward enough; we understood there was a ladder all the way up. It began at the foot of a limestone cliff, past a sign reading 'Military Zone – No Access'. Thirteen steel flights bolted to the largely vertical face, with occasional rungs missing, took us up 322 metres (according to our chart). About halfway up the ladder, Jenny – a few rungs below the captain – was heard uttering mutinous remarks but was persuaded that it was easier to keep going up. There were of course

stupendous views as we sat huddled atop the pinnacle by the red-painted beacon. Tropicbirds and grey noddies fluttered all around us, apparently amazed to see anyone here, while large iguanas eyed us more stolidly. The descent, as we had supposed, was much more intimidating than the climb up.

Fernando was a little tropical paradise. There were deserted sand beaches – one, the Praia do Sancho, was reached via a less challenging ladder climb down through a pothole – where dolphins came to swim with us, and a small village where you could buy exotic fruits for next to nothing. We made a friend called Ziza who daily ransacked his garden for us, plying us with armfuls of starfruit, spring onions, peppers and, most wonderful of all, maracujá (passionfruit). Suffering from the heat, we spent much time at the *Pousada Esmeralda* in the village, bravely trying out our Portuguese on

The eastern extremity of Fernando de Noronha, Santo Antônio bay upper centre

Vila dos Remedios, Fernando de Noronha

the kindly owner. '*Muito refrescante!*' (very refreshing) turned out to be as useful a phrase for us in Brazil as '*Oishi!*' (delicious) is in Japan.

As you'd expect from its location, Fernando was one of the first outliers of the Americas seen by Europeans, possibly as early as 1500; Amerigo Vespucci was an early visitor. Later, sundry pirates – including the Welshman Black Bart – used this as a hideout. And in February 1832, on her outward voyage to Patagonia, the *Beagle* (of course) called in. Captain Fitzroy had been tasked with confirming the island's exact longitude by means of his array of 22 chronometers. Darwin was interested by the 'exceedingly steep' O Pico but, anxious to experience for the first time the lush tropics of which he had heard so much, was disappointed:

'We had no gaudy birds, no hummingbirds. No large flowers.'

Fernando served as a prison island up until the 1950s and, like those other oceanic islands we've visited – St Helena,

Ascension, Cocos Keeling – a waystation for transoceanic cables. We poked around the vintage buildings that remain: a colonial-era church with peeling walls, a fine governor's mansion and a fort with (oddly) British cannon in the gunports. Ziza couldn't tell us anything about that, but he was excited in that the entire archipelago was about to be declared a National Park; tourists would soon flood in, he hoped (and they have).

We were sad to leave after the seven days we were allowed. It was 370 miles and a four-day sail on to Fortaleza, on the mainland, the last few hours of which we spent dodging strange local fishing boats known as jangadas. These are low wooden platforms – more raft than boat – with only a few centimetres of freeboard and enormous lateen sails that give them a turn of speed in very light winds. The design and the name originate from southern India, an interesting example of technology transfer in the days of sail. Many of the sails bore the names of sponsors – oil companies – and we learned that there is an annual regatta in which fishermen from all over north-eastern Brazil compete fiercely.

Fortaleza with its population of 2 million was intimidatingly large from seaward; we had not been anywhere like this for months. And we'd been warned. In Fernando we'd made friends with Thomas and Erica, from Greece. Their vessel – *Conqueror* – was 23-foot-long and little more than a dinghy. With four of us seated in their cockpit over drinks, you had to put your feet up on the opposite side, because sea water came up the cockpit drains. They had no means of cooking, no sextant, let alone a SatNav, and had crossed the Atlantic from Spain using a page torn out from a school atlas and a hiking compass. These were intrepid young people.

Thomas and Erica had been to Fortaleza already, but when we asked for advice, they were not encouraging. *Conqueror* had been broken into and Erica had been threatened with violence.

'No, no,' said her partner, shaking his head grimly. 'We never go there again.'

Checking in at the posh Iate Club de Fortaleza seemed to confirm our worst fears. The tie-wearing duty officer at reception was friendly enough. But after handing us a form that told us we may not use the 'swimming poll' he pointed out a section that read 'several times thieves have stolen all he can'. Going over to the window of his office, he pointed out a rusting, ramshackle freighter anchored 100 metres or so beyond *Tarka*, flying the blue-and-white Salvadorean flag. It was full, he said, of illegal Portuguese migrants

Climbing to the summit of O Pico

awaiting word on their status in Brazil. The story seemed an unlikely one. But we nodded seriously when in a classic gesture that is common to Spanish-speakers, he pointed theatrically at his own right eye and said: '*Olho vivo!*' (watch out).

We were assigned a security guard, a thin grizzled man of at least 70:

'This is Heitor. He will remain on your vessel when you are on shore. And we recommend that he stay on board at night as well. Of course, you will need to feed him. But…' (this sotto voce) 'you should not supply him with any alcohol.'

Heitor saluted us sharply with one hand, a shotgun in the other. We tried to look as though this was a normal practice and smiled in welcome to our new friend. He mumbled something interrogative under his breath to the official, who turned back to us:

'Ah yes. Heitor would just like to remind you that if he uses any ammunition, that will be on your account.'

IF YOU GO…

ENTRY FORMALITIES

Citizens of the USA, Canada and Australia will be required, as of April 2025, to obtain an e-visa for Brazil in advance; UK and EU citizens could obtain visas on arrival. Visas are for 90 days, extendable once.

Foreign yachts are not normally boarded by officials, but formalities on land are time-consuming; smart dress is required (no shorts/T-shirts/flip flops). Officials in Fernando de Noronha, Salvador (Bahia), Recife and Rio are used to dealing with yachts; in other locations they may expect you to employ an agent.

In most ports, immigration (NEPON/ Federal Police), customs (Receita Federal), health and the port captain (Capitania dos Portos) should be visited (in that order – in reverse when clearing out). Customs require a Declaration of Goods, preferably to be filled in prior to visiting: **www.edbv.**

receita.fazenda.gov.br/edbv-viajante/ **pages/selecionarAcao/selecionarAcao.jsf.** Movement between ports must be cleared with the Capitania for every stop; if moving between states the federal police must also be informed.

At Fernando, the port captain (whose office overlooks the beach) co-ordinates all formalities; VHF Ch 12/**porto@noronha. pe.gov.br**. Costs are high. There is a daily fee for the boat (US$55), a daily fee per capita (US$16) and a third fee for the Marine National Reserve (US$65pp for ten days; the Reserve covers 65 per cent of the shoreline). Cash (Reals only) or credit card.

GETTING THERE

Under sail, Fernando is best approached from the east. Approach from the Caribbean is difficult, bucking prevailing winds and a

A Jangada off Fortaleza

strong north-west-flowing current. There are frequent flights to/from the Brazilian mainland.

DISTANCES

Fernando to Fortaleza, 360 miles; Fernando to Recife, 300 miles; Ascension to Fernando, 1,100 miles.

WEATHER

The island lies within the south-east trade wind belt and has a rainy season from February to July, when average wind speeds decrease slightly. The temperature range is 25°C to 30°C year-round. There has only ever been one cyclone. Forecasting is good; for regional forecasts see **www.marinha.mil. br/chm/dados-do-smm-meteoromarinha/ previsao-24-horas.**

ANCHORAGE

Baía Santo Antônio, GPS 03°49'.922S 032°24'.542W; depth 6 metres. Subject to swell from the north-east; if the swell should turn to the north-west, landing becomes dangerous. Land in the lee of the stone breakwater.

GENERAL

Population 3,000. There are small shops, a bank; fresh fruit is readily available. The recent development of high-end tourism means prices are high, but the authorities limit visitors to a maximum of 500 at one time. The island has become a diving destination, known for its warm waters and excellent visibility. Baía dos Golfinhos has a permanent resident dolphin population.

CHARTS

BA 388, Islands off the East Coast of Brazil; BR 52, Proximidades do Arquipélago de Fernando de Noronha.

REFERENCES

Morgan, Tom.
(1) *South Atlantic Circuit*; and
(2) *Havens and Anchorages, A Companion to 'The South Atlantic Circuit'*. RCC Pilotage Foundation. Dorset, UK, 2002.

(3) Balette, Michel. *Brazil Cruising Guide.* RCC Pilotage Foundation. Dorset, UK, 2010.

(4) Hill, Annie. *Brazil and Beyond.* Easton, USA: Tiller Publishing, 2000.

(5) Ceccon, Marcal. *Cruising the Coast of Brazil.* Available from the author, **rapunzel@ netmogi.com.br**; 2008. (For Fernando)

(6) *South Africa to the Caribbean.* RCC Pilotage Foundation. Dorset, UK, 2019; free at **https://rccpf.org.uk/pilots/177/South-Africa-to-the-Caribbean.**

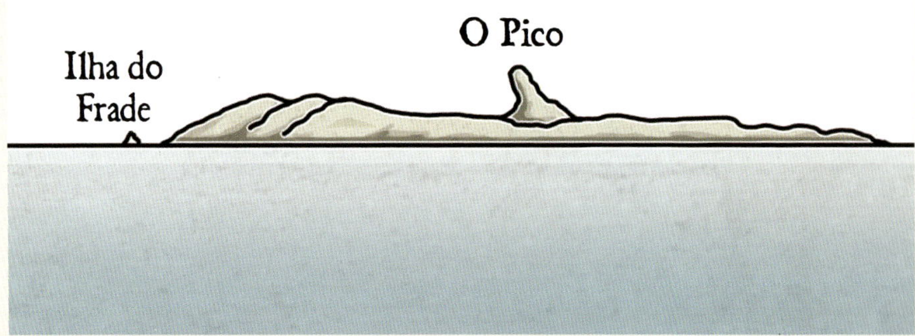

VIEW FROM 12 NM OUT FROM THE NE

PRAIA CANTAGALO, ANGRA DOS REIS

BRAZIL

Oh, I'd love to roll to Rio,
Some Day Before I'm Old!

Like Kipling, we'd always dreamed of sailing into Rio de Janeiro, one of the world's great harbours, up there with Cape Town, Hong Kong and Sydney. And the landfall did not disappoint.

We were 22 days out from St Helena. At 5.30am the sun was still below the horizon astern. The distinctive outline of the Sugarloaf was black against a panorama of glittering city lights. Behind it rose the sharper and higher peak of the Corcovado, the still-floodlit Christ with its outstretched arms visible against the slowly lightening sky. The wind had fallen calm, so as the sun inched upwards I cranked up our engine. I called Jenny on deck, to share the developing view.

'I can smell the land. Beautiful, it must be sandalwood,' I said.

Jenny sniffed. She looked back into the cabin.

Bosun Bird at anchor below the Sugarloaf, with the Corcovado as a backdrop

Botafogo Bay and the Iate Clube do Rio de Janeiro

'I don't think that's the land,' she said. 'It's coming from the engine.'

I switched off. For the next hour, we rolled uneasily in the swell while – down below – I wrestled to push back into place the steel shaft of the engine's raw-water pump, which had worked free from its bearings. It had bored an impressively neat, smoking hole in the wooden engine cover. As we motored past the old fortress on Ilha Laje and into the shelter of Guanabara Bay, Jenny was deputed to stay below and – with a hammer – tap the shaft back into position whenever it showed signs of edging forward again.

We anchored at the very foot of the Sugarloaf, in Urca Bay. We remembered not only Fortaleza, but our honeymoon in Rio, when we'd been mugged on Copacabana beach. We stripped down the exterior of the boat, locking up securely before warily rowing ashore. We were greeted by a respectable-looking man sitting on the beach wall, sipping Antartida beer from a cooler. We asked if this was a safe place to land. 'More or less,'

he said. 'But you should lock the dinghy. And don't leave those oars around.'

For the next several days, whenever we went into town, we carried the two white pine oars. They made getting on and off the bus awkward, and we attracted strange looks when we took them into a movie theatre with us. But the one time when it looked as though we might be in for another mugging, the menacing group of four youths backed off as soon as we both adopted belligerent stances, oars in hand.

Surprisingly few foreign yachts call in at Rio, except on long-distance races. It was already November and the evidently underworked and overqualified customs officer whose responsibility it was to issue us with a temporary import license told us he had only processed 33 for the year so far. Then to immigration, in an echoing warehouse in the docks that, on the occasions cruise ships call, is used for disembarkation. Next to health, here located behind an unmarked steel door and up a staircase at Warehouse 18, reached via a workers' bus that ran the length of the docks. We were asked if we felt all right and were given a fine-looking 'certificate of pratique', which entitled us to take down our yellow Q flag. Finally to the port captaincy, a branch of the navy. Most ports in Brazil have such a presence, and at each, you must check in and out, obtaining clearance for the next destination. In compensation for this rigmarole, I was pleased to note that on all official documentation in Brazil, I appeared either as 'Master' or 'Commander,' occasionally both. Jenny was less pleased; the only options for her were 'Cook' or 'Engineer'.

Returning from our first day ashore, we found the dinghy intact but wondered whether it might be wiser and safer to seek a mooring buoy and access to land at the nearby Iate Clube do Rio de Janeiro. The receptionist didn't quite sniff at the sight of us, oars and all, but looked like he wanted to:

'You are most welcome, sir. Visitors may use the facilities of the club with a signed introduction from three members in good standing and following consideration of your application by the committee, which meets monthly. Would you care for an application form?'

We said we'd think about that. After half an hour of enjoying the air-conditioning, we left unobtrusively.

Later, we would find that this attitude towards foreign cruisers was typical in Brazil. In this country sailing was an activity for the mega-rich. Nobody wanted to behold among the huge power boats and three-spreader super-yachts a cruising boat with its chunky lines, a weed-encumbered waterline

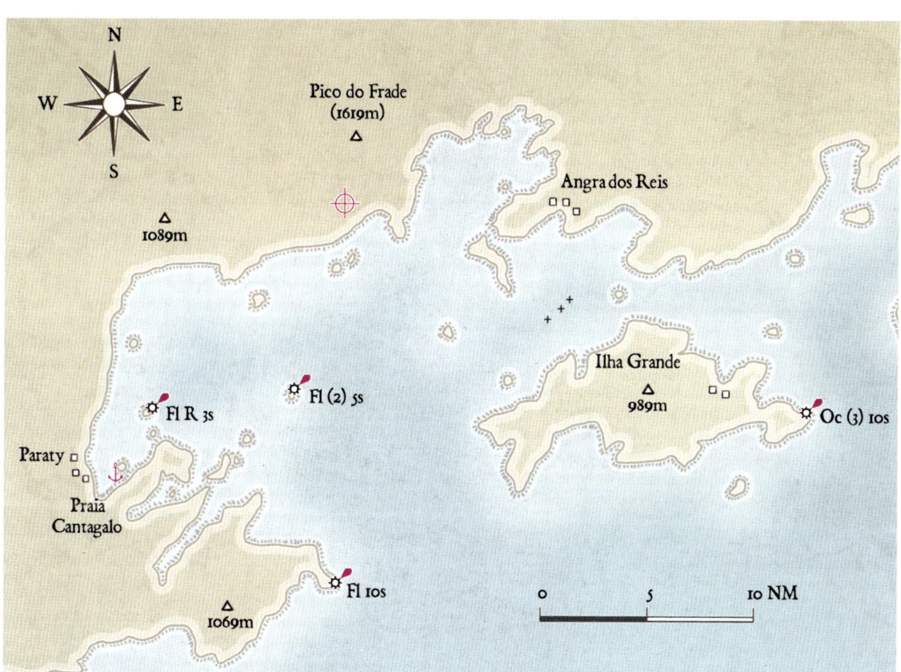

Praia Cantagalo, Angra dos Reis, Brazil
23° S 44° 30' W

and clumsy self-steering gear on the stern. Least of all did members wish to encounter hirsute foreigners in T-shirts, ragged shorts and flip-flops, looking for somewhere to do their laundry.

We survived Rio intact, but a few days in a big city is usually enough for us. On the beach where we first landed was a bar called the Garota da Urca[18] (presumably a reference to the 'Girl From (nearby) Ipanema'. Every evening large crowds gathered on its terrace and the party would begin. On Friday night I couldn't sleep as a particular song on the karaoke machine seemed to be on a continuous loop. It seemed familiar. But I only recognised it for sure when, on the tenth or twelfth repetition, the crowd sang the chorus in accented English: 'More, much more than thees, I did it my way…'

We left in the morning for a sail 60 miles to the west. We passed the great sweep of Copacabana beach, its white crescent of sand backed by modern high-rises, then Ipanema and São Conrado. Behind the last beach rose the distinctive peak known as Pedra da Gávea (Squaresail Mountain), proudly climbed by Darwin on the *Beagle*'s outward voyage. By dawn we were off Angra dos Reis (the Bay of Kings).

We spent the next ten days cruising the spectacular verdant islands and inlets of this region, sailing only very short distances. We anchored every night in a different cove – each with dense tropical jungle tumbling steeply to the shore itself, toucans, mirror-flat calms and warm swimming. Occasionally a fishing boat would pull in late at night;

and at the weekend there were some more power boats and yachts around, as the São Paulo crowd materialised. But after the hustle and stress of Rio this was tranquillity. Our final stop was off the beautiful old colonial town of Paraty.

Founded in 1597, Paraty boomed once gold was discovered in the hinterland of Minas Gerais province; it became the seaward terminus of a road from Ouro Preto and Diamantina known as the Caminho do Ouro (Gold Road), at which the Portuguese galleons were loaded. They'd sail first to Rio, where convoys would be assembled, then onwards to Lisbon. But so conducive was the deeply indented coastline of Angra dos Reis to pirate hideouts that, eventually, a safer route from the mines to the (then) capital was found. Once-opulent Paraty fell into gentle decline.

It's now a colonial jewel, decreed a UNESCO World Heritage site in 2016. The town is so close to the water and so low that the streets flood at high tide (an efficient means of clearing them out), and the old centre has been declared car-free.

Our anchorage here was marked on the chart as Praia Cantagalo ('Singing Rooster Beach'); it was also known, more aptly, as Praia dos Vagabundos. On shore was the 'International Yacht Club': an abandoned and shuttered house by a small and isolated sandy beach, with a spring channelled into a hose. It had come to be used as an informal gathering spot for foreign yachties.

Over laundry we made friends with Adriana, a young Black Brazilian woman who lived alone on a tiny white

---

18 'The Girl from Urca.'

The Paraty waterfront

catamaran, a remarkable exception to the national sailing profile. Adriana had a low, sensual and husky voice. Once we'd met up a few times, I got up the nerve to tell her in my best Portuñol that whenever we'd been to Rio over the years, we'd always been struck by the similar-sounding voice of the announcer at Galeão airport. The quietly soothing, soft manner in which she would report that Varig Flight 206 to Manaus was unavoidably delayed, or that the noon Areolíneas Argentinas shuttle to Buenos Aires was cancelled, had won her legions of fans, and – we'd read – an international award.

'Oh yes!' Adriana laughed. 'She's very famous. But you know what? The newspaper did a report about a year ago. It turns out she's a *solterona* – an old maid – of about 70. Everyone was so disappointed. The men, at least.'

We also met Horacio, the single-handed skipper of *Marie Galante*, from Puerto Madryn, Argentina. Tanned and wiry, he was very friendly and more than happy to regale us with accounts of sailing the wild and chilly waters of Patagonia, into which we would soon be headed. Sooner or later, when yachties swap stories, they become accounts of storms, catastrophes narrowly avoided or actual disaster. Horacio's stories were all in this vein, accompanied by belly laughs and much use of 'Che'.

In between, he insisted that we visit his home port, famously founded in the mid-19th century by Welsh pioneers.

'I'm sure it's a very interesting place,' I said. 'But isn't it a lee shore in anything except a westerly? And there's no harbour…'

Horacio reluctantly admitted this was so. And he went on to tell us of sundry yachts that had been blown on to the beach when the wind moved into the east.

Rowing back in the balmy Brazilian night air to *Bosun Bird*, the only sound was the frogs croaking. The sea was glassy still and the stars were reflected in it. You could see the darkened bell tower of the old Paraty church and a few golden lights in the windows of the colonial houses on the waterfront.

Patagonia seemed awfully forbidding.

IF YOU GO...

For entry formalities to Brazil and references see Chapter 43, pages 281 and 282.

GETTING THERE

Under sail (probably overnight from Rio), approach is best from the east; a current of 0.7 to 1 knot consistently runs to the west and south-west, parallel to the coast. Angra dos Reis and Paraty can easily be accessed overland from Rio.

DISTANCE

Rio de Janeiro to Praia Cantagalo (Paraty), 100 miles.

WEATHER

South of 20°S, the south-east trades take on a more easterly and northeasterly aspect, running parallel to the coast. December to March are the hottest and wettest months here, average temperatures 24°C (Jan) to 18°C (July).

ANCHORAGE

Praia Cantagalo, GPS 23°13'.446S 44°41'.592W, depth 5 metres; it is 1 mile by dinghy to the Paraty waterfront. Land on the sand beach; fresh water available.

GENERAL

Paraty (pron. Para-CHEE) is a small, tourist-dependent town with some basic services. More services are available at the town of Angra dos Reis, in the north-eastern corner of the bay (25 miles).

CHARTS

BA 3970 Rio de Janeiro to Ilha de Sao Sebastiao; BR 1633, Baía da Ilha Grande Parte Oeste.

At anchor, Angra dos Reis

PUERTO DESEADO

ARGENTINA

Bosun Bird was deep into the Roaring Forties, the course due south. By staying close to the coastline of Argentine Patagonia, we'd avoided heavy seas and we'd even had to use the engine a few times when the westerly winds briefly died.

A niggling worry developed. Every time I turned the ignition key, there were unfamiliar vibrations. We emptied both cockpit lockers in the hope of identifying something that might have shifted and that could be provoking the new noise. After two days a minute examination revealed that a bolt on one of the four engine mounts (the L-shaped brackets that secure the body of the engine to the boat) had sheared. The engine was effectively supported by only three mounts and was now unsteady. The bolt in question was inaccessible and had left half its body embedded in the engine.

The weather forecast was favourable for carrying on, past the entrance to the Strait of Magellan and into the Beagle Channel, 400 miles from our current position. But we knew we would need the engine for entering tiny anchorages in the Beagle. We scrutinised our charts and with reluctance decided to backtrack

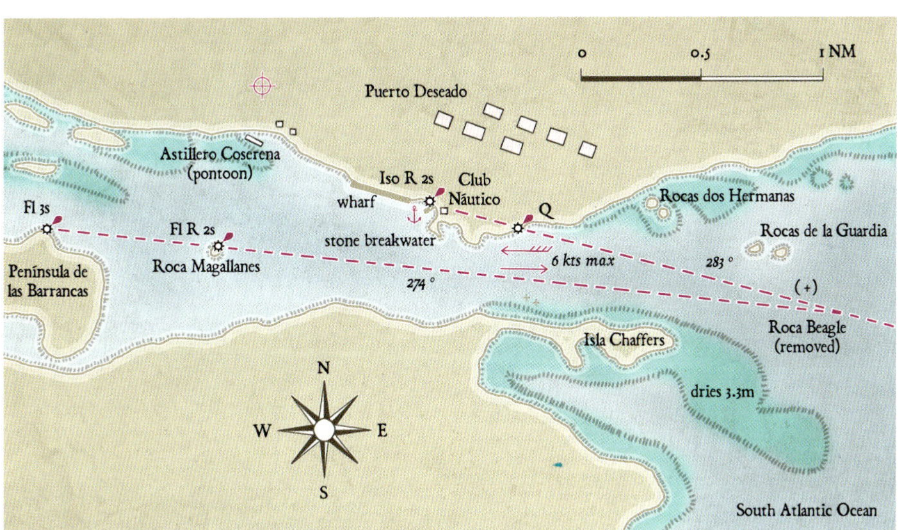

PUERTO DESEADO, ARGENTINA
47° 45' S 65° 55' W

20 miles and try to effect repairs in the last easily accessible refuge on the Patagonian coast: Puerto Deseado.

Magellan stopped here in 1520 on the first circumnavigation of the globe, to see if this inlet (technically a ria, or flooded river – unique in South America) could be the hoped-for passage to the Pacific. But it was named (in 1584) after the flagship of Sir Thomas Cavendish, the *Desire*. According to one theory, it was a member of his largely Welsh crew who gave to the quaint, ungainly birds that here abound, the name 'pen gwyn' (white head, in Welsh).

But getting into the harbour wouldn't be plain sailing. Captain Fitzroy (uncharacteristically) twice put the *Beagle* on a rock in the middle of Port Desire's entrance channel. The blurry photocopy we had of a 1963 Admiralty chart showed 'Roca Beagle' clearly. By it was an enigmatic handwritten annotation in pencil: 'Blown Away'. But the main obstacle would be Deseado's large tidal

range – about 5 metres – and the near-constant race in the entrance channel. The current would run up to 5 or 6 knots, briefly slowing to reverse itself around high and low water.

We arrived off the entrance as dusk fell. The current was likely near slack at the time, but this set of narrows, between reefs, was not one to attempt at night. We anchored off, entirely exposed to any wind from the north or east. It was a restless night as a northeasterly duly built up, with unlimited fetch. By dawn *Bosun Bird* was bucking, her bows dipping under the oncoming waves. More by adrenaline than strength we were able to retrieve the anchor and, as the time for the next slack approached, we set off into the entrance, half under sail and half under the power of our rattling engine.

We'd get to know Deseado well. Soon people were greeting us on the main street of this small 'wild west' Patagonian town and enquiring keenly in shops as to how our '*problemita*' with

The town wharf in a strong westerly, seen from our mooring

Sailing south into the Roaring Forties

the '*patas*' (literally paws, here used to denote the engine mounts) was going. Our land base for operations was the local Club Náutico, off which we occupied one of two moorings laid for visiting yachts. With its bar run by two Brazilian sisters, it doubled every afternoon as the broadcast centre for Deseado FM and the local cable TV station. When there wasn't much happening on TV (which was most of the time), the camera was focused on *Bosun Bird*, bobbing just offshore.

We would trek daily to the cluttered and dark workshop of Coco, the town's sole diesel mechanic. Coco was nearly 70 and not in great health. In his younger days he had been one of the top mechanics on the Argentine motor racing circuit, specialising in tuning hot rods (same term in Spanish). He rarely appeared at the shop before noon, by which time there was a line-up to consult him. Much of the afternoon would be spent in companionable mate (tea) sessions with anyone who happened to show up. We squatted around a gas stove in one corner, under a grimy picture of the 1978 River Plate soccer team: 'The best ever.' Coco would assure us emphatically. 'Boca? A bunch of upstarts. And don't get me started on that Maradona…'

The only other decoration was a calendar dated 2002, featuring a skimpily clad Miss Dayco Fanbelts.

Coco knew his stuff. He pondered our problem long and hard, made trips on board to inspect the engine in situ, and for his final session, worked with us until 1am. He would accept only token payment. The critical moment came when we needed to move the boat to the commercial wharf, decouple the

With Coco the mechanic

engine, move it forwards and – with mains power – drill out the recalcitrant bolt. The wind picked up as we lay alongside. As we crunched against the wall in a heavy chop, it fell to Jenny to stabilise the engine (which was swinging from the mainsheet, just inside the cabin) while I scrambled to replace a mooring line that had torn away. Coco, on his knees, stabbed at the stub of the bolt with his drill. When all was done, Pedro El Tornero (the 'lathe man') realigned the engine and the Brazilian sisters plied exhausted and battered Jenny with feijoada.

When we first arrived, there was one other yacht in: our German friend Mark, aboard *Zanzibar*, whom we had met in Mar del Plata and who had beaten us here by a day or two. He had chosen an offshore route and had taken a thrashing. His canvas spray dodger was wrecked, stanchions were bent by the force of waves breaking over him, and his crew for the passage, a young Israeli, had hightailed it out of Deseado within minutes of arriving, swearing never to go near the sea again. But Mark's adventures were not yet over. After a few days he set off again, bound for Punta Arenas on the Strait of Magellan (an alternative route to the one we were taking, shorter but less scenic and with some difficult stretches of tidal rapids). We had a farewell coffee with him at our favourite *confitería*, the *Santa Cruz*, and thought we would not be seeing him again, at least for a while.

Ten days later, we were amazed to see *Zanzibar* once again entering Deseado, this time under sail; given the difficulty associated with doing this, we assumed he had lost the use of his engine. Back at the *Santa Cruz* and obviously relieved to be alive and to tell his story, Mark told us the grisly details: a saga of storm-force winds, a grounding off Rio Gallegos and mechanical problems. 'But I'm not going south again,' Mark concluded. 'Panama has got to be easier than this.'

Mark hired a crane to hoist his boat out for repairs. His vacated mooring was soon occupied by *Harrier of Down*, a bright yellow Peterson 26 crewed by the very English Julian Mustoe. Julian was retracing (rather approximately) the voyage of the *Beagle* around the world and was able to point out exactly where she had anchored. Fitzroy's journal includes an engraving, itself taken from a painting made by Conrad Conrad Martens on Christmas Day, 1833.

Darwin encountered large herds of guanaco here (many can still be seen) and recounts 'ransacking' (his term) an Indian grave. He spends days roaming the pampas while the men work on the *Beagle*. He is struck by the sheer immensity, the emptiness of the windswept plains around him. With much time to think, he begins to question for the first time his captain's conviction – and the common wisdom of the time – that the Earth was only 5,000 or so years old. He recalls Shelley:

> *…all seems eternal now.*
> *The wilderness has a mysterious*
> *tongue,*
> *Which teaches awful doubt.*

Our preoccupations were more mundane. The engine was fixed. But we were obsessed by our own awful doubt over when to leave Puerto Deseado. We agonised over weather predictions in the internet café and checked in repeatedly via SSB radio with Les, our meteorological guru in the Falklands. Finally, we made a decision to go for it on the evening tide, one Friday.

As we turned south again into the gathering dusk, *Atao* – a large French yacht that we'd seen moored on the other side of the inlet – overtook us. Jean and Francine waved at us from their cockpit. They'd called in to Deseado for an equally pressing but quite different reason. They had five children, all under the age of eight.

'Can you imagine the laundry?' Francine had said when we'd run into her in town, laden with bulging black bin bags.

Evening on the south shore

IF YOU GO…

ENTRY FORMALITIES

Citizens of most countries are granted a 90-day visa for Argentina, on arrival.

The first (and key) authority to be contacted when entering by yacht (and when moving between any port) is the Prefectura Naval (Coastguard), reachable on VHF Ch 9 or 16. For entry and every movement, you require authority and must submit a detailed crew/vessel list – *Rol de despacho* – downloadable at **www.argentina.gob.ar/despacho-de-embarcaciones-deportivas.**

With copies of this form duly stamped by the Prefectura, then visit immigration, customs (where permission to import the vessel is granted) and health.

Underway in Argentine waters, you are required to report your position daily by radio or email to one of four Prefectura offices, in Buenos Aires (**contrasebaires@prefecturanaval.gov.ar**), Mar del Plata (**mpla@prefecturanaval.gov.ar**), Comodoro Rivadavia (**criv@prefecturanaval.gov.ar**) or Ushuaia (**ushu@prefecturanaval.gov.ar**); frequencies are on the form. It is advisable to keep a record of such contacts.

Prior to leaving the country, you may be subject to a safety inspection by the Prefectura.

Vessels entering from (or travelling to) the Falklands/Malvinas require special authorisation; the relevant law and a request form can be found at **www.malvinense.com.ar/smalvi/10/1547.htm**. Seven days' notice required.

The Yacht Club Argentino (YCA) maintains three marinas in the Buenos Aires area and one at Mar del Plata; they are welcoming and will assist with formalities: **www.yca.org.ar/home/institucional/sedes/**.

GETTING THERE

The dominant winds along the Patagonian coast are westerlies, meaning that approach from either north or south is possible; so as to minimise rough seas, most vessels hug the coastline. Entry to Puerto Deseado should be timed for slack (approx. at high/low tide); the maximum current is 6 knots. There is a lit entry range (274°T). If the wind is steady in the west it is possible to wait at anchor in the outer bay. There are frequent buses north and south, but no airport.

DISTANCES

Mar del Plata to Puerto Deseado, 685 miles; Puerto Deseado to Ushuaia, 550 miles.

WEATHER

Westerlies blow all year, with only occasional south-easterly interruptions ('sudestadas'). As lows pass to the south, the wind shifts from north-west to south-west and intensifies, often to 40 to 50 knots. Föhn winds blowing down the slopes of the Andes sometimes exacerbate north-westerlies; they are known as *Zondas*. In summer the temperature range is 11°C to 20°C.

Black oystercatcher

ANCHORAGES

South of Roca Foca (conditional), GPS 47°46'.11S 65°50'.07W, depth 15 metres. There is a single mooring buoy for visitors off the Club Náutico at GPS 47°45'.38S 65°54'.22W. The club monitors VHF Ch 16. With permission, it may be possible to tie up at the Astillero Coserena shipyard pontoon (north side preferrable), one mile to the west of the club on the Ria's north bank; call on VHF Ch 16. It is also possible to anchor on the south shore in the lee of Peninsula de las Barrancas (which is in fact an island); this shoreline is completely undeveloped.

GENERAL

Population 10,000. Most services, including banking, are available. The Prefectura is behind the main wharf (Muelle Fiscal) on Avenida España (Ruta 281).

CHARTS

BA 1302, Cabo Guardian to Punta Nava (out of print; replacement BA 3334 lacks harbour plan); Arg H-360, Rada Puerto Deseado; Arg H-361, Río Deseado-Puerto Deseado. These paper charts may not be GPS compliant.

REFERENCE

Rolfo, Mariolina and Ardrizzi, Giorgio ('The Italians'). *Patagonia and Tierra del Fuego, Nautical Guide (3rd edn)*. Rome, Italy: Nutrimenti Mare, 2016.

Gauchos honoring the Virgin Mary in a street parade

SPANIARD HARBOUR, BAHIA AGUIRRE

ARGENTINA

Below 40 degrees there is no law;
Below 50 there is no God.
(Cape Horners' adage)

We were closing in on 54°30' south, at the northern entrance of the Strait of Le Maire. This was the critical point on our passage through Patagonian waters: the gap between Tierra del Fuego and Staten Island, after which we'd be able to turn west towards the more sheltered waters of the Beagle Channel. We needed to be there at the right time or face a contrary current of 8 knots near Cabo San Diego. Above all we needed to avoid the kind of wind-against-current situation that creates waves of 10 metres in height. Le Maire has sunk more ships than Cape Horn, 100 miles further on.

At 3.49am we hit our GPS waypoint; we were dead on time. Less positively, it was a moonless, overcast night, with snow squalls. As we coasted on, we could see neither of the key lighthouses that mark the two sides of the channel, let alone land itself. Instead, phosphorescent wave crests were breaking all around us. Every few minutes, although the wind was quite steady and remained astern of us, there would be a flurry of breakers, with one wave train suddenly appearing from a new direction to meet the more regular pattern. These were 'whirlpool' effects caused by the current rushing along with us. One or two bone-chilling breakers climbed into the cockpit.

Spaniard Harbour, Bahia Aguirre, Argentina
⊕ 55° S 65° W

As dawn came up, the wind eased and, out of the murk, we made out the faint lights of a cruise ship heading north. It was bound for New Island in the Falklands, the surprised watch officer told us when we called him up. And then the mist started to lift on the starboard side. There, tantalisingly revealed for a few minutes at a time as the clouds swirled in then out, were the steep and menacing mountains of the very tip of Tierra del Fuego.

We weren't through yet, though. Now the wind turned and built to 20 knots, on the nose. We had wind against current. I recalled the account by pioneer Lucas Bridges, in *Uttermost Part of the Earth*, of his mother Mary braving this Strait in a little sailing ship in 1871. Twice they were blown back:

It is difficult to describe the mountainous waves made steeper by the world-famous tide rip in those Straits, or the nights hove to and battened down, when water pounds on the deck or swills about in the bilge, and the creaking of timbers and spars is accompanied by the roar of the gale in the rigging, and the occasional machine-gun rattle of the storm sails when, instead of filling, they shake in the wind.

At anchor, Spaniard Harbour

Beating our way out of the Strait of Le Maire, Tierra del Fuego off the bows

The 380-mile passage from the Falklands took Mary 40 days.

All day we tacked anxiously back and forth across the southern entrance of the Strait. For hours our GPS showed we were making no progress, or maybe half a knot. We became far too familiar with the distinctive Sail Rocks. Jenny was despondent and wondered if we should peel away and run downwind to Port Stanley. But as evening came on, the adverse current weakened. We started to inch our way west, the uninhabited shores of Tierra del Fuego's Mitre Peninsula now to the north of us.

By midnight, it looked as though we had a chance of making safe haven in Bahía Aguirre, a large indentation that gives some shelter from the south-westerly gales that blow straight up from the Horn. Breaking our rule against making night entries, we felt our way in, using the depth sounder and straining

our eyes in the dark. The moment the anchor went down at 1.30am in Spaniard Harbour – a nook in the north-western corner of the bay – marked the end of the most stressful 24 hours we'd ever passed at sea. The night was again miserable with rain and wind, and no stars were visible. But we celebrated giddily with glasses of cheap red wine.

Spaniard Harbour was beautiful, wild and scary. We were past the worst, but there were still many more miles to windward before we would reach truly sheltered waters in the Beagle Channel. Just around that rocky point off our beam, there was nothing between us and Antarctica. It felt like we were hanging on to the bottom of the world. And it wasn't as though the place had a very happy history.

All of the first European settlers in this part of the world – including Lucas Bridges' parents – were missionaries, who saw the hardy and aggressive aboriginal peoples of Tierra del Fuego and its channels as one of the last great challenges remaining for any evangelical worth his salt.

One of the earliest was Allen Gardiner, who had made converts to his muscular Christianity in Zululand, New Guinea and Bolivia before trying his luck here. In December 1850 Gardiner had himself put ashore with six companions at Banner Cove, Picton Island, at the eastern entrance of the Beagle Channel. Here they hoped to establish a mission among relatives and descendants of the famous Fuegian Indian – Jemmy Button – whom Fitzroy had years before taken to England aboard the *Beagle*. But barely had the ship that brought them disappeared over the horizon than a horrific oversight came to light: they

had left all their ammunition, which they would need for hunting and/or for self-defence, aboard the *Ocean Queen*. Within days the party was under siege by Indians, and they had to retreat to their small boats for safety. Eventually they fled, leaving on a large rock the painted message: 'Go to Spaniard Harbour; March 1851', this in hope of some rescue party miraculously appearing.

Winter set in at their new refuge, 40 miles east of Picton. One of their boats was lost in a storm. In an exceptionally high tide most of the supplies, which they were keeping in a cave, were ruined. All of the party started to show signs of scurvy; all they could find to eat were shellfish, seaweed and the odd dead seabird. One by one, they died. On 26 August 1851, Gardiner's assistant wrote a last testament, stating that he would

The old estancia, Spaniard Harbour

not change his situation with anyone on earth. He concluded: 'I am happy beyond words.' Gardiner himself wrote his last words on 5 September, apparently in a similar state of religious ecstasy. All the bodies were found a year later by a passing ship.

Gardiner's cave can still be seen behind the beach. There are two or three semi-derelict buildings remaining from an estancia that was last a going concern in the 1970s; a caretaker occasionally visits to repair the fences. When I ventured ashore, two horses, starved for company, rushed over excitedly to meet me. The British Admiralty pilot book for the area notes that the nearest permanent human settlement is Ushuaia, 'five days' hard ride'.

We spent nearly a week at Spaniard Harbour, waiting for some respite from the westerlies outside. Every morning we would check in to the cruisers' net for the best weather estimates. At last, the break came: we made an overnight dash to Picton.

Allen Gardiner's desperate message on the rock at Picton has long since faded, and there are no longer any aggressive natives stoning passing boats. Quite the contrary. Barely had we anchored and run stern lines ashore in Banner Cove than the crew of a fishing boat, the *Macarena*, came over and asked if we would like some *centolla* (king crab). In front of us, they pulled the eight 30-centimetre-long legs off each of two enormous and discomfited crabs. In return they were happy to accept our last remaining cask of Argentine red; we'd drunk the rest at Spaniard Harbour.

At anchor in a westerly gale, Spaniard Harbour

IF YOU GO…

For entry formalities see Chapter 45, page 294.

GETTING THERE

The wind is almost invariably westerly, which makes for a beat from the south exit of the Strait of Le Maire into the bay and onwards to Puerto Williams (Chile) or Ushuaia (Argentina). There is no easy overland access.

DISTANCES

Puerto Deseado to Spaniard Harbour, 509 miles; Spaniard Harbour to Puerto Williams (Chile), 73 miles; Spaniard Harbour to Ushuaia (Argentina), 90 miles.

Centolla (King crab), Banner Cove

WEATHER

The westerlies are strongest in summer, and at the end of the passage of a front (ie from the south-west). It is advisable to wait for moderate conditions if proceeding further west from here. Good forecasting can be obtained from the Chilean navy; forecasts are broadcast twice daily in Spanish by coast radio stations on 2738 and 4146kHz and may be picked up/requested from this vicinity on VHF from the small Chilean base at Isla Snipe, north-west of Isla Picton.

ANCHORAGE

Spaniard Harbour/Puerto Español, GPS 54°55'.00S 65° 57'.94W, depth 15 metres. If not in use, it is possible to tie to an Argentine navy buoy off Punta Pique (south extremity of the bay) at GPS 54°55'.70S 65°58'.30W. There is nearly always surf on the beach. There is no protection here from (rare) easterly winds.

GENERAL

A history of territorial disputes between Argentina and Chile means that the waters in this vicinity are considered sensitive; both navies patrol regularly. Assume you have been seen; fishing boats will likely report you. On no account land on Chilean territory before clearing in at Puerto Williams. Similarly, it is illegal to land again in Argentina if you have already cleared out of the country.

CHARTS

BA 559, Anchorages in Tierra del Fuego (out of print; number reassigned); Arg H-419- A, De Cabo Buen Suceso a Cabo San Pio.

PART V

NORTH ATLANTIC
AND CARIBBEAN

QUEBEC HARBOUR, MICHIPICOTEN ISLAND, LAKE SUPERIOR

CANADA

As we left the Apostle Islands on the Wisconsin shore of Lake Superior, Jenny asked me if I'd taken my seasickness pills:

'No… Who gets seasick on a lake?'

Well, it turns out I do. It would be an overnight sail – 82 miles, to be precise – to the western tip of Isle Royale. As the sun sank behind us, the wind was building to 25 knots, the seas to 1.5 metres. As we usually do when sailing dead downwind, we were rolling heavily, the dimly lit compass swinging dizzyingly on its gimbal. Eyeing the bucket, I decided to dispense with dinner.

I should have known better than to skip the Stugeron. Superior is enormous (350 miles by 160) and cold, so much so

QUEBEC HARBOUR, MICHIPICOTEN ISLAND, LAKE SUPERIOR, CANADA
47° 40' N 85° 50' W

that it generates its own weather systems and winter gales powerful enough to slow the big Lakers that ply between Duluth and Sault Sainte Marie ('The Soo'). I recalled the haunting ballad by Gordon Lightfoot, that every Canadian grows up with: 'The Wreck of the Edmund Fitzgerald'.[19]

Just before dawn, we made out the Rock of Ages light, on the reef of the same name; we coasted past it, into the more tranquil waters of Washington Harbor, Isle Royale. The next few days of exploration of this 110-kilometre-long island, which is on the US side of the border, set the tone for weeks: hiking in the boreal forest of the interior, scrambling along smooth, tideless granite 'beaches', glimpsing moose, beaver and porcupines. In the evening the call of loons echoed across still and lonely bays. One night as the moon came up, we heard wolves howling. There was a pair of friendly park rangers at a place called Windigo, but apart from this we saw no one. This, they told us, is the most inaccessible (and least-visited) National Park in the Lower 48.

We sailed from bay to bay on Isle Royale's north shore, stopping to explore an abandoned copper mine at a location first mined by Native Americans 5,000 years ago, then crossed into Canadian waters and made for Rossport, where we planned to restock.

We quickly discovered that this is one of those places that is only shown on maps because there is a large empty space to fill. There were 20 or 30 houses spread along the waterfront, with no one to be seen apart from a man sunning himself in his string vest in an overgrown garden. He sleepily informed that the nearest shop was at Thunder Bay, 200 kilometres west. No, there was no bus. Yes, the Canadian Pacific Railway line passed just behind town, but there'd been no passenger service since the 1970s. The man invited us with a wave to make the most of the blackberry bushes that were threatening to envelop his house. In the log Jenny glumly concluded her entry on Rossport with the remark: 'No liquor store.'

At the Slate Islands, the water was clear and still; we could see the bottom in 6 metres. And clean: by now we had for weeks been drinking straight from the lake. In a tiny cove at Allouez Island, our next stop, we spent the days picking blueberries and, sunburned, dared to go for a swim. This was a mistake: the average water temperature in Superior is only 4.5°C.

One afternoon at Allouez our halyards began to rattle and the lines holding us into the shore called for adjustment; black thunderclouds loomed. It was time to move to somewhere less exposed. We made for a long, thin bay over on the mainland – Pulpwood (Playter) Harbour – within the Pukaskwa National Park. Presumably there had once been a logging industry here, but you wouldn't have known it. This was one of the wilder and emptier places we have ever been. We passed two stormy

---

19 Lightfoot, Gordon. 'The Wreck of the Edmund Fitzgerald', from the album *Summertime Dream*. © Reprise Records, 1976. On YouTube at: www.youtube.com/watch?v=PHoK6ojmGZA

Previous pages: Quebec Harbour

Pulpwood harbour, Pukaskwa National Park

days looking through the binoculars for Beach Blobs: mostly these were beavers, sometimes porcupines, but sometimes the less mobile ones would turn out just to be dark pieces of driftwood. Although there is no tide on Superior, there is seiche: a surge that is created by persistent winds from the same direction (in this case westerlies) and which, once risen, then oscillates slowly back and forth, the length of the lake. This we noticed when, a day into the gale, we observed Blobs that had previously been dry but were now half-underwater.

Once the wind was down, we had a series of fast and rolly beam reaches south to Quebec Harbour, on Michipicoten Island. The island's name is an Ojibwe word meaning Big Bluffs. Here at last we came across a few more people: a handful of sports fishermen in their runabouts, camping in grassy

meadows above the beach. There are no longer any permanent inhabitants on Michipicoten, but once, back in the 1880s, there was a copper mine here that employed upwards of 200 people, with a post office and a medical clinic. That went bust. Then in the 1930s Purvis Fisheries set up shop at Quebec Harbour, taking advantage of the Depression-era market for cheap Lake Superior fish: long since bust as well.

There remain a few buildings from the fishing era. We poked around the old Purvis offices, which smelled of hornets' nests and dust. Along the shoreline several wrecks were visible: *Captain Jim*, the rusting iron ribs of the *Billy Blake*, and a 150-foot steamer called the *Hiram R Dixon* that burned to the waterline in 1903. One morning a damp fog blanketed the bay; it was a reminder that summer was half-gone. Bob, the skipper of *Boomalong* – an

Quebec Harbour

old tug he'd converted into a pleasure boat – invited us to warm our hands over coffee in his snug little wheelhouse. He'd been coming here to fish for 20 years or so and in real life was a university lecturer.

'The people we call Ojibwe,' he told us, 'actually call themselves Anishinaabe. It means The True People, I'm told, or Beings Made From Nothing. To them this was always a mysterious place, that kept disappearing in the mist when they approached by canoe. They said it was the work of Gitchi Manitou, the Great Creator… Plenty of the old folks still believe.'

A few days later, using a hand-drawn map Bob had made for us, we rowed out from our anchorage at Sinclair Cove, on the mainland, to a place known to the Ojibwe as Agawa. Here, on a great rock wall that rises almost vertically from the water's edge, is a large set of red ochre paintings. Some are simple discs whose meaning is unclear, but there are also canoes and clearly recognisable animals such as moose, bear and caribou. The pictographs are probably 400 years old, coincidentally around the time that Frenchman Étienne Brûlé made his way up from the St Lawrence and became the first European to see the Upper (Supérieur) Lake.

The sharpest painting is of an odd spined and horned animal with a cat-like face, complete with whiskers. This – say today's Ojibwe elders – is Mishipeshu, the Great Lynx and the spirit of the water. According to legend, Mishipeshu, whose home was Michipicoten Island, could work for or against humans. He could calm the lake, or he could bring great storms by thrashing his tail.

Somewhere off Agawa, I recalled, is where the *Edmund Fitzgerald*, bound for The Soo, went to the bottom on the black night of 10 November 1975. At 730 feet in length and 26,000 tons, she was at the time the largest ship ever to have sailed the Great Lakes. There were 29 men on board and no survivors.

'Mishipeshu,' I mused to Jenny as we rowed home. 'It makes you think.'

Mishipeshu, the Great Lynx (Agawa)

IF YOU GO…

ENTRY FORMALITIES

For information on entry formalities to Canada, see Chapter 12, page 88.

For Lake Superior. The USA/Canada border runs in a south-east/north-west direction through Lake Superior; Michipicoten Island is in Canadian waters.

Cross-border regulations for pleasure craft plying the Great Lakes change frequently. Official US ports of entry on Superior are Duluth/Superior and Sault Sainte Marie, but entry to Isle Royale (USA) from Canada can usually also be made – in summer only – at both Rock Harbor and Windigo; check **www. nps.gov/isro/planyourvisit/customs.htm**.

Canadian ports of entry on Lake Superior are Thunder Bay and Sault Sainte Marie; if you wish to proceed directly from the US side to remoter locations in Canada, seek in advance a Remote Area Border Crossing Permit; see **www.cbsa-asfc.gc.ca/prog/canpass/rabc-pfre/menu-eng.html**.

For an overview of yacht entry regulations, including penalties for non-compliance, see **www.cbsa-asfc.gc.ca/travel-voyage/pb-pp-eng.html**.

GETTING THERE

A sailboat can work its way up through the other Great Lakes, via locks, from the Gulf of St Lawrence to Sault Sainte Marie and Lake Superior. There are numerous places where trailerable boats may be launched: the principal towns on Lake Superior are Sault Sainte Marie (Canada/USA), Thunder Bay (Canada) and Duluth (USA). Yachts can be chartered in Bayfield, Wisconsin. For access by commercial craft to Isle Royale, see **www.**

Boomalong tied up at Quebec Harbour

nps.gov/isro/planyourvisit/directions.htm; Isle Royale is closed to visitors in winter.

DISTANCES

Sault Sainte Marie to Quebec Harbour, Michipicoten, 121 miles; Duluth to Quebec Harbour, 349 miles.

WEATHER

In summer, a high pressure system builds over Lake Superior, favouring west to east passages under sail along the north (Canadian) shore, vice-versa on the south (USA) shore. Fog is common, especially in late summer. The lake is exceptionally cold. In winter 60 per cent of the surface freezes over; ice coverage peaks in February. Both the US and the Canadian Coastguard provide detailed VHF weather forecasting/reporting.

ANCHORAGE

Quebec Harbour, Michipicoten. Enter using a pair of ranges and via a narrow buoyed channel. East anchorage (off the old settlement): GPS 47°43'.0882N 85° 46'.5821W, depth 4 metres; West anchorage: GPS 47°42'.5963N 85°49'.0493W, depth 2 metres. NB: do not confuse Quebec Harbour with Michipicoten Harbour (on the mainland, to the north-east).

OTHER ANCHORAGES

Washington Harbor, Isle Royale, USA: GPS 47°54'.8574N 89° 09'.7902W, depth 9 metres; Rossport: GPS 48°49'.9189N 87°31'.1435W, depth 13 metres; McGreevy Harbour, Slate Islands: GPS 48°39'.4238N 87° 00'.7527W, depth 4 metres; Allouez Island (tight one-boat anchorage; use shorelines); enter from the north-north-east to GPS 48°41'.0978N 86°36'.7776W, depth 5 metres; Pulpwood (Playter) Harbour: GPS 48°34'.7391N 86°15'.9348W, depth 17 metres; Sinclair Cove: GPS 47°22'.4811N 84°42'.2308W, depth 3 metres.

GENERAL

There are no services on Michipicoten Island; there are a few private houses that are inhabited in the summer only. The island is one of the last refuges of the boreal woodland caribou, of which only a few dozen survive.

CHARTS

CHS 2309, Cape Gargantua to Otter Head; CHS 2315, Harbours on the East Shore of Lake Superior: Quebec Harbour.

REFERENCES

(1) Dahl, Bonnie. *Superior Way: The Cruising Guide to Lake Superior (4th edn)*. Duluth, USA: Lake Superior Port Cities, 2008.

(2) *Richardson's Lake Superior Chartbook and Cruising Guide (4th edn)*. New Bedford, USA: Maptech/Richardson's Publishing, 2011.

Abandoned buildings, Quebec Harbour

ANSE AUX PETITES ILES, SAGUENAY FJORD – QUEBEC

CANADA

You might think that sailing down the St Lawrence River from Lake Ontario to the open Atlantic would be a breeze: just drift the 450 miles downstream from Kingston to Rimouski, in light westerlies, admiring old Montreal and Quebec City on the way and hopefully spotting a few whales as you reach the sea.

The first couple of days as we wended our way through the Thousand Islands (which actually number about 2,000) and into the river itself were tranquil enough. Running in 8-knot winds, boosted by the 2-knot current and with Canada to port, the USA to starboard, we passed the huge island homes of 19th-century barons. Here was Boldt Castle, built by hotel magnate George Boldt for his wife Louise, abandoned when she died; a little further downstream was the equally extravagant Singer Castle (as in the sewing machines).

Legend has it that one day the Boldts were out for a cruise on their steam yacht

Approaching Quebec

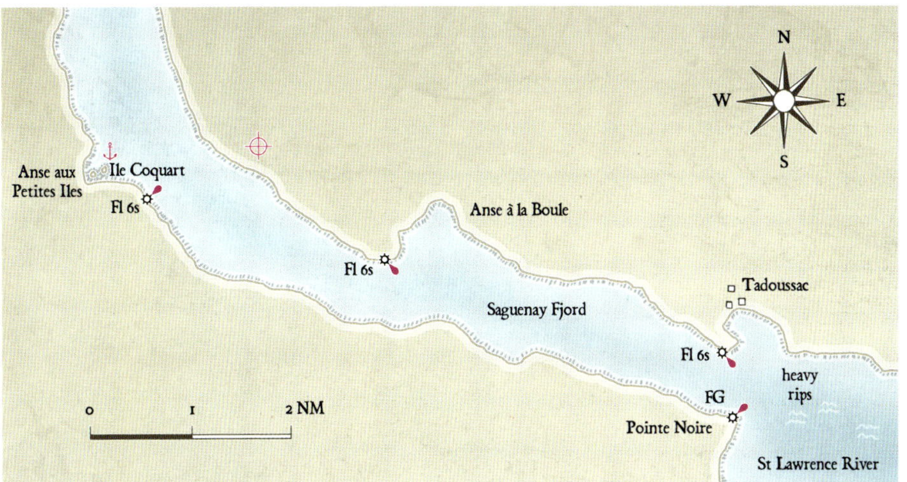

Anse aux Petites Iles, Saguenay Fjord, Quebec, Canada
48° 10' N 69° 50' W

among these islands, and it was time for lunch. The cook, who doubled as the chef at George's Waldorf Astoria, forgot to bring any salad dressing for their lunch. He improvised with what was on board – mayonnaise, ketchup, pickle relish, Worcestershire sauce and an egg – and thus was born Thousand Island dressing.

The first lock – Iroquois – was disconcertingly easy. We rafted up to a small workboat, entered the upstream gates and, before they had even closed, the downstream set was open. Lake Ontario was so low this summer that there was no need for a controlled drop. Over the next couple of days we passed through two more locks – Eisenhower and Snell – and soon we were on Lake Saint Francis, looking forward to a good sail in relatively open water. But there were rumbles of thunder astern, the wind picked up from 5 knots to 35 in a few minutes and – with a bang – our mainsail blew apart, with a 3-metre-long rip. The wind subsided to a manageable 15 knots, but by now there was lightning and torrential rain. Running under our Number Two jib, we limped into Salaberry de Valleyfield to dry off and locate a sailmaker.

More locks – Beauharnois, Saint Lambert, Sainte-Catherine – led us around Montreal. By now we were old hands at tying up to the clever floating yellow bollards that keep you in place as the water level sinks. At each lock (this was before the days of cell phones) we took advantage of waiting periods to land and call the sailmaker we'd found, listening to his diagnosis and eventually making arrangements to pick up the repaired main at a point downstream. At Saint Lambert the wait was ten hours: the up-bound *Grant Carrier* had lost control in the lock and hit the ship arrester at the upstream end. It took that long to fix both the lock gate and his mechanical issue.

Below Montreal strong, steady westerly winds kicked in. They allowed for fast running and demanded concentration. We kept having to gybe to avoid oncoming ships in the main channel but, with all seven locks now behind us and the river flowing freely, the stress was more about the tide. At the

Richelieu Rapids, the St Lawrence briefly narrows from a mile to a 300-metre-wide dredged channel; on an ebb tide it flows close to 10 knots. We arrived too late for slack and spent an uneasy night anchored off the village of Saint Charles des Grondines, where the current kept our anchor line tight.

The river began to widen definitively once we'd passed the dramatic ramparts of Quebec City. Needing both wind and tide in our favour, we had little time for tourism ashore, but in compensation we found ourselves anchoring in unexpected, picturesque out-of-the way corners waiting for that combination. This is old Quebec. The bucolic Ile d'Orléans, which took a day to slide by us, was the first part of New France to be colonised, starting in 1650. It was said that if you opened a Quebec phone book (for there were still such things in those days), more than half the names you'd find could be traced to those pioneers. The coast gradually became more rugged, the cliffs higher. We started to see guillemots and murres: signs of the ocean ahead. There was a smell of salt in the air.

Below the quaintly named Iles du Pot à l'Eau de Vie (Brandy Pot Islands) we had space to tack at leisure: the St Lawrence was now 10 miles across. The currents here were perplexing, unpredictable. As we worked our way over towards the north shore and the turn-off into the Saguenay fjord, we found ourselves in sudden overfalls, accelerating first one way, then being set back the other.

The turbulence meant rich pickings, not just for the seabirds but for whales. With an afternoon to spare, we anchored on the Batture aux Alouettes shoal and got out a cetacean identification guide. First there were what looked like a smattering of tiny icebergs that kept sinking. Easy: they could only be belugas. Then a pair of minkes, cruising a long line of foam. The much larger ones over there must be fin whales. And then the big prize: something enormous and a lot slower. Glance at it for a moment and you might think there was a rock out there, mottled and bluish. A puff of steam and it disappeared. Could it have been a blue?

Jacques Cartier reported on the abundant whales in these waters in 1535, while a later explorer – Samuel de Champlain, in 1603 – dwelt in more detail on a cove at the entrance of the fjord, 'capable of sheltering ten or twelve ships'. The bay Champlain described now hosts the village of Tadoussac and a disproportionately grand hotel overlooking the water. White and red, reminiscent of the infamous Overlook Hotel from *The Shining*, it dates from

At anchor, Anse aux Petites Iles

On the shores of the St Lawrence, near Rimouski

1864 but was rebuilt in 1941 under the direction of Montreal shipping millionaire William Coverdale, who stuffed it with art treasures.

We anchored that evening at a safe distance off the beach – there's a tidal range here of 8 metres – and treated ourselves to a drink in the grand but dark main bar of the old hotel. 'Remember to not talk politics to anyone,' Jenny had said, reminding me that the Saguenay region is the heartland of Quebec separatism. She need not have worried. There were just a few elderly gents in suits, sitting half asleep in overstuffed leather armchairs. One was reading the (English-language) *Montreal Gazette*; they were clearly Anglos. Anyway, they were unlikely to engage in conversation with a pair of underdressed cruisers who could have done with a shower.

Champlain's local Montagnais (Innu) guides pointed up the Saguenay and said it led eventually to a 'great northern bay', reached after many days of travel. Likely they meant Hudson Bay, then unknown to Europeans. But the explorer only ventured 10 or 12 leagues along the waterway and judged the terrain too forbidding to warrant further attention.

Next morning, we followed in his wake.

The Saguenay fjord's often sheer granite walls are a clue to its great depth; it can be difficult to find anywhere to anchor. But after some casting about we chose a pristine location in Anse aux Petites Iles, stern-tied to Ile Coquart (Black Eye Island). We made it our base for three days. Evenings and early mornings, it was still here with only the call of loons to disturb the peace. There was a chill in the air at these hours, for the sun does not penetrate far even in summer, and there was mist on the water. We explored our tiny island and rowed over to the mainland. This is a national park, and there were wooden tent platforms in the forest behind a narrow beach. There could be no path in or out of here; you would have to come in by kayak.

At last we'd found the tranquillity we'd envisaged when we left Lake Ontario. Jenny agreed and added: 'And the great thing is, we don't have to sail back.'

A few days later, as planned, we'd be hauling *Tarka* out at Rimouski and putting her on a flatbed. To paraphrase that old saw about the comparative virtues of sailing and flying: 'There's nothing that goes upstream like a Mack truck.'

IF YOU GO…

For information on entry formalities to Canada, see Chapter 12, page 88.

For Anse aux Petites Iles, Quebec. There are approximately 16 Telephone Reporting Sites-Marine (TRS-M) where foreign yachts may check into Quebec if arriving from abroad. The nearest TRS-Ms to Tadoussac are at Quebec, Saguenay and Baie Comeau. The skipper (only) should land and call toll free to 1-888-226-7277, from the indicated phone. If no further verification is required, you will be given a report number. For the full list of TRS-M sites see **www.cbsa-asfc.gc.ca/do-rb/services/trsm-sdtm-eng.html** and filter by Province.

For an overview of yacht entry regulations, including penalties for non-compliance, see **www.cbsa-asfc.gc.ca/travel-voyage/pb-pp-eng.html**.

GETTING THERE

The current is the key factor in planning any voyage on the St Lawrence. Between Lake Ontario and Montreal, it is eastbound, usually at less than 2 knots. Below Montreal, tide combines with current to give eight or more hours of ebb, reaching up to 7 knots. The incoming flood is hardly noticeable until (if eastbound) you are below Quebec. In a word, it is much easier to sail down the St Lawrence than up it. Used in conjunction with tide tables, the *Atlas of Tidal*

The sun coming up over the St Lawrence

The Hotel Tadoussac

Currents for the St Lawrence Estuary, free at **www.charts.gc.ca/publications/atlas-eng.html**, is a vital tool for planning a passage.

DISTANCES

Kingston (Ontario) to Tadoussac, 430 miles; Quebec to Tadoussac, 132 miles; Tadoussac to Anse aux Petites Iles, 7 miles.

WEATHER

The funnelling effect of the river and mountains in the valley of the St Lawrence means that winds are almost always south-westerly, very occasionally the reverse. Thunderstorms are common on the upper St Lawrence in summer. In the Saguenay fjord, winds follow the inlet and usually blow down-fjord; outflow winds become very strong when high pressure becomes established over the continent (mainly in winter). *The Secrets of the St Lawrence – Marine Weather Guide,* is an excellent resource, available free online at **www.publications. gc.ca/site/eng/9.924000/publication.html**.

ANCHORAGE

Anse aux Petites Iles, GPS 48°09'.66N 69°52'.404W; depth 15 metres; stern-tie close to the north side of Ile Coquart. The bottom drops off steeply: barely 100 metres to the east, the depth is 165 metres.

GENERAL

The village of Tadoussac (pop 800) has a 30-slip marina and some basic services; there is a vehicle ferry across the fjord here, and a daily bus service to/from Quebec and Montreal. Tadoussac is a popular destination for whale-watching in the summer. Fifty miles up the fjord, the town of Saguenay (pop. 145,000) has all services; there are marinas and a yacht club. The fjord frequently freezes over January to March.

CHART

CHS 1203, Tadoussac à/to Cap Eternité.

REFERENCES

(1) Sacco, Michel. *Cruising Guide; St Lawrence River and Quebec Waterways (3rd edn).* Quebec, Canada: L'Escale Nautique 2019.

(2) Nautisme Quebec. *Nautiguide,* published annually, free at most marinas (in French) or online at **www.nautismequebec.com/outils-et-initiatives/nautiguide/**.

MAN O'WAR BAY

TOBAGO

We were not sorry to leave Fortaleza (Brazil), bound for the Caribbean. One night there had been gunfire just across the anchorage. We were sadly unsurprised a few years later to read of the murder of sailing icon Peter Blake, moored off an island in the mouth of the Amazon.

Every day, it was squally and overcast, but we made good progress up the north-eastern coast of the continent, boosted by a favourable current that sometimes reached 3 knots. One day, 20 miles offshore – we saw no land the entire way – we found ourselves in powerful eddies and rips and we became aware that the water was fresh, presumably pouring out from the Amazon.

Good sun sights were scarce. Eight days out, we thought we might be on the latitude of Devil's Island, which sounded like an interesting place to visit. But we were far from certain; it seemed wiser to push on. We rummaged around for some coloured nylon scraps, looked up the flag for Trinidad and Tobago, and Jenny began stitching. On the evening of Day 13 we began to pick up cricket commentary on the radio –

the West Indies were playing England at Edgbaston, England – and next afternoon, 1,665 miles on from Fortaleza, the green hills behind Scarborough, Tobago came into view.

It's always a pleasant shock, after days and days at sea, to land and just let a new culture bombard you: everything seems so novel and fresh. A set of large handwritten placards by the steps where we landed advertised upcoming shows, from calypso star Black Stalin to 'Scherherazad – Striptease Dancer'. At the Tobago Race Club, bets were being accepted 'on Local and English Races Only'; a man emerged counting a stack of T & T dollars; he waved them jubilantly at us. A large and colourful mural on a street corner caricatured South African premier PW Botha (apartheid was not yet dead) and shouted, 'Cry Blood, Africa!'

The officials were all correct, friendly and well-disposed to offer advice – when we asked – about up-and-coming calypso and Soca stars. Following their recommendations, De Mighty Trini's catchy calypso hit 'Sailing?' became our anthem.[20]

---

20 De Mighty Trini. *'Sailing?'*, from the album *Sailing?*. © JW Productions, 1988. On YouTube at: www.youtube.com/watch?v=9NJkGKEgvlc

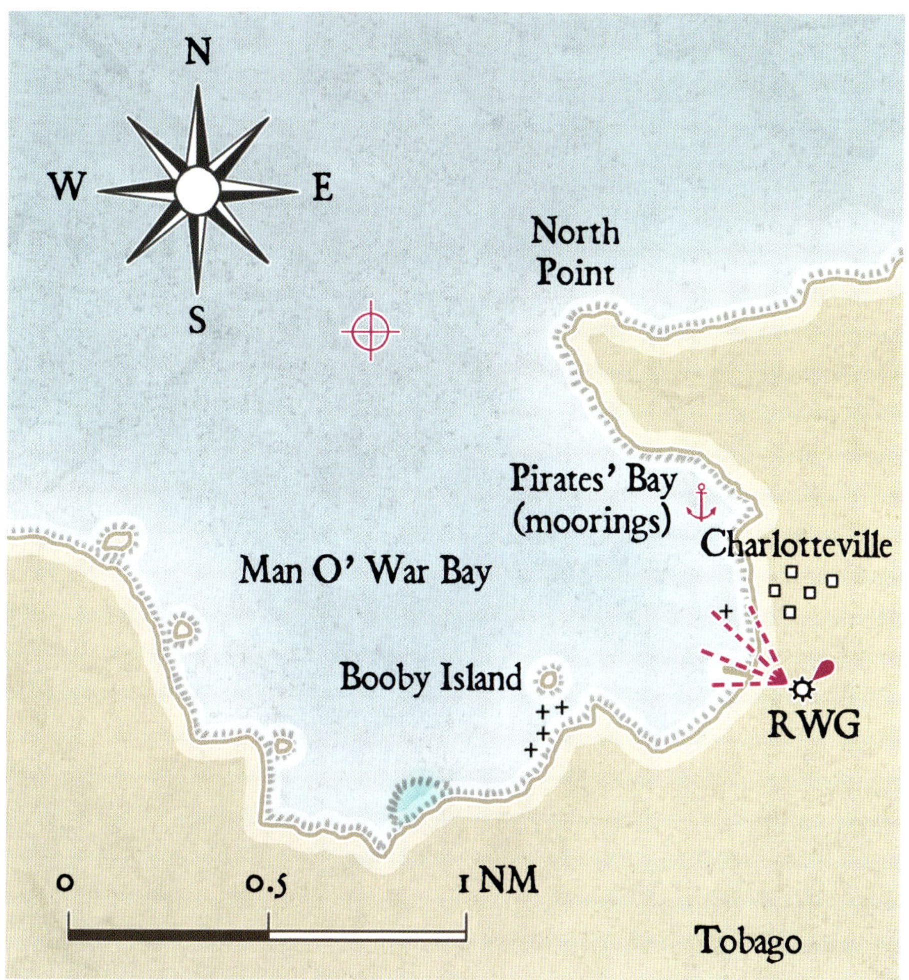

Man O' War Bay, Tobago
⊕ 11° 20' N 60° 34' W

We moved from Scarborough to Store Bay, on the south-western tip of the island. Non-sailing friends often imagine that cruising is one non-stop holiday, as you go from beach to beach. But our few days here were more typical of the reality. We detected that a strand was working loose from our wire forestay: a sign of incipient failure. The loss of a backstay you can survive (the mainsail itself will hold the mast up), but if the forestay breaks, the mast will come down. So, we spent most of two days working to replace it. Jenny, being much lighter than me, was winched to the masthead for the most difficult work. Things were not made easier by boats whose wake left us rocking and well-meaning marine passers-by who kept asking us what we were doing.

Store Bay was popular mainly with locals, but one day we met a young Canadian from Vancouver, Elise, who was (her term) 'shacked up' for the duration of her holiday with a dreadlocked Tobago man called John. Both she and John were intrigued with our lifestyle: how did we afford it? How

Reaching into Man O'War Bay

much did a boat cost? Did you have to be an expert? They came out for dinner one evening on the boat and we were touched when Elise produced a little handmade card she'd made after I'd mentioned it was Jenny's birthday. We kept in touch for years. We sensed Elise's interest had been piqued, but she couldn't quite make up her mind – and she never did.

We worked our way up the west coast; all of the quirky and/or English names on the chart – London Bridge Rock, Englishman's Bay, Bulldog Shoal – reminding us of Ascension, St Helena and the days when the Royal Navy ruled these waters. A few miles out, we stopped for the night at Plymouth. Any decent anchorage in the Windwards, we would soon learn, has fortifications from the British era, and here was no exception. Fort James, constructed starting in 1760, overlooks Great Courland Bay; it first saw action in repelling rebellious

slaves, and then fell into French hands for a short period. Nearby is another of those interesting colonial-era grave inscriptions. On a black slab are inscribed the mysterious words:

Beneath these walls are deposited the body of Mrs. Betty Stiven and her child. She was the beloved wife of Alex B Stiven. To the end of his days (he) will deplore her death, which happened upon the 25th November 1783 in the 23rd year of her age. What was remarkable of her, she was a mother without knowing it, and a wife without letting her husband know it except by her kind indulgence to him.

We'd been tempted to Miss Trim's Roti Shop in Plymouth by her menu, which included not only Seamoss, but Callaloo Soup and the intriguing Buss Up Shut Roti. She couldn't explain the meaning of this last term. Later we would learn it is the vernacular for 'Busted Up Shirt', on account of the way in which, for this dish, the flatbread (roti) is beaten with a wooden spoon until it resembles a rumpled old shirt. But Miss Trim was confident about Betty's enigmatic epitaph:

'Obvious, sah. She a coloured slave, livin' wid her white master. But didn't dare remind him, cos otherwise he slap her. Den she have a baby, yeah? But die in the act. Least, that's what ah tink…'

Near the northern tip of the island is steep-sided Man O'War Bay, not named in honour of a ship but rather in remembrance of a similarly shaped cove on the coast of Dorset. It is wide and spacious and was deserted that day, with a light offshore breeze blowing. So we sailed our anchor in without bothering to start the engine. Only later, as we worked our way up the chain of the Windward Islands from Grenada to Montserrat, would we realise how rare it is to find a scenic, safe… and empty

anchorage in the Caribbean. At 80 windward miles away, Tobago is further than most of the charter yachts based in Grenada wish to go.

Man O'War and Charlotteville became our home for a week. One afternoon, we watched a cricket match on the green: Charlotteville CC versus the T & T Army. The players wore whites, the umpires shorts and T-shirts. The great West Indian cricketing personality of that time was Michael Holding, a fast bowler known as 'Whispering Death'. It was clear that every bowler on the pitch wished to emulate him, taking run-ups so long that our fellow spectators could hardly contain themselves:

'Dis Army bowler, he not careful, he gonna get lost in town…'

Jenny was tolerant but not greatly taken with the game. Only three wickets fell. For one, she was looking the other way; for the second she had wandered off to find a cold lollipop. And for the third she did not realise the man was out until he was walking off the pitch.

Cricket at Charlotteville

IF YOU GO…

ENTRY FORMALITIES

Visitors of most nationalities are granted 90-day visas upon arrival in Trinidad and Tobago, extendable once. Entry to Tobago can be made either at Scarborough or Charlotteville; it is not necessary first to visit Trinidad.

In advance of your arrival, fill in a Float Plan, available through the Yacht Services Association of Trinidad and Tobago (a non-governmental body tasked by the government to take care of incoming yachts): **www.ysatt. com/yacht_entry.php**. Send by email to the multiple addresses listed.

Off the port of entry, call the T & T Coastguard on North Post Radio, VHF Ch 16 or SSB 2182kHz. Fly your Q flag. You may be instructed to await boarding by health authorities; if not, they should be the first call and will issue a Health Clearance Certificate, required by customs and immigration. There are significant fees should you not time your entry to and departure from territorial waters within office hours/weekdays.

Vessels travelling to Tobago from Trinidad are required to check out of Port of Spain but may be given permission to anchor at Store Bay and travel overland to Scarborough to clear in.

Moderately smart dress is expected when conducting paperwork; no shorts/T-shirts.

Note: there have been occasional attacks on yachts travelling between Grenada and Trinidad, apparently by Venezuela-based pirates, most recently in 2019. Some yachts choose to make this passage in company. See **www.safetyandsecuritynet.org/passage-precautions/**.

GETTING THERE

If aiming for Tobago, the winter trades make for a gruelling beat to windward from nearly all the Caribbean islands (except Barbados and possibly St Vincent), made harder by a strong westbound current. Approach from Brazil, the Guyanas or across the Atlantic

Man O'War Bay

The waterfront at Charlotteville

is straightforward. Tobago can be reached by ferry from Trinidad (three hours). Many airlines fly in via Port of Spain; Caribbean Airlines flies direct from the USA.

DISTANCES

Chaguaramas (Trinidad) to Man O'War Bay, 90 miles; St George's (Grenada) to Man O'War Bay, 92 miles; Bridgetown (Barbados) to Man O'War Bay, 120 miles.

WEATHER

The trade winds here blow from the east, most strongly from January to June. Tobago lies on the southern limit of average hurricane tracks but has no anchorage that would be tenable in a rotating storm. Many yachts retreat to Chaguaramas (Trinidad) for the hurricane season.

ANCHORAGE

Pirates' Bay, Man O'War Bay, GPS 11°19'.711N 60°33'.141W; depth 12 metres. Fifteen mooring buoys have been installed in this area so as to minimise damage to coral. They are administered by the non-profit Environmental Research Institute of Charlotteville (ERIC); bookable; fees apply; **www.tobago-moorings. com**. This corner of Man O'War is well protected, but swell enters and can make

landing difficult; from the beach at Pirates' Bay it is a 20-minute walk through the rainforest to the village.

GENERAL

Charlotteville is a small fishing village with few services, but there are several restaurants and guest houses. It is a port of entry. In 2020 Northeastern Tobago was declared a UNESCO Biosphere Reserve; see **www. unesco.org/en/articles/north-east-tobago-declared-unesco-biosphere-reserve**. Snorkelling is good. Tobago, compared with other islands in the eastern Caribbean (including Trinidad), is relatively safe. The island should not be confused with the Tobago Cays (in St Vincent, 90 miles to the north-west).

CHARTS

BA 477, Tobago and Approaches; Imray B-4 (includes detail of Man O'War Bay).

REFERENCES

(1) Doyle, Chris. *The Cruising Guide to Trinidad and Tobago, Plus Barbados and Guyana (4th edn)*. Dunedin, USA. Cruising Guide Publications, 2013.

(2) Pavlidis, Stephen J. *A Cruising Guide to Trinidad and Tobago*. Melbourne, USA: Seaworthy, 2003.

CAYO HERRADURA, ISLA LA TORTUGA

VENEZUELA

June too soon
July stand by
August a must
September you'll remember
October all over

This is a rhyme that everyone in the Caribbean knows, to remind themselves of the approach of the hurricane season. Climate change means it's not as reliable a guide as it once was, but for many years June has seen cruisers seeking a mooring in one of the Caribbean's few hurricane holes; or heading south, below 10 degrees.

In happier times, Venezuela was the default destination: wonderful empty beaches on the offshore islands, a mainland coastline deeply indented with jungly coves and toucans in the trees, friendly people. And – if yours was a power boat – fuel cheaper than bottled water.

People who tell you that the trade winds blow constantly and predictably in the eastern Caribbean, and that it's

Approaching Cayo Herradura

Cayo Herradura, Isla La Tortuga, Venezuela
⊕ 11° N 65° 15' W

always sunny, are wrong. We spent days hanging around in the crowded anchorage at St George's, Grenada, waiting for the passage of a tropical wave – a trough that brings heavy clouds, thunderstorms, squalls and a shift in the wind from east to south-east – before we decided it was the right time to make our move to Venezuelan waters. It was just two days before that 'July stand by' warning was due to kick in.

Los Testigos, a small group of near-desert islands 90 miles to the south-west, was our first stop. They could not have been a greater contrast to buzzing Grenada. There were eight or ten cruising boats scattered among three anchorages, each of which had its own sandy beach and colourful snorkelling among the fringing rocks. We spent the days swimming or walking in the dry, scrub-covered hills on the biggest island: a few cacti, perhaps refreshed by the tropical wave, were flowering. From the 250-metre summit we could see all the way to Margarita Island, 40 miles to

the west, and to the mainland of South America. There was a small village that consisted of a few makeshift fishermen's shacks and a more substantial pair of buildings that housed a three-person navy detachment. The young Teniente was wearing shorts and a T-shirt with holes: he barely glanced at our papers and wished us a happy stay in Venezuela; we should check in more formally at Margarita, he said.

Life for the fishermen looked to be hard. Then was no naturally occurring water in the islands; no electricity. Lacking ice, they would dry their catch in the open, which made for a stench around the settlement and great clouds of flies. When a second tropical wave came through, everyone rushed to bring in the fish and, instead, put out big blue plastic drums wherever drips accumulated. We took advantage of it to let our dinghy accumulate a few centimetres of water and used it as a bathtub.

Pampatar, the most popular anchorage on Isla Margarita, was in those days a

Venezuelan tourist trap and one of those not-especially-attractive places to which cruising boats gravitate in large numbers and become inexplicably rooted. One enterprising husband-and-wife crew who spoke Spanish had taken advantage of this phenomenon and offered a service called Shore Base. They would take your paperwork around the necessary stops – customs, immigration and so on – for a fee of 350 Bolivars (the actual fees involved totalled 30 Bs). We very much prefer to do such things ourselves. This is all part of cruising life and while some officials can be difficult, we usually find that with a few polite words and a little flattery about their country, we make new friends.

But Pampatar, we had to admit, had its uses. We'd been experiencing problems for months with our alternator. The Electro Auto Margarita saved us. Chief mechanic Miguel confirmed my diagnosis that the regulator – a little box on the back – was at fault. No, he didn't have another in stock, he said. But then, after some thought, he said 'a Fiat will do'. He asked us to wait, went out of the front door of his workshop and looked up and down the street. We watched him walk away and around the corner. He was back 20 minutes later, with a used regulator, wires and all. We were sure Miguel had simply lifted it from an unsuspecting car owner. But it worked.

We sailed out to the islands again, this time to La Blanquilla. There is a picture-perfect cove on the western side of this island – described by cruising doyen Don Street as the most beautiful beach in the Caribbean – that is known as the Bahía del Americano. The gringo in question was long gone, the house he had built in ruins, the airstrip to which he once flew his millionaire friends overgrown and unusable. We had the place to ourselves. One night we made a fire with driftwood gathered from the beach, baking two large potatoes in foil in the embers, accompanied by a can of beans. As the fire died, we watched the stars setting over the empty ocean to the west.

At La Tortuga, reached after another night sail – this time to the south-west – we anchored first at Playa Caldera. Two fishermen and a young boy came out to see us. They presented us with a *mero* – a grouper – and Jenny went below to find what we could offer in return. Counterintuitively, it was two small tins featuring Charlie the Tuna, which had been with us for at least two years, that lit their eyes up. As they prepared to head back, one of the men hesitated, then said: '*Oiga…* Listen, if you see anything, or hear anything in the night, don't worry. But don't come out. *Me entiende*? Understand?'

Later that day, we came across the wreckage of two light planes on a makeshift landing strip behind the shacks on shore. No, those planes were not the result of poor flying by Caracas playboys, we learned. La Tortuga was a transit point for drugs bound for Florida; the wrecks represented a couple of shipments gone wrong. The noises we should ignore would be from clandestine night landings and/or high-speed launches.

We moved to a location the fishermen recommended, where no one would '*molestar*' us: Cayo Herradura (Horsehoe Key), a low, flat island off the north-west corner of the big island.

When I think back, years later and after 70,000 miles at sea, it seems to me that of the hundreds of places we have dropped our anchor, this one was especially memorable. We could see our chain as it snaked away on the white sand bottom. There were kilometres of shimmering pristine beaches, pelicans at the shoreline, manta rays and angel fish in the shallows. As we snorkelled, we could hear the parrotfish munching on coral. We brought on board a few of the more interesting (uninhabited) shells we found, along with the jaws of a shark that must have fallen victim to the fishermen a year or two earlier. There was even an interesting if enigmatic morsel of history, something I always appreciate. Wedged among coral rocks and old conch shells behind the beach was a cracked plaque that told us that German polymath and explorer Alexander von Humboldt was at Cayo Herradura in July 1799.

There were signs even in 1988 that paradise was threatened: the two wrecked aircraft, the fishermen's warning. And since our season off the coast of Venezuela, the country's economy has collapsed. Amid political chaos, millions of people have become refugees in neighbouring countries; poverty has taken hold. Narcotraffickers rule and violent crime has rocketed. Every Western government exhorts its nationals to stay away.

I take consolation in the fact that Colombia's reputation in those days was equally, or more, frightening. Colombia has pulled through and it is safer now than it has been for many years. Cartagena has become a must on the cruising circuit. Venezuela will pull through, too.

The upper jaw of the shark is on the wall by our dining table at our home on Salt Spring Island in British Columbia as I sit writing this, the shells are on the windowsills. They remind me every day of distant anchorages under starry skies.

Bahía del Americano, La Blanquilla

IF YOU GO…

ENTRY FORMALITIES

At the time of writing, all nationalities entering Venezuela by sea or overland required a visa in advance; apply at the nearest embassy. For air arrivals, EU and certain other nationalities did not, but Canadians and Americans did. These regulations are in flux; check for updates.

Entering at Los Testigos, notify the navy personnel, who will forward your details to Caracas/Isla Margarita. At Margarita (Pampatar), it is necessary to clear in person with the port captain, immigration, the National Guard and customs.

GETTING THERE

Under sail, Venezuela's offshore islands are best approached from the east. Isla Margarita can be reached by air or ferry, but the outer islands are not accessible except by private vessels (which visit from the mainland, especially at weekends). In former times, Pampatar and Puerto La Cruz were popular assembly points for foreign yachts. A few yachts still visit the Los Roques archipelago.

DISTANCES

St George's (Grenada) to Los Testigos, 80 miles; Los Testigos to Pampatar, 46 miles; Pampatar to Cayo Herradura, 100 miles; La Blanquilla to Cayo Herradura, 66 miles; Cayo Herradura to Puerto la Cruz, 65 miles.

WEATHER

In winter the trade winds blow strongly between east and south-east. In summer, winds are much lighter and more variable; calms are common at night and in the early morning, especially near the mainland. Venezuela is south of the normal hurricane belt, but hurricanes to the north still affect the weather.

ANCHORAGES

Cayo Herradura, GPS 10°59'.533N 65° 22'.782W, depth 3 metres; Playa Caldera (La Tortuga), GPS 10°57'.330N 65°13'.667W, depth 3 metres.

GENERAL

There are no services, and no water on Los Testigos, La Blanquilla or La Tortuga (but there is now a small 'eco' resort at Playa La Caldera, La Tortuga). On account of security considerations, consult widely if you decide to go.

CHARTS

Imray D14: Islas Los Testigos, Isla La Tortuga; La Blanquilla.

REFERENCES

Doyle, Chris.
(1) *Sailor's Guide to a Venezuela Cruise*; and (2) *Cruising Guide to Venezuela and Bonaire (3rd edn)*. Cruising Guide Publications, Dunedin. USA,1990/2007

(3) Street, Don. *Street's Cruising Guide to the Eastern Caribbean: Vol IV – Venezuela and the ABC Islands*, New York, USA. WW Norton, 1989. (Donald Street recently passed away; it is unlikely his book will be updated, absent some improvement in the security situation).

(4) Virlogeux, Francoise. *Guide des Petites Antilles, Venezuela, Vol. 1*. Paris, France. Editions du Pen Duick, 1983 (in French).

A NOTE ON CHARTS

Most governmental hydrographic agencies[21] are rapidly moving away from paper charts and into the production of electronic (digital) charts. But progress is uneven and common standards and formats are yet to be agreed. For the purpose of brevity and consistency – and recognising that many cruisers still hold an inventory of paper charts – references in this book are to paper charts.

Digital charts come in two formats:

A Raster Navigational Chart (RNC) is an electronic picture of a pre-existing paper chart; it carries no additional information (but a position can be read by moving a cursor).

An Electronic Navigational Chart (ENC) is a 'smart chart', which means the user can click on different features – such as a light or buoy – to retrieve additional information not available in paper or raster charts but contained in Pilot Books or Sailing Directions. They are also known as vector charts and can be integrated with other navigational systems such as radar, GPS, course and speed. ENC catalogue numbers are usually unrelated to paper chart catalogue numbers.

The International Hydrographic Organization (IHO), an intergovernmental organisation that co-ordinates the activities of national hydrographic offices and promotes uniformity in nautical charts and documents, has developed standards to describe how ENCs should be produced. The S-57 'Transfer Standard for Digital Hydrographic Data' is the current IHO recommended standard, but compliance is incomplete. It has also developed the S-100 'Universal Hydrographic Data Model' to cater for future demands for digital products and services.

Hydrographic agencies also offer a wide range of other products: Pilot Books (Sailing Directions; in Spanish 'Derroteros'), Lists of Lights, Tide tables, Notices to Mariners (chart updates) etc. These are now almost always available digitally. As the use of ENCs becomes more widespread and the related technology develops, much of the information in these publications will be integrated into the ENCs, and separate products are likely to become obsolete.

An increasing number of cruisers make use of Google Maps/Earth, which has the advantages of being free, extremely accurate in terms of GPS, informative regarding land features and surprisingly useful in indicating likely depths in coral waters. Downsides are the fact that navigational aids are not shown and in a few parts of the world the imagery

---

21 While governments maintain a near-monopoly on charting, an exception has long been Imray. Targeting the recreational/cruising market, Imray for many years produced its own paper charts for popular cruising areas, based on official data but augmented by in-house cartographers; www.imray. com/products/product-types/Charts/. A number of commercial companies – Navionics, Standard Horizon, C-Map – now buy, repackage and resell the data from ENCs. Imray offers raster versions of its own paper charts.

remains poor. Excellent bandwidth is required for real-time use. Certain software packages allow for satellite images from Google Maps/Earth to be overlaid on ENCs.

An alternative (free) gateway to satellite imagery is **https://satellites.pro/**; unlike Google Earth/Maps, images here are not dated.

Services offered by the world's major hydrographic services are listed here: **https://marine-charts.com/marine-hydrographic-offices/**.

Charting information for destinations in this book is provided below.

Argentina (Arg)
- Catalogue for paper and electronic charts (ENC): **http://www.hidro.gov.ar/nautica/cartasnauticas.asp**
- Raster versions of most of Argentina's paper charts may be downloaded free at: **http://www.hidro.gob.ar/**
- Note inconsistency in web addresses: gob/gov.

Australia (AHO; Aus)
- Catalogues for all formats of Australian charts are available at: **www.hydro.gov.au/prodserv/paper/charts.htm**

Brazil (BR)
- Catalogue of Brazilian paper charts: **https://cartasnauticasbrasil.com.br/**
- Brazilian electronic charts (ENC) are marketed through the International Centre for ENC's (IC-ENC): **www.ic-enc.org/**
- Raster versions of most of Brazil's paper charts may be downloaded free at: **www.marinha.mil.br/chm/dados-do-segnav/cartas-raster**

Canada (CHS)
- Catalogues for all formats of Canadian charts are available at: **www.charts.gc.ca/charts-cartes/chart-index-carte-eng.html**

Chile (SHOAC)
- Catalogue for paper charts and ENC: **https://tienda.shoa.cl/**
- *Atlas Hidrográfico De Chile (8th edn)*, 2020 – miniature versions of all Chilean charts in ring-binder form; just about useable, with a magnifying glass. Older editions are in a larger format, hardback. Available through the above portal.

Cook Islands (NZ/CK)
- Land Information New Zealand (LINZ), the country's hydrographic agency, produces and maintains charts on behalf of the Cook Islands.
- The LINZ catalogue of paper and ENC charts is available at: **www.charts.linz.govt.nz/charts**

Fiji (F)

- The Fiji Hydrographic Service *(6 Amra Street, P.O. Box 12387, Walu Bay, Suva. Level 2, Amra Court building, Suva Fiji)* produces charts; these are costly and not easily available.
- Catalogue/source: **www.yachthelpmarinesupplies.com/store/fiji-charts**

France (SHOM); includes French Polynesia

- Catalogues for all formats of French charts are available at: **https://diffusion. shom.fr/cartes/cartes-marines.html**

Japan (JHA)

- Japan Hydrographic Agency (**www.jha.or.jp/en/shop/products/nautical/ index.html**) charts have the Prefix 'W'; there exist a few charts in English, with the prefix 'JP'.
- As well as regular charts, the Agency produces a 12-volume 'S-Guide' of Chartlets, numbered H800-W to H812-W. These are now out of print, but pdf versions of the same books are available (for a fee); each volume contains 50 or more harbour Chartlets. For online sales, volumes are divided into groups of ten to fifteen Chartlets: **www.jha.or.jp/en/shop/products/smallcraft/index.html**

Namibia – see South Africa.

Rodrigues and Mauritius

- India is the Chart Producer nation for Rodrigues and Mauritius. The current portfolio consists of 12 paper navigational charts and 14 ENCs. For the list, see: **https://housing.govmu.org/Pages/Dept%20and%20Org/Divisions/Survey/ Mauritius-Hydrographic-Service.aspx**

Samoa (NZ/WS)

- Land Information New Zealand (LINZ), the country's hydrographic agency, produces and maintains charts on behalf of Samoa.
- The LINZ catalogue of paper and ENC charts is available at: **www.charts.linz. govt.nz/charts**

Solomon Islands (SLB)

- In 2017 Australia became the Primary Charting Authority for the Solomons; navigation charts and a catalogue are now published under the 'SLB' prefix.
- Catalogue for paper charts: **www.hydro.gov.au/webapps/jsp/charts/ SLBchartlist.jsp**
- Catalogue for electronic (ENC) charts: **www.hydro.gov.au/webapps/jsp/ charts/SBenclist.jsp**

South Africa (SAN) and Namibia

- Charts for both South Africa and Namibia are produced by the South African Navy Hydrographic Office, based in Cape Town. The current portfolio (2024) consists of 109 paper charts, 57 ENCs and nine other publications.
- Catalogue for paper charts: **www.sanho.co.za/products/paper_charts.htm**
- Catalogue for ENC charts: **www.sanho.co.za/products/general.htm**

Tonga (NZ/TO)

- Land Information New Zealand (LINZ), the country's hydrographic agency, produces and maintains charts on behalf of Tonga.
- The LINZ catalogue of paper and ENC charts is available at: **www.charts.linz.govt.nz/charts**

United Kingdom (BA)

UK charts are often known as (British) Admiralty charts and are produced by the UK Hydrographic Office, an agency associated with the Ministry of Defence. It lists over 3,500 Standard Nautical Charts (SNCs; ie paper) and 14,000 Electronic Navigational Charts (ENCs) in its portfolio – more than any other agency. Unlike NOAA/NGA charts, BA charts are subject to copyright. Most BA charts are now metric; as a rule, any chart in colour will be metric.

For the full catalogue (SNCs and ENCs), see: **www.admiralty.co.uk/publications/admiralty-digital-catalogue**

For 200 years, BA charts have been the default chart for offshore sailors. But it is now phasing out coverage of certain less-travelled areas outside UK waters. Sometimes – for example in the case of Vanuatu – there is no capable national authority ready to step in, meaning coverage lapses.

Confusingly, as BA charts are replaced, updated or phased out, their number is assigned to new and quite unrelated charts. For example Chart BA 1462 formerly referred to Port Resolution, Tanna Island, Vanuatu; now it depicts Harbours on the North and East Coasts of Scotland.

An Admiralty publication of particular use to offshore cruisers is *Ocean Passages for the World* (NP136), see: **https://www.admiralty.co.uk/publications/publications-and-reference-guides/ocean-passages-for-the-world**. This volume contains a short section on optimal routes for passages under sail, as well as a set of useful charts on wind patterns, currents etc.

Like the NGA, the Admiralty publishes Pilot (Routeing) Charts, but – at a cost of GBP18 for each individual chart – they are scarcely a bargain compared to the NGA equivalent, which is free: **www.admiralty.co.uk/charts/planning-charts/routeing-charts.**

USA (NOAA/NGA/DMA)

Charts for the United States are produced and marketed by the National Ocean and Atmospheric Administration (NOAA). For international waters, the Defence Mapping Agency (DMA) was formerly responsible for mapping; in 1996, it was absorbed into the National Geospatial-Intelligence Agency (NGA). Older US charts for international waters may bear the prefix DMA, more modern ones NGA.

Nearly all NOAA paper/raster nautical charts show depths in feet or fathoms; however, IHO ENC product specifications state that for electronic charts, depths must be encoded in metres. Neither NOAA nor NGA charts are subject to copyright.

- NGA paper charts are available through dealers, for example: **www.nauticalchartsonline.com/charts/NGA**
- Catalogue of NOAA paper/raster and ENCs: **https://charts.noaa.gov/ InteractiveCatalog/nrnc.shtml**

NOAA has started to cancel individual paper/raster charts and will shut down all production and maintenance of traditional paper nautical charts and the associated raster chart products and services by January 2025. To partly replace these charts, NOAA has developed an online application (NOAA Custom Chart or NCC) that enables users to create their own customised nautical charts directly from the latest NOAA ENC data. These charts are in pdf format and can be printed. See: **https:// nauticalcharts.noaa.gov/charts/noaa-custom-charts.html**.

Of particular interest to offshore cruisers are the sets of Pilot Charts published by the NGA. They depict averages in prevailing winds and currents, air and sea temperatures, wave heights, ice limits, visibility, barometric pressure, and weather conditions at different times of the year. The NGA Atlas of Pilot Charts comprises five volumes, one for each major oceanic region. Each volume is an atlas of 12 pilot charts – one for each month – depicting observed and averaged conditions. These can be downloaded free at: **https://msi.nga.mil/Publications/APC**.

ACKNOWLEDGEMENTS

A warm thank you is owed to Liz Multon at Adlard Coles for accepting the original concept for this book with such enthusiasm and shepherding it through to completion with unfailingly helpful suggestions.

My thanks as well to Kate Savage for her careful edits; and to Phil Beresford for his thoughtful selection and layout of the images.

Richard Thomson, meanwhile, took my clumsily drawn charts and sketches, bravely interpreted my near-illegible annotations, and with great patience and care transformed them into works of art; it no doubt helped that he is an accomplished sailor in his own right.

Last, but by no means least, it will be more than evident to the reader that without the lifetime of support given to me by my quietly-spoken but intrepid crew and admiral – Jenny – I would never have set to sea in the first place, let alone put 70,000 miles under the keel.